Comparing
the Literatures

David Damrosch

Comparing the Literatures

Literary Studies in a Global Age

PRINCETON UNIVERSITY PRESS

Princeton and Oxford

Contents

Illustrations

Acknowledgments

During the dozen years that this book has been percolating, I have amassed debts whose full acknowledgment would substantially increase the book's size. I have tried out these ideas in lectures in some forty countries and have gotten many helpful suggestions in the process. Here I might mention several sets of talks that extended the discussion beyond a single session, with warm thanks to Suradech Chotiudompant at Chulalongkorn University, Chen Yongguo at Tsinghua, Mads Rosendahl Thomsen and Christian Dahl at Aarhus and the University of Copenhagen, Péter David-házi at Eötvös Loránd and the Hungarian Academy of Sciences, Mitsuyoshi Numano at the University of Tokyo, and Gisèle Sapiro at the École des Hautes Études en Sciences Sociales. Perhaps these names can stand for another two hundred.

Versions of sections of these chapters first appeared in the Saussy and Heise reports for the American Comparative Literature Association, the *ADE Bulletin*, the *Canadian Review of Comparative Literature*, Bermann and Porter's *A Companion to Translation Studies*, *The Comparatist*, *Comparative Critical Studies*, *Comparative Literature Studies*, *European Review*, Moser and Simonis's *Figuren des Globalen*, *MLQ*, *Modern Philology*, *Neohelicon*, Hayot and Walkowitz's *A New Vocabulary for Global Modernism*, *PMLA*, *The Routledge Companion to World Literature*, and *Translation Studies*.

The following chapters owe much to conversations with my students, with participants and colleagues at the annual sessions of the Institute for World Literature, and during the meetings of the ACLA. Martin Puchner generously read and commented on the full manuscript, as did Delia Ungureanu, who also recommended the Chinese painting *Discussing the Divine Comedy with Dante* as the book's cover image. I am grateful for sometimes *very* lively conversations with Emily Apter, Susan Bassnett, Sandra Bermann, Homi Bhabha, the late and deeply lamented Svetlana

Boym, Pheng Cheah, Amanda Claybaugh, my brother Leo Damrosch, Wiebke Denecke, Theo D'haen, John Hamilton, Eric Hayot, Ursula Heise, Djelal Kadir, Franco Moretti, Stephen Owen, Orhan Pamuk, Katharina Piechocki, Sheldon Pollock, Bruce Robbins, Haun Saussy, Gayatri Spivak, Galin Tihanov, Lawrence Venuti, Rebecca Walkowitz, Saul Zaritt, and Zhang Longxi. I am grateful as well to Young-hae Chang and Marc Voge, to Edward Kim, and to Samuel Whitehead for their kind permission to use their images. The saintly patience and sound advice of my editor Anne Savarese have kept this book on track, and Daniel Simon's judicious copyediting has improved the resulting manuscript throughout. My wife, Lori Fisler Damrosch, has been stalwart in her loving support throughout the years.

This book would not exist without the generosity of my teachers in college and graduate school. I have previously dedicated a book to Michael Holquist; here I will mention four other names among many, each representing a different kind of debt. As an assistant professor with many set responsibilities, Margaret Ferguson made time to do a tutorial on Homer, Virgil, and Milton. Peter Brooks's classes offered a compelling blend of theoretical sophistication and close reading, in open-ended but still focused seminar discussions. W. Kelly Simpson made learning Middle Egyptian a chance to encounter a very distant culture from multiple perspectives, from art and archaeology to political history to exceptionally close readings, down to the level of individual hieroglyphs and the likely provenance of a scribe's handwriting. Finally, Nils Alstrup Dahl was a living link to the Enlightenment tradition of biblical scholarship, in which philology and hermeneutics went hand in hand. His characteristic expression of satisfaction with a piece of evidence was "It's clear," while an ill-founded observation would be met with its opposite: "*Well* . . . that's not *so* clear." Clarity has been a prime virtue for me ever since.

It seems appropriate that these very different teachers, incomparable in both senses of the word, should have made me a comparatist.

Comparing
the Literatures

Introduction

Late one night, half a century ago, as a graduate student in comparative literature neared the date of his doctoral oral exam, his wife dreamed they were woken up by the sound of a truck and a knock on the door. When her husband went downstairs to answer it, he found a pair of workmen, in overalls, who proved to be two of his examiners, Harry Levin and Renato Poggioli. Recounting this dream in 1968 in his presidential address to the American Comparative Literature Association, Harry Levin reported that "the student reacted with that *savoir-faire* which is always so happy a feature of dreams. He simply remounted the stairs and reported to his wife, 'The men are here to compare the literature'" ("Comparing the Literature," 6). This book is intended to answer the question behind the young woman's dream: Just what was her husband doing with his life? And as for ourselves, how should we go about plying the comparatist's trade today? How can we best address the many disparate literatures now at play in literary studies, and what do we really mean by "comparing" them?

Comparing the Literatures is addressed not only to students and faculty in comparative literature programs, but to anyone interested in incorporating a comparative dimension into their work. Insofar as "comparative literature" signifies working across national boundaries, a growing number of scholars in national literature departments are becoming comparatists to a significant degree: a study of Walcott's *Omeros* and Joyce's *Ulysses* is as much a comparative project as a study of Joyce and Homer. Comparatists have classically crossed linguistic as well as geographical borders, but studies within individual languages increasingly involve comparative explorations: of varieties of "weird English" (Ch'ien), of Francophone transculturations, of standard versus colloquial Arabics. A recent anthology of literature in Portuguese includes work from Angola,

Cape Verde, East Timor, Goa, Guinea-Bissau, Macau, and Mozambique, as well as Brazil and Portugal. Even to speak of "the Lusophone world" would be an oversimplification for the anthology's editors, who gave it the plural title *Mundos em português* (Buescu and Mata, 2017). Furthermore, the contemporary concern with issues of migration and diaspora has heightened attention to the presence of multiple languages within national cultures, which were never as monolingual as the ideology of the "national language" supposed. For many of us today, comparison begins at home.

While questions of comparative method and purpose are now broadly shared across literary and cultural studies, the challenges of comparison become particularly acute within the discipline of comparative literature. As the Dutch comparatist Joep Leerssen has asked, "What is the unit of comparison? Is it the language community or its awkward sister, the race? Is it a given 'society' at a given stage of its 'development'?" He notes that these alternatives were widely debated in the nineteenth century and are still in the air, "as is the almost palpable reluctance to spell out precisely what terms like language or race or a literature called 'comparative' actually, specifically mean" ("Comparing What, Precisely?" 207). The solutions that comparatists have found over the years—and also their confusions and their outright failures—can provide instructive lessons for broad-based literary studies in general.

The challenge of defining what, precisely, comparatists do has only increased since Harry Levin's day, an era in which the discipline was imbued with assumptions that limited but also delimited the field, providing relatively clear parameters for teaching, research, and program requirements. Most comparatists focused on a handful of major western European powers, and within those literatures their emphasis was on the high-humanist tradition of the aristocratic past and its middle-class heritage. This was already a very considerable domain for even an entire department to encompass. In 1960 Werner Friederich, founder of the *Yearbook of Comparative and General Literature*, noted wryly that the term "world literature" was rarely being applied to much of the world:

Apart from the fact that such a presumptuous term makes for shallowness and partisanship which should not be tolerated in a good university, it is simply bad public relations to use this term and to offend more than half of humanity. . . . Sometimes, in flippant moments, I think we should call our programs NATO Literatures—yet even that would be extravagant, for we do not usually deal with more than one fourth of the 15 NATO-Nations. ("On the Integrity of Our Planning," 14–15)

Friederich, however, wasn't calling for an expansion of the field of comparative literature; instead, he recommended dropping the term "world literature" altogether.

Even within the favored few NATO-Literatures, women's writing, minority writers, and popular literature or film—to say nothing of that infant medium, television—weren't yet seriously competing for attention with Virgil, Dante, Flaubert, and Joyce. The internet, with its cyberworld of digital media, didn't yet exist; it was only in 1969, a year after Levin recounted his oneiric anecdote, that a graduate student at UCLA transmitted the first message through the early ARPANET, then being developed with funding transferred by the Department of Defense from its ballistic missile program.

The intellectual boundaries of comparative literature were seconded by social norms. Levin's mostly male colleagues might be amused by the gendered incomprehension of the dreaming wife, but today women far outnumber men in literature PhD programs, and many more women—both scholars and writers—appear in the following chapters than would have been found in a comparable survey fifty or even twenty-five years ago. Nor are marriages still assumed to be heterosexual, and a recent survey of my department's students yielded self-identifications under three different categories, "Male," "Female," and "Other." Levin's anecdote also played on the incongruous idea that Ivy League faculty could morph into maintenance men. The class-based humor of this metamorphosis may look darker today to the many adjunct (or, now, "clinical") faculty who can feel all too much like migrant blue-collar workers. The difficulties of securing a tenure-track job affect all fields, but they have a special urgency for comparatists: will jobs, never plentiful, dry up altogether as beleaguered literature departments pull back to nationally defined core fields?

Comparatists have long played a central role in the import-export trade in literary theory, but as theoretical perspectives take hold in many different venues, does the discipline still have a distinctive identity and purpose? Older discussions of "The Crisis of Comparative Literature" (Wellek) or "Criticism and Crisis" (de Man) have given way to stark accounts of disciplinary death (Spivak) and "Exquisite Cadavers" (Saussy). Perhaps it is a sign of the times that vampires and zombies have been the subject of recent seminars at the ACLA's conferences. Are the undead poised for promotion from objects of study to a membership category? Friends with Death Benefits?

As if these problems weren't enough, the humanities at large are under severe strain, buffeted by declining enrollments as STEM fields garner more and more interest from college students and their anxious parents. Meanwhile, cash-poor governments reduce funding for any areas that don't lend themselves to corporate partnerships, a situation that has gotten a good deal worse since Bill Readings surveyed *The University in Ruins* in 1996. Both humanistic values and the internationalism so central to comparative studies are under attack today by metastasizing ethnonationalisms in many parts of the world, not least the United States. These problems don't just haunt graduate students' dreams but are the waking concerns of students and faculty alike.

Despite all these challenges, comparative studies are thriving in many ways. The very pressures besetting national literature programs give them good reason to hire people who can teach courses that reach outward from their core literatures, and globalization gives increasing fluidity to national traditions themselves. Whereas the comparatists of the postwar era felt a mission to help put a war-weary Europe back together, we now have an expanding set of equally compelling needs, from the crises of migration and of the environment to the worldwide rise of inequality, together with violent conflicts that have the United States involved in an Orwellian state of perpetual war. The polarization of political discourse, and the general shortening of people's Twitter-fed attention spans, give literature a vital role in helping all of us to think more deeply and to envision ways the world could be remade. Literature's utopias, dystopias, and heterotopias are needed more than ever today.

If the study of Renaissance poetry and bourgeois novels could once have seemed a kind of escapism or high-toned consumerism, today the careful reading of challenging literary works has something of the oppositional force of the slow food movement in a world dominated by artery-clogging fast food. The globalizing forces that have given the world McDonald's and McFiction also bring us a far wider range of alternative literary worlds, both old and new, giving us new kinds of aesthetic pleasure as well as broader ethical and political perspectives, challenging us to make effective use of an ever-widening range of comparisons. All these changes, both positive and negative, require us to rethink the ways we read, the ways we organize our programs, and the ways we carry on virtually every aspect of our scholarly life and work.

A period of conceptual and institutional ferment represents a time of danger and a time of opportunity. The kind of training that Harry Levin and René Wellek gave their students will no longer suffice even for market purposes, much less for making the most of the intellectual possibilities opening up for us in a global vision of the world's literary production. Yet many programs in comparative literature took shape in the 1950s and 1960s and have not been fully rethought since then. Major intellectual changes came with the rise of literary theory in the late 1960s and then the waves of feminist, postcolonial, and cultural studies, yet most programs have evolved through a series of ad hoc incremental steps. By now they have become motley enterprises, trying to convey—or confine—a rapidly evolving discipline within aging intellectual and programmatic structures. Even otherwise progressive thinkers sometimes seem deeply wedded to doing what they were doing twenty or thirty years ago.

Patchwork repairs can be stitched together for quite a while (here the zombies could make themselves useful), but they are likely to pull apart in a period of tectonic change. Comparative literature today is experiencing a paradigm shift of the sort that occurs only once or twice in a century, and an effective response will require us to rethink the grounds of comparison from the ground up. If we keep on doing what we've been doing, our ideas will look ever more threadbare, our methods amateurish, our results scattershot. Departments and deans will have good reason to pull back, promoting narrower but better focused work within the individual major literary traditions, if they don't abandon foreign literatures outright. Graduate students already feel increasing pressure to cut back intellectually, as they find themselves caught in the crosswinds of an ever-expanding intellectual mandate amid a contracting material economy. Stipends stagnate, debts mount up, and associate deans deny housing extensions as they press students to get up and out, all at a time when there is more to learn than ever before. Maybe there just isn't time—or funding—to master that third language, still less to start a fourth? Maybe those wider comparisons should be dropped from the dissertation? Wouldn't it be better to stick with two neighboring national traditions, one period, one genre, a manageable comparison of three or four novels, using the familiar theoretical framework your adviser was taught thirty years ago?

These pressures make this the best possible time to think freshly about comparative studies, as we have compelling ethical and practical reasons to move beyond business as usual. What tools do we need to have in our toolboxes today? What resources should we draw on as we respond to the changes sweeping across literary studies, the humanities, and the public sphere? One of my themes will be that our global literary aspirations need to be matched by greater engagement with the rich variety of comparative scholarship across the past two centuries and in many parts of the globe, from Brazil to the Balkans to China and Japan. American comparatists can be farseeing in their literary vision but oddly myopic in their scholarly attention, largely ignoring the wider world of comparative work beyond our borders. Elsewhere, comparatists often follow developments in the United States and two or three western European countries but may not look farther afield; a genuinely global grasp of comparative studies lags far behind the steady expansion of our literary awareness. This book is written within a U.S.-American context but with regular reference to initiatives and formations abroad.[1]

---

[1] Even when discussions elsewhere have been translated, they are often neglected within the Anglosphere, and many valuable studies have never been translated at all. I use translations whenever they are available (with occasional modifications); the translations are my own when I quote from a work whose title is given only in French, German, Italian, Spanish, Catalan, or Portuguese.

Our institutional arrangements are a critical part of this story, and we need to become more aware of what our practices do both for and to their practitioners. In a time of strain and flux, these arrangements cease to be mere matters of convenience and become the focus of high-stakes contests over definition and control. Equally important are the assumptions that often go uncontested, reinforcing ossified hierarchies and relations of authority, sustaining an academic politics that can be very different from our own self-image. As Mary Douglas argued in her incisive late book *How Institutions Think*, institutions powerfully shape the questions scholars ask, the ways we approach those questions, and the answers we find. The following chapters take up key issues that people doing comparative work need to rethink today, working both within and against our institutional and disciplinary constraints, whether we are in a department of comparative literature or are undertaking a comparative project from a different home base. There is no single set of languages, canon of texts, or body of theory that every comparatist needs to know, but each of us ought to get a good sense of the options available to us under each of these categories, and to know what we're doing when we make our choices of materials and methods.

One of the crucial things that we should know is how we relate to our predecessors. *Comparing the Literatures* offers a broadly historical sweep from the turn of the nineteenth century to the present, looking particularly at turning points in the lives and work of people who remain vitally relevant for our present concerns and debates. The border-crossing discipline of comparative literature has attracted a fair share of borderline personalities, restless souls unwilling to accept the confinement of more closely bounded fields of study. These are often people whose background has set them askew from their society, even if they haven't emigrated outright. Their work has been shaped as much by struggles with colleagues— and with their own inner demons—as by purely intellectual concerns.

From autobiographical sketches to full-scale memoirs, comparatists have had a good deal to say about themselves, in an accumulating body of writing that represents a neglected resource for the study of the problems and promise of comparative studies going forward. Out of modesty, embarrassment, or sheer narcissism, scholarly memoirists sometimes downplay these conflicts, coating them with a patina of nostalgia or self-deprecating humor, while other accounts are darkly colored by long-cherished grudges. Yet an attentive reading can find instructive lessons in these writings, and equally in the confessional undercurrents that well up between the lines of sober textual explications, whether we hear the traumatic echoes of war and exile reverberating through Erich Auerbach's *Mimesis* or tease out the uncanny mixture of concealment and confession in Paul de Man's coolly seductive essays.

Looking at scholarly activists from Johann Gottfried Herder and Germaine de Staël to Gayatri Spivak, Franco Moretti, and other contemporaries, we can gain insight into the personal and political stakes in the longstanding debates over comparative studies. With the perspective of time, we can better see continuities among people who would once have seemed diametrically opposed, and we may more readily observe problems that persist in our own work but that can be harder to recognize when we're in the midst of them ourselves. Every reader of this book will have an individual set of formative figures to explore, a group only partially overlapping with the people presented here, not only foundational figures but also influential teachers, whether or not they are among the names usually invoked in our journals. As Charles Bernheimer instructed the contributors to the ACLA's 1993 report on the discipline, "Situate your subject!"—meaning our subject position as well as whatever subject we were treating.

My own perspective is that of someone raised and teaching in the United States, though also with a strong awareness of German Jewish immigrant roots, and with parents who vividly recalled their early days in the Philippines, where they met. I am a liberal humanist by outlook, struggling as many of us are to make sense of an increasingly illiberal world. In theoretical terms, I am a structuralist in recovery. A lingering structuralism fuels a continuing interest both in literary forms and in programmatic structures, while the "recovery" aspect has given this book a much more pronounced political cast than it would have had if I'd written it closer to my student years in the 1970s, when textuality frequently eclipsed history, at least in the Department of Comparative Literature at Yale. Even then, studying ancient Near Eastern and colonial-era Mesoamerican literatures brought me into close contact with scholars for whom material culture was a central concern, in fields that provided constant reminders of how many artifacts, and lives, have been lost in the course of ancient and modern imperial adventures alike.

Working frequently in earlier periods, I am concerned about the steady drift of literary studies toward a heavy concentration on the past two centuries, even the past fifty years: just 1 percent of the history of literacy to date. We have become increasingly adept at deconstructing racism, imperialism, and more recently speciesism while ignoring the creeping *presentism* in much of our work. Yet even to understand the consequences of modern imperialisms, for instance, it is helpful to attend to the many empires that came before them. In "Prolegomena to a Cosmopolitanism in Deep Time," Bruce Robbins has called for a "temporal cosmopolitanism" that would compare the literatures of such disparate empires as the Persian, the Ottoman, and the Chinese together with the later European empires, without either romanticizing precapitalist empires or letting the European ones off the hook. In the following chapters, I draw as often from older periods as from the past century when I bring forward literary examples—actually comparing some literature—to illustrate a question of method or approach. These examples range from Shulgi of Ur in the late third millennium BCE to Ovid and Apuleius in Rome, Murasaki Shikibu in Heian Japan and Higuchi Ichiyō in the Meiji Period, James Joyce, J.R.R. Tolkien, and Marguerite Yourcenar in the twentieth century, and contemporary global writers including Yoko Tawada and the Korean American internet duo Young-Hae Chang Heavy Industries.

A running theme in this book will be the long-standing tension between inclusive and exclusive visions of comparative study. This tension has surfaced at every level—socially, ideologically, institutionally, in terms of the literature being studied, and in terms of theoretical approaches. Comparative literature has roots in the disparate perspectives of the aristocratic de Staël and the populist Herder, evolving through the nineteenth century in unstable combinations of cosmopolitanism and nationalism. These early trends have translated institutionally into comparatists' passive-aggressive relations to national literature departments, into Ivy League condescension to Midwestern state schools, and into internecine conflicts between Europeanists versus postcolonialists versus students of world literature. These oppositions too often yield exclusivist position-takings that limit our ability to build solidarity as we all struggle within our institutions and in our wider society. We need to brush the discipline's history against the grain: to see why promising avenues were shut down a century and more ago; to recover common grounds of comparison from differing perspectives; to realize how many writers remain neglected—or are newly eclipsed—in our seemingly ever-expansive era; and to consider how we can reconfigure our persistently conservative institutional practices in order to realize comparative literature's progressive goals.

Not formed around any set literary canon, critical method, or institutional structure, comparative literature is the sum of its answers to the vexed questions that arise when we look closely into its organizing principles. With political debate becoming increasingly polarized in our troubled times, I have found it useful to take an extended look at the varied politics of comparative studies. This is a running theme throughout the book and is highlighted in chapter 3, which follows the initial chapters on origins and emigrations and then leads into the disciplinary terms "theories," "languages," "literatures," "worlds," and "comparisons," with each chapter building on the previous ones. A discipline's agenda in a typical decade could be shaped by debates over any one of these key terms; today we confront them all at once. If we fail to find creative ways to deal with these disputed questions, comparative literature will disintegrate amid their competing vectors. Conversely, however, the social and intellectual upheavals we face can prompt us toward a deeper understanding of the discipline's achievements, its persistent internal contradictions, and its future possibilities.

My central theme is that there is a history that everyone interested in comparative study ought to possess, and a cluster of perennial questions that each of us should come to terms with, whatever our institutional location, whether we are full-time or periodic comparatists, and however variously each of us may formulate the syllabi we design, the research questions we ask, and the ways we seek to intervene on our campuses and in society at large. Sixty years ago, in the sparkling "Polemical Introduction" to *Anatomy of Criticism* (1957), Northrop Frye insisted that any discipline worth its salt should be conceivable as "a coherent and systematic study, the elementary principles of which could be explained to any intelligent nineteen-year-old" (14). To build support for comparative study in difficult times, we need to do better at formulating our principles and explaining them to intelligent nineteen-year-olds, to our puzzled life partners, and to harried fiftysomething deans.

This is what any discipline needs to do. We shouldn't fear—or flatter ourselves—that comparative literature has become so expansive and various that it can no longer be conceived as a discipline at all but instead has become an "Indiscipline" (Ferris), some "wraithlike" entity (Saussy) haunting Bill Readings's University in Ruins. Northrop Frye's response to the theoretically unreflective close readings of the 1950s was to situate the work of practical criticism within a broad framework, a poetics of literature. So too, introducing the 2006 ACLA report, Haun Saussy proposed that the discipline "needs, as its manual of procedures, not a theory (a philosophy or an ideology) but a poetics (an elucidation of the art of making, as applied to its own practices)" ("Exquisite Cadavers," 23–24). In the following chapters, surveying comparative literature's history, its present tensions, and its future prospects, I attempt to reframe the exfoliating variety of comparative studies today. An anatomy of comparison, you might say; a disciplinary poetics.

1

Origins

A Tale of Two Libraries

If you retrace Lord Byron's footsteps down the tree-shaded allée leading to the Château de Coppet, just outside Geneva, you will reach the residence of the woman Byron came there to see: Anne Louise Germaine Necker, Baronne de Staël-Holstein. Philosophe, novelist, and pioneering feminist, Madame de Staël was a leading figure in the early history of comparative literature. The chateau is now in the hands of the tenth generation of her family to own the property, and it is little changed from her day, though light bulbs have replaced the wax tapers in the candelabras. In the opulent rooms open to the public, the furnishings are still those de Staël used when she entertained her many visitors in the years when she held forth at Coppet after Napoleon banished her from Paris.

Ascending the sweeping stone staircase, you can listen for the echoes of the harp once played by Madame de Récamier—displayed in the room reserved for her visits—and in de Staël's own bedroom inspect the full-length portrait of her late lover John Rocca, twenty-two years her junior, elegantly posed in his blue silk hussar's uniform before his Arabian stallion, "Sultan." Downstairs, the Grand Salon is hung with the Aubusson tapestries that a succession of Europe's leading poets, philosophers, and politicians could admire if their attention wandered from the ceaseless flow of de Staël's brilliant, seductive, intense conversation. Next to the Grand Salon stands the library, its lofty bookcases crowned with garlands and busts of Virgil, Demosthenes, and Diderot.

A very different result would attend a search for the library of Johann Gottfried Herder, one of the dominant thinkers of his era and de Staël's greatest counterpart in the early elaboration of comparative literary studies. His childhood home in the Prussian backwater of Mohrungen hasn't survived, but his longtime residence in Weimar still stands: a pleasant three-story house with just enough space for Herder and his wife, their eight children, and his books. Over the years the great philosopher assembled one of the best private libraries in Europe, an encyclopedic collection of literature, philosophy, theology, and history in eight languages. This library, however, can no longer be seen, and not only because the house is now divided into private apartments. Herder's modest salary as superintendent of clergy at Weimar was inadequate for the large family's expenses, and late in life his financial difficulties were exacerbated by a son's addiction to gambling. Following Herder's death in 1803, his grieving widow was forced to sell the books at auction to pay off some of their debts.

The history of comparative literature is in many respects a history of archives—of libraries and collections preserved or lost, studied or forgotten, sometimes rediscovered, sometimes not. Perhaps the first library ever created specifically to house and study foreign texts was established by the Tang Dynasty monk Xuanzang in 645 CE when he returned from his epochal "journey to the western regions"—India—to collect Buddhist manuscripts. He little realized that he would become a literary hero in his own right a millennium later, in Wu Cheng'en's masterpiece *Journey to the West*. Closer in time, the discipline has immediate roots in the collection, study, and translation of ancient manuscripts by classicists and biblical scholars in Europe. The foundations of comparative literature were established by the comparative philology that began in Renaissance Italy and spread to many parts of Enlightenment Europe, a history detailed in James Turner's *Philology: The Forgotten Origins of the Modern Humanities* (2015).

The European philologists' work was given a dramatically global turn in the 1780s by the great linguist Sir William Jones. Raised bilingually in English and Welsh, Jones had mastered Greek, Latin, Persian, Hebrew, and Arabic while still in his twenties, sometimes signing his name in Arabic as Youns Uksfardi ("Jones of Oxford"). After being posted to Calcutta as a judge on the colonial Supreme Court of Judicature, he immersed himself in Sanskrit studies whenever he could spare time from his judicial duties. He soon realized the commonality of many European languages with Sanskrit—a language "of a wonderful structure; more perfect than the *Greek*, more copious than the *Latin*, and more exquisitely refined than either," as he memorably declared in his "Third Anniversary Discourse" to the Asiatic Society of Bengal, which he'd founded in 1784.

It is thanks to the work of Jones and his followers that the German comparatist Max Koch could write a century later that "comparative literary history, like comparative philology, gained a sure footing only with the inclusion of the Oriental, particularly Indian, material" ("Introduction," 72). Baidik Bhattacharya has emphasized that any genealogy of comparative literature should include the Asiatic Society's work ("On Comparatism in the Colony"). More broadly, a non-Eurocentric comparatism can draw on philological traditions from China and Japan to the Arab world, as Sheldon Pollock and his contributors have shown in their collection *World Philology* (2015). In chapter 4, we will look at Kālidāsa's *Meghadūta*, first translated by William Jones's disciple Horace Hayman Wilson; a comparative history of philology could well counterpoint Master Xuanzang's Sanskrit translations with those by Jones and Wilson a millennium later.

Issues of antiquity versus modernity, of travel and translation, and of the urge to recover the past while controlling the imperial present will recur repeatedly in the following chapters. The European philologists were more interested in language than in literature per se, but their methods and discoveries fed directly into the comparative literary studies that began to appear at the turn of the nineteenth century, notably in the immensely influential works of Herder and de Staël. Herder was deeply influenced by Robert Lowth's *De sacra poesi Hebraeorum* (1753), a pioneering study of what we would now call comparative poetics. Lowth's assessment of biblical poetry over against the Greek and Roman classics inspired Herder's studies of Hebrew poetry and of Asian traditions, while both Herder and de Staël drew on the findings of classical philology in formulating their ideas on the relations of ancient and modern literature.

They shared broadly common Enlightenment roots, but in their lives and work Herder and de Staël display a series of binary oppositions of Saussurean proportions: Johann Gottfried Herder, philosopher-preacher of humble German origins, the great promoter of folk poetry, an ardent apostle of German nationalism, a committed Lutheran and devoted family man, struggling to make ends meet; across the Rhine, the wealthy aristocrat Germaine de Staël, famous for her Parisian salon, something of a freethinker, something more of a libertine (her five children had four different fathers), a widely traveled cosmopolitan but devoted to her glittering life in Paris, until Napoleon forced her into exile in her moated chateau on the shore of Lac Léman.

The oppositions soften considerably upon closer inspection. Neither Herder nor de Staël was a prisoner of their sex. Herder worked in close partnership with his wife, Caroline, and de Staël developed many of her ideas in dialogue with her lover Benjamin Constant. Both she and Herder wrote for women as well as men, and both were creative writers—Herder a talented poet, de Staël a best-selling novelist—who explored social and political themes in their prolific writings. These include genre-defying works that interweave literary analysis, philosophical inquiry, and fervent political discussion, centrally concerned with the challenge of leading an ethical life in chaotic times.

Despite her wealth, moreover, de Staël was a borderline figure in more than one way. She was acutely aware of her precarious position as a woman active in the public sphere, and she was only a generation removed from Herder's own modest social background. Herder's father was a church sexton and schoolteacher; de Staël's mother was the daughter of a Swiss parish priest. Her father, Jacques Necker, was responsible for the family's recent prominence, having moved from Geneva to Paris at age fifteen to seek his fortune. Like Jews, Protestants could engage in interest-bearing financial practices forbidden to Catholics, and in his twenties and thirties Necker enjoyed a meteoric rise as a banker and speculator. He became Louis XVI's finance minister, a position he lost in 1781 during a financial crisis brought on by his policy of supporting the American Revolution via high-interest loans, but he remained a voice for reform in the years leading up to the French Revolution. The Château de Coppet dated back to the thirteenth century, but it only came into the family when Necker bought the property as his country estate in 1784, when his daughter was eighteen.

As a Protestant growing up in Paris, daughter of a nouveau riche financier, Germaine Necker found herself in an ambiguous relationship with the aristocratic culture around her. Her parents couldn't countenance her marrying a Catholic, and so they didn't take the usual route of buying their way into the French aristocracy through marriage. When their daughter turned twenty, they settled for an impoverished but Protestant Swedish nobleman on the verge of middle age, and so Germaine Necker became Madame la Baronne de Staël-Holstein. Her father bought the grateful groom an ambassadorship to France so that the newlyweds wouldn't have to live in the baron's homeland.

Herder too had a complicated relationship to the aristocracy. A commoner by birth, a populist by conviction, and a man of deep personal piety, Herder spent most of his career awkwardly ensconced in court circles as an employee of the libertine Carl August von Sachsen-Weimar. The grand duke of this little duchy (roughly the size of Rhode Island) was a generous patron of the arts, but he took a dim view of the revolutionary changes sweeping over France. Herder's relations with his patron became increasingly strained after he refused to offer prayers in church for the French royal family after their imprisonment in 1789.

Both Herder and de Staël were lifelong opponents of despotism. De Staël's first book, published in 1788 when she was twenty-two, was an encomium to the republican ideals of the Genevan Jean-Jacques Rousseau; his portrait hangs to this day in the Grand Salon at Coppet. In 1792 Herder celebrated the early Provençal poets for creating a poetry "whose purpose and goal was *freedom of thought*"—his italics—breaking the yoke of the "despotism" of Latin (*Briefe zu Beförderung der Humanität*, 482). He went farther in a passage deleted from subsequent editions of the book, declaring that "there is only one class in the state, the *Volk* (not the rabble); the king belongs to it as well as the peasant" (768–69).

Both Herder and de Staël welcomed the advent of the French Revolution, only to recoil at the mounting violence capped by Robespierre's Reign of Terror, the state-sponsored bloodbath that gave the world the very term "terrorism." During the revolution de Staël took great risks, and spent large sums in bribes, to smuggle endangered friends out of France. She enjoyed a period of substantial political influence during the late 1790s, but her days in Paris were numbered after she opposed Napoleon's assumption of dictatorial powers in 1799. It is no coincidence that Herder and de Staël wrote two of their most ambitious comparative works—his multivolume *Briefe zu Beförderung der Humanität* (1792–97) and her *De la littérature: Considérée dans ses rapports avec les institutions sociales* (1800)—during this tumultuous period, as they sought alternatives to the warring despotisms that surrounded them.

The Tongue, This Little Limb

Language and literature are closely bound up with ethics and politics throughout Herder's multifaceted writings, from his very first works— *How Philosophy Can Become More Universal and Useful for the Benefit of the People* (1765) and *Fragments on Recent German Literature* (1767–68)— through his *Treatise on the Origin of Language* (a foundational work for comparative philology), to his *Outline of a Philosophy of History* (a second field-creating work), and on to such later writings as *The Effect of Poetry on Ethics* and his *Letters for the Furtherance of Humanity*. In these works, and in his major collections of *Volkslieder* (1774–79), Herder developed his highly influential ideas on the intimate relation between language, literature, and national identity—"the Herder effect," as Pascale Casanova has called it (*The World Republic of Letters*, 75).

Germany in the eighteenth century was notably lacking in political unity of the sort enjoyed by France or England; Sachsen-Weimar was just one of some three hundred miniature polities (the number kept shifting) wedged in between Prussia and Austria. There were also substantial German-speaking minorities in many other regions, from Hungary to Pennsylvania to Argentina; Herder began his own career teaching school in the German community in Riga, Latvia. He published his first books during his Riga years (1764–69), when he began to seek the unity of German culture in its language and its literature, particularly the literature of *das Volk*—the people as a whole, not simply the peasantry or commoners. What distinguished true *Volkspoesie* for Herder was not a specific class origin but rather its embodiment of a people's aspirations, their culture, their landscape and environment.

In the preface to his first collection of *Volkslieder* (1774), Herder argued that the wellspring of European poetry could be found in the popular ballads and songs of the Middle Ages. He praises the English poets in particular (with his characteristic use of fervent italics) for staying in touch with their artistic roots: "The greatest singers and favorites of the Muses, *Chaucer* and *Spenser, Shakespear* and *Milton, Philip Sidney* and *Selden*—how can I, how shall I describe them?—were *enthusiasts for the old songs* . . . the root and core of the nation" (18–19). And woe betide the artist—or the scholar—who undervalues the old songs:

> Anyone who dismisses them and has no feeling for them shows that he is so inundated in the trumpery of aping the foreign, or so transfixed by the senseless fool's gold of foreign mimicry, that he has ceased to value or have any feeling for what is the very *body of the nation.* And so a grafted foreign seedling or a leaf fluttering in the wind gets the name of *an all-time virtuoso of the latest taste! a Thinker!* (19)

In an essay on Shakespeare, Herder stresses the playwright's homegrown virtues: his colloquial language, his accessibility to a wide audience, and his lack of concern for artificial rules of art. Fundamentally, this means that Shakespeare wasn't French. "The question I really want to ask," Herder declares, in tones dripping with irony, "is whether anything in the world possibly surpasses the sleek, classical thing that the Corneilles, Racines, and Voltaires have produced, the series of beautiful *scenes, dialogues, verses,* and *rhymes* with their *measure, decorum,* and *brilliance?*" ("Shakespeare," 295). French drama is deadened by "this outward conformity, this effigy treading the boards," yet "every country in Europe is besotted with this slick superficiality and continues to ape it" (295).

Herder's sarcastic term for imitation, *Nachäfferei* ("aping after"), is a pointed rejoinder to the *Nachahmung* or pious imitation of the ancients promoted by his older contemporary Johann Joachim Winckelmann, whose *Über die Nachahmung der griechischen Malerei und Bildhauerkunst*

(1755) had championed classical Greek art as the model through which German artists could return to natural simplicity and escape the weight of French neoclassicism. By contrast, Herder elaborated a vision of England as a powerful countermodel to modern France and ancient Greece alike. Shakespeare (and by extension Goethe, Schiller, or Herder himself) could go beyond Sophocles and Racine, not by trying to imitate either of them, but instead by finding new forms of expression that would be as responsive to their age and environment as the Greek and French tragedians were to theirs.

Yet was Herder really offering an escape from imitation, or was he merely relocating the objects of emulation across the English Channel? As Ulrich Beil has noted, Herder placed his successors in "what we would now call a *double bind:* it seemed that the Germans were to be set right through imitation (of England) to free themselves from the curse of imitation and establish an autonomous national culture" ("Zwischen Fremdbestimmung und Universalitätsanspruch," 277). The most influential German literary historian of the nineteenth century, Georg Gottfried Gervinus, argued that the way out of this double bind was to set aside foreign models altogether. Gervinus embodied his perspective in his massive *Geschichte der poetischen National-Literatur der Deutschen*, which appeared in five volumes from 1835 to 1842. His was an oxymoronic title, proclaiming the "poetic national-literature" of a people who didn't have a nation to call their own. In his fourth volume, Gervinus criticizes Herder for not having the courage of his national convictions, shrewdly noting that even Herder's project of collecting folk poetry was an imitative enterprise, inspired by Thomas Percy's *Reliques of Ancient English Poetry* (1765). To Gervinus, Herder's internationalism merely represented an attempt to disguise his dependence on his English predecessor. "It seemed too poor to be an English Percy," Gervinus writes, "and so he undertook to avoid so common an influence by assembling the treasures of the entire world" (quoted in Beil, 276n.63).

Yet Herder's internationalism was neither a reflexive Anglophilia nor an anxious Francophobia; instead, it was the fruit of deep reflection on the uncertainties of cultural belonging in a radically relativistic world. Language and literature may be the best index of national identity, but

Herder understood language, literature, and national identity itself as common products of ceaseless flux:

> Poetry is a Proteus among the peoples; it changes its form according to the people's language, customs, habits, according to their temperament, the climate, even according to their accent.
>
> As nations migrate, as languages mix themselves together and change, as new matters stir men, as their inclinations take another direction and their endeavors another aim, as new models influence their combination of images and concepts, even as the tongue, this little limb, moves differently and the ear accustoms itself to different sounds: so too the art of poetry changes not only among different nations, but also within one people. (*Briefe zu Beförderung*, 572)

Just how confidently can anyone speak of "one people" at all, if the very tongue is so vulnerable to change? Herder's enthusiasm for cultural difference is tinged by an undercurrent of fear, an anxiety in the face of a variety too great to be encompassed by any concept whatever. "How it always frightens me," he confesses, "whenever I hear an entire nation or era characterized in a few words: for what a huge mass of differences is bundled up in the word *Nation*, or the *Middle Ages*, or *antiquity and modernity*!" (493).

Herder's relativism allows him to assert that each national culture should be assessed on its own terms. Yet even as he rescues Shakespeare from Parisian and Athenian standards alike, Herder is left pondering the evanescence of any artist's work beyond its immediate environment. His Shakespeare essay leads to a melancholy conclusion that anticipates Shelley's "Ozymandias":

> Sadder and more important is the thought that even this great creator of history and the world soul grows older every day, that the words and customs and categories of the age wither and fall like autumnal leaves, that we are already so removed from these great ruins of the age of chivalry. . . . And soon, perhaps, as everything is obliterated and tends in different directions, even his drama will become quite incapable of living performance, will become the dilapidated

remains of a colossus, of a pyramid, which all gaze upon with wonder and none understands. ("Shakespeare," 307)

Herder's melancholy was no mere pose; he suffered a mental breakdown
around this time.

A deeply divided personality, Herder was capable of intense friendships
and bitter estrangements, most notably with—and then from—Goethe. He
met the young poet in Strasbourg in 1770 and inspired him to move beyond a derivative classicism to the intensely personal poetry of the "Sturm
und Drang" movement, of which they became founders. It was then
through Goethe's good offices that Carl August appointed Herder in 1776
as supervisor of clergy in Weimar, and for twenty years Herder and Goethe
were close friends. Their friendship was troubled, however, by Herder's
distaste for Goethe's immorality (Goethe and the grand duke were never
happier than when venturing off together in search of village maidens to
seduce) and by Herder's sense of being neglected by his increasingly famous friend.

Herder struggled throughout his life to hold his various selves together,
but the divisions that were personally so painful added originality and
complexity to his thought. A poet and a philosopher, a theologian and a
philologist, he was impatient with received ideas and methods. He was
among the first to assert that the Song of Songs is a secular poem and not
a religious text, and he did pioneering textual work in establishing the
historical order of the gospels. Philosophically, he was heavily influenced
by the young Immanuel Kant, under whom he studied at Königsberg,
but also by the poetic theologian Johann Georg Hamann, self-styled "Prussian Pan" and "Mystic of the North," who attacked Enlightenment rationality in an oracular, aphoristic style (Zaremba, *Johann Gottfried Herder*,
40–48). Throughout his writings, Herder sought to reconcile secular philosophy and mystical theology, systematic thought and a deep suspicion
of all systems. An engaging but often polemical writer, he composed some
of his liveliest essays out of rage at new works by his former mentor Kant,
whom he accused of fostering a heartless rationality divorced from real
life—"a swindle," "a pure-impure reason," a "transcendental barbarism . . .
dwelling in an empyrean high above all nature and experience" (*Briefe*

zu Beförderung, 793). These are judgments that Herder issued in print; he was still more biting in a letter to Jean Paul, dismissing Kantian philosophy as intellectual masturbation: "*Onanismus* der rein-unreinen Vernunft" (*Briefe Gesamtausgabe* 7:425).

The constant mutation of thought, expression, and values meant for Herder that philosophical introspection is bound to go off the rails unless it is constantly tested against the varieties of social experience. This could best be done through study of different people's languages and customs. Comparative philology expanded in Herder's vision into a proto-anthropology, another discipline of which he was a founder. He first developed the thesis later elaborated by Sapir and Whorf that language strongly shapes thought, and he repeatedly turned to literature as the royal road to cultural understanding, able to preserve the thoughts and the values of past and present cultures alike. The comparative study of literature was a key means by which Herder sought to forge a synthesis of local identity and common humanity. As Jérôme David has emphasized,

> *Humanität* is a goal for Herder, that of a *Menschheit* that wants to honor the free will given by God. Let us not forget that Herder was a pastor. This *Humanität* is among other things a collective process. . . . There is no longer an essence of humanity but rather an incessant effort of collectivities seeking, each in its own fashion, to become more fully humane. (*Spectres de Goethe*, 46–49)

Herder's collections of *Volkslieder* brought together poems from many countries, enabling him to argue both for the distinctive strength of German literature and also for its connection to a wider, even universal cultural continuum. Combating dismissive views of medieval German writing, he declares that "to those—so genteel, refined, and jaded—who judge and blithely condemn, I merely reply with the example of every neighboring nation. Without a doubt, the Gauls, the English, and all the more the Nordic peoples were *Volk*, merely *Volk*! *Volk* like the German *Volk*!" (*Volkslieder*, 18). Herder's conception of *das Volk* has none of the racist connotations it would take on in later treatments. What he sought through comparative study was both to highlight the integrity of German culture and to combat any nationalistic vanity, stressing the common humanity of which any particular culture is just one expression. His is thus a nationalist internationalism, grounded in the elemental structures of linguistic kinship as expressed through the personal, regional, and national inflections of "the tongue, this little limb."

Falling Back into Life

If Herder gives us a prime case of early comparatism in a semiperipheral location, Germaine de Staël was situated at the very heart of European culture. Born and raised in Paris, she never lost her sense of Paris as the center of the world, even after extended travels in Italy, England, Germany, and Russia. The pleasures of the Château de Coppet, and the stimulation of arguing with Goethe and Schiller in Weimar, were pallid substitutes for life in the *ville lumière*. As she remarks in her book *Ten Years of Exile*, "Montaigne said, 'I am French through Paris.' If such was his thought three hundred years ago, what would it be with so many witty people gathered in the same city since then, and so many accustomed to using their wit for the pleasure of conversation?" (28). Napoleon knew that banishment to the provinces could break a true Parisian's spirit, less visibly but just as effectively as imprisonment in the Bastille. "In the long run," de Staël says, "residence forty leagues from the capital . . . weakens most exiles" (29).

De Staël developed her ideas on literature and society under the shadow of her exclusion from the Parisian circles essential to her intellectual vitality and even her mental health. After Napoleon seized power in 1799, de Staël, Constant, and their embattled circle of liberal friends came into increasingly open conflict with the first consul, soon to be self-crowned emperor. The tipping-point came in January 1800, when Constant gave a speech in Parliament praising liberty and all but openly denouncing Napoleon. De Staël's salon was a breeding place for liberal sentiments, and her relationship with Constant was common knowledge. In *Ten Years of Exile*, de Staël reports that, having helped her lover write his speech, "I could not help but fear what might happen to me in consequence. I was vulnerable through my taste for society" (28). She had a soiree planned for the evening after Constant gave his speech, and the consequences quickly became apparent: "I was to have a number of people in my home whose company I enjoyed a great deal but who were partial to the new government. I received ten notes of excuse at five o'clock. I withstood the first and second well enough, but when those notes followed one after the other I began to feel uneasy" (29).

She wasn't yet banished outright, but social ostracism was its own form of psychological torture. This was all the more painful for someone subject to what she calls "ennui," speaking of it in a way that we would today label depression:

> The specter of *ennui* has pursued me all my life; it is through that terror that I might have been capable of bowing to tyranny, had this weakness not yielded to the example of my father, to his blood running in my veins. Be that as it may, Bonaparte was quite familiar with my weakness as well as everyone else's, for he is perfectly aware of everyone's bad side, since that is what brings them under his subjection. (28)

Later, in exile, she contemplated suicide, though characteristically she channeled her depression into writing a long essay weighing and then dismissing the arguments in its favor. She begins the essay by noting that reflection is the best remedy for suffering, "just as a patient can turn over on a sickbed, seeking to find the least painful position" ("Réflexions sur le suicide," 345).

The looming threat of exile is the context in which she wrote *De la littérature: Considérée dans ses rapports avec les institutions sociales*, which she drafted in the months after Napoleon forced her to shut down her salon. In taking up this topic, de Staël accomplished several purposes at once: to refresh her mind by thinking about literature, one of her great passions; to assert the importance of women's contributions to public life; to advance her critique of authoritarianism by indirect means; and, not least, to restore her place in Parisian society. The book brilliantly accomplished all these goals:

> Toward the spring of 1800 I published my work on literature, and its success fully restored me to favor in society; my salon was peopled once more, and I rediscovered the pleasure of conversation;

and conversation in Paris, I admit, has always been the most stimulating of all for me. There was not a word about Bonaparte in my
book on literature, and yet the most liberal sentiments were, I believe, expressed vigorously. But at the time Bonaparte was still far
from being able to shackle the freedom of the press as he can now.
(*Ten Years of Exile*, 34)

De Staël's book returned to the "querelle des Anciens et des Modernes"
that had raged a century before: should modern art and literature be based
on imitation of the ancients, or did the progress in science and in understanding require new forms of expression? In a chapter on "The General
Spirit of Modern Literature," de Staël begins by acknowledging the importance of classical models. "The principle of the fine arts, imitation,"
she remarks, "does not admit of unlimited perfection; the moderns, in this
respect, can never do more than follow the path traced out by the ancients" (*De la littérature*, 11). Yet she positions herself squarely on the side
of the moderns, and not simply to rehearse arguments formerly made by
a mostly male group of thinkers. Her emphasis is on "a new development
of sensibility and a deepened knowledge of character," which she sees as
deriving from the improved status of women in modern society:

> The ancients esteemed men as their friends, while they considered
> women merely as slaves brought up for that unhappy state. Indeed,
> most women almost deserved that appellation; their minds were not
> furnished with a single idea, nor were they enlightened by one gen-
> erous sentiment. . . . Only the moderns, acknowledging other talents
> and other ties, have been able to express that sense of predilection
> that can incline a lifelong destiny toward the sentiments of love. (11)

A century earlier the *querelle* had focused on the reigning genres of drama,
epic, and lyric poetry, but by de Staël's time the novel was coming into
prominence. Novels were generally regarded as light and even immoral
entertainment (women were said to read the racier romances "with one
hand"), but de Staël recognizes the novel as the quintessential expression
of modernity:

> Novels, those varied productions of the modern spirit, were a genre
> almost entirely unknown to the ancients. They did compose a few

pastorals in the form of novels, at a time when the Greeks endeav-
ored to find means of relaxation amid servitude. But before women
had created an interest in private life, matters of love had little ability to excite the curiosity of men, whose time was almost entirely
occupied by political pursuits. (11)

In de Staël's analysis, later echoed by Virginia Woolf in *A Room of One's
Own*, women writers gain insight from their position as a dominated
class in patriarchal society: "Women discovered in the human character
a myriad of nuances that the need to dominate, or the fear of being
dominated, led them to perceive; they supplied dramatic talents with
new and moving secrets" (11). These deepened perceptions enrich literature and then enter the public sphere of philosophical discourse: "Every
sentiment to which they were permitted to devote themselves—the fear
of death, the regrets of life, unlimited devotion, resentment without
end—enriched literature with new expressions. . . . It is for this reason
that the modern moralists have, in general, so much more finesse and
sagacity in the knowledge of mankind than did the moralists of antiquity" (12).

The modern novel, expressing a feminized moral sensibility, thus gives
rise to "those ideas that were not to be found until women had been accorded a kind of civil equality" (12). Yet de Staël is well aware that women
still have only "a kind" of civil equality, and that her age had yet to achieve
the freedoms long sought by republican thinkers from Rousseau to her
father to Constant and herself. In a world rife with inequality and ever-
renewed despotisms, the private sphere remains the breeding ground of
progress, and literature is needed to point the way forward:

> We must not compare modern virtues with those of the ancients in
> their public life; it is only in free countries that there can exist that
> constant duty and that generous relation between the citizens and
> their country. It is true that, under a despotic government, custom
> or prejudice may still inspire some brilliant acts of military cour-
> age; but the continued and painful attention given to civil affairs
> and legislative virtues, the disinterested sacrifice of one's whole
> life to the public sphere, can only exist where there is a real passion

for liberty. It is therefore in private qualities, in philanthropic sentiments, and in a few superior writings, that we should examine moral progress. (14)

De la littérature had a great impact in valorizing women's writing over against the prestige of the dominant male tradition, and de Staël's emphasis on literature's responsiveness to its society gave her work considerable relevance for peripheral locales far from France. To give one example, her book was taken up in the 1830s in the journal *Niterói: Revista Brasileira*. As Antonio Candido characterizes the journal's adaptation of her ideas, "a new country, such as Brazil, must create its own literature, for which it must before anything else reject classical influences in order to open itself to local inspirations" (*Formação da literatura brasileira*, 2:296). Among the journal's contributors, Candido quotes J. M. Pereira da Silva, a future founder of the Academia Brasileira da Letras:

> At the beginning of the century, Romantic poetry raised its victorious standard everywhere in Europe; in France, in Italy, which hitherto had thrown themselves into the embrace of an entirely imitative poetry. . . . In Brazil, however, this poetic revolution was never fully felt; our bards renounced their fatherland . . . becoming mere imitators of unrelated thoughts and ideas. (2:296–97)

For Pereira da Silva, urging his countrymen to join the poetic revolution, a de Staëlean Romanticism becomes the force that can displace France itself as the object of imitative desire.

De la littérature was the first of several major works in which de Staël used literature to develop progressive ideas through cross-cultural analysis. She pursued these goals in her novel *Corinne, ou l'Italie* (1807) and in her penetrating study of modern German culture, *De l'Allemagne* (1810), which introduced German Romanticism to France and sought to counter French stereotypes of their Teutonic neighbors. As Albert Guérard has put it, "She was among the first to discover that the Germans were Germans, and not simply benighted human beings who, through sheer perversity, refused to speak French" (*Preface to World Literature*, 347). These works, however, were written not in France but during the decade of exile that began when Napoleon banished her in 1803, a period that ended only with his defeat at Waterloo.

De Staël could never have contented herself for long with hosting a purely literary salon. She held strong political opinions, was impatient of tact and discretion, and often got carried away in the flow of her ideas. Interlocutors as eminent as Byron and Goethe struggled to get in a word edgewise. She had honed the French art of the barbed aphorism—Napoleon signed peace treaties, she later wrote, with "the care Polyphemus took to count the sheep as he admitted them to his cave" (*Ten Years of Exile*, 51)—and comments made among friends had a tendency to get around. Her restored salon soon attracted renewed hostility from the first consul: "The existence of a woman people visit for her wit and her literary reputation is nothing much, but this nothing much did not depend on him, and that was sufficient for his wanting to crush it" (58). Her fault wasn't mere independence; Bonaparte was well aware that her visitors included many of his opponents. Hence he "persecuted me with meticulous care and inflexible asperity at an ever-increasing pace" (1).

Left unfinished at her death, *Ten Years of Exile* gives a chilling portrait of a tyrant who established what was probably the first modern cult of personality. Here, the blending of old and new modes takes on a sinister cast, described with a novelist's eye for detail: "in his dress, as in the political situation of the day, a mixture of the old and new regimes was seen. He had outfits made all of gold, straight hair, short legs and a large head, as well as something hard to describe that was awkward and arrogant, scornful and diffident, that seemed to combine all the parvenu's lack of charm with all the tyrant's boldness" (51). She says that Napoleon's smile "was more like a metal spring than a natural reaction," but it was considered charming by his adherents, who sought any assurance of his favor and who fixated on his every attribute. "I recall a member of the Institute," she continues, "a Councilor of State, telling me seriously that the First Consul's fingernails were perfectly formed" (51).

The counselors who were hanging on Napoleon's smile and admiring his fingernails were becoming cogs in the machinery of a despotic economy:

At a mint in Petersburg, I was struck by the violence of machines driven by a single will; those hammers, those anvils, seem like people, or rather voracious animals, and if you tried to resist their force, it would annihilate you. However, all that apparent fury is calculated, and those springs operate by the movement of a single arm. In my mind's eye, this is the image of Bonaparte's tyranny; he causes the death of thousands of men, just as these wheels strike coins, and his agents, for the most part, are as insensitive as this wood and this iron that fulfill their function without relying on themselves for guidance. The invisible momentum of these machines comes from a will at once diabolical and mathematical that transforms moral life into a servile tool. (48–49)

The outlines of the new regime were already evident to de Staël when she wrote *De la littérature*. Though she acknowledged that Napoleon had brought order after the chaos of the revolution, she felt that the fall of Robespierre was leading not to a free republic but to a new and more insidious form of tyranny.

Even as she sought literary means to advance the cause of progress, de Staël was haunted by her awareness of the limited effect that any novelist or critic could have in a world in which progress of any kind was difficult to discern. In concluding her chapter on "The General Spirit of Modern Literature," de Staël cites an eloquent speech in 1766 by a member of the French Parliament who successfully argued for the posthumous reversal of a death sentence unjustly imposed on his father. She starts to draw a positive conclusion from this example— "Thus the century has progressed toward the conquest of liberty; for virtue is always its herald"—only to be brought up short by more recent memories:

Alas! How shall we banish the painful contrast which so forcibly strikes the imagination? One crime was recollected during a long succession of years; but we have since witnessed numberless cruelties committed and forgotten almost at the same moment! And it was under the shadow of the Republic, the noblest, the most glorious, and the proudest institution of the human mind, that those execrable crimes have been committed! Ah! How difficult do we find it to repel those melancholy ideas; every time we reflect upon the destiny of man, the revolution appears before us! (15)

Comparison here reaches its limit, collapsing into unbridgeable contrast: one bright moment in 1766—the year of de Staël's birth—pales before the chaos and repression that have predominated ever since. Though she is careful to speak only of the revolution, there is a pointed absence of any suggestion that things have improved under Napoleon. If recent history offers no consolation, a comparative search for principles or historical patterns may be equally futile. "In vain do we transport our spirit back over times long past, in vain do we desire to comprehend recent events and lasting works within the eternal connection of abstract patterns," de Staël concludes. "Reflection no longer has the strength to sustain us; we have to fall back into life" (15–16). De Staël should be on any comparatist's reading list today, for her pioneering analyses of the relations of literature to social institutions, for her emphasis on literature's ethical and political force, and also for her sobering reflections on the limits of what criticism can accomplish before we fall back into life.

The Principle of Polyglottism

In writing about literature in its relations to social institutions, one institution that de Staël didn't mention was the university. Higher education wasn't a major force for social change in her day, but over the course of the nineteenth century, first in Germany and then elsewhere, colleges and universities became places for sustained intellectual inquiry. The social change that couldn't be achieved by caffeinated conversation in aristocratic salons might be brought about by extended research and the inculcation of new ideas in a younger generation. The outlines of the modern university were emerging, and a growing number of fields were becoming academic disciplines, among them *littérature comparée* or *vergleichende Literaturwissenschaft*. We can see this development in the work of two scholars who built on the legacy of Herder and de Staël as they helped establish comparative literature as an institutional field of study: the Transylvanian comparatist Hugo Meltzl, principal editor of the first journal of comparative literature, the *Acta Comparationis Litterarum Universarum* (1877–88), and the Irish scholar Hutcheson Macaulay Posnett, who established the discipline's name in English with the publication of his book *Comparative Literature* in 1886.

Posnett's and Meltzl's methods diverged dramatically, but they both sought alternatives to the dominant modes of literary and cultural study, the nationalistic and the cosmopolitan. Writing from borderline positions both culturally and institutionally, Posnett and Meltzl understood the ease with which cosmopolitanism could collapse into its seeming opposite, becoming a form of imperial nationalism. Both in their complex personal positions and in their intellectual agendas, Meltzl and Posnett offer important early models for a global comparatism today, even as the eclipse of their projects offers cautionary lessons we should still heed.

The tension between nationalism and cosmopolitanism was already present in comparative philology. Supranational in method, philology was often strongly nationalistic in its emphases. In the revolutionary year 1848 the great philologist Jacob Grimm published an influential *Geschichte der deutschen Sprache* in two volumes. He intended this history of the German language to demonstrate the true unity of "our unnaturally divided fatherland," as he put it in a dedication to Gervinus, the historian who had criticized Herder for his insufficient nationalism. In his dedication, Grimm speaks of Goethe not as the proponent of *Weltliteratur* but as the very embodiment of German identity: "without him we never truly feel ourselves as Germans, so strong is the native power of national language and poetry" (*Geschichte*, 1:iv). Grimm's history had a contemporary agenda: he eloquently evokes "the people's freedom, which nothing can hinder any longer, of which the very birds twitter on the rooftops," adding, "O, that it would come soon and never withdraw from us!" (1:iv–v). Carrying Gervinus's nationalism into the linguistic realm, Grimm proclaims the triumph of the German language, seen in the sound shifts emphasized in his "Grimm's Law":

Since the close of the first century the weakness of the Roman Empire had become manifest (even though its flame still flickered from time to time), and among the unconquerable Germans the awareness of their unstoppable advance into every region of Europe had grown ever stronger. . . . How else could it be, but that so forceful a mobilization of the people would stir up their language as well, shaking it out of its accustomed pathways and exalting it? Do not a certain courage and pride lie in the strengthening of voiced stop into voiceless stop, and voiceless stop into fricative? (1:306–7)

Such philological nationalism could be countered by cosmopolitan perspectives, yet cosmopolitanism itself was often a projected form of nationalism. Thus the poet and translator August Wilhelm Schlegel wrote in 1804:

Universalism, cosmopolitanism is the true German trait. For a long time our lack of a unified direction has placed us in an inferior position in relation to the limited and therefore more effective national tendencies of other peoples. But this lack, if transformed into something positive, becomes the totality of all directions and will establish superiority on our side. It is therefore not an all too sanguine hope, I believe, to think the time close when German will be the general language of communication of all civilized nations. (Quoted in Koch, "Introduction," 74)

That same year, Schlegel joined de Staël's household at Coppet as tutor to her children. He remained part of her inner circle until her death in 1817, then took up a professorship in Bonn, where he devoted himself primarily to Oriental studies and set up a printing shop for Sanskrit texts. Sir William Jones's enthusiasm for Sanskrit was having lasting results.

By the 1870s, the unstoppable march of German fricatives had yielded a unified and powerful Germany, and as Schlegel had hoped, German was becoming a crucial language, at least for international scholarly exchange if not for civilization as a whole. Yet German speakers outside German territories still found themselves in complex situations of divided or multiple cultural loyalties. This was very much the case for Hugo Meltzl, who was born in 1846 among the German-speaking minority in Transylvania. Meltzl was born into a well-to-do merchant family and attended Unitarian and Lutheran schools in his hometown and in the provincial capital of Kolozsvár, also known as Cluj or Klausenburg—a city whose shifting names already tell a tale of ethnic intermingling and competition among

Hungarians, Romanians, and Germans. Now part of Romania, the city was rebaptized in 1974 as Cluj-Napoca, to the greater glory of the Ceauşescu regime in honor of the region's early history as a Roman colony.

Meltzl learned Hungarian and Romanian only in school, where he concentrated on German philosophy and literature while also trying his hand at writing poetry. Both a Hungarian patriot and a cultural internationalist, he had a Herderian interest in folk poetry, including the songs of the Transylvanian Roma. He went to Leipzig and Heidelberg for college and graduate study, writing a doctoral dissertation on Schopenhauer. Upon receiving his degree in 1872 at age twenty-six, he returned to Cluj to become a professor of German language and literature at the new Franz-Joseph-Universität. Named for the Habsburg emperor, the university had been founded that year with a double purpose: to spread the influence of German culture in the eastern wing of the empire and at the same time to promote "Magyarization," which in practice meant increasing the sway of Hungarian over Romanian culture in this ethnically mixed region. It is in this context that a locally born, Heidelberg-trained academic could be chosen for a professorship despite his lack of prior experience.

The youngest of the university's forty faculty, Meltzl found himself coexisting with colleagues who espoused varying forms of nationalism and differing degrees of imperialism, together with some cosmopolitan idealists such as himself. Most important among these was the oldest member of the faculty, the Hungarian polymath Samuel Brassai (1800–1897), a professor of comparative philology and also a mathematician, botanist, and theologian. Well into his eighties, Brassai continued to publish books on algebra, Sanskrit linguistics, and theology. In 1877 the two scholars joined together to found the world's first journal of comparative literature, which they conceived as a venue for international communication and exchange.

At first they published their journal under a triple Hungarian/German/French title, *Összehasonlító Irodalomtörténelmi Lapok / Zeitschrift für vergleichende Litteratur / Journal d'histoire des littératures comparées*. Rapidly moving beyond an emphasis on national comparisons, they began a "New Series" in 1879 under the expansive Latin title *Acta Comparationis Litterarum Universarum*, or "Journal for the Comparison of the Totality of

Literature," in Haun Saussy's apt translation ("Exquisite Cadavers," 9). With Brassai already in his mid-seventies, Meltzl did most of the actual editing; he became the journal's sole editor upon Brassai's retirement in 1883. Throughout its eleven years of existence, the journal was a shoestring operation, largely funded by Meltzl and Brassai themselves. Yet the editors made up in enthusiasm what they lacked in resources.

In an introductory essay, Meltzl set forth the editors' intention as nothing less than "the *reform of literary history*, a reform long awaited and long overdue which is possible only through an extensive application of *the comparative principle*" ("Present Tasks," 42, his italics). He argued that Goethe's cosmopolitan conception of *Weltliteratur* had been pressed into the service of narrowly nationalistic concerns, and he wished to rescue the idea of world literature from an emphasis on a nation's absorption of foreign influences and its own impact abroad: "A journal like ours, then, must be devoted at the same time to the art of translation and to the Goethean *Weltliteratur* (a term which German literary historians, particularly Gervinus, have thoroughly misunderstood). . . . As every unbiased man of letters knows, modern literary history, as generally practiced today, is nothing but an *ancilla historiae politicae*, or even an *ancilla nationis*" (42)—a handmaid of political history or even of the nation itself.

As a telling example of the myopic distortions involved in such nationalistic literary history, Meltzl cites studies of the aubade, whose origin German literary historians traced to Wolfram von Eschenbach, ignoring the fact that "Lieder of this type were sung eighteen centuries ago in China (as those contained in the *Shih Ching*) and are frequently found among the folksongs of modern peoples, for instance, the Hungarians" (43). Meltzl's example reveals the double strategy by which his journal would seek to counter the literary nationalism of the European great powers: first, by widening the field to include masterpieces of other cultures (China, in this example), and second, by expanding the European arena to include the literatures of smaller countries: in this instance, not at all randomly, Hungary. Where Schlegel and Goethe had looked forward to German taking a leading role in cultural exchange, Meltzl and Brassai sought to showcase languages and literatures usually overlooked from great-power perspectives.

Throughout the nineteenth century, the scholarly bias toward the literatures of a few major powers was reinforced by a bias toward major languages. Writers living in Hungary and writing in Hungarian were thus doubly disadvantaged, a dilemma emphasized at the century's end by the Danish comparatist Georg Brandes in a skeptical essay on *Weltlitera-tur* (1899). He had spent a lifetime working to modernize and liberalize Danish literature by introducing the major European literatures, most famously in his multivolume *Hovedstrømninger i det nittende Aarhundre-des Litteratur* (1872–90, Main Currents of Nineteenth-Century Litera-ture), which treated the literatures of England, France, Germany, and Italy. These main currents didn't include his own rivulet of Denmark, but he was tireless in promoting interest abroad in Ibsen and Kierkegaard, the Scandinavian writers he felt had the best chance at attracting wide recognition. By 1899, though, Brandes was exasperated with the endless uphill battle, which he describes in military language:

> It is incontestable that writers of different countries and languages occupy enormously different positions where their chances of obtain-ing worldwide fame, or even a moderate degree of recognition, are concerned. The most favorably situated are the French writers, al-though the French language occupies only the fifth rank in terms of its extent. When a writer has succeeded in France, he is known throughout the world. English and Germans, who can count on an immense public if they are successful, take second place. . . . But who-ever writes in Finnish, Hungarian, Swedish, Danish, Dutch, Greek or the like is obviously poorly placed in the universal struggle for fame. In this competition he lacks the major weapon, a language—which is, for a writer, almost everything. ("World Literature," 61)

Both Meltzl's Hungarian and Brandes's Danish appear in his list of the chronically disadvantaged. These disparities continue to this day. The Danish scholar Mads Rosendahl Thomsen has discussed the situation of "lonely canonicals," writers from small countries who may be almost alone in achieving recognition abroad (*Mapping World Literature*, 48). So too in his *Memoir of Hungary*, the novelist Sándor Márai wrote of his

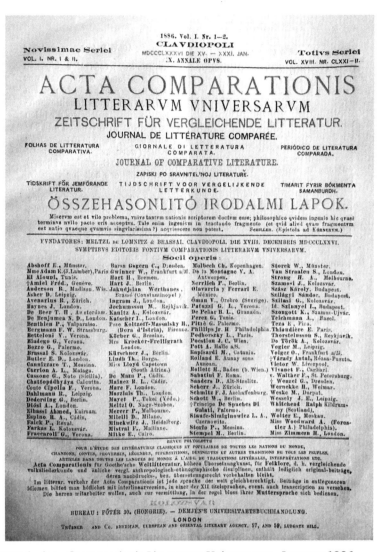

FIGURE 1. *Acta Comparationis Litterarum Universarum*, January 1886.

"destiny" as a writer in a language incomprehensible abroad: "What was this destiny? Loneliness" (316).

Meltzl and Brassai hoped that their journal could level the playing field by bringing more languages into play. This desire led to their most dramatic editorial decision: to admit ten (and eventually twelve) "official languages" for their articles. They printed the journal's title in all their official languages (figure 1). In the first issues, the Hungarian title came at the top, but soon it was dropped down, evidently so as not to put off readers abroad; it now came last on the masthead, in medium-sized type, "like a modest innkeeper following his guests," as Meltzl put it in an 1879 note ("An unsere Leser," 18). Antonio Martí Monterde has observed, "Meltzl is aware that, due to the peculiar situation of its language amid Europe's plurilingualism, Hungary represents an almost absolute alterity in the very middle of Europe; any relation between Hungarian literature and other literatures is marked by this difference" (*Un somni europeo*, 314).

In keeping with their polyglot emphasis, Meltzl and Brassai established an editorial board of global scope, with members not only from Hungary and Germany but also from Australia, Egypt, England, France, Holland, Iceland, India, Italy, Japan, Poland, Portugal, Sweden, Switzerland, Turkey, and the United States. By assembling so wide-ranging a team, and by founding their journal on "the Principle of Polyglottism," the editors sought at once to protect the individuality of smaller literatures and to explode nationalistic exclusivity. As Meltzl said in his inaugural essay on "Present Tasks of Comparative Literature,"

> By now, every nation demands its own "world literature" without quite knowing what is meant by it. By now, every nation considers itself, for one good reason or another, superior to all other nations. . . . This unhealthy "national principle" therefore constitutes the fundamental premise of the entire spiritual life of modern Europe. . . . Instead of giving free rein to polyglottism and reaping the fruits in the future (fruits that it would certainly bring), every nation today insists on the strictest monoglottism, by considering its own language superior or even destined to rule supreme. This is a childish competition whose result will finally be that all of them remain— inferior. (46)

The *Acta Comparationis Litterarum Universarum* was intended to set this situation right, both by its radical plurilingualism and also by its literary strategies. Meltzl and Brassai developed a two-pronged approach: first, to compare masterpieces of world literature (mostly composed in large countries with highly developed literary cultures), and second, through a Herderian emphasis on oral and folk materials. The study of folk songs became a centerpiece of the journal's project, a powerful way to level the playing field for countries not yet on the map of world masterpieces.

Meltzl was attempting a synthesis of Goethe's elitist globalism with Herder's populist emphasis on the folk, making the *Acta* more a refinement within German cultural debates than an alternative to them. In its broad outlines, moreover, the journal's program can be seen, as David Marno has argued, as presenting Hungarian literature as a visible but subordinate strand within Austro-Hungarian culture, "a last position accessible to someone who wants to advocate the literature of a country that had lost its war for national independence just two decades earlier," while implicitly furthering the empire's suppression of Croatian, Czech, Romanian, Serbian, and Slovakian, none of which figured among the journal's many official languages ("The Monstrosity of Literature," 40–41).

Operating within the German cultural diaspora and the Austro-Hungarian empire, Meltzl nonetheless set his sights well beyond the limits of imperial cultural politics. In his inaugural essay, Meltzl urges attention to "the spiritual life of 'literatureless peoples,' as we might call them, whose ethnic individuality should not be impinged upon by the wrong kind of missionary zeal." He goes on to condemn a recent Russian *ukaz* that had prohibited the literary use of Ukrainian in Ukraine—a region where the politics of language remain violently contested to this day. Meltzl is outraged by the Russian decree: "It would appear as the greatest sin against the Holy Spirit even if it were directed only against the folksongs of an obscure horde of Kirghizes instead of a people of fifteen million" (46). It was evidently Russia's censorship of minor literatures that caused Meltzl to exclude Russian from his journal's roster of "official languages"—a remarkable decision, really, to punish Russia by banishing its language from the pages of a young journal of enormous ambition but limited readership.

Meltzl was probably the first person ever to use an ecological metaphor to describe less-spoken languages and their literatures as endangered species: "In a time when certain animal species such as the mountain goat and the European bison are protected against extinction by elaborate and strict laws, the willful extinction of a human species (or its literature, which amounts to the same thing) should be impossible" (46). The *Acta* opposed great-power hegemony and sought to protect the literatures of smaller nations, promoting contact and mutual appreciation of traditions whose distinctness should be preserved and even enhanced in the process. Though he was personally an eminently cosmopolitan figure, Meltzl was nonetheless concerned to distance his project from a major-power cosmopolitanism. "It should be obvious," he wrote,

> that these polyglot efforts have nothing in common with any kind of universal fraternization or similar international *nephelokokkugia* [Cloud-Cuckoo-Land]. The ideals of Comparative Literature have nothing to do with foggy, "cosmopolitanizing" theories; the high aims (not to say tendencies) of a journal like ours would be gravely misunderstood or intentionally misrepresented if anybody expected us to infringe upon the national uniqueness of a people. . . . It is, on the contrary, the *purely national of all nations* that Comparative Literature means to cultivate lovingly. . . . Our secret motto is: nationality as the individuality of a people should be regarded as sacred and inviolable. Therefore, a people, be it ever so insignificant politically, is and will remain, from the standpoint of Comparative Literature, as important as the largest nation. (45)

The Relativity of Literature

A few years after Meltzl issued his stirring call to action, Hutcheson Macaulay Posnett took a different approach in the first book in English devoted to the new discipline. Posnett doesn't appear to have known of Meltzl or his journal, but from his position in Ireland he developed his own critique of a centralizing cosmopolitanism. Born in 1855, Posnett studied classical philology and law at Trinity College, Dublin, where he became a tutor while also practicing law in Dublin. He wrote on law and on historical method before turning to his study of comparative literature, which he completed just before sailing for New Zealand, where he had been appointed to the chair in classical philology at the University of Auckland. There he taught philology, English, French, and law, returning five years later to his legal career in Ireland.

Posnett's methods were diametrically opposed to Meltzl's: he worked on his own rather than with a group, amassing a mountain of evidence through wide and somewhat scattershot reading, relying often on translation rather than concerning himself with polyglottism. Yet his perspective was as global as Meltzl's: he gave substantial space to India, China, and the Arab world as well as to the ancient Mediterranean and modern Europe, and he sought worldwide correlations of literary and social developments that enabled him to give equal weight to folk literature and to literary masterpieces. In his hands, comparatism became an ethical and even social ideal, allowing him to appreciate a wide variety of literatures on their own terms, instead of ignoring or assimilating whatever differed from European norms. Natalie Melas has observed that for Posnett "comparison itself turns out to be a prominent measure of social progress: the more a society advances—that is, expands and specializes—the more it brings under the purview of comparison" (*All the Difference in the World*, 21). Yet a comparative interest in other literary traditions didn't mean a leveling cosmopolitanism, which Posnett identified particularly with France:

> In the literature of France, since the firm establishment of centralized monarchy in the seventeenth century, we everywhere feel the presence of that centralizing spirit which in the Académie Française found a local habitation and a name . . . capable of its best defence from the standpoint of cosmopolitan culture. From this standpoint national centres like Paris and its Academy become the best substitute for a world-centre which differences of language and national character cannot permit. (343–44)

Posnett here anticipates Pascale Casanova's perspective in *The World Republic of Letters*, but he contrasts Parisian cosmopolitanism unfavorably with a more decentralized and regionally varied British culture:

> the true makers of national literature are the actions and thoughts of the nation itself; the place of these can never be taken by the sympathies of a cultured class too wide to be national, or those of a central academy too refined to be provincial. . . . Here, then, we have two types of national literature—the English, blending local and central elements of national life without losing national unity

in local distinctions such as Italy and Germany have known too well; the French, centralizing its life in Paris, and so tending to prefer cosmopolitan ideals. (345)

Posnett considered cosmopolitanism an imperial nationalism writ large. Long before Benedict Anderson's *Imagined Communities*, Posnett argued that national identity is a fiction, useful in various ways but not to be taken literally: "What is a 'nation'? . . . The word 'nation' points to kinship and a body of kinsmen as the primary idea and fact marked by 'nationality.' . . . But the 'nations' of modern Europe have left these little groups so far behind that their culture has either forgotten the nationality of common kinship, or learned to treat it as an ideal splendidly false" (339–40).

Posnett attacked neoclassicism along with cosmopolitanism, and for comparable reasons. If nations aren't essential unities, neither are human beings. Like Herder, he asserted that there can be no single set of norms governing the artistic productions of differing groups:

> Literature, however rude, however cultured, expresses the feelings and thoughts of men and women. . . . It is incumbent, therefore, on the champions of universal literary ideas to discover the existence of some universal human nature which, unaffected by the differences of language, social organisation, sex, climate, and similar causes, has been at all times and in all places the keystone of literary architecture. Is there one universal type of human character embracing and reconciling all the conflicting differences of human types in the living world and in its historical or prehistoric past? Can really scientific reasons be advanced in support of the sentimental belief in that colossal personage called "man," whose abstract unity is allowed to put on new phases of external form, but whose "essence" is declared to remain unaltered? (21)

These considerations introduce Posnett's chapter "Relativity of Literature," in which he asserts that literary production varies with the stages of social life. In a passage echoing de Staël's views, he illustrates relativity through the differing status of women in premodern and modern times. "The careful study of any literature possessing a history sufficiently long," he writes, "reveals the most diverse treatment of female character." He adduces examples from India, China, ancient Israel, Greece, and Rome, and he observes that even in ancient Greece, "the women of the *Iliad* and *Odyssey*—Helen, Andromache, Nausicaa—bring before us social relations very different from those of Aristophanes' women" (25).

Admittedly, Posnett envisioned cultural relativity in a schematic way, in a thoroughgoing scientism fully in keeping with his book's publication in an "International Scientific Series," where it appeared together with volumes on evolutionary theory, volcanoes, psychology, and jellyfish. Building on the work of the early sociologist Herbert Spencer and the legal historian Sir Henry Maine, Posnett adopted a worldwide evolutionary scheme, summarized by Joep Leerssen as the progression "from clan-system to the city-state, on to the nation and finally to a universal culture and 'world literature'" (*Komparatistik in Großbrittanien*, 61). Interestingly, though, Leerssen here misremembers the progression that Posnett actually gave, for Posnett saw world literature as arising in imperial settings in late antiquity, long *before* the birth of the modern nation. In his chapter on world literature, Posnett notes that his ordering might seem counterintuitive, but he insists that the facts bear him out: "it may be said that our order of treatment . . . is not in harmony with prevailing ideas of literary development. Why not pass, it may be asked, from the city commonwealth to the nation, and from national literatures reach the universalism of world-literature?" (240). He answers that world literature first developed in the Hellenistic world—where the term "cosmopolitan" was invented—and then in the supranational religious communities of Christianity and Islam, and so he treats the "days of world-empire and world-literature" before turning to the modern national literatures (241). Posnett is thus already aware that "there has probably never been a cosmopolitanism that did not have colonialism lurking somewhere in the vicinity" (Robbins and Horta, *Cosmopolitanisms*, 4).

In keeping with his anticosmopolitanism, Posnett assesses world literature in decidedly mixed terms. Freed from exclusive attachment to their home locality, the Hellenistic writers were able to develop a new appreciation for nature, and they also enjoyed a heightened sense of individuality. Yet they also lost an organic connection to a community, instead concocting artificial constructions for distant readers: "The leading mark of world-literature . . . is the severance of literature from defined social groups—the universalizing of literature, if we may use such an expression" (238). He thus anticipates the complaints leveled today against "global lit," as with Vittorio Coletti's critique of "la progressiva de-nazionalizzazione del romanzo" (*Romanzo mondo,* 2). Yet Posnett's model for a rootless cosmopolitanism is the Hellenistic world and its imperial Roman aftermath: "A society of such limited sympathies and unlimited selfishness was unsuited to the production of song," but only for satire and for Alexandrian commentaries (266). Warming to his theme, two pages later he denies the Roman Empire any good literature at all: "If imagination depends on the existence of some genuine sense of human brotherhood, be it wide as the world or narrow as the clan, we must admit that the social life of Imperial Rome was such as must destroy any literature" (268).

Posnett's discussion of imperial world literature was informed by his own position within the British Empire. Blaž Zabel has uncovered a series of letters that Posnett contributed over the years to Irish and English newspapers. He described himself as "a moderate Liberal" and supported Home Rule in Ireland, and he proposed that the colonies should play a major role in the reformation of the British Empire. As Zabel says, "Posnett's peripheral position not only shaped his political stance, but also influenced his understanding of literature and literary systems" ("Posnett," 2). As Leerssen puts it, Posnett was developing "something which one might call imperial multiculturalism," in a vision of world literature that "seems to be uncannily foreshadowing, from a colonial context, the postcolonial paradigm in which the term is now gaining new importance" ("Some Notes," 113, 115). Publishing his work as he moved from the inner to the outer margins of the British Empire, Posnett saw clearly the dangers of a hegemonic cosmopolitanism.

On the Borderlands of Science and Literature

How successful were Posnett and Meltzl in achieving their global goals? Posnett was bitterly disappointed that his book failed to win many adherents. It attracted the attention of assorted comparatists in Europe and the

United States, and it was soon translated into Japanese, but it didn't spark any broad-based reconstitution of literary studies. A brilliant, querulous autodidact, Posnett had read his way so far beyond the bounds of ordinary academic training that few were prepared to follow his lead, and for his part he made little effort to engage with contemporary scholarship. Indeed, his preface frames his position as both methodologically and geographically marginal. He begins by roundly declaring: "To assume a position on the border-lands of Science and Literature is perhaps to provoke the hostility of both the great parties into which our modern thinkers and educationists may be divided" (v), and he ends his preface by alluding to his shifting geographical position: "Should errors of print or matter have escaped the author's notice, he would beg his readers to remember that this work was passing through the press just as he was on the eve of leaving this country for New Zealand" (vii).

Posnett's global perspective—perhaps coupled with impatience with Irish academia—may have led him to seek the appointment at Auckland, yet his move took him far from the Continental venues where the new discipline of comparative literature was being developed, and he made no further substantial contribution to literary studies. He returned to the subject once more, fifteen years later, in an article on "The Science of Comparative Literature," in which he recalled his pioneering role in coining the name "comparative literature" and expressed his annoyance that scholars had largely ignored him while pursuing narrower concerns.

Meltzl's journal was more directly engaged with the scholarly community, and its international board collectively had the linguistic knowledge that Posnett lacked. But how did Meltzl's polyglottism work in practice? If it had truly been written in a dozen languages, the journal could not have been comprehensible to more than a handful of readers at most, and in actual practice the journal's working languages were chiefly two: German and Hungarian. In examining the articles written in four volumes covering the years 1879–82, I find that half of all the articles (76 out of 156) were written in German, while 20 percent were written in Hungarian. The remaining 30 percent of the articles were written mostly in English, French, or Italian. No articles at all appeared in the "official" languages of Icelandic and Polish. Poems from around the world were regularly given in the original, but always with a translation into one of the journal's dominant languages. So the journal's polyglottism was far more limited in practice than in theory, and yet even so it appears to have had a limiting effect on the journal's readership. The Hungarian scholar Árpád Berczik has found that in its best year the *Acta* achieved a circulation of only a hundred copies, a number that declined in the journal's later years ("Hugó von Meltzl").

For its select readership, however, the *Acta* provided a lively venue for the sharing of ideas and information among its far-flung correspondents, and the journal gave Meltzl an opportunity to work out his strategies for the promotion of Hungarian literature on the world stage. Meltzl considered that Hungary had produced one writer of genuinely world-class stature: Sándor Petöfi, poet-hero of Hungary's failed struggle for independence in 1848–49, who had died on the battlefield at the age of twenty-six. Over the course of his journal's life, Meltzl arranged for translations of poems by Petöfi into no fewer than thirty-two languages. Through these translations and in a series of essays on Petöfi's work, he sought to show a global public that here was a Hungarian poet who deserved a place at the table of world literature, much as Georg Brandes began doing for Kierkegaard with a book in German on him in 1877—the year of the *Acta*'s founding— and would go on to do with Ibsen as well.

Rather than seek to promote other Hungarian writers of (in his view) lesser literary merit than Petöfi, Meltzl placed his second great stress on his region's contribution to world folk poetry, showcasing lyrics not only in Hungarian but also in Romanian, and several times including Roma folk songs. The first English translation of Romanian folk songs was published in New York by one of his contributors (Phillips, *Volk-songs*). In his journal, Meltzl delighted in finding the circulation of folk motifs across wide geographical areas. In an article on "Islaendisch-Sizilianische Volks-tradition," he discusses a lyric found in similar forms in Iceland, Sicily, and Hungary, concluding: "Das sind die wunder der vergl. litteratur!" ("These are the marvels of comp. lit.!" [117–18]). No one but Meltzl would ever have thought to identify—or invent—an "Icelandic-Sicilian folk tradition," bypassing any metropolitan center whatever. In the journal's second volume, Meltzl issued a call for contributions to an ambitious anthology (never realized), to be named *Encyclopaedia of the World's Poetry*. Merging his two emphases, Meltzl asked his contributors to send in two poems from every country in the world: one folk poem and one literary work, each of them to be given in the original and in "a literal interlinear translation in one of the European languages" (2:177).

By these means Meltzl was working out a practical mode of comparison on a worldwide basis, creatively negotiating the cultural politics of relations between small and large literary powers. It is ironic, then, that his journal's impact was limited by national factors as well as by its polyglottism. Equally serious was the growth of comparative study in France and Germany. According to Árpád Berczik, the death blow to Meltzl's struggling journal was the appearance in 1887 of a rival journal, published in Berlin under the editorship of Max Koch, a professor at Marburg. Meltzl complained that this new publication seemed intended to siphon off readers and contributors from his journal, and he felt that Koch's title was suspiciously close to the *Acta*'s own German title. Though Meltzl had studied in Germany and likely knew Koch, it was particularly galling that he learned of the new journal only through newspaper reports. In a plaintive editorial note, Meltzl tried to rally his readers, not precisely to boycott his new rival, but at least to remain his readers as well:

> We have recently learned from news reports that a journal of comparative literary history is supposed to be starting publication in Berlin. As pleased as we are that even in Goethe's homeland this great branch of comparative literature . . . is finding a freestanding home, we must equally lament the—surely coincidental!—choice of a title, which is bound to cause much confusion with the German title of the *Acta Comparationis*. We therefore wish here to plead in advance for care to be taken, so that at least the learned public may note the difference between the *Zeitschrift für vergleichende Litteratur* (since January 1877) and the *Zeitschrift für vergleichende Litteraturgeschichte* (since Summer 1886). (Berczik, "Hugó von Meltzl," 98–99)

Koch's journal must have struck Meltzl not only as a personal affront but as a real step backward. Written entirely in German, its articles were almost exclusively by German scholars—one of whom was a member of

Meltzl's own editorial board—and their emphasis was on literary relations with Germany. The first issue, for example, featured articles on Goethe, Uhland, Kleist, and Lessing, while also including articles on Chinese poetry and African fables. The Berlin journal treated folk poetry as well, and if Meltzl felt that Koch was trying to steal his thunder, he could hardly have thought it a coincidence that several of these treatments focused on folklore from his own region. The very first issue included an article on a theme from *Tristan* as found in Roma and Romanian poetry, while the next issue featured a prominent article "Zur Litteratur and Charakteristik der magyarischen Folklore."

Neither article mentions Meltzl or his journal at all, nor does Koch's inaugural essay. Koch ranges widely over the tasks of comparative study (source study, aesthetics, comparative literary history, interarts comparison, and folklore), and he mentions dozens of precursors from the seventeenth century to his own day, almost exclusively Germans. He concludes by emphasizing the national value of comparative study: "German literature and the advancement of its historical understanding will form the starting point and the center of gravity for the endeavors of the *Zeitschrift für vergleichende Litteraturgeschichte*" ("Introduction," 12). Based in a center of scholarly life and exchange, the Berlin journal was not only more nationalistic than Meltzl's; it was also better in terms of scholarly protocols. Koch was able to attract more distinguished contributors, to publish more full-scale essays than Meltzl could afford to print, and to reach many more readers. Meltzl kept the *Acta* going for another year after the Berlin journal appeared but then gave up; Koch's journal had won out.

Koch appeared to be stealing Meltzl's thunder, and his journal certainly represented a very different approach. Whereas Meltzl championed polyglottism and inveighed against great-power cosmopolitanism, Koch advanced a cosmopolitan universalism grounded in a single major European language, his own. Yet in its own way his journal was working to foster a European and even global awareness among its German readers. Koch's interest in Hungarian and Romanian folk songs wasn't merely strategic but stemmed from his own Herderian enthusiasm for the world's literary expression. As he says in his introductory essay, Herder understood *Volkspoesie* "in its unity not confined either in time or by borders"

("Introduction," 4). Koch praises Karl Goedicke's study *Every-Man, Homulus und Hekastus: Ein Beitrag zur internationalen Litteraturgeschichte* (1865) for revealing deep connections between Asia and Europe, likely transmitted orally as well as through lost literary means, whereby Buddhist and Persian materials came to infuse medieval European legends and tales.

By the 1880s the study of India's literatures had expanded beyond Sanskrit into the Indian vernaculars. An essay by Hermann Oesterley in the inaugural issue discusses an eight-part Tamil tale, "Die Abenteuer des Guru Paramártan," and follows the analysis with a translation of the story (1:48–72). Another article, Richard Meyer's "Über den Refrain," is an essay in comparative poetics that presents the refrain as the kernel of all poetry, drawing on Sanskrit, Arabic, and African traditions as well as classical Greece. In the context of today's interest in animal studies, it is noteworthy that Meyer proposes that great apes' cries of greeting to the rising sun are a form of protopoetry, though he leaves the connection an open question—not wishing, he says, to seem "ultradarwinianisch" (36). German *Nachäfferei* could now share the stage with actual apes.

If Koch's journal had a more global perspective than has sometimes been supposed, Meltzl's *Acta*, conversely, had nationalist tendencies of its own. Though many of his contributors were internationalists, others were far more concerned to promote their own national tradition. The journal's Albanian contributor, Thimi Mitko, for instance, was a committed ethnonationalist, though his perspective was somewhat softened in the journal's cosmopolitan framing. Levente Szabó has observed that "the Albanian case is one of the instances which can show the diverse (and often divergent) strata and the composite, sometimes eclectic nature of *ACLU* that often makes binary terms like nationalism and cosmopolitanism come together in less binary, but more fragmented, intricate and complex ways" ("Negotiating World Literature," 44).

The early history of comparative studies includes Herder's nationalist internationalism, de Staël's feminist cosmopolitanism, Posnett's social evolutionism, Meltzl's utopian polyglottism, and Koch's strategically German comparatism as well. This history is neither a linear story of progress nor a war of attrition between cosmopolitan comparatists and their nationalistic rivals. Instead, we see the early comparatists' shifting attempts to mediate their own internal mixtures of internationalism and national belonging, to wrestle with intractable problems of language and translation, to look at European literature as a whole, and to take account of the new worlds opened up by agents of empire and the much older literatures uncovered by Egyptologists and Assyriologists. By the century's end, an international network of scholars was working to understand both European and non-European literatures in their own contexts and in relation to literatures elsewhere. Their collective work set the stage for the growth of the discipline far from the precincts either of the Asiatic Society of Bengal or of the University of Berlin. It would soon be Chinese scholars who led the way in revolutionizing language, and society itself, through comparative literary studies.

2

Emigrations

During the summer of 1915, a small circle of Chinese students at a rural university hotly debated the crucial literary and linguistic questions of their day. Should classical Chinese be abandoned in favor of the vernacular language spoken by common people? Should the Chinese script itself be retained, or simplified, or replaced outright by romanization? Should contemporary writers continue to use classical literary forms, or did new social conditions require new modes of writing, inspired by European novels and plays? Far from Beijing or Shanghai, the friends were hammering out their ideas with great intensity, and their discussions would soon have a tremendous impact in China's "New Culture" movement. Yet for all their modernism, like centuries of literati before them they pressed their points home in poems and in late-night drinking sessions. Brilliant and polemical, arrogant and self-mocking, they were testing the limits of language and of friendship alike.

Their debates continued throughout the school year and reached a climax the next summer when a classically minded member of the group, Mei Chin-chuang, accused his friend Hu Hung-hsing of merely recycling stale ideas from Tolstoy. Hu replied with a long poem written entirely in the vernacular, at once demonstrating the possibilities of a supposedly subliterary language and also trying to lower the temperature of the debate a little:

"The man has leisure, the weather is also cool,"
Old Mei has entered the battlefield.
Banging on the table, cursing Hu Shih,
Saying that his words are really too ridiculous.

[. . .]

Old Mei rambles on, old Hu laughs heartily.
Let's regain our calm equanimity, what kind of a debate is this!
Words are not new or old, but they may be dead or alive.
(Hu, *Autobiographical Account*, 171–72)

Mei wasn't persuaded. Nor was their friend Jen Shu-yung, who called Hu's poem "a total failure" and asked: "Considering your great talents and capacities, why do you reject the main road and insist on frivolous bypaths, to plant beautiful flowers among the thorns?" (173–75). Undaunted, Hu formulated his ideas for "a literary revolution" in a manifesto, written in formal literary Chinese, based on eight succinct principles: "Don't use clichés," "Don't groan without being sick," "Don't imitate the ancients" (Chou, *Hu Shih*, 149). Writing under his Darwinian pen name, Hu "Shih," or "fittest" (as in "the survival of the fittest"), Hu published his "Preliminary Discussion of Literary Reform" in January 1917 in the new Shanghai journal *La Jeunesse*, whose French title proudly announced its westernizing internationalism. There would be no turning back after that.

What is particularly striking about the exchanges between Hu Shih and his friends is that they didn't take place outside Shanghai or Xiamen but at Cornell University. They continued the debate via sporadic meetings and frequent letters after Mei went on to graduate study at Harvard and Hu moved to Columbia to pursue a PhD in philosophy under the direction of John Dewey. Their debate had heated up after Hu criticized Jen for using archaisms in a poem about a boating mishap on Lake Cayuga, involving Jen, Mei, and "Miss Ch'en Heng-che" (Hu, *Autobiographical Account*, 169). He had originally come to Cornell from Shanghai in 1910 to study agriculture, but his assigned area of focus, pomology, while no doubt useful for apple farmers in upstate New York, seemed completely irrelevant for life back home in China. He changed to literature and philosophy in his second year, and after receiving his BA he began graduate studies in philosophy before transferring down to Columbia. His manifesto for a literary revolution became a rallying point for cultural reform, and Hu found himself a celebrity when he returned to teach in Beijing in 1918. As his friend Lin Yutang wrote in a memoir, "Hu Shih returned with national acclaim to join Peking University, and I was at

Tsinghua to greet him. It was an electrifying experience" (*From Pagan to Christian*, 44).

It is possible to tell this story as a conversion narrative, in which Hu Shih comes to America, discovers European literature and American pragmatism, then returns home to spread the gospel of westernization. He certainly learned a great deal from his Cornell courses in philosophy and in English, French, and German literature—a virtual major in comparative literature—and then from Dewey at Columbia. Yet as we can see from Hu's exchanges with Mei and Jen, he was developing his ideas first and foremost in a circle of fellow émigrés concerned with China's cultural history and modern needs. When Mei accused him of promoting warmed-over Tolstoyism, Hu later wrote, "I laughed aloud when I heard this. I said that I was talking of Chinese literature entirely from the Chinese point of view, and that I was not [at] all interested or concerned with the opinions of the European or Western critics" (*Autobiographical Account*, 168).

Emigrants have always played a major role in the history of comparative literature, from Madame de Staël writing *De l'Allemagne* during her Napoleonic exile down to such influential contemporary critics as Edward Said, George Steiner, Julia Kristeva, Gayatri Spivak, and Franco Moretti. Particularly in the United States, special attention has often been given to the role played by midcentury émigrés from Europe, including Erich Auerbach, Leo Spitzer, René Wellek, and Paul de Man, in an era when few American scholars had ever received formal training in comparative studies. Yet a full picture of these immigrations shouldn't be confined to a few great men, as has often been the case. Natalie Melas remarked in 2006 that "I have encountered no discussion, whether biographical or analytical, of women's experience in the rise of the discipline of comparative literature or in its institutional life" (*All the Difference in the World*, 13). Margaret Higonnet had published her important collection *Borderwork: Feminist Engagements with Comparative Literature* in 1994, but her contributors' focus was on women writers and on feminist literary theory rather than on their own experiences. In this chapter we will look not only at Auerbach and Spitzer but also at Lilian R. Furst, whose family fled Vienna in 1938 and who published a memoir with the resonant name *Home Is Somewhere Else*; chapter 3 will begin with the Armenian émigré Anna Balakian. Higonnet remarks in *Borderwork*, "Reading at the crossroads, reading along the borderlands of silence, is the work that confronts both comparative literature and feminist criticism today" ("Introduction," 16).

Beyond these figures, the case of Hu Shih and his friends shows us that these emigrations didn't begin only in midcentury, and they didn't only involve Europeans. Nor was it always a question of permanent resettlement. Hu Shih's eight years in the United States gave him a decisive period of reflection on his home culture, to which he always intended to return. Looking at Hu Shih and at Lin Yutang, we see an additional dimension of comparative study throughout the century: it was often elaborated by people who saw themselves as public intellectuals. Though Hu and Lin both spent periods as professors of literature and as leaders of academic institutions, they were involved in a wide range of other activities, including journalism, literary writing, and government service. Their more popular writings as well as their academic scholarship had a lasting influence on comparative literature, developing many of the terms still being explored in East/West and postcolonial studies today.

Hu Shih's Literary Revolution

Both Hu Shih and Lin Yutang were born comparatists, raised amid interwoven and competing cultural strands. Hu's father was a Neo-Confucianist, a believer in science and progress who also taught his children calligraphy and the Confucian classics, including the *Book of Songs* as well as the *Analects* and the *Classic of Filial Piety*. Poetry and filial piety merged in "Poems for Learning to Become a Man," a collection that he assembled for his son and copied out with his own brush. These poems promoted Confucian precepts as giving timeless guidance in life:

As recorded in the Classics and documents,
As taught by teachers and scholars,
The Way of being a man has no other arts:
Examine principle, and extend knowledge,
Return to the self, and make your actions real,
Study diligently, and never depart from the Tao.
(*Autobiographical Account*, 62)

Hu's mother, on the other hand, wasn't a Confucian rationalist but a devout Buddhist, and she warned him that misbehavior could result in his reincarnation as a pig or a dog (88).

Even as Hu Shih had to negotiate between different Chinese traditions, Western culture was becoming a presence in his life. Combining his parents' teachings, young Hu constructed a cardboard Confucian temple, using a Noontime Tea box as its inner shrine, festooned with classical couplets on silver and gold paper. He encountered his first work of Chinese fiction, a tattered copy of *Water Margin* partly eaten by rats, among the trash tossed into a Standard Oil Company kerosene crate (67). By his early teens, he was reading Western literature, philosophy, and history in Chinese retranslations from Japanese, and it was Thomas Huxley's *Evolution and Ethics* that inspired his pen name of "fittest." The Confucian exhortation to "study diligently and never depart from the Tao" actually entailed a progressive series of departures for him; he left home at age twelve to study in Shanghai—"a small child alone and lonely, protected only by a loving mother's affection, something of a habit of diligence, and a bit of skepticism" (92)—and then crossed the Pacific at age eighteen for his sojourn at Cornell and then Columbia.

Hu Shih's American education gave him a comparatist's outlook, but in later life he never did extended work on foreign literatures. Instead, his studies abroad gave him a new purchase on his home tradition. In his debates with his friends at Cornell, he cited Dante, Chaucer, and Martin Luther as founders of vernacular literatures, and he says that thanks to those writers, "I finally understood clearly the history of Chinese literature, now realized that Chinese literature in the vernacular . . . constituted the orthodox literary tradition of China, [and] represented the natural direction in the development of the Chinese literary revolution" (162).

Hu Shih's work undercuts any pure opposition between comparative literature and the study of a national tradition. For Hu, there was no question of abandoning Chinese traditions in order to adopt Western modes, or of creating a cosmopolitan alternative to nationalism. Instead, the European vernacular revolution provided a comparative perspective from which to serve China by reassessing the Chinese tradition itself.

He went on to pursue this project in many books and essays, including seminal studies of *The Story of the Stone*. As he later said of the three centuries of prior commentators on Ming Dynasty fiction, "These classic scholars lacked external materials for comparison and reference. . . . Without comparative material, without reference material from the outside, it was almost impossible for these scholars to understand what they were studying" ("Reminiscences," 245).

Hu was closely associated with the New Culture movement of the 1910s and 1920s, a period in which the traditional concept of literature as part of a broader framework of *wen* (order, harmony, culture) was being redefined along Western lines as *wenxue*, "literature" as a distinct and autonomous mode of imaginative writing. Yet Hu's conception of his role was never belletristic, and it remained more within the realm of *wen* than of the new *wenxue*. His writing freely crossed the boundaries of literature, philosophy, and history, as well as the divisions between scholarly analysis and activist journalism. Already during his Cornell years, he became a sought-after speaker for American audiences interested in understanding contemporary China and its turbulent politics. He transferred to Columbia after Cornell cut off his fellowship, as his advisers felt that he was going around giving speeches when he should have been devoting himself to his coursework. For his part, Hu saw his activities as complementary, and he remained loyal in many ways to his father's neo-Confucianism, taking a "cultural-intellectualist approach" to addressing social concerns (Chou, *Hu Shih*, 116).

Hu Shih's loyalty to his paternal legacy was deepened by a formative tragedy: when he was not quite four years old, his father died while away on government service. In his father's final letter home, "his last instructions to me urged me to pursue my studies diligently. These scant few lines have had a great influence on me throughout my life" (*Autobiographical Account*, 60). By that time, Hu's father had already taught him seven hundred Chinese characters, each written out on a sheet of red paper: "These characters, all of which my father had written with his own hand, my mother preserved her entire life, these square red sheets of paper being the most spiritual mementoes of the life of the three of us together" (59–60). Weeping, she would tell her son, "You must follow in your father's footsteps. In my whole life, I have known only this one perfect man, you must learn to be like him, must not bring disgrace on him" (73–74). Writing, public service, and filial duty were already inseparably connected for the four-year-old boy.

Hu Shih's scholarship and journalism were closely bound up with his public role as a leader in building a modern China. Under Chiang Kai-shek's government in the 1930s and early 1940s, he served for several years as president of Peking University, where he tried unsuccessfully to mediate when the Kuomintang repressed student protests. Later he was China's ambassador to Washington and then to the nascent United Nations, and he served in the National Assembly from 1947 to 1962, first in Beijing and then in Taiwan after 1949. He had written a series of essays in 1919 on the theme "Study More Problems, Talk Less of Isms," arguing that China's Marxists were dwelling in a world of abstractions rather than dealing with practical issues. Yet he was never a Kuomintang party man. As early as 1929 he sharply criticized the Kuomintang for corruption and for violating human rights, and as Chiang Kai-shek's ambassador to the United States in 1938–42, he traveled around the country to raise support for China's struggles against Japan but rarely mentioned Chiang or the Kuomintang. Throughout his life, Hu insisted that political action needed to be based on careful thought grounded in deep cultural training. He wrote in 1916 that "I do not condemn revolutions. . . . But I do not favor premature revolutions, because they are usually wasteful and therefore unfruitful. . . . My personal attitude is: 'Come what may, let us educate the people'" (Chou, *Hu Shih*, 113).

Second Sister's Admonition

A culturally varied upbringing and an education abroad set Hu Shih's friend Lin Yutang on a very different trajectory. Born in 1895, Lin was the son of devout Christians; his father, in fact, was a pastor. Like Hu's father, though, Pastor Lin was also a Confucianist. He taught his children calligraphy and the Confucian classics, even as he cherished an ambition for his sons to study one day in Oxford or Berlin. Lin grew up reading the

Confucian *Book of Songs* along with translations of Walter Scott, Victor Hugo, and *The Thousand and One Nights*. As a teenager, he was sent to study English at a missionary school, St. John's College in Shanghai. "Though it was Episcopalian," he later wrote, "its sacred mission for the majority of the students was to produce successful compradores for the Shanghai tycoons" (*From Pagan to Christian*, 29). Lin's love of literature soon outweighed his economic and spiritual interests alike; invited to speak in church when home on vacation, he shocked his father by giving a talk on "The Bible as Literature" (30).

After graduation Lin moved to Beijing in 1916 to teach English at Tsinghua University, but he began to feel ashamed of his limited knowledge of Chinese literary and cultural traditions. He drifted away from Christianity and became closely involved with the New Culture movement, while also reading extensively in classical and vernacular Chinese writing. Then in 1919 he won a fellowship to study comparative literature at Harvard. His parents wanted to see him married first, and they arranged a marriage for him; the honeymoon trip for the newly introduced newlyweds was their sea voyage to America.

Their experience in Cambridge proved to be a true idyll. As Lin recalled in his *Memoirs of an Octogenarian*, "It was so sweet, Hong and I the two living together, living our lives alone" (45). They found an apartment near the massive new Widener Library, where Lin rejoiced in the freedom of the stacks: "I always maintained a university should be a jungle where monkeys should be let loose to pick and choose from a feast of nuts from any tree he wants and swing and jump to other branches. His monkey sense will tell him what nut is good and eatable. I was having a riot of a banquet. To me the Widener Library was Harvard and Harvard was the Widener Library" (40). Here Lin both evokes and remakes the traditional Buddhist image of "the monkey of the mind," which is supposed to be quieted by meditation, not indulged in leaping about from thought to thought.

Lin was preparing to write his MA thesis and proceed to doctoral studies when an administrator back in Beijing arbitrarily canceled his fellowship. Half a century later, Lin recalled this sudden reversal with unconcealed bitterness: "Dr. Sze was cutting off my neck. Never have I exulted so much on anybody's death, when later I learned Dr. Sze had committed suicide" (41). Lin's professors recommended him to a temporary post teaching Shakespeare in Jena, after which Lin and his wife proceeded to Leipzig, where he earned a PhD in comparative philology. Somewhat disturbed by the activities of a "nymphomaniac" landlady (53)—thin walls?—Lin delved deeply into classical Chinese as well as Germanic linguistics and textual criticism, then returned to China in 1923 as a professor of English at Peking University.

Lin came back to a country in the midst of wrenching conflicts. He fled Beijing in 1926 amid a purge of leftist intellectuals by the warlords who then controlled northern China. ("When the local general had two editors shot before midnight we knew that he meant business" [63].) He ended up in Shanghai, where after a brief period of service in Sun Yat-sen's Nationalist Party, he became disillusioned with party politics and decided to devote himself to writing. He established a series of cultural journals and became a prolific essayist in both Chinese and English. In his memoir, he draws a direct link between his growing political independence and his search for an intimate, undogmatic style:

> I had established myself as an independent critic, neither a Kuomintang man, nor for Chiang Kai-shek, and at times a merciless critic. I had dared to say what cautious critics refrained for the sake of pacifying everybody. At the same time, I had been developing a style, the secret of which is [to] take your reader into confidence, a style you feel like talking to an old friend in your unbuttoned words. All the books I have written have this characteristic which has a charm of its own. It brings the reader closer to you. (69)

Lin might well have made his entire career in Shanghai but for a suggestion from Pearl Buck, then teaching in Nanjing, who was visiting Shanghai in 1933 with her American editor and lover Richard Walsh. She had just won the Pulitzer Prize for her novel *The Good Earth* (the Nobel would follow a few years later), and she saw Lin as an ally in mediating between China and the West. At her suggestion, Lin wrote (in English) *My Country and My People*, the first of his books of cross-cultural exposition and explanation. Published in New York by Walsh in 1935, it became a number 1 *New York Times* best seller—a first for a book by an East Asian—and stayed on the best-seller lists for a remarkable fifty weeks. The next year Lin and his family moved to New York.

In the years that followed, Lin Yutang established himself as the world's foremost exponent of East/West cultural comparison, writing a series of essayistic books and several novels, most translated into a dozen or more languages. He lived in the United States for three decades before moving to Taiwan late in life, but like Hu Shih he remained loyal to his prerevolutionary upbringing in the world of *wen* rather than *wenxue*. In such works as *The Importance of Living, The Wisdom of China and India,* and *On the Wisdom of America* he seamlessly brought together insights from philosophers, novelists, and poets. He was always skeptical of academic specialization and theoretical system-building, advancing the Daoist philosophy of yin and yang as truer to life than overly schematic and rationalist philosophies, whether Kantian or Confucian. "I am by habit a Confucian," he remarks in *The Pleasures of a Nonconformist*, "but by nature a Taoist. Taoism has more soul" (72).

Lin Yutang's comparative method can be seen as an adaptation of the yin-yang pattern of complementary opposites, each of which has a spot of the opposite at its heart. Deliberately unsystematic, Lin could combine universalism and cultural specificity within the same essay. In a chapter of *The Pleasures of a Nonconformist* on "Chinese Humanism and the Modern World," he remarks: "There is a certain pathos about Chinese humanism and a certain cheerfulness in acceptance of life. It reminds me of the ethics of Marcus Aurelius" (104). Here, time and space almost disappear in a universal humanism, but three pages later, Lin emphasizes a deep and almost ineluctable cultural difference. "I think a nation's culture is more or less the result of a racial temperament," he declares; "foreign cultural ideas may be superimposed on a nation, but unless they are in accord with its innermost instincts, they will not become a real factor in the life of the nation. . . . More often it happens that it is the racial temperament which alters the cultural ideas" (107). This statement can be applied to Lin's sense of himself; his Confucian habits and Taoist temperament persisted despite his years studying comparative literature and philology at Harvard and in Leipzig.

In an essay written in Shanghai in the early 1930s, "The English Think in Chinese," he adopts a pseudo-Orientalist puzzlement at the mysterious West and its violence-ridden civilization: "I am going to speak of my impressions of the white man," he says. "Everyone knows that Europe is in a mess. . . . We are forced to ask ourselves, 'What are the psychological limitations of the Europeans which make peace so difficult in Europe?'" (*Confucius Saw Nancy*, 94–95). Whereas Hu Shih's Western training gave him a comparative perspective on China, Lin asserts that his Chinese perspective gives him privileged access to the English mind: "I think, as a Chinese, I can understand the English character better than Englishmen understand themselves." This cross-cultural insight is possible because the English and the Chinese share a fundamental commonality—a lack of logic: "Both peoples have a profound distrust of logic and are extremely suspicious of arguments that are too perfect. . . . All Englishmen love a good liar, and so do the Chinese. We love to call a thing by anything except its right name." The English "never allow themselves to be lost in their own thoughts and logical abstractions," and Lin finds when dealing with an Englishman that "there is an inevitability about his words and actions and gestures when he is not looking like a dumb, persecuted animal" (97, 105). There is no hint of the subaltern in Lin's satirically laced praise of the English—or the Sino-English—character.

Lin used cultural products of all sorts, from art to furniture to clothing, to illustrate the essence of a civilization's values; he wrote essays on subjects as various as "The Chinese Temper," "On Sitting in Chairs," and "How I Bought a Toothbrush." In revolutionary circumstances, many Chinese intellectuals grew impatient with Lin's essays on everyday subjects, which his friend Lu Xun dismissed as "bric-à-brac for the bourgeoisie" (Denton, "Lu Xun Biography"). Yet Lin's attention to mundane practicalities inspired him to work for years on developing and then manufacturing the first functional Chinese typewriter. Its invention required solving a complex set of intellectual and practical challenges, which Thomas Mullaney details in *The Chinese Typewriter*, in a chapter centered on Lin's invention. Figure 2 shows Lin with his daughter Lin Tai-yi demonstrating the typewriter, in one of many write-ups in the popular press in 1947. Before long, as Jing Tsu has discussed in *Sound and Script in the Chinese*

CHINESE TYPEWRITER CAN PRINT 90,000 CHARACTERS

FIGURE 2. Lin Yutang with Lin Tai-yi demonstrating his typewriter. "Chinese Typewriter Can Print 90,000 Characters." *Popular Mechanics*, December 1947, p. 143.

Diaspora, the U.S. military took an active interest in Lin's invention as they began to develop a program in mechanical translation, in "a race for informational advantage" against the Soviet Union (73).

The war inspired Lin's boldest attempt at cross-cultural diplomacy, *Between Tears and Laughter*, which he published in 1943 in an attempt to rally American support for China against its Japanese occupiers. Characteristically, Lin begins by avoiding a polemical tone, seeking "a real communion of the spirit" with his readers "in an unbuttoned mood, collar and tie loose, as by a friend's fireside" (1). Yet he swiftly mounts a sharp critique of the Roosevelt administration for its weak support of China's struggle to drive the Japanese from Manchuria. Quoting a speech in which Roosevelt claimed to be strongly backing China while offering only token assistance, Lin says that "it was the last straw, and broke the camel of easy-paced Chinese patience. It was a slap in the face, and stunned me into a half-daze" (2).

Lin knew that the wartime American public would hardly welcome his attacks on Roosevelt as a liar and on Winston Churchill as a British imperialist, and so he employed several strategies to frame his critique for a resistant public. A comparative approach is signaled at the very outset by a trio of epigraphs, all emphasizing the necessity of wise reflection in order to build a peaceful world. These epithets are taken from Mencius, Socrates, and, strikingly, Eleanor Roosevelt, who is enlisted as an authority only pages before Lin mounts his critique of her husband's duplicity. Throughout the book, Lin attempts to rise above his evident anger; after lambasting Roosevelt's temporizing speech, he claims that "I am no longer angry; only the stupidity of it all is a little boring" (5). But a page later this world-weary posture wears thin: "I do not believe in an automatic millennium that is going to blossom out of this spiritual desert. I smell too many corpses around" (6).

Having mobilized Eleanor Roosevelt against her husband, Lin turns to classical Greece to ground his treatment of Churchill. He compares the British prime minister to Pericles leading Athens into a self-destructive war in hopes of preserving an unsustainable empire, a comparison that recalls Plato's dark portrayal in *Gorgias* of Pericles as a war-mongering demagogue. Anticipating his readers' likely reaction to this view of Churchill, then being lionized in the American press as the British bulldog facing down Hitler, Lin insists that "I am not anti-English; I am anti-idiots of any nationality, including my own" (34). He returns to the attack on Churchill toward the end of the book, damning him with mocking praise: "If I do not misinterpret Winston Churchill, he is fighting a twentieth-century war in order to take off his boots after the war and climb back into a nineteenth-century bed, comfortably mattressed in India, Singapore, and Hong Kong. He has the admirable tenacity of the English bulldog, and also its intelligence" (185). In terms that anticipate Orwell's *1984*, Lin perceives that the war is being waged as much to preserve an aging imperial order as to defeat the Axis powers, and he urges his readers to acknowledge China and the Soviet Union as equal partners in creating a viable postwar world.

Lin's readers weren't persuaded. *Between Tears and Laughter* was dismissed by reviewers and sold poorly. Yet both before and after the war, Lin pursued his quest to forge a cosmopolitan wisdom, drawing on Eastern and Western sources, ancient and modern. Erich Auerbach spent the war years writing *Mimesis* in an attempt to put European culture back together, but Lin was seeking to envision a fully global postwar world order, and he continued this project in such books as *The Wisdom of Lao-tse* (1948), *On the Wisdom of America* (1950), and *The Importance of Understanding* (1960). As Suoqiao Qian has argued in *Liberal Cosmopolitan: Lin Yutang and Middling Chinese Modernity*, Lin's worldly cosmopolitanism can be newly relevant today, in a post–Cold War world.

Almost by definition, comparatists are people blessed, or afflicted, with double vision. Lin Yutang recognized in himself a whole series of oppositions: novelist and philosopher, dreamer and inventor, universalist and essentialist. In traditional yin-yang theory, the principles of activity and passivity are coded as male and female, but Lin liked to think of himself as combining both active and passive principles: "As an apostle of the philosophy of Loafing, he claims he is the hardest working man in China outside President and Madame Chiang Kai-shek" (*Memoirs of an Octogenarian*, 3). Already in his early essay "On Sitting in Chairs"—written during a period of typically intense productivity—he makes inactivity into his prime activity: "I want to write about the philosophy of sitting in chairs because I have a reputation for lolling. Now there are many lollers among my friends and acquaintances, but somehow I have acquired a special reputation for lolling, at least in the Chinese literary world" (*Confucius Saw Nancy*, 60–61). With his love of everyday domesticity—his inventions included a toothbrush that could dispense its own toothpaste—Lin understood that an equitable world order should begin at home. He encouraged his daughters in intellectual pursuits, and all three became writers. The best known was his middle daughter, Lin Tai-yi (shown with her father and his typewriter in figure 2), who wrote several novels in English as well as a biography of her father in Chinese.

At once relaxed and driven, a meditative Taoist and a pragmatic Confucian, Lin Yutang was formed by a dual family heritage, both male and female. Together with the memory of his father, who had introduced him to the Bible and to Confucius, Lin carried on the legacy of his favorite older sister. He describes his attachment to her in his memoir *From Pagan to Christian* (1959). Not otherwise named, his second sister (who would in fact have been called Second Sister within the family) was a voracious reader. She read translated Western novels to her younger brother, and before long they were making up their own Sherlock Holmes mystery tales and acting them out. This sister was eager to go away to a women's college, but "my father would not think of it. My sister pleaded and coaxed and made promises, but my father said, 'No.' To me it was dreadful. . . . And so my sister drifted and drifted teaching in Amoy and waiting to get married" (26–27). The excuse was the high cost of college, but she would likely have gotten a fellowship; higher education simply wasn't for a girl.

In a symbolically overdetermined scene of departure, Lin left for St. John's College on the very day of his sister's wedding. As he was leaving, "my sister took forty cents from the pocket of her bridal dress and gave it to me. She said at parting, with tears in her eyes, 'Ho-lok, you have a chance to go to college. Your sister, being a girl, can't. Do not abuse your opportunity. Make up your mind to be a good man, a useful man, and a famous man'" (28). Decades later, Lin was startled to see (or to think he saw) a double of his sister on an American movie screen, in an uncanny overlay of prerevolutionary China and postwar Hollywood: "My sister was talented and had an expression of intelligent delicacy like Deborah Kerr, so much so that when I first saw the latter on the screen a few years ago, my heart skipped a beat and I clutched the arm of my daughter and exclaimed, 'There, that is how my second sister looked!'" (26). Clearly, he had told his daughters about their talented aunt; perhaps this daughter was none other than the future novelist Lin Tai-yi, who herself would be Second Sister in their household. She would have grown up hearing the story, but she couldn't have met her aunt, because the wedding day was the last time her father ever saw her. After quoting Second Sister's parting words, Lin tersely states: "She died of bubonic plague two years later, but those words are still ringing in my ears." He adds: "I tell these things because they have so much to do with the influences that shape a man's moral being" (28).

That is how he told this story in 1959; but he returned to this traumatic valediction at the end of his life, in his *Memoirs of an Octogenarian* (1975). In a chapter entitled "My Childhood," he describes his sister as "my mentor and companion," saying that "we practically grew up together, she teaching me and admonishing me" (18). Almost inadvertently, he strays into recalling her beauty: "My second sister had vivacious eyes, and a set of very even white teeth. To her fellow students she was regarded as a beauty, but this was not what I was going to tell about. She was brilliant in her studies and should be going to a college. But my father had other sons to support; for a son, yes, but for a girl, no" (18).

Now writing more than sixty years after the event, he repeats his sister's parting words of regret and admonition, then expands on his reaction: "Knowing her desire so well, I felt the full force of these simple words. It made me guilty about the whole thing. They burned into my heart with the oppressive weight of a great load, so that I had the feeling I was going to college in her place." He next speaks of her death, but now adds a chilling final detail: "When I returned to Poa-ah next year, she had died of bubonic plague, with an embryo already eight months old." A sober comment ends the chapter on his youth: "These things are so deep they cannot be forgotten" (19).

His sister's parting injunction to him to become a good man, a useful man, and a famous man resulted in a profoundly ethical outlook, a series of patented inventions, and forty-eight books. Throughout Lin Yutang's life and work, comparative study bridged a host of distances and differences: between East and West, antiquity and modernity, men and women, philosophy and literature, scholarship and popular writing, reflective detachment and social engagement. And perhaps one day in a Manhattan movie theater, his daughter the budding novelist could merge with Deborah Kerr to bring Second Sister, however briefly, back to life.

Home Is Somewhere Else

The scholars who emigrated from Europe in midcentury were in a very different situation from Hu Shih and Lin Yutang, but their experiences were formative for postwar comparative literature in the United States. Their exilic displacement has often been described in positive terms, as a *translatio studii* enabling a great scholar to build a new life and to revive the discipline from a new perspective, as in Emily Apter's discussion of Leo Spitzer in "Global Translatio" or the essays collected in Stauth and Birtek's *'Istanbul': Geistige Wanderungen aus der 'Welt in Scherben'*.

Speaking of the impact of Wellek and Poggioli on American comparative studies, Harry Levin remarked in 1968 that "their synonymous Christian names"—René and Renato—"portended a renascence" ("Comparing the Literature," 7). Had he thought to add a woman to his list of influential émigrés, Lilian Renée Furst could equally have been included.

A closer look at the midcentury émigrés reveals a more troubled picture. The academics who escaped pogroms and death camps were very much aware of their good fortune, and the most fortunate among them pursued thriving careers in the postwar years. In the United States, émigrés such as Auerbach, Spitzer, Wellek, and the Armenian immigrant Anna Balakian exerted a decisive influence on the discipline, perhaps more than they would have had if they'd returned to their home environments in Germany, Austria, Czechoslovakia, and Turkey. Yet even the fortunate few were marked by the traumas of their dislocations. Their struggles to reconstruct their lives are worth our attention today, as we seek to resituate comparative studies in a world of radically unequal global flows of people, capital, and cultural products of all kinds.

To begin with Lilian Furst, she was a prolific and significant scholar, author of dozens of essays, several anthologies, and fifteen books, including late in life a study of novels of forced emigration, *Random Destinations* (2005). Her title is deliberately ironic, as "destination" implies destiny or at least some settled intent, rather than the randomness and unsettledness that she explores in a range of wartime and postwar fictions, including works by Anita Desai, Ruth Prawer Jhabvala, and W. G. Sebald. Completed a decade earlier, her memoir *Home Is Somewhere Else* gives personal expression to the experience of dislocation, which began when she was seven years old and never really ended.

Furst was born in Vienna in 1931, daughter of a Hungarian father and a Polish mother; her parents had worked their way up from poverty to build a successful practice as dentists, a few blocks away from the Freuds in Berggasse. In an essay on "Freud and Vienna," Furst describes the tenuous status of Freud's parents, who like her own parents gave their children nonbiblical names so as not to sound too Jewish. She observes that Freud was only four years old when his family moved to Vienna, where he lived for the next seventy-seven years, and yet "paradoxically, however, at some level he remained an outsider, a 'Zugeraster' in Viennese dialect; the word, a corruption of 'zugereist' (traveled there) was the common denotation for immigrants, particularly the East European Jews who flocked to the city in the late 19th and early 20th centuries" (49). The same term could be applied to Furst herself, except that immigration and relocation were repeated experiences for her, almost a way of life.

Home Is Somewhere Else: An Autobiography in Two Voices (1994) is a dual memoir, based on a manuscript that her father had written in retirement in the early 1970s, into which Furst inserted alternating chapters giving her own sometimes quite different memories of the events her father recounts.[1] In her first chapter, she describes a primal scene of life thrown out of joint:

> My first distinct independent memory is of the day the Nazis marched into Vienna in March 1938. March in Vienna is usually rather cold, gray, and inhospitable, but on that day the sun was shining and the sky was of the deep blue I now associate with North Carolina or California. I remember so well leaning out of the window of our apartment on the Maria-Theresienstrasse trying to see what was going on. . . . Both the maids had gone out to join the crowds, while my parents huddled in their office, conferring in whispers. (13)

She recalls that "the public jubilation outside was in stark contrast with the silence within. The daily round of life had ceased in the face of this event that I was witnessing. The pervasive atmosphere of mourning in our home was eerie and ominous" (14).

Soon her parents determined to flee—"forced to become flotsam," as her father puts it (73)—and after an agonizing series of attempts to find refuge, they managed to reach England, where Furst grew up. She won a scholarship to Cambridge, then secured teaching positions in Belfast and then Manchester before moving to the United States in 1971, accompanied by her now-widowed father. She had become almost

---

[1] Interestingly, in the German translation, the "two voices" become a singular "Jewish fate": *Daheim ist anderswo: Ein jüdisches Schicksal erinnert von Vater und Tochter.*

incurably restless, however, and after teaching at Dartmouth she taught for varying periods at Harvard and at the Universities of Oregon and Texas, Case Western Reserve University, and Stanford. Her father accompanied her, and Furst says that "through our multiple moves, in addition to our status as strangers in the land, we formed an island of otherness wherever we went" (212). He never objected to pulling up stakes yet again, though he once ruefully remarked, "It's a pity God put down our bread in so many little piles in so many different places" (221). After his death in 1985, Furst finally settled down at the University of North Carolina for the remaining quarter-century of her life. Having written a series of pathbreaking comparative studies of Romanticism, naturalism, and realism, in her late sixties she became a founder of the field of narrative medicine, in works such as *Between Doctors and Patients: The Changing Balance of Power* (1998), *Just Talk: Narratives of Psychotherapy* (1999), and *Medical Progress and Social Reality* (2000), which includes discussion of the struggle of women to find acceptance in medicine.

To the end of her life, Furst's experience of exile infused her scholarship. Her 2005 study *Random Destinations* begins with a prologue in which she describes leaving Vienna in 1938 with her parents on a train that also carried a group of Jewish children bound for a Kindertransport ship. "How they stared at me, the only child walking along the corridor of that train securely gripping her father's hand! This autobiographical experience together with the oral history I picked up from my parents and their friends forms the extraneous frame and the impetus to this study" (xi). In the body of the book, Furst emphasizes ordinary experience in ways that anticipate today's discussions of the migration crisis: "Through their predilection for the remarkable, not to say exceptional, cases the sociohistorical studies tend to distort the overall picture of the average escapee's difficulties, efforts, and occasional failures in the process of resettlement" (11). Most memoirs similarly overemphasize success, as the writers "express pride in overcoming obstacles and often gratitude to their host country" (13).

Furst finds a counterbalancing force in novels, which "concede the malaise, the sense of distance and apartness from their second homes, which persist for many escapees" (194). She concludes that "while the sociological studies provide much valuable information about escapees' outer, public paths, the fictions allow revealing insights into the scars on the souls of these 'shards from the explosion'" (195). She emphasized literature's ability to convey traumatic experience in other works as well, including *Idioms of Distress: Psychosomatic Disorders in Medical and Imaginative Literature* (2003), which moves from hysteria in Freud's time to contemporary eating disorders. In her late turn to medical humanities, she found a way to connect her literary skills to the medical profession that her parents had hoped she'd pursue.

Despite all her success, in *Home Is Somewhere Else* she says that "even now, an American citizen, tenured in a major university, holder of an endowed chair," with savings, investments, and many publications, "still I am liable to agonies of anxiety and insomnia because, alone, at some level, I still feel so terribly vulnerable to the contingencies of an untrustworthy world" (23–24). She returns to this theme at the end of her memoir, describing her life in Chapel Hill:

> My neighbors play golf and bridge, and walk their dogs, and talk with passion about "the game." I don't understand what matters to them any more than they understand what matters to me. . . . In the great melting pot that this county is said to be, I have somehow not melted; on the contrary, I have become more myself, and thereby more other. I am not in exile from anywhere; the worlds I knew have gone, and I mourn their disappearance as I do that of the family I would have had. A student with bright red curly hair and glasses had a curious fascination for me, and it was some weeks before I realized that she reminded me of the cousin I last saw when I was six and she eight; she vanished in Treblinka. (217)

Now she ends the book, and her final words recall the large red J—for *Juden*—stamped on her family's exit visa next to the Nazi swastika: "Home is where my things are. Home is nowhere. Maybe home is beyond the grave. . . . I float on the periphery, at home yet not truly so in Europe, Great Britain, or the United States. My geographical roots are shallow; only those created by the brand mark of the red 'J' run deep into my being" (217).

After Istanbul

As Lilian Furst's memoir shows, migrancy can be a lifelong experience, resonating in the minds and hearts even of people who become well established in their oxymoronic home away from home. In the case of the two comparatists whose exilic experiences have been most often discussed, Leo Spitzer and Erich Auerbach, attention has primarily been paid to their time in Istanbul, as though it was during those years that they experienced the pain of dislocation before returning to the fold of Western academia with their prestigious appointments at Johns Hopkins and at Yale. They were less willing than Furst to openly register their lasting pain, but they too struggled to find their footing in the United States and to master the anxiety and grief that they felt over everything, and everyone, they'd left behind.

Istanbul was certainly a crucial turning point for both Spitzer and Auerbach. Many readings of their work, beginning with Geoffrey Green's *Literary Criticism and the Structures of History* (1983), have been informed by the drama of their Nazi-era exile, the period so movingly evoked by Auerbach in the postwar epilogue to *Mimesis*, almost as an aside: "I may also mention that the book was written during the war and at Istanbul, where the libraries are not well equipped for European studies" (557). The German original underscores the Istanbul setting: not "where" but *hier* the libraries are not well equipped (518). He claims to mention this fact only to excuse his paucity of reference to existing scholarship: "The lack of technical literature and periodicals may also serve to explain why my book has no notes" (557). Yet the book is a magnificent recovery of his lost European world, as he indicates in his closing lines: "I hope that my study will reach its readers—both my surviving friends of former years [*meine überlebenden Freunde von einst*] as well as all the others for whom it was intended. And may it contribute to bringing together again those whose love for our western history has serenely persevered" (557).

Auerbach allows that he might never have managed to write his masterwork if he'd had to consult the vast range of relevant studies he would have had available in Germany, but this seems as much an excuse as a factual necessity. He chose, after all, to have no footnotes at all, despite the presence of a good number of studies in the Istanbul library and in his own collection. He had brought many books with him, and as his son Clemens later recalled, he supplemented his library with extensive purchases when he spent five weeks back in Germany in 1937, spending down his savings by buying books, as Jews weren't allowed to take money out of the country (Clemens Auerbach, "Summer 1937," 495).[2]

Beyond the liberation from scholarly protocols, Istanbul offered a fresh vantage point: Edward Said has argued that *Mimesis* is "a work whose conditions and circumstances of existence are not immediately derived from the culture it describes with such extraordinary insight and brilliance but built rather on an agonizing distance from it" ("Secular Criticism," 8). Following Said, Emily Apter describes both Auerbach and Spitzer as practicing "a 'resistance' philology" in Istanbul ("Global Translatio," 274), though she also notes in Said's account a certain tendency toward "the fetish of exile." As she says, "the record shows that Auerbach was in pretty good cosmopolitan company during his Istanbul sojourn" (275). Kader Konuk has shown in *East-West Mimesis* how integrated Auerbach was among the German Jewish academic community in Istanbul. He wrote to a friend in June 1946, near the end of his stay:

> Among the many agreeable features of our present circumstances . . . one of the most important is that we share them with a great number of fellow sufferers, emigrants of all kinds, most of them also at the university, many of them very clever and likeable. Things really haven't gone so badly for us, other than that we've become quite poor . . . but those are bourgeois concerns. (Vialon, *Erich Auerbachs Briefe*, 70)

As an example of their straitened circumstances, Auerbach remarks that he and his wife have recently had to sell their piano.

Auerbach was deeply engaged in building literary studies at the University of Istanbul during his eleven years there (1936–47). In the foreword

---

[2] Auerbach took up the chair in Istanbul vacated by Spitzer, who himself had an extensive personal library. His Hopkins colleague Richard Macksey has told me that when Spitzer received news of a fire onboard the ship that was bringing his wife and son to America, he reacted with alarm: "My books!"

to a newly established Turkish journal of Romance studies, he speaks proudly of the steady increase in enrollments, and he says that his best students "have thrown themselves into their studies with great eagerness and energy and have overcome every technical difficulty" ("Über das Studium der Romanistik in Istanbul," 91). In an essay on Auerbach and Spitzer, "Heimat im Exil," Yasemin Özbek has noted their success in getting several of their assistants out of Germany to Istanbul, where they formed the core of an intellectual circle under their mentors' direction. In Spitzer's case, he was able to further re-create his German life by bringing along Rosemarie Burkart, who was his lover as well as his research assistant.

All in all, Auerbach and Spitzer felt relatively at home during their Istanbul years; America proved to be a far more foreign environment for both of them. Before finding posts in Princeton and then at Yale, Auerbach first washed up in central Pennsylvania, where Penn State was just beginning its transition from an agricultural state college to a national university. Writing to Werner Krauss soon after his arrival in January 1948, Auerbach described State College as "a little provincial town with a huge state university (12,000 students) and no real College," adding that he'd been hired to help build up the humanities in an institution where "the Liberal Arts have been completely neglected until now" (Vialon, *Erich Auerbachs Briefe*, 47).

Though State College, Pennsylvania, was a far cry from either Marburg or Istanbul, Auerbach would readily have stayed on, but the university decided to let him go at the end of his initial contract. The reason: Auerbach was suffering from hypertension, and the dean didn't want to make a long-term commitment to a potential invalid. Djelal Kadir has uncovered Auerbach's personnel file at Penn State, including the letter from the doctor describing him as a bad risk. In "Auerbach's Scar," Kadir quotes a letter that Auerbach wrote to his dean after receiving this news:

> We had a very cordial talk with Dr. Glenn, but, as I expected, he can do nothing in my case. I am extremely grateful to you that you are willing to write to your friends about a possible position for me. I want to mention, in this connection, that there might be possibilities not only in the field of Romance philology and literature, but

also in Comparative Literature, or even German. Thank you very much. Yours sincerely, Auerbach. (25)

As Kadir says, "The case file is amply articulate, intentionally and otherwise, on a bureaucratic process worthy of Kafka. And the circumspect conversion, in Auerbach's final sentence, of his undeniable qualifications into hypothetical 'possibilities' is not an insignificant index to his own self-effacement and dislocation within a precarious locus" (25). The great Romance philologist's willingness to teach "even" German speaks volumes.

Dismissed from Penn State, Auerbach managed to secure appointments at the Institute for Advanced Study at Princeton and then at Yale, but he never really acclimated to American culture, or even to the English language. Writing from New Haven in 1951 to Siegfried Kracauer, who had written him a warm letter in English, Auerbach apologized for replying in German: "As you see, I still cannot truly accustom myself to writing you in English" (Barck and Treml, 484). As Monica Jansen and Clemens Arts have observed, even during his final years at Yale, "Auerbach seems always to have remained something of 'a stranger in a strange land'" ("L'approdo americano," 75). A deep anxiety persisted beneath the surface of the unruffled calm that Auerbach projects in the closing words of *Mimesis*. Mary Ann Caws, who was his student at Yale, has recalled that in seminars he would often have two cigarettes burning at once—one in his hand, a second one forgotten in his ashtray. Late in 1955 he wrote to Kracauer that he had accomplished little in the previous several months: "that first of March, when I visited you at the art gallery, was the start of a kind of depression that lingered on for quite a while" (Barck and Treml, 486). Perhaps contributing to his depression, his hypertension persisted; it killed him two years later.

Leo Spitzer had left Germany and then Istanbul well before the war. He was free of Auerbach's health problems, and he had the good fortune to secure a chair directly at Johns Hopkins, the American university founded directly on German principles, located not in rural Pennsylvania but in the bustling city of Baltimore. Yet he too experienced his departure for America more as the loss of Europe than as the gain of the New World. He was deeply torn on boarding ship in 1936, only partly because he was leaving behind Rosemarie Burkart, for whom he'd been unable to secure American residency papers. In a letter to Kurt Vossler that December, at the end of his first semester at Hopkins, he speaks in melancholy terms of the parting, not just from her (*"ein* lieber und geliebter Mensch"), but from his German milieu, almost as if he'd still been living in Germany while in Istanbul:

> The departure from Istanbul was a most melancholy experience. For I sensed that I was taking leave of almost everything that matters to me apart from family and scholarship: a German milieu, Europe, ancient culture, *one* lovely and beloved person, many young fellow workers, intelligent students—even including the Turks, who bade me farewell as an honored professor would be in Germany (a farewell lecture on my part, a dinner from the Rector, an evening of dancing). The moment when the ship got under way, and the friends and students who—with one, the most grief-stricken, exception—had clustered together at the dock now began to disappear, while behind them the Genoa Tower stood in the dusk like a landmark of the Roman world, was one of the most difficult of my life. (Hausmann, *Vom Strudel*, 314–15)

At Hopkins, Spitzer continued, "Here everything is fine, polite, peaceful, accommodating—but cool and glassy at heart." He was unimpressed by his new surroundings and apparently unsure of how to relate to Baltimore's minority population: "Baltimore is a Bonn the size of Cologne"— this was not a compliment—"with parks and villas but no Rhine or ocean and without anything noteworthy at all. Nothing but rows of long, tedious streets, with hardly any sidewalks, as everyone has their autos; 25 percent of the inhabitants are Negroes" (318). He found the students at Hopkins "industrious, of course, but not very original, and in particular with little sense of intellectual history and little feel for beauty" (319). Clearly, Spitzer had his work cut out for him if he was going to inculcate the historical and aesthetic values that meant everything to him.

Like Lilian Furst, however, Spitzer was determined to make himself at home "somewhere else" as best he could, and he threw himself into the task. He started writing primarily in English, and unlike most émigré comparatists he took an active interest in American literature and culture, much as he had in Turkish while in Istanbul. His *Essays on English and American Literature* even includes a boldly speculative essay on "American Advertising Explained as Popular Art," in which he analyzes a Sunkist orange juice ad in terms of Renaissance iconography. This was no mere *jeu d'esprit;* in a footnote, he says that studying the Sunkist ad gave him "the first avenue (a 'philological' avenue) leading toward the understanding of the unwritten text of the American way of life" (249).

Even as he strove to build a new life in America, he made exceptional efforts to connect his past and present. In 1948 he published a collection entitled *Essays in Historical Semantics*, consisting of three essays written in English and three prewar essays in German. Remarkably, he decided to leave the German essays untranslated; in a foreword, he says that "such a presentation seemed fitting in view of my desire to attract scholars in German and English toward that common stock of European semantics that informs their own vocabulary: in this volume all nations will appear as citizens of 'quella Roma onde Cristo è Romano'" (13–14). It is appropriate that he closes this justification with an (untranslated) line from his exilic forebear Dante, whose Christianity the Jewish émigré translates into the Rome of Romance philology.[3]

Particularly revealing is the autobiographical title essay of Spitzer's collection *Linguistics and Literary History*, also published in 1948. He begins by asserting that a life story can erase the difference of decades and of continents, even as he proposes that individual experiences profoundly shape a scholar's identity:

> I have chosen the autobiographical way because my personal situation in Europe forty years ago was not, I believe, essentially different from the one with which I see the young scholar of today (and in this country) generally faced. I chose to relate to you my own experiences also because the basic approach of the individual scholar,

[3] This line is spoken by Beatrice atop Mount Purgatory before she takes Dante to Paradise: "then you will be with me forever a citizen / of that Rome where Christ is a Roman" (*Purgatorio* 32, 99–100). Perhaps Spitzer was recalling the lines written in his guest book in Cologne by none other than Erich Auerbach, whom he had invited to give a lecture in 1932. Auerbach wrote: "Unser Gegenstand ist nicht die Kunde von Sein und Kultur, sondern 'das Rom, in dem Christus Römer ist'" (Our object is not the message of Being and Culture but "that Rome, where Christ is a Roman") (Gumbrecht, *Vom Leben und Sterben*, 164).

conditioned as it is by his first experiences, by his *Erlebnis*, as the Germans say, determines his method: *Methode ist Erlebnis*, Gundolf has said. (1)

So far, so good, but then he makes a startling analogy: "In fact, I would advise every older scholar to tell his public the basic experiences underlying his methods, his *Mein Kampf*, as it were—without dictatorial connotations, of course" (1).

What could Spitzer possibly have intended by this comparison? In an essay on Spitzer, "Methode ist Erlebnis"—a title drawn from this passage—in his book *Vom Leben und Sterben der großen Romanisten*, Hans Ulrich Gumbrecht is frankly astonished. "The play on Adolf Hitler's book," he says, "makes it clear that in 1948 Spitzer had still not yet begun to reflect seriously on the horrors of the Third Reich" (129). Something else must be going on, though, as Spitzer's letters of the 1940s show that he was intensely aware of the depredations of the Nazis who had forced him from his homeland, and after the war ended, he was unsparing in condemning those scholars who had accommodated themselves to the regime. Like Vladimir Nabokov, whom he resembles in many ways—he even celebrates "butterfly-words" in his essay—Spitzer asserts a sovereign command of language, the freedom of a world of words. His statement can be compared to his friend Victor Klemperer's dissection of the *Lingua Tertii Imperii*: Spitzer isn't going to let Hitler gain control over a *single word* of German—not even the title of Hitler's infamous apologia, whose meaning is reduced to "dictatorial connotations," nothing more, ready to be relegated to the ash heap of history.

And yet, as with Nabokov, persisting memories of trauma lie behind the Olympian façade. Though *Linguistics and Literary History* came out only in 1948, the book bears a foreword dated September 1945 (vi). Spitzer likely wrote the title essay that summer, and at a deep level it represents a coming to terms with his life in the wake of the final collapse of the Third Reich and Hitler's suicide that April. Thus Spitzer frames his essay in response to the German crisis of language and culture, but there is another dimension to this passage. He is writing for his new American audience, and here we have to unravel the complexities of that relation. Beneath Spitzer's nostalgic evocation of "the gay and orderly, skeptic and sentimental, Catholic and pagan Vienna of yore" (2), there runs a current of anxiety: just how can he make himself at home in this strange new world? Can he connect to postwar America at all? We can already see this concern in Spitzer's foreword to his collection. "I dedicate this first book of mine printed in America," he says,

> to Assistant Professor ANNA GRANVILLE HATCHER who is an outstanding American scholar in the too little cultivated field of syntax— which, in her case, is expanded into stylistic and cultural history— and who could thus teach me, not only the intricacies of English syntax and stylistics, but some of the more recondite features of American culture and of its particular moral, logical, and aesthetic aspirations: a knowledge without which all endeavors of the philologist to explain poetry to an American public must fail completely. (v)

Note the absolutes in this sentence: without such a guide, not just some efforts but any effort at all must—not may—fail, and it must fail completely.

In fact, Spitzer's efforts failed even with Anna Hatcher. He had helped his star pupil finish her dissertation, had it published by the Johns Hopkins University Press, got her hired and then tenured in his own department. She also became his lover, replacing the lost Rosemarie Burkart; for years, Richard Macksey has told me, the two had lunch together every day in the faculty club, arriving late and lingering in the half-empty room. Upon his retirement, she co-edited a festschrift for him, and after his death she prepared an unfinished book of his for publication. There could be no more devoted disciple—but she could never match his philological skills, his cosmopolitan flair, or his poetic sensibility. Her own awareness of this fact can be seen in the dedication of her first book, the published version of her dissertation, *Reflexive Verbs: Latin, Old French, Modern French* (1942):

To

LEO SPITZER

WHO BELIEVES THAT LANGUAGE IS POETRY

I DEDICATE THIS LABOR BASED ON STATISTICAL COMPILATION

IN WHICH THE FIGURES SEEMED, SOMEHOW,

TO ADD UP TO POETRY.

Sadly, they don't.

Try as he might, in every way and on every level, Spitzer could never get close enough to his students to bridge the gulf between the gay and orderly Vienna of his youth and the gray urban grid of postwar Baltimore. According to Richard Macksey, who studied with Spitzer in the 1950s, his graduate students were awed but bewildered by his unpredictable interpretations: they would sit in his seminars, wondering what he would come up with next. The problem was perhaps as much a matter of personality as of cultural difference: Spitzer loved to make discoveries that no one else could find. Introducing his festschrift, Henri Peyre put the matter in warmly affectionate terms. When discussing a text, Peyre said,

> Spitzer's very face radiates joy. To read, to rummage around, to perceive enigmas invisible to others, to construct some new hypothesis on the spot—one senses that this gives him an utterly youthful pleasure [*un plaisir tout juvénile*]. . . . In an age besotted with contemplating its tragic self, in a profession that doesn't lack stern-faced crusaders and timid moralists astray in the garden of beauty, fearful of its too great delights, it is a noble boast for this often-exiled man that he has never lost the appetite for the elevated pleasure [*jouissance supérieure*] with which language and literature should be enjoyed. ("Avant-propos," 7)

Pulling hidden enigmas out of texts gave Spitzer great pleasure, but it is no wonder that he had difficulty communicating his intuitive method to his students.

A sense of unbridgeable distance underlies "Linguistics and Literary History." After recounting his intellectual autobiography and explicating his philological method, he concludes, finally, that there is no way to teach the method; one just needs to live it: "the capacity for this feeling is, again, deeply anchored in the previous life and education of the critic, and not only in his scholarly education: in order to keep his soul ready for his scholarly task he must have already made choices, in ordering his life, of what I would call a moral nature" (29). But in the essay's conclusion, he regrets that he can never be part of his students' daily lives:

"I have sometimes wondered if my 'explication de texte' in the university classroom, where I strive to create an atmosphere suitable for the appreciation of the work of art, would not have succeeded much better if that atmosphere had been present at the breakfast table of my students" (29).

Spitzer's problem was less an agonizing distance from Europe than a tantalizing *proximity* to the American life around him, a milieu in which, like Lilian Furst, he could never feel truly at home. Fifteen years into his sojourn at Hopkins, Spitzer still viewed his new academic world with an outsider's eye. In a plenary address to the Modern Language Association, "The Formation of the American Humanist," published in *PMLA* in 1951, he asks why no excellent young philologists are emerging from any of the American universities. A first explanation he offers is that American academics give their students *too much advice*, thereby stifling their natural independence and creativity; he notes with pride that he wrote his own dissertation without a word of feedback from his mentor Wilhelm Meyer-Lübke from the day his prospectus was approved until the day he submitted the completed dissertation. Then comes a second, and still more surprising, explanation: "to make things worse—I hesitate to say it, but I shall say it—our students marry too early." Though he grants that such marriages protect the (now evidently male) graduate students from "the soiling effect on mind and body of prostitution and debauchery" (!), he wishes that "the young scholar should keep himself as long as possible 'disponible,'" instead of having to "shoulder his moral responsibilities and submit to the necessities contingent on married life and children (and God knows how exacting American wives and children sometimes are!)" (41). To these detrimental factors, Spitzer adds a third: new PhDs in America are all expected to teach as well as to be scholars, rather than being trained on one track or the other. He recommends adopting the German system in which a minority of elite graduate students could devote themselves to scholarship in the honored role of *Privatdozent*, free of most responsibilities for teaching and administration.

Spitzer admits that his readers aren't likely to favor these opinions, so different from the egalitarian ideals of the American system. He anticipates their reaction in stark terms: "You may have decided," he says, "that consequently, as the saying goes, 'I should go back where I came from.' But I do not wish to go back, I wish to stay in this country that I love" (47). He defends his critique as an expression of his love affair with America itself: "Is it not understandable that a relationship deliberately based on choice may inspire, at the same time, more passion and more criticism than an inherited relationship?" (47). He argues that a synthesis of American egalitarianism and European elitism will serve scholarship better than saddling every graduate student and assistant professor with heavy teaching loads.

Strange though his ideas must have sounded at the time, over the next generation many American universities did begin to offer better fellowship packages, to create postdocs, and to lighten the teaching load for junior faculty—albeit partly by the expanded use of poorly paid adjuncts with few benefits and little stability, in an abusive two-tiered system that Spitzer would likely have considered less honest and more unequal than the open elitism of the German universities. As for the burdens posed by young scholars' family responsibilities, it would be decades before universities began to institute parental leave policies and to extend tenure clocks for parents of young children. Institutionally as well as intellectually, Spitzer's migrant perspective gave him a prescient angle of vision.

Spitzer strove in a host of essays during his American years to inculcate his unique blend of philology and literary analysis. In his hands, stylistics became a compelling elaboration of Herder's intimate linkage of language and identity, now personal as well as cultural. In "Linguistics and Literary History," he challenges us to attend closely to what is most distinctive in a writer's style. As a prime example, he gives a passage from Rabelais, on whose extravagant neologisms he had written his *Habilitationsschrift* in Vienna thirty-five years before. "Just listen to the inscription on the *abbaye de Thélème*," he says,

> that Renaissance convent of his shaping, from which Rabelais excludes the hypocrites:

> Cy n'entrez pas, hypocrites, bigots,
> Vieux matagotz, marmiteux, borsoufles,
> Torcoulx, badaux, plus que n'estoient les Gotz,

Ny Ostrogotz, precurseurs des magotz,
Haires, cagotz, cafars empantouflez,
Gueux mitoufles, frapars escorniflez,
Befflez, enflez, fagoteurs de tabus;
Tirez ailleurs pour vendre vos abus. (17)

He comments that most French scholars would see this passage simply as mediocre poetry based on the genre of a barker's harangue, yet he experiences it very differently:

> But I can never read these lines without being frightened, and I am shaken in this very moment by the horror emanating from this accumulation of -*fl*- and -*got*- clusters—of sounds which, in themselves, and taken separately, are quite harmless, of words grouped together, bristling with Rabelais' hatred of hypocrisy—that greatest of all crimes against life . . . as shattering now as at the hour when Rabelais begot these word-monsters. (17–18)

What can we make of this explanation? Lacking Spitzer's decades of philological training, his devotion to phonemes and morphemes, can we really share his terror at these *fl* and *got* clusters? I certainly wasn't frightened by them when I read Rabelais as a teenager, and I was no more shattered the first several times I read Spitzer's essay; his reading seemed forced, exaggerated. But then I noticed that he asks us to *listen* to the lines; and how should we hear them?

The Abbaye de Thélème depicted at the close of the first book of *Gargantua and Pantagruel* is a humanist ideal, a cross between an aristocratic chateau and More's *Utopia*, which had been published two decades before. It is a refuge for rational discourse and virtuous pleasures, secured by excluding the hypocrites who might undermine the abbey's harmonious order. I suppose that the poem would have been read by professors in fin-de-siècle Paris or Vienna in a tone of urbane mockery. The unstoppable flow of language will drive the hapless hypocrites away, much as the power of music drives the wicked Monostatos from Sarastro's enlightened temple in *Die Zauberflöte*, composed in Mozart's own gay and orderly Vienna a century before Spitzer's birth. Read in this way, the passage conveys none of the horror that Spitzer says he feels. But several pages later, he gives us a different way to read, hinting at the psychic trauma that underlies his reaction. Suppose that in place of "hypocrites" and "maggots" you substitute the word "Jews." And what if Rabelais's greatest modern successor had been doing just that?

"Now, who are the descendants of Rabelais?" Spitzer asks (22). His answer, for "our own time": Louis-Ferdinand Céline. And not just any Céline, but the author of *Bagatelles pour un massacre*, which had become a best seller in Vichy France. Spitzer quotes a passage that, he says, "can be compared with the apocalyptic inscription over the portal of Thélème":

> Penser "sozial!" cela veut dire dans la pratique, en termes bien crus: "penser juif! pour les juifs! par les juifs, sous les juifs!" Rien d'autre! Tout le surplus immense des mots, le vrombissant verbiage socialitico-humanitaro-scientifique, tout le cosmique carafouillage de l'impératif despotique juif n'est que l'enrobage mirageux, le charabia fatras poussif, la sauce orientale pour ces encoulés d'aryens, la fricassée terminologique pour rire, pour l'adulation des "aveulis blancs," ivrognes rampants, intouchables, qui s'en foutrent, à bite que veux-tu, s'en mystifient, s'en baffrent à crever. (22)

After quoting this diatribe against a Jewish plot for world domination through social and scientific inquiry, Spitzer somberly concludes: "Words and reality fall apart. This is really a *voyage au bout du monde*: not to the oracle of Bacbuc but to chaos, to the end of language as an expression of thought" (22). This is how he wants us to *hear* Rabelais, not just read him: with the violence that a Céline—or a Hitler—would give to the explosive *fl* and *got* clusters that seek to expel the foreign Gotz and the maggoty Ostragotz from the humanist utopia.[4]

Spitzer was by no means an antihumanist, and he was no determinist. In a 1944 essay on "Geistesgeschichte vs. History of Ideas as Applied to Hitlerism," he roundly rejected a claim by his Hopkins colleague Arthur Lovejoy that Nazi ideology was a direct outgrowth of Romantic ideas of

---

[4] To hear how the Rabelais passage would likely have been read in Spitzer's youth as compared to how he was evidently hearing it in the 1940s, see David Damrosch and Katharina Piechocki, "Spitzer's Rabelais" (YouTube).

organicism, dynamism, and national essence. Yet he shared with Lovejoy an emphasis on the historical roots of social formations, and he had an abiding concern with the uses and abuses of language. As early as 1918, he had published an urgent appeal, *Fremdwörterhatz und Fremdvölkerhaß: Eine Streitschrift gegen die Sprachreinigung* ("hunting foreignisms and hating foreigners: a polemic against linguistic cleansing"). Composed in 1945, "Linguistics and Literary History" can be compared to Horkheimer and Adorno's *Dialectic of Enlightenment*, written in their own American exile and published the previous year. Taken in a wrong direction, the dialectic of Renaissance humanism can lead down from the Abbaye de Thélème to the gates of Auschwitz.

As Spitzer remarks in his critique of Lovejoy, "A scholarly text, as well as a poem, may have overtones; and listening to them is an essential part of reading" ("Geistesgeschichte," 198). If we read Leo Spitzer, Lilian Furst, and their contemporaries with our ears as well as our eyes open to their historical and political contexts, they have much to teach us today, not only about the history of the migrant discipline of comparative literature but about the double-edged sword of language. A renewed "resistance philology" can help us navigate our shifting relations to our home culture and to those we encounter in the wider world, amid the complex mixture of civilization and barbarism that these troubled scholars saw everywhere around them.

3

Politics

The comparatists who reshaped the field in the United States during the 1950s and 1960s were driven by a sense of mission. Theirs was a utopian perspective, well expressed by Anna Balakian, who became a leading figure in both the American and the International Comparative Literature Associations; the ICLA's Balakian Prize for first books is named in her honor. In a late essay, "How and Why I Became a Comparatist" (1994), she describes her family's emigration in 1921 from Turkey to western Europe and eventually to the United States. She recalls that "when finally our movements came to rest in America, I had by age ten developed a deep sense, through personal experience, of the distinctions between international, national, and multicultural relationships." She was already attuned to the politics of language: "German in a German-speaking city was a national experience; German in New Britain, Connecticut, USA was a ghetto phenomenon" (75).

When her family left Constantinople, six-year-old Anna clung to her beginning French primer, and she always regarded French as the language of "my mind's awakening" (76). Once settled in the United States, like many immigrants she found in public education a route to upward mobility. She majored in French at Hunter College in New York, which was then still a women's college focused on teacher training. She went on to Columbia, intending to take an MA in French and become a high school teacher. Yet her life's path was altered by two forces: a mentor and a conference. At Columbia, she came under the wing of the comparatist Paul Hazard, who was dividing his time between Columbia and the Collège de France. He encouraged her to do a doctorate, after which she began teaching French at Syracuse University. She would have remained a professor of French but for an unexpected turn of events: in 1958 Werner Friederich invited her to the pivotal second meeting of the newly formed ICLA, which he was organizing at the University of North Carolina at Chapel Hill. Balakian was tempted to go, but she wasn't sure of her qualifications:

> But was I a Comparatist? In fact what was a Comparatist? It was a man (I did not know of any women in the field) of infinite knowledge in literature and philosophy, like the late Paul Hazard, and expert in several languages, with a refined and developed *Weltanschauung* and wisdom acquired through a life devoted to reading and scholarly probing. . . . Could I call myself a Comparatist just because I had wandered across Europe at an early age? (77)

Balakian writes that "what really prompted me to explore my potential as a Comparatist was the fact that I had been nurturing a deep-seated pacifism," based in "a revulsion against all national confrontations and ethnic antagonisms" (77). She leaves tacit the likely origins of this revulsion in the Armenian genocide and her family's flight from Turkey amid a renewed wave of ethnic cleansing. Displaced into western Europe and then the United States, she found in surrealism a new basis for developing her radical internationalism:

> Naively and perhaps with the idealism of youth, I thought of Comparative Literature as an antidote to excessive nationalism, and surrealism was the one literature that was reacting against national divisions and even overcoming the barriers between the arts. I thought, innocently, that with the perspectives of Comparative Literature and the dissemination of the principles of surrealism we could change the world. . . . So I bought a ticket and made a small financial investment that was to shape the rest of my life. (77–78)

Changing the World

Many comparatists sought to change the world in the postwar years, a time of rapid expansion in higher education and optimism about America's role in fostering international cooperation and understanding. In the lead article for the inaugural issue of the *Yearbook of Comparative and General Literature* in 1952, Henri Peyre was moved to speak in terms of manifest destiny: "In the last two or three decades, new duties devolved upon this country: it fell to the lot of America to be, not only the greatest power on this planet, but the obvious link between Europe and Asia, and between the past and future of mankind" ("A Glance," 1). Peyre had emigrated from France in 1925, soon after receiving his degrees from the Sorbonne and the University of Paris, and his pride in his adopted country was undimmed in 1952. He adduces several reasons why America could become "the paradise for Comparative Literature," including the nation's "motley" multiethnic composition and "an enviable freedom from national prejudice." But the first factor he cites is institutional: "American universities have been less narrowly fettered with hidebound traditions than those of an older continent and have proved hospitable to new subjects"—albeit, he cautions, "to the point of being accused of an exaggerated fondness for temporary vogues and whimsical fads" (1).

Whether unfettered or faddish, comparative literature was caught up in broad changes in American higher education. These affected all disciplines but had distinctive effects on the new field, whose growth occurred at the confluence of two broad movements: the postwar explosion of college enrollments and Cold War competition. Two governmental initiatives in particular had a decisive impact: the Servicemen's Readjustment Act of 1944—better known as the G.I. Bill—and the National Defense Education Act, passed by Congress in the wake of the Soviet launch of *Sputnik* in 1957. Appropriately, the NDEA was signed into law by President Eisenhower on September 2, 1958, just a week before the ICLA met in Chapel Hill. Comparatists quickly took note of the opportunities offered by the act, which supported foreign-language study and created a series of area studies programs. At its first conference in 1962, the newly formed American Comparative Literature Association invited a program officer, James Blessing, to give a plenary talk on the act. Three years later, the act's importance for the growing discipline was singled out in the opening words of the influential "Report on Professional Standards" prepared for ACLA by the committee chaired by Harry Levin: "The recent proliferation of Comparative Literature, in colleges and universities throughout the country, could hardly have materialized without the support of the National Defense Education Act" ("Levin Report," 21).

James Blessing's address to the ACLA was published in the inaugural issue of *Comparative Literature Studies*, the quarterly journal that joined Friederich's *Yearbook*, and the ACLA itself, as demonstrating that the discipline was setting down solid roots in the American academic landscape. In his address, Blessing remarked "what a pleasure it is to think that a representative of the Federal Government should have anything at all to spend half an hour saying to the American Comparative Literature Association," adding—quite possibly sincerely—"and how delightful to be that representative" ("Comparative Literature and Title IV," 133). Blessing's listeners were delighted in turn by his report that the act's Title IV fellowship program was already funding 20 percent of all graduate students in comparative literature, a discipline that the government favored as "especially adapted to the preparation of college and university teachers" (130), thanks to its intellectual breadth and its emphasis on languages. Yet even as comparatists were receiving Blessing's blessing, the NDEA was giving greater support to the act's Title VI, which developed area studies programs in the service of Cold War rivalries. Though in principle the Title VI funding should have been well suited for comparative literature, its emphasis was on languages and regions far from the discipline's purview in that era.

Such an emphasis remains to this day. The website of the Department of Education includes a celebratory essay on its area studies programs, which notes that "prior to the passage of the act, few of the languages spoken by more than three-fourths of the world's population were being offered in the United States and not enough scholars were available to perform research in such languages or to teach them. . . . Hindi, for example, was being studied by only twenty-three students in the United States in 1958." The example of Hindi is far from random: "At that time, India was the world's largest democracy and leader of the Nonaligned Movement of approximately 120 countries. Vowing to maintain independence from either side of the Cold War, the countries of the Nonaligned Movement made many joint stands against U.S. and Western European intervention in the world and enjoyed Soviet support" ("History of Title VI").

Given the act's political purposes, the area studies programs were devoted to regions outside western Europe, still the center of comparative studies. The Title VI centers became dominated by political scientists and economists with few literary scholars included, a disciplinary division of labor that reinforced the disconnection of comparative literature from programs in non-western-European cultures. As a result, Blessing devoted his ACLA talk only to the smaller Title IV fellowship program, and he further remarked that the funding for both the Title IV and Title VI programs amounted in 1961 to just $12.4 million. That figure could seem impressive to poorly funded humanists, but it was only a pittance in the nearly $700 million in federal funding that year for university research and graduate training. "Such disparity," Blessing remarked, "undermines the position of the humanities in many subtle ways" (131). Comparatists weren't just in bed with the State Department and the Pentagon; they were having to share the bed with the scientists who were hogging the blankets and the balance sheets.

To change the world as Anna Balakian and her friends sought to do, they would have to begin with an almost equally daunting task—changing the university. As if the inexorable growth of the sciences weren't enough of a problem, the comparatists also had to contend with their rivals in the existing literature departments. In the United States as elsewhere, those departments remained closely tied to the nineteenth-century nationalism of their origins. Most literary scholars had little interest in broadly international work, and many were hostile to the antinationalistic perspective of comparatists like Balakian. Any discussion of the politics of comparative studies, then, needs to have a dual focus on institutional politics as well as the wider political scene, and here a postcolonial perspective is particularly germane.

In the turbulent year of 1968, American higher education was analyzed in postcolonial terms in a seminal study, *The Academic Revolution*, by the sociologists Christopher Jencks and David Riesman. The revolutionary struggles underway around the country and in Indochina give a context for their study of the reshaping of American higher education in the previous two decades. They approached the academic revolution as a social phenomenon that both resulted from and enhanced seismic shifts in the

American population and economy, as higher education became a significant vector of upward mobility, particularly for rural and working-class whites and to a lesser but growing extent for ethnic minorities. With these emphases in mind, Jencks and Riesman studied not only elite private universities but also public, Catholic, and historically black institutions. In their book they are critical of the emphasis on research that was fueling much of the system's expansion. Here the actors would include the National Science Foundation as well as the NDEA, along with such private funders as the Rockefeller and Ford Foundations. Jencks and Riesman saw these often technocratic initiatives as leading to the dominance of graduate education in academia, hindering the social revolution at the crucial undergraduate level. It is in this connection that their anticolonial perspective comes to the fore:

> We are troubled by the fact that the graduate schools have an essentially imperial relationship with many of the institutions and subcultures on their borders, particularly the undergraduate colleges. Their apparent successes depend in many cases on exploiting these underdeveloped territories. First, the graduate schools import the colleges' most valuable "raw material," i.e. gifted BAs. They train these men [sic] as scholars. The best of them they keep for themselves; the rest they export to the colleges whence they came, to become teachers. (515)

They weren't optimistic that this neocolonial relationship was likely to change anytime soon: "We see little prospect that the graduate imperium will yield to outbreaks of unrest among the natives in the undergraduate colleges. If decolonization comes in our time—and we doubt that it will—it will come as a result of strong initiatives from dissidents within the graduate schools themselves" (516).

Jencks and Riesman's analysis applies with particular force to comparative literature. Many of its programs were established purely at the graduate level, on the grounds that undergraduates simply didn't know enough to do serious comparative work. Once they had completed their training in two or three languages and literatures, such students could rise to the higher level of graduate study in comparative literature.

The discipline's elitism extended from students to colleagues. Very much in Jencks and Riesman's terms, the surrounding language and literature departments were expected to provide comparative literature with its raw materials: language training, primary texts, and prospective graduate students. Levin's 1965 "Report on Professional Standards," and its successor the 1975 Greene Report, emphasized that programs should only be established in institutions with "an existing strength in language departments and libraries to which not very many colleges, and indeed not every university, can be fairly expected to measure up" ("Levin Report," 21). In both reports, comparative literature depends on commerce with its related—or tributary—departments, but the deal is based on a hierarchical division of labor.

Literary theory was becoming the crucible in which the raw materials of literary texts were to be refined before being sold back to purchasers in the many departments, colleges, and universities that couldn't "measure up" to the comparatists' high standards. A similar elitism prevailed within the discipline itself, with a handful of East Coast departments setting the tone for the rest. Thus the majority of faculty on both the Levin and the Greene committees were not just white men (two out of seventeen were women) but professors trained or teaching (or both) at Yale or Harvard. Reflecting the boom in Continental theory then getting underway, the Levin Report recommended that comparative literature programs give graduate students a common basis for their work in disparate literatures by offering "one or two basic courses—let us say, proseminars in theory of literature and in textual methods or technical problems" (23). If those enticing courses in "textual methods or technical problems" were ever mounted at all, they were soon eclipsed by the theory proseminar as the gateway requirement in many programs.

By this time, the American comparatists felt that they had not only established themselves in the United States but had gained an ascendancy over their counterparts in Europe. The battle to establish the American programs' legitimacy had been waged throughout the 1950s, and many of the native-born or newly minted Americans saw themselves as having won a decisive victory at the Chapel Hill ICLA meeting that changed Balakian's life. There the "American" perspective was summed up in no uncertain terms by the Czech émigré René Wellek. In his plenary speech, "The Crisis of Comparative Literature," Wellek mocked the "French school" as limited to positivistic studies of the mere "foreign trade of literature," far below the broad horizons of true comparative studies. "In its methods and methodological reflections," he acidly stated, "comparative literature has become a stagnant backwater" (292). He argued that comparatists must rise above nationalistically inflected positivism by understanding the intrinsic qualities of the literary work "as a stratified structure of signs and meanings" (293). In a heartfelt peroration, he stated:

Once we grasp the nature of art and poetry, its victory over human mortality and destiny, its creation of a new world of the imagination, national vanities will disappear. Man, universal man, man everywhere and at all times, in all his variety, emerges and literary scholarship ceases to be an antiquarian pastime, a calculus of national credits and debts and even a mapping of networks of relationships. Literary scholarship becomes an act of the imagination, like art itself, and thus a preserver and creator of the highest values of mankind. (295)

Exploring man, universal man in all "his" variety, by the mid-1960s American comparatists were confident in their victory over the Europeans' putatively narrow focus on "national credits and debts." The Levin Report even denied that any conflict remained with "the French school," arguing that the discipline in America was characterized by its thoroughgoing internationalism and its friendly relations with comparatists abroad (25).

A major factor in the eclipse of the French school was again institutional. In France, as in most other countries, the discipline was constrained by the hegemony of the national literature, whereas the wartime émigrés were pleasantly surprised to find that the American universities had no departments of American literature at all. Instead, in a ghostly vestige of British colonialism, Americanists were (and usually still are) folded into English departments dominated by British literature, with few faculty lines despite their high enrollments. Like most English professors, the émigré comparatists didn't think that America had produced enough significant literature to require much attention. As Wellek declared in "The Crisis of

Comparative Literature," literary jingoism was rare in the United States, "which, on the whole, has been immune to it partly because it had less to boast of" (289). Thus American literature posed little threat, and comparative literature in the United States was on a roll, expanding at a rate unthinkable anywhere in Europe.

Directly anticipating today's discussions of literary centers and peripheries, the Levin Report concludes by tracing the discipline's movement from periphery to center within academia. "A generation ago," the report says, comparative literature "would have been looked upon as at best a supplement to the national literary histories, and as such a luxury for most academic communities. However, as the literary and linguistic disciplines have reconsidered their criteria and reorganized their curricula, it has been moving from the periphery toward a more and more centralizing role" (25). The report generously says that the relationship "should be one of close collaboration, rather than rivalry" (25), but this will now be a collaboration of the "more and more central" discipline with its ever more peripheral neighbors.

Levin's committee proposed that whatever its specific structure, "Comparative Literature must always be embodied in a kind of interdepartment" (22). Almost all American programs have indeed become interdepartments in this sense, even if they have departmental status and a core of full-time faculty. This interconnectivity provides variety and flexibility for students, and it gives jointly appointed faculty a welcome opportunity to teach beyond their obligations in their primary department. These arrangements, though, are often more beneficial for the tenured faculty than for their younger colleagues, who may have to please two tenure committees with very different goals and expectations. Graduate students in particular can fall between the cracks—or into the yawning gulfs—between departments. They can find their teaching opportunities limited or their fellowships cut if departments decide to favor one of "their own" students over an interloper from outside, or even over a student who is housed in their department but who works mostly with faculty in other departments.

This was brought home to me not long after I started teaching at Columbia as an assistant professor, when the best of our first-year comparatists suddenly had his fellowship taken away at the end of his MA year.

Fluent in five languages, he had done brilliantly in all his courses, but he had mostly worked with faculty outside his (and my) home department of English and Comparative Literature. Fellowship funding was tight for the PhD program, and our departmental graduate committee chose to devote their limited funds to students better known to them and their senior colleagues. The problem wasn't only with the department; it lay equally at the door of the interdepartmental Program in Comparative Literature— or would have, if we'd had a room of our own. The program had long been run on a quite informal basis by a genial medievalist, W.T.H. Jackson. He was an excellent scholar but a feckless administrator, and when chairing the German department had been known by his younger colleagues as "What The Hell Jackson." Edward Said had recently taken over as director of the program, but the comparative literature doctoral subcommittee remained focused on approving orals lists and thesis proposals. No one was following the money.

Said and the other senior faculty who were best positioned to improve matters were largely unaware of the problem, since their favorite students would get funded as a matter of course. After rallying support for our suddenly penniless student, I was able to get his funding restored, and I began serving as the program's first-ever director of graduate studies. For the next twenty years, I also made a point of serving on my department's graduate committee, to make sure that comparatists applying through the department would have an advocate in admissions and that once on campus their interests would be protected. Though academic politics is more often satirized in novels than theorized in the pages of *Critical Inquiry*, such departmental diplomacy is often critical to a program's success.

Along with its interdepartmental struggles, comparative literature has long experienced ideological and methodological strife of its own. During the 1950s as now, the discipline was home to sharply competing interests and views. René Wellek's fiery speech in Chapel Hill can't have pleased his host, Werner Friederich, who had studied at the Sorbonne before emigrating to the United States. Four years after the 1958 congress, Friederich wrote a memorial tribute in the *Yearbook* to his Sorbonne teacher Ferdinand Baldensperger, one of the figures whom Wellek had signaled out for particular scorn for his "attention to minor authors and to the bygone fashions of literary taste" ("The Crisis," 286). In his tribute, Fried-erich unrepentantly wrote that he regarded his teachers at the Sorbonne "as the very soul of their branch of learning" ("Ferdinand Baldensperger," 41). At the Sorbonne, as in most programs of the prewar era, the practice of *littérature comparée* presupposed relatively self-contained national lit-eratures as the basis of comparison. In turning from national traditions to "universal" theoretical concerns, Wellek was actually reinventing him-self as much as he was trying to shoulder his rivals aside. His own 1931 doctoral dissertation at Princeton, *Immanuel Kant in England, 1793–1836*, would have fit rather comfortably within the "foreign trade" model he mocked in 1958, but by then he had set his sights on higher goals.

The broader perspectives promised by theory were still chiefly derived from the literatures of a handful of countries. Even when discussing a gen-eral question of poetics or a broad literary movement, most comparatists continued to draw their examples almost exclusively from the major powers of western Europe. Thus Wellek's *The Romantic Age* (1955) dealt solely with Germany, France, Italy, and England—the same four countries that Georg Brandes had studied in the 1870s in his *Major Currents of Nineteenth-century Literature*. In this context, Wellek's lack of Arabic or Chinese was no more a disadvantage for his studies of "universal man in all his variety" than his native fluency in Czech was an advantage. He actually wrote periodically on Czech literature, but never as a comparat-ist. When he gave a lecture in 1963 on "Czech Literature at the Crossroads of Europe," he was speaking not at a meeting of the ACLA but to the Czechoslovak Society of Arts and Sciences. He was then serving as the second president of the society, an academic and cultural organization that had been founded in Washington five years before and was devoted to building solidarity and intellectual exchange among the Czech and Slova-kian exile communities. On the occasion of his address, the society made him a birthday present of a collected volume of his *Essays on Czech Liter-ature*. Yet only Prague theory, and not Czech literature, figured in Wellek's studies in comparative literature.

Most comparatists in America were primarily appointed in a national literature department, and they often chafed against the deep-rooted na-tionalism of their noncomparatist colleagues. Albert Guérard spoke for many in 1958 when he used religious language to condemn "the nation-alistic heresy" in a lead article for the *Yearbook of Comparative and General Literature* ("Comparative Literature?" 4). The comparatists' nation-based internationalism both grounded their discipline and also limited its reach, as they evolved a kind of passive-aggressive relation to the national literature departments on which they drew for faculty, students, and materials. The great majority of literary scholars were fully ensconced within a single linguistic or national tradition, and they didn't take kindly to being offered the role of native informants—or compradores—for an imperial comparative literature. Few would have read with pleasure the 1975 ACLA "Report on Standards," chaired by Wellek's colleague and former student Thomas Greene, which was explicit in its hegemonic enthusiasm:

> When the Comparative Literature movement gathered strength in the U.S. during the two decades following World War II, it was dedicated to high goals. It wanted to stand, and in large part did stand, for a new internationalism: for broader perspectives, for larger contexts in the tracking of motifs, themes, and types as well as larger understandings of genres and modes. . . . Within the academy, it wanted to bring together the respective European language departments in a new cooperation, reawakening them to the unity of their common endeavor, and embodying that unity in various ways, both customary and creative. . . . This vision of a fresh and central academic discipline was ambitious in the noblest sense. It remains our common inheritance. (Greene Report, 28)

It is a wonderful thing for comparatists to enjoy broader perspectives, larger contexts, and larger understandings as they develop a fresh, central, noble, and ambitious discipline, but few outside the charmed circle could have relished their characterization, by implication, as narrower, smaller, staler, peripheral, plebeian, and unambitious.

A fair number of the foreign literature faculty in the United States were immigrants themselves, but they weren't too pleased to have carpetbaggers touch down in their well-tended fields to pick up some supplies. Then too, even émigré scholars weren't always hospitable to immigrants of the wrong sort. Writing at age eighty-eight in 1994, René Wellek vividly recalled arriving in Northampton, Massachusetts, in 1928 to be interviewed for a lectureship in German at Smith College. He was met at the train station by the department chair, Ernst Heinrich Mensel, a German-born medievalist: "When I left the train Mr. Mensel saw me getting out and walked up to me with his hands stretched out and said (I swear that these were his first words): 'I see you are not a Jew.'" Wellek comments that "If I had been a Jew, Mr. Mensel would have taken me on a tour of the campus but sent me back to New York" ("Memoirs of the Profession," 3).

Faced with the skepticism of their possibly narrower but certainly more numerous colleagues, the 1965 and 1975 "Standards" committees sought to defend their grounds of comparison and to secure their borders, fearing that the very success of comparative literature programs risked dilution of the entire enterprise and the erosion of its elite status. As the Greene Report darkly remarked, "There is cause, we believe, for serious concern, in transforming our discipline, that we not debase those values on which it is founded. The slippage of standards, once allowed to accelerate, would be difficult to arrest. . . . In at least some colleges and universities, Comparative Literature seems to be purveyed in the style of a smorgasbord at bargain rates" (31). The Armenian immigrant Anna Balakian used a startling analogy in making a similar complaint in 1994: "The barriers have come down completely and there is total permissiveness in declaring oneself a Comparatist. We have arrived on dangerous ground. We are threatened," she warned, "with a host of scholars crossing over without union cards" (84).

The (Euro-)American Comparative Literature Association

Carefully policing its members' union cards and green cards—their Greene cards?—the ACLA remained a small organization through the 1980s, and during the 1960s the political urgency of the 1950s gradually began to fade. The issues of European conflict and postwar reconstruction that were so vital to the émigrés were distant from their American students, and some of the émigrés themselves were happy to finally get away from the cultural politics of the Nazi era. Paul de Man gives a particularly vivid case in point, as will be discussed in the next chapter, but even René Wellek kept his ongoing Czech involvements separate from his comparative studies, emphasizing stratified structures of signs and meanings over any direct political concerns.

The discipline's West-Eurocentrism was regrettable but not too surprising in the postwar decades. What is more remarkable is that the discipline was not only Eurocentric but also *Amerifugal*, as we might say. Not only the émigrés but even American-born comparatists rarely worked on American literature. In their dissociation from the host culture, they showed an inverse limitation to the pattern in most other places, where comparative study has often been closely tied to work in the national tradition. Even today, a significant proportion of comparative work in most countries is devoted to relations between the national tradition and a few foreign literatures, as can be seen at the annual meetings of the German or Brazilian comparative literature associations, in the pages of the *Jadavpur Journal of Comparative Literature*, or most of the Chinese journals in the field. This emphasis has often limited the range of languages, countries, and topics taken up by comparatists in many parts of the world, but it has at least given comparative study a clearer and more direct connection to national life. Anna Balakian may have wanted to change the world, but Hu Shih had more impact on changing China. If the United States offered an unusual opportunity for broader-based studies, it was at the price of a pervasive dissociation from American literature and from the country's cultural and political debates.

In the final paragraph of his essay on "The Crisis of Comparative Literature," René Wellek accepts this trade-off:

> We still can remain good patriots and even nationalists, but the debit and credit system will have ceased to matter. Illusions about cultural expansion may disappear as may also illusions about world reconciliation by literary scholarship. Here, in America, looking from the other shore at Europe as a whole we may easily achieve a certain detachment, though we may have to pay the price of uprootedness and spiritual exile. (295)

It is entirely understandable that Wellek, Lilian Furst, and their fellow émigrés never lost their sense of uprootedness, but what of their American students? To take the examples of several Americans who became my teachers in the department founded by Wellek, Peter Brooks was born in New York, Thomas Greene came from New Jersey, Michael Holquist from Illinois, Lowry Nelson from Utah, and A. Bartlett Giamatti—a future president of Yale and then commissioner of Major League Baseball—grew up in South Hadley, Massachusetts. All five made their careers in the country of their birth, yet they all specialized in European literature, and only Peter Brooks periodically wrote on figures such as Henry James or William Faulkner. Why did they do so little with the literature of their own country?

This pattern was more than the sum of their individual choices; it reflects the sorting mechanisms built into literature departments around the country. With scarcely any Americanists working in comparative literature, undergraduates interested in American literature would go into English departments (or then the newer American Studies departments) and would rarely think of comparative literature as an option. For their part, comparatists on graduate admissions committees looked for students who shared their interests and rarely opted for the occasional stray Americanist who might apply to their program. In *How Institutions Think*, Mary Douglas writes: "Institutions create shadowed places in which nothing can be seen and no questions asked. They make other areas show finely discriminated detail, which is closely scrutinized and ordered. . . . Institutions systematically direct individual memory and channel our perceptions into forms compatible with the relations they authorize" (69). As she mordantly remarks, "Institutions have the pathetic megalomania of the computer whose whole vision of the world is its own program" (92).

For many years the world vision of American comparative literature had little connection to American literary life, and the social engagements that gave rise to antiwar activism and to new programs in African American and women's studies were far from the discipline's center of concern. This institutional sorting was reinforced by the comparatists' commitment to working in two or three languages beyond English. Outside the elite prep schools, most American high school students studied only one other language beyond English, or none at all. Even in college, real proficiency was usually gained only in a single language such as French—an accomplishment that could impress an English department's admissions committee but that would fall short of the expectations of comparative literature programs. The Americans who gravitated to them were thus people who differed from almost all their classmates in their greater linguistic skills, and they often differed as well through experiences of dislocation from their local upbringing.

Some comparatists were children of émigrés, of diplomats, or (like myself) of missionaries, and they could absorb an international outlook from their families. Yet to take the examples of Greene, Nelson, and Giamatti, all three were raised entirely in the United States, and only Giamatti had a relatively recent heritage connection to Europe. Even that was two generations removed. His paternal grandparents had emigrated from Naples in 1900, becoming part of the working-class Italian American community in New Haven. Giamatti's father became a professor of Italian at Mount Holyoke, specializing in Dante. It was only a step farther for his son to become a comparatist—once he abandoned his boyhood dream of playing for the Boston Red Sox—with an emphasis on English and Italian Renaissance literature. It is notable that both father and son gravitated toward premodern rather than to modern literature; Europe had become distant from them in time as well as space.

A. Bartlett Giamatti was named after his two grandfathers, but no one called him by his Italian first name, Angelo. Everyone knew him as "Bart," the name taken from his maternal grandfather, Bartlett Walton, scion of a wealthy New England manufacturing family and a graduate of Andover and Harvard. After Giamatti became president of Yale, his predecessor Kingman Brewster commented:

> Had the backgrounds of his parents been reversed, the President of Yale would be Bartlett A. Walton, and he probably would not have been pictured recently with a laughing and voluptuously gowned Sophia Loren in newspapers across the country at a tribute given them in Washington by the National Italian-American Foundation. Nor might published profiles say that he uses his hands when he talks, which he does no more than his predecessor. (Valerio, *Bart*, 10–11)

Giamatti's dual family background paved the way for his decision to become a comparatist, but neither Thomas Greene nor Lowry Nelson had a living memory of an immigrant heritage. Both, however, came to literary studies from parochial origins that they had decisively left behind. Born in Provo, Utah, Nelson was the son of a Mormon elder who became a professor of sociology in Minnesota and a specialist in Cuban society. The elder Lowry Nelson (after whom his son was named) had a painful falling-out with the Church of Jesus Christ of Latter-day Saints in 1947—the year his son graduated from Harvard—after the head of missions wrote to ask whether there were enough Cubans "of pure white blood" to be suitable candidates for conversion. In a series of eloquent letters, Nelson struggled to persuade the Mormon hierarchy to abandon their racial policy. The dispute reached the desk of the president of the church, seventy-seven-year-old G. Albert Smith (a great-grandnephew of Joseph Smith himself), who warned that "you are too fine a man to permit yourself to be led off from the principles of the Gospel by worldly learning." Even more than his father, Lowry Nelson Jr. went on to a life in pursuit of worldly learning; not long after his retirement from Yale, he died of a stroke in Estonia while researching Russian symbolist poetry.[1]

Thomas Greene's family history was less dramatic but equally decisive. He was born in 1926 in a small town in central New Jersey, where his parents ran a motel. After high school he went off to Principia College in Elsah, Illinois, a college for Christian Scientists whose five hundred students almost outnumber the townspeople of Elsah today. Though Greene's parents probably expected Principia to strengthen their son's commitment to Christian Science, it was there that he got his first taste of a wider world. As he later wrote, he was profoundly influenced by a charismatic misfit on the faculty, a former ballet dancer who had toured (and probably been involved) with Anna Pavlova. "At Principia he ostensibly taught the history of the fine arts, but he actually taught the wonder of civilization. He was an elegant, subtle, lonely man who pronounced with ardor

---

[1] The astonishing exchange of letters between the LDS Church authorities and the senior Lowry Nelson is preserved at Utah State University and can be found online at www .mormonstories.org/other/Lowry_Nelson_1st_Presidency_Exchange.pdf.

luminous unfamiliar names: Piero della Francesca, Isadora Duncan, Henri Matisse, Virginia Woolf, Martha Graham. From him I first learned to love a city I had not yet seen—Paris." He concludes his brief tribute by saying, "I set his name down here with posthumous piety: Frank Parker" ("Versions of a Discipline," 38).

Greene was drafted in the waning months of World War II. The army sent him to Yale for nine months to study Japanese and then to Korea—"where I could *not* prudently use the Japanese I had learned," as he wryly notes (38). The G.I. Bill then enabled him to return to Yale to finish his college education, whereupon he won a Fulbright Fellowship to do a PhD in French at the Sorbonne. There he met and married his wife, but he never completed his dissertation on the early avant-garde poet Lautréamont, after struggling to cope with "a French academic bureaucracy that finally defeated me" (40). He returned to Yale and shifted from modern literature to the Renaissance and from French to comparative literature, writing his dissertation under Wellek and Auerbach.

Greene held strong political views. In a memorial tribute after his death in 2003, David Quint said that

> Of all my professors in the sixties and seventies, he is the only one I know of who handed in his draft card during a protest against the Vietnam War in Washington. . . . He was an unabashed liberal, a one-time ward-heeler for the Democratic Party in New Haven. He hated our present political situation; he had nothing good to say about a particular Yale graduate [George W. Bush] in the highest office of the land. ("Thomas M. Greene")

I don't recall that Greene ever mentioned his political views in his classes on Shakespeare and on Renaissance lyric, which were devoted to intensive engagement with the poetry. Most of the speakers at his memorial emphasized Greene's ethical commitment, rather than politics as such. David Quint too turned to religion after discussing Greene's politics, saying that his classes "evoked an intense feeling of mourning for how much we had lost of the cultural traditions and mental worlds of the past. We felt as if we were being led by a priestly hierophant who was summoning up the past and its great writers to speak to us, to span the abyss of time."

Greene's profoundly ethical outlook was the ground of his academic work, as of his politics outside the classroom. The two emphases came together in retirement, when he founded Open End Theater, a program for inner-city high school students in New Haven, who would stage a pressing personal or social problem and then engage with the audience to debate how the characters should resolve it. In his open-ended scholarship as well, Greene's example can remind us that it is not only through direct discussion of political themes that comparatists do political work. A committed internationalism remains a hallmark of comparative studies today, and at a time of resurgent nativism in many parts of the world, a multilingual internationalism remains a critical dimension of our political engagement, whatever specific brand of politics we espouse.

From Law to Liberty

A prime example of seriously, though obliquely, engaged scholarship at midcentury is Northrop Frye's *Anatomy of Criticism* (1957). With its emphasis on atemporal symbolic patterns, the *Anatomy* paved the way for the explosive success of French structuralism in the American market a decade later, and it was the single most cited work of North American scholarship from the late 1950s through the 1970s. Frye was active institutionally as well, founding the comparative literature program at the University of Toronto and later becoming president of the Modern Language Association. His tireless work on Canadian literature made him an influence on writers such as Margaret Atwood, and he became a household name in Canada. Frye is probably the only North American literary critic ever to have been featured on a postage stamp.

In a prefatory note to the *Anatomy*, Frye presents his project as "pure critical theory," concerned with developing principles of literary symbolism into "a much larger theoretical structure" (xiii) that could serve as the basis for a scientific literary criticism. This note is followed by Frye's "Polemical Introduction," in which he declares: "It is necessary that scholars and public critics should continue to make their contributions to criticism. It is not necessary that the thing they contribute to should be invisible, as the coral island is invisible to the polyp" (12). Warming to his theme, a few pages later Frye openly mocks the vogue for new-critical close readings of individual works: "the critic is assumed to have no conceptual framework: it is simply his job to take a poem into which a poet has diligently stuffed a specific number of beauties or effects, and complacently extract them one by one, like his prototype Little Jack Horner" (17–18).

Frye had been ordained a minister in the United Church of Christ before turning to literary studies, and biblical typology was a prime model for his archetypal criticism, but he asserts that literature's symbolic structures are distinct from any social, religious, or political message an author might have in mind. He shows no interest in biblical theology; instead, the Bible shows a structural progression "from law to liberty" (181), which it shares with secular comedy from Aristophanes to Bernard Shaw. Similarly, when Frye refers to works built around political themes, his interest is in genre, plot structures, and quasi-Jungian archetypes; politics as such falls away. Thus when he discusses *Major Barbara*, he doesn't mention Shaw's satire of the Salvation Army's coercive reformism or the seductive social planning of the arms manufacturer Andrew Undershaft, who creates a munitions workers' paradise. Instead, Frye evokes Shaw's "brilliant parody of a *cognitio*" at the end of the play, which involves a revelation that Undershaft's son-in-law is also his cousin, enabling him to break a rule against appointing an immediate family member as successor. "It sounds complicated," Frye remarks, "but the plots of comedy often are complicated because there is something inherently absurd about complications," and the dénouement shows that "comedy regularly illustrates a victory of arbitrary plot over consistency of character" (170). In principle, a political reading could perfectly well take account of a play's underlying structures, but in discussing Ibsen a few pages later Frye offers an outright denial of modern politics in favor of timeless dramatic devices: "When in *Ghosts* and *Little Eyolf* Ibsen employed the old chestnut about the object of the hero's affections being his sister (a theme as old as Menander), his startled hearers took it for a portent of social revolution" (181).

Yet it would be a mistake to think of Frye as an apolitical writer. Though he sidelines openly political themes, throughout the *Anatomy* he finds a progressive, even revolutionary, force in literature's imaginative power—a view very much in keeping with the surrealist ideas that so attracted Anna Balakian. Frye argues that literature provides a crucial counter to the repressive forces of custom and conventionality promoted in stereotyped commercial and political speech. In this respect the *Anatomy* fits squarely within the postwar skepticism of manipulative rhetoric, whether the Nazi euphemisms and buzzwords dissected by Victor Klemperer in *LTI—Notizbuch eines Philologen* (1947) or Big Brother's "Newspeak" in Orwell's *1984*. But Frye is unusual in extending his critique to his fellow literary critics, both past and present. As he says of Matthew Arnold, "It is not hard to see prejudice in Arnold, because his views have dated: it is a little harder when 'high seriousness' becomes 'maturity,' or some other powerful persuader of more recent critical rhetoric" (22). Frye's ironic labeling of these terms as "powerful persuaders" echoes *The Hidden Persuaders*, Vance Packard's attack on Madison Avenue advertising, also published in 1957.

Frye rejects what he sees as critical business as usual, which he parodies in financial terms: "That wealthy investor Mr. Eliot, after dumping Milton on the market, is now buying him again; Donne has probably reached his peak and will begin to taper off; Tennyson may be in for a slight flutter but the Shelley stocks are still bearish. This sort of thing cannot be part of any systematic study" (18). For Frye, "every deliberately constructed hierarchy of values in literature known to me is based on a concealed social, moral, or intellectual analogy." He continues:

> The various pretexts for minimizing the communicative power of certain writers, that they are obscure or obscene or nihilistic or reactionary or what not, generally turn out to be disguises for a feeling that the views of decorum held by the ascendant social or intellectual class ought to be either maintained or challenged. . . . A selective approach to tradition, then, invariably has some ultra-critical joker concealed in it. There is no question of accepting the whole of literature as the basis of study, but a tradition (or, of course, "the" tradition) is abstracted from it and attached to contemporary social values, being then used to document those values. (23)

In Frye's view, literature offers our best hope for individual freedom and for social progress, once it is freed from attachment to a set aesthetic or moral code.

Frye is heir to Shelley's belief that poets are the unacknowledged legislators of the world, giving us the imaginative impetus to conceive a better world than the one we find ourselves in. But with a difference: for Frye, it is no longer the poet but the critic who plays this role. Writers are often caught in their own (or their patrons') ideologies, and they may be seduced by their imagination into utopian fantasies of little practical value. It is the critic whose wide reading reveals literature's deeper truths, of which the individual authors are dimly aware at best. "For better or worse," he asserts, the critic is "the pioneer of education and the shaper of cultural tradition" (4). Aided by the pioneering critic, the reader can achieve the freedom that literature enables, through an inversion of the profits flowing from consumers to producers under capitalism:

> It is the consumer, not the producer, who benefits by culture, the consumer who becomes humanized and liberally educated. There is no reason why a great poet should be a wise and good man, or even a tolerable human being, but there is every reason why his reader should be improved in his humanity as a result of reading him. Hence while the production of culture may be, like ritual, a half-involuntary imitation of organic rhythms or processes, the response to culture is, like myth, a revolutionary act of consciousness. (344)

The study of literary conventions is the royal road to freedom from conventionality itself.

In principle, all modes and all genres should be of equal value for a scientific criticism, but throughout the *Anatomy* it is clear that Frye's deepest sympathies lie with comedy, and particularly with satire. He is at his most eloquent in evoking the values of Menippean satire, a genre he sees as including Apuleius, Rabelais, Robert Burton's *Anatomy of Melancholy*, and even *Alice in Wonderland*. Frye could almost be characterizing his own *Anatomy* when he describes Burton's, in which "society is studied in terms of the intellectual pattern provided by the conception of melancholy, a symposium of books replaces dialogue, and the result is the most comprehensive survey of human life in one book that English literature had seen since Chaucer," complete with digressions on "the miseries of scholars" and "satire on the *philosophus gloriosus*" (311). Throughout the *Anatomy*, Frye emphasizes "the theme of the absurd or irrational law that the action of comedy moves toward breaking," often "the whim of a bemused tyrant whose will is law" (169). "The society emerging at the conclusion of comedy" represents "a kind of moral norm, or pragmatically free society," achieved through a movement "from a society controlled by habit, ritual bondage, arbitrary law and the older characters to a society controlled by youth and pragmatic freedom" (169).

Frye's book advances a poetics of liberation. "At the center of liberal education," he declares, "something surely ought to get liberated" (93). He returns to this theme in the book's passionate conclusion: "The ethical purpose of a liberal education is to liberate, which can only mean to make one capable of conceiving society as free, classless, and urbane." Frye knows that this is a utopian ideal: "No such society exists," he continues, "which is one reason why a liberal education must be deeply concerned with works of imagination" (347). Though poets often strive to convey socially accepted moral truths, "poetry continually tends to right its own balance, to return to the pattern of desire and away from the conventional and moral. It usually does this in satire. . . . The qualities that morality and religion usually call ribald, obscene, subversive, lewd, and blasphemous have an essential place in literature" (156). In its emphasis on the freeing of libidinal desire as prologue to social liberation, *Anatomy of Criticism* has a good deal in common with Herbert Marcuse's *Eros and Civilization* (1955) and Norman O. Brown's *Life against Death* (1959).

As a comparatist Frye was a theorist, but as a Canadian he was an activist. He was outspoken in supporting antiwar protesters during the Vietnam War and in opposing South African apartheid, to the extent that he was subjected to surveillance by the intelligence service of the Royal Canadian Mounted Police. The Mounties didn't track his literary activism, but it was equally pronounced. He wrote extensively about Canadian literature, urging writers to give up their provincial "garrison mentality" and their conformity with social norms. In 1962 he gave a series of radio talks to present his ideas to a general audience, which was published by the Canadian Broadcasting Company as *The Educated Imagination* (1963). Frye's title significantly revises the title of Lionel Trilling's best-selling *The Liberal Imagination* (1950): a comprehensive liberal education takes the place of Trilling's focus on the reader's individual encounter with a few exemplary works.

Like Wellek, Frye left his own literature out of his comparative studies. No Canadians appear among the nearly three hundred writers in the *Anatomy*'s index, though unlike most comparatists in the United States, Frye does include many U.S.-American writers. Yet his archetypal method wasn't dependent on the "great tradition" of a major power; it could apply as readily to Margaret Atwood or Robertson Davies as to Shakespeare and Dante. As he says in his radio broadcasts, "The constructs of the imagination tell us things about human life that we don't get in any other way. That's why it's important for Canadians to pay particular attention to Canadian literature, even when the imported brands are better seasoned" (*The Educated Imagination*, 53). Taken together, Canadian and foreign literature can open out the world that his listeners see around them. He invites them to imagine walking down a Toronto street, "Bloor or Granville or St. Catherine or Portage Avenue," observing the conventionality of everything they see, from shop signs to men's crewcuts to the lipstick and eye shadow "that women put on because they want to conventionalize their faces, or 'look nice,' as they say" (34). "All this convention is pressing towards uniformity or likeness," he remarks, in terms anticipating Herbert Marcuse's next book, *One-Dimensional Man* (1964). In a typically off-centered observation, he adds that the only exceptions "are people who have decided to conform to different conventions, like nuns or beatniks" (34–35).

In contrast to Marcuse's utopian plea for negative thinking by unconventional outsiders, Frye takes a pragmatic view that there can be no social life without convention. Literature itself is built on conventions, but with a saving difference: when we read attentively, "this time we notice that they are conventions, because we're not so used to them. These conventions seem to have something to do with making literature as unlike life as possible"—having people speak in rhymed couplets, bringing unicorns to life, or giving every mystery a satisfying solution (35). Literature's alternative worlds can help us see through the repressive conventions that society presents as the natural order of things and to envision other ways our world could be—a theme to which we will return in chapter 7. Frye's perspective can be compared to the Russian formalists' emphasis on the revolutionary force of defamiliarization, as seen in such essays as Viktor Shklovsky's "Art as Technique" (1917). Among Frye's contemporaries, his view comes close to that of Adorno, who sought in art an alternative to the seductions of totalitarian rhetoric and bourgeois conventionality alike. Adorno memorably remarked in 1951, "Art is magic delivered from the lie of being truth" (*Minima Moralia*, 222).

Frye was a resolute progressive, but like Wellek and Greene he left his political activism outside the classroom. The disengagement of most comparatists of their generation from direct political questions influenced both their textual analyses and also their choice of works to study. Only after I finished graduate school did I learn that the author of *The Importance of Being Earnest* and "The Decay of Lying" had also written "The Soul of Man Under Socialism." Conrad's *Heart of Darkness* was usually discussed in the 1960s and '70s as an existential confrontation with the unknown, or at most as a stirring denunciation of colonialism, without exploring the text's problematic representation of Africa and Africans. As for theoretical approaches, the structuralist and then poststructuralist theories that dominated the 1970s were often radical in their European contexts, but they were typically presented in the United States in formalist terms, in what Frank Lentricchia sardonically labeled "the New New Criticism" in *After the New Criticism* (1980). Lentricchia was an Americanist teaching in California, where leftist politics had come to the fore beginning in the late 1960s, but formalism predominated in most comparative literature programs through the 1970s. Thus in my student years at Yale, we read Georg Lukács's *Theory of the Novel* rather than his *History and Class Consciousness*, and we read Roland Barthes's *S/Z* as a narratological tour de force, with no attention to Barthes's slyly subversive sexual politics—an occlusion of critical attention that D. A. Miller would later analyze in *Bringing Out Roland Barthes* (1992). Miller received his PhD from Yale in 1977 with a dissertation on problems of narrative closure in Jane Austen, George Eliot, and Stendhal; it was only later that he would become a prominent queer theorist and would expand his interests beyond Europe to include American culture, writing books about Broadway musicals and American film.

In 1976 the young Jonathan Culler did assign us two books by the leftist philosopher-critic Kenneth Burke, in a graduate seminar on "Models of Discourse and Tropological Operations." (Bliss was it in that dawn to be alive, and to be studying models of discourse and tropological operations!) Yet in keeping with the emphases of Culler's prizewinning *Structuralist Poetics*, published the previous year, what we read were Burke's densely argued *The Grammar of Motives* and *The Rhetoric of Motives*, rather than more political works such as *Attitudes toward History* or "The Rhetoric of Hitler's *Battle*." That 1939 essay was political both in its theme and in its purpose; Burke framed his analysis of Hitler's rhetoric with an all too prescient warning that Hitler's debasement of religious discourse could well find successors in America. It is this essay by Burke that I assign today, together with excerpts from *Mein Kampf*, in a class on "The Philosopher and the Tyrant," in which we look at modes of authoritarian discourse from antiquity to our troubled present day.

Enter Foucault

Given the discipline's distance from American culture, the waves of activism that arose in the 1960s had less effect in most comparative literature programs than in the more politically attuned English or French departments and the new programs in women's and ethnic studies. Things changed quickly in the late 1970s. During his first semester as a visiting professor of French at Berkeley in 1975, Michel Foucault was almost unknown in the United States and his lectures were sparsely attended, but by 1980 he had become a celebrity, filling a 2,000-seat lecture hall. Foucault was a prime mover in shifting an ethical criticism to an openly political emphasis. In an interview published in the Berkeley student newspaper that fall, he remarked: "In a sense, I am a moralist, insofar as I believe that one of the tasks, one of the meanings of human existence—the source of human freedom—is never to accept anything as definitive, untouchable, obvious, or immobile. No aspect of reality should be allowed to become a definitive and inhuman law for us." So far, Frye would readily agree, but Foucault continued: "We have to rise up against all forms of power—but not just power in the narrow sense of the word, referring to the power of a government or of one social group over another: these are only a few particular instances of power" (Bess, "Power, Moral Values, and the Intellectual").

One of the first comparatists in America to make sustained use of Foucault was Edward Said. Beginning in the mid-1970s, he mounted an enormously influential attack on depoliticized approaches to literature and intellectual life, building on an eclectic group of thinkers from Vico to Marx and from Auerbach to Gramsci and Foucault. As closely identified as he became with the Palestinian struggle and with postcolonial literary studies, however, Said didn't begin as an oppositional critic. He was born in 1935 to a well-to-do Palestinian Christian family based in Cairo, where he was educated under the British colonial system, including at a school where the use of Arabic was forbidden. At home the family spoke Arabic and English interchangeably, and Said developed a deep love of British and French literature; like the young Lin Yutang in Shanghai, he knew more about European literature than about his own tradition. Throughout his life he remained devoted to canonical British and French writers, from Jonathan Swift to Austen, Conrad, and Proust; "I'm a canon man, after all," as he remarked at a conference in his honor at NYU in 1995.

His father had become an American citizen when living in the United States after the First World War. He sent his son at age sixteen to the elite Mount Hermon boarding school in Northfield, Massachusetts, whose school song, as it happens, is a setting of William Blake's poem "Jerusalem." There Said developed his skills as a pianist and graduated at the top of his class, then studied English at Princeton, where he was drawn to the New Critic R. P. Blackmur. He went on to do a PhD in English at Harvard, writing a dissertation on Conrad. On receiving his degree in 1963, he joined the department of English and Comparative Literature at Columbia, where he taught for forty years until his death in 2003.

The Columbia department was hospitable to socially inflected scholarship. A dominant figure was Lionel Trilling, who wrote extensively on Marx and Freud, as did his former student Steven Marcus, and both were involved with *Partisan Review,* the leading outlet for the New York Intellectuals. Yet Trilling's liberalism was expressed more in ideas than in action. As the historian Thomas Bender has written, "wary as he was of activism and commitment, he encouraged a worldly and sophisticated hesitation" ("Lionel Trilling and American Life," 326). While the faculty could debate issues of race and ethnicity, the debaters couldn't be too ethnic themselves. In a retrospective essay after his death, Diana Trilling remarked that "in appearance and name," her husband could seem suitable to be hired as the department's first-ever Jewish faculty member, whereas if he'd been named "Israel" Trilling after his mother's father, he probably wouldn't have gotten the offer ("Lionel Trilling," 44). Two decades later, A. Bartlett Giamatti was more readily accepted at Yale than Angelo B. Giamatti might have been, and the Columbia department that hired the Conrad specialist Edward W. Said wouldn't likely have taken a chance on the Palestinian activist E. Wadie Said.[2]

Conrad remained a central figure for Said, but the book that grew out of his dissertation, *Joseph Conrad and the Fiction of Autobiography* (1966), is a psychological study very much in keeping with the existentialist emphasis of the day. The terms "colonialism," "imperialism," and "empire" don't appear in the index. While Said was deeply concerned with the tensions between Conrad's foreignness and his English fiction, he focused on "the difficulties of Conrad's spiritual life" in "a phenomenological exploration of Conrad's consciousness" (5, 7).

Said turned from literary history to literary theory in his second book, *Beginnings: Intention and Method* (1975), which locates modernism as a turning point in which the given circumstances and inheritances of people's lives, their "filiations," came to seem bankrupt and writers increasingly formed new social and cultural affiliations of their own. The book's focus is still literary and philosophical rather than political, exploring inaugural strategies in works by Vico, Dickens, Nietzsche, Hopkins,

---

[2] Not unlike Steven Marcus, who grew up as a poor Jewish boy in the Bronx but developed a high Victorian persona (and a lifelong British accent) during two years at Cambridge, Said had a fondness for woolen greatcoats and bespoke tweeds. He might almost have been describing himself in 1983 when he characterized Conrad as taking on "the adopted identity of an émigré-turned-English-gentleman" ("Secular Criticism," 19).

Freud, Conrad, and Proust, building on a wide range of structuralist and poststructuralist thinkers. Said uses Foucault's idea of an epistemic shift in post-Enlightenment discourse to argue for modern thinkers' need to break out of established modes of thought, but *Beginnings* emphasizes general challenges to authority rather than developing any outright political critique. In his preface, Said offers a vision of self-aware criticism that Northrop Frye could readily have endorsed; "if there is one especially urgent claim to be made for criticism," he says, "it is in that constant re-experience of beginning and beginning-again whose force is neither to give rise to authority nor to promote orthodoxy but to stimulate self-conscious and situated activity, activity with aims non-coercive and communal" (xiv).

Beginnings was a work on the cusp of structuralism and poststructuralism, with affinities to narratological works such as Frank Kermode's *The Sense of an Ending* (1967) or, a few years later, Peter Brooks's *Reading for the Plot: Design and Intention in Narrative* (1984). Yet in contrast to Kermode and Brooks, Said was showing how writers could destabilize narrative designs and intentions from the get-go, and the Johns Hopkins journal *Diacritics* devoted an issue to discussing *Beginnings* in relation to deconstructive theory. In his contribution, J. Hillis Miller emphasized the book's affinities with de Manian aporias, while two other contributors argued that Said hadn't taken deconstruction's insights sufficiently to heart. Only one essayist, Hayden White, perceived that the book was "a political allegory" ("Criticism as Cultural Politics," 19).

In a long and illuminating interview included in the issue, Said pointed to this political dimension, saying that in *Beginnings* "I was examining the way in which one launches oneself from contemplation to a sort of worldly action," yet he noted that "much of the answer to that is left very implicit in the book" ("Interview," 39). Though he expressed impatience with being read in terms of endless aporias, he did ally himself with aspects of the work of the "Yale School" identified with de Man, Hillis Miller, Geoffrey Hartman, and Harold Bloom. Interestingly, he singled out Bloom for praise. "Whatever his political beliefs," he remarked, "he's hit on something I find absolutely true: that human activity, and the production of work, does not, cannot take place without power relationships of the sort he talks about in poetry. One doesn't just write: one writes against, or in opposition to, or in some dialectical relationship with other writers and writing, or other activity, or other objects" (35).

The interview gives a fascinating glimpse of a mind at a decisive turning point. After growing up in Cairo, with occasional trips to Jerusalem and family vacations in Lebanon, Said lived in the United States from age sixteen onward; the struggles in Israel/Palestine seemed increasingly distant as he pursued his studies and started his career. A year after he published his Conrad book, however, the Arab-Israeli War of 1967 jolted him into direct political action, even as he continued his daily life as a professor of English and comparative literature. In the 1976 interview, Said spoke of finding himself at "a difficult juncture." As he told the interviewer,

> I lead a pretty uncontroversial life in a big university, and I've done a fair amount of work which has always been plugged into the established channels. That's a function of a certain education, the appearance of a certain social background. Yet I lead another life, which most other literary people say nothing about. . . . My whole background in the Middle East, my frequent and sometimes protracted visits there, my political involvement: all this exists in a totally different box from the one out of which I pop as a literary critic, professor, etc. Now the second, and older, life is encroaching fairly seriously on the other one, and this is a difficult juncture for me. (39)

It can't have been easy to experience his disparate selves popping out of different boxes, but Said seized the opportunity this confusing situation presented. He told the interviewer that "there are links between the two worlds which I for one am beginning to exploit in my own work" (39), and he described his project in *Orientalism*, which he was then completing. He concluded by saying that

> I feel myself to be writing from an interesting position. I am an Oriental writing back at the Orientalists, who for so long have thrived upon our silence. I am also writing *to* them, as it were, by dismantling the structure of their discipline, showing its meta-historical,

institutional, anti-empirical, and ideological biases. Finally, I feel myself to be writing for compatriots and colleagues about matters of common concern. (47)

Writing both for his compatriots and for his colleagues, Said was finding a way to bring his two audiences, as well as his two selves, together.

From Said to Spivak

During the following years Said continued to refine his ideas in a host of essays and books, notably in *The World, the Text, and the Critic* (1983)—a title that recalls his long-ago Anglican baptism, in which the infant Edward would have been enjoined to renounce the world, the flesh, and the devil, but now with the text in place of the flesh and the critic in place of the devil. The collection's lead essay, "Secular Criticism," offers a pointed critique of a detached humanism in which "the approved practice of high culture is marginal to the serious political concerns of society. This has given rise to a cult of professional expertise whose effect in general has been pernicious. For the intellectual class, expertise has usually been a service rendered, and sold, to the central authority of society" (3). Said argues that "It is not practicing criticism either to validate the status quo or to join up with a priestly caste of acolytes and dogmatic metaphysicians" (5). Frye could have used that formulation, but Said goes further, insisting that "the realities of power and authority—as well as the resistances offered by men, women, and social movements to institutions, authorities, and orthodoxies—are the realities that make texts possible, that deliver them to their readers, that solicit the attention of critics" (5).

He urges his readers to become more aware of our confinement in the institutional structures of power that uphold our work, which he sees as having neutralized the radicalism of Continental theory as it was being imported to America. "The intellectual origins of literary theory in Europe were, I think it is accurate to say, insurrectionary," he says:

And yet something happened, perhaps inevitably. From being a bold interventionary movement across lines of specialization, American literary theory of the late seventies had retreated into the labyrinth of "textuality," dragging along with it the most recent apostles of European revolutionary textuality—Derrida and Foucault—whose trans-Atlantic canonization and domestication they themselves seemed sadly enough to be encouraging. (3)

He returns to the attack in an essay reprinted near the end of the collection, "Reflections on Recent American 'Left' Literary Criticism," which had first been published in 1979 in *boundary 2* as the lead essay in an issue devoted to "The Problems of Reading." In that essay he gives a scathing critique of revolutionary gestures without real political consequences:

> [N]ow we find that a new criticism adopting a position and a rhetoric of opposition to what is considered to be established or conservative academic scholarship consciously takes on the function of the left-wing in politics, and argues *as if* for the radicalization of thought, practice and perhaps even of society by means not so much of what it does and produces, but by means of what it says about itself and its opponents. (12)

Limiting themselves to "the academic matter of literature, to the existing institutions for teaching and employing students of literature," Said says, these critics have succumbed "to the often ridiculous and always self-flattering notion that their discussions and debates have a supremely important bearing upon crucial interests affecting humankind. In accepting these confinements the putative Left, no less than the Right, is very far from playing a left-wing role" (13). Said's chief exhibit for such pseudo-oppositional rhetoric is Paul de Man. He says that "corrosive irony is really de Man's central problematic as a critic: he is always interested in showing that when critics and/or poets believe themselves to be stating something they are really revealing—critics unwittingly, poets wittingly—the impossible premises of stating anything at all, the so-called aporias of thought to which de Man believes all great literature always returns" (16).

Said went farther in a lead essay for a special issue of *Critical Inquiry* in 1982. The subject was "The Politics of Interpretation," with nine essays by Said and other leading figures, including Hayden White, Stanley Cavell, and Julia Kristeva, followed by five responses. In Said's essay, "Opponents, Audiences, Constituencies, and Community," his target wasn't just domesticated French theory but contemporary criticism at large, from American New Criticism to the French *nouvelle critique*. On both sides of the Atlantic, he argued, "an interest in expanding the constituency lost out to a wish for abstract correctness and methodological rigor within a quasi-monastic order. Critics read each other and cared about little else" (6). Derrida was now as much to blame as de Man; "it has always seemed to me that the supreme irony of what Derrida has called logocentrism is that its critique, deconstruction, is as insistent, as monotonous, and as inadvertently systematizing as logocentrism itself" (9).

The first of the five respondents was Gayatri Chakravorty Spivak. Having come from India to pursue graduate studies at Cornell, she had written her dissertation on Yeats under de Man's direction, then took a job in 1965 as an assistant professor at the University of Iowa. In 1967 she had chanced upon Derrida's *De la grammatologie*—one of three books published that year by the then little-known Algerian-French philosopher—and she had decided to try translating it. *Of Grammatology* appeared in 1976, prefaced by her eighty-page analytical introduction, which established her as a leading exponent of deconstructive thought and as someone not inclined toward critical business as usual. In her response in the *Critical Inquiry* issue on "The Politics of Interpretation," she pointedly pluralized the issue's theme in her own title, "The Politics of Interpretations." While she fully agreed with Said that criticism should be politically engaged, she sharply countered his broad-brush portrayal of apolitical deconstructive theory, declaring that his essay at times seemed like "a tirade against the folly or knavery of the practitioners of the discipline" (263). She further argued that, as "a star within a star system," Said was blind to the real political work being done in less elite settings, whether in journals such as *Radical Teacher* or as seen "in course syllabi, in newsletters, and increasingly on the rolls of young teachers denied tenure" (267).

Whereas Said's concern in his essay was with academics' relation to the larger culture, Spivak's response turned to the politics within academia itself. The postcolonial perspective that had been just an analogy for Jencks and Riesman was a different matter for a scholar born in Calcutta five years before independence, and it was different as well for a young woman entering a male-dominated profession. It is symptomatic that of the fourteen contributors to the *Critical Inquiry* issue, she was the only woman apart from Kristeva and the only person of non-European origin apart from Said, and hence the sole contributor at the intersection of these two marginal positions. Her early work on Yeats hadn't been marked by questions either of gender or of empire, but following the publication of her Derrida translation she began to think seriously about these two dimensions, in relation both to literary theory and to pedagogy.

Three essays from 1981 can give a good picture of Spivak's rapidly evolving views. In "Finding Feminist Readings: Dante–Yeats," she describes an unsettling moment in 1977 at a symposium on feminist literary criticism, where a speaker gave a paper on Dante's *La Vita Nuova* without discussing the sexism of the tradition within which Dante was writing. An assistant professor in the audience raised a skeptical question:

> "How can a woman learn to praise this text?" Before the speaker could answer, a distinguished woman present in the audience said, with authority: "Because the text deconstructs itself, the author is not responsible for what the text seems to say." I was deeply troubled by that exchange. Here is male authority, I thought, being invoked by a woman to silence another woman's politics. (43)

Before her eyes, deconstruction was being mobilized to limit the disruptive potential of deconstruction itself. "All that summer and fall the problem haunted me," Spivak says, "and that Christmas I thought I had found a formulation for it: deconstruction in the narrow sense domesticates deconstruction in the general sense" (45). Like Said, she argues that "to read no more than allegories of unreadability is to ignore the heterogeneity and asymmetry of the 'material'" (64), but she sees other possibilities in a deconstructive approach, which she illustrates through a discussion of Dante and Yeats. Looking at their deeply contradictory attitudes toward the women in their lives and in their writing, she proposes that "feminist alternative readings might well question the normative rigor of specialist mainstream scholarship through a dramatization of the autobiographical vulnerability of their provenance" (46).

A second essay of 1981, "Reading the World: Literary Study in the 80s," was given as a talk to the College English Association, and in this context Spivak turned from conference settings to explore the interplay of vulnerability and authority in the classroom. She describes a recent experience in teaching an honors seminar at the University of Texas at Austin:

> At the first class meeting, the young men and women sat, as did I, in movable chairs around a hollow square of four oblong tables. I was a little late for the second class meeting. The students had left the same chair empty, and thus given me a chance to introduce to them the theme that . . . history and the institutions of power and authority are stronger than the limits of personal good will. If you deny them, they will get in through the back door. (674)

She pointed out to the students that the seminar setting masked a system of hierarchies that affected their relations with her and with the rest of the student body. They had been admitted to an honors program that gave them privileged access to the seminar, nominally a space of free and equal exchange, yet the students had instinctively reproduced the hierarchy that the seminar setting had appeared to erase. She told them, "Because I warmed that particular chair with my bottom the last time, I seem to have baptized it as the seat of authority and you have left it empty for me. Your historical-institutional imperatives are proving stronger than your personal good will" (674). Any Southern Baptists in the class might have been disconcerted by her unusual form of baptism, but she certainly got her point across. She concludes her essay by proposing "that a literary study that can graduate into the 80s might teach itself to attend to the dialectical and continuous crosshatching of ideology and literary language. Further, that such an activity, learned in the classroom, should slide without a sense of rupture into an active and involved reading of the social text within which the student and teacher of literature are caught" (676–77).

A third essay from the same year marked Spivak's growing interest in exploring a deconstructive feminism beyond Europe and America. This was her first translation of a story by the Bengali writer Mahasweta Devi, "Draupadi," which appeared in *Critical Inquiry* in an issue on "Writing and Sexual Difference." Spivak's translation, again with a substantial introduction, was the only contribution with a non-Western focus. In her introduction, Spivak writes, "I translated this Bengali short story into English as much for the sake of its villain, Senanayak, as for its title character" ("Draupadi," 381). Senanayak is an intelligence officer tasked with tracking down and interrogating Maoist insurgents who have rebelled against the Indian government in West Bengal. No cartoon villain, Senanayak is a pluralist and an aesthete; he reads Shakespeare and anti-Fascist literature and sympathizes with the rebels. Draupadi is the object of his pursuit, but even after she is caught, stripped naked, and repeatedly raped, she defiantly refuses to betray her comrades or even to feel shame.

Strikingly, in her introduction to the story Spivak doesn't simply take Draupadi's side against the patriarchal order but registers an uneasy connection to the aesthete-interrogator Senanayak. As Devi describes him— using terms taken directly from English, which Spivak italicizes in her translation—"Whatever his *practice*, in *theory* he respects the opposition. . . . Thus he understood them by (*theoretically*) becoming one of them. He hopes to write on all this in the future" (394). Spivak comments: "Correspondingly, we grieve for our Third-World sisters; we grieve and rejoice that they must lose themselves and become as much like us as possible in order to be 'free'; we congratulate ourselves on our specialists' knowledge of them" (381). Writing both within and against the feminism of "our own academic and First-World enclosure," she stresses that "we will not be able to speak to the women out there if we depend completely on conferences and anthologies by Western-trained informants. As I see their photographs in women's-studies journals or on book jackets—indeed, as I look in the glass—it is Senanayak with his anti-Fascist paperback that I behold" (382).

Spivak says that Devi "invites us to begin effacing that image" through her fundamentally deconstructive narrative: "The story is a moment caught between two deconstructive formulas: on the one hand, a law that is formulated with a view to its own transgression, on the other, the undoing of the binary opposition between the intellectual and the rural struggles" (382, 386). In Spivak's hands, deconstruction was regaining its political edge, taking it well beyond the limits that Said, or probably Derrida himself, would have anticipated.

In looking back at comparative studies from the 1940s to the 1980s, the story is more complicated than a forward march from aestheticism to political engagement, or from a conservative humanism to a thoroughgoing radicalism. Anna Balakian spent her life working on André Breton and other surrealists who were both aesthetically and politically radical, even though she inveighed in her later years against what she saw as poststructuralist dogmatism and narrow identity politics.[3] Conversely, the resolutely progressive Edward Said worked mostly on major canonical European writers, often using methods of close reading that he first developed at Princeton under R. P. Blackmur's guidance. In "Secular Criticism," even as he presses for a more politically engaged scholarship, he notes that "it may seem odd, but it is true, that in such matters as culture and scholarship I am often in reasonable sympathy with conservative attitudes" (22). Gayatri Spivak was equally aware of her complex position of "Marginality in the Teaching Machine," as she titled an essay in 1988. There she speaks in terms that critically recall Said's *Beginnings* but that would also apply to herself—and to many of us, her readers: "If the 'somewhere' that one begins from is the most privileged site of a neocolonial educational system, in an institute for the training of teachers, funded by the state, does that gesture of convenience not become the normative point of departure? Does not participation in such a privileged and authoritative apparatus require the greatest vigilance?" (64).

From Anna Balakian and Northrop Frye to Edward Said and Gayatri Spivak, all the figures we have been looking at in this chapter have wanted

---

[3] She details her objections in *The Snowflake on the Belfry: Dogma and Disquietude in the Critical Arena* (1994). In her essay "How and Why I Became a Comparatist," her impatience with postcolonial perspectives surfaces in an insistence on regarding Aimé Césaire purely "as a francophone surrealist who happened to be born in Martinique" (82).

to change the world, beginning with their classrooms and moving outward to their departments, the discipline, and the world at large. Despite their very real and sometimes sharp disagreements, the work of all these comparatists assorts well with the injunction that Said brings forward in the conclusion to "Secular Criticism," in which he argues that critics must always be suspicious of any dogmatic orthodoxy: "For in the main—and here I shall be explicit—criticism must think of itself as life-enhancing and constitutively opposed to every form of tyranny, domination, and abuse; its social goals are noncoercive knowledge produced in the interests of human freedom" (29).

4

Theories

Writing in October 1988 in New York's *Village Voice Literary Supplement,* Edward Said celebrated the fact that poststructuralist, Marxist, and feminist perspectives had expanded the literary canon to include such major but neglected writers as Chinua Achebe and Zora Neale Hurston, and yet he declared that "much of the energy has gone out of literary theory itself" ("News of the World," 14). The problem was that criticism had become a self-enclosed academic game: "the fussy formalism, the tiresome wheel-spinning and elaboration, the triumphalist professionalization of some theoretical work has gone too far to be interesting" (14). It is unclear just how interesting fussy formalism and tiresome wheel-spinning would have been even *before* they went too far, but Said wasn't alone in feeling that the many theoretical approaches which had come into play during the previous two decades hadn't produced the clarity of vision that Wellek and Frye had hoped for, much less the wider political impact that Said was seeking to achieve.

His essay was the first entry in a section entitled "Where Do We Go from Here?" This was a set of statements by critics including Geoffrey Hartman, Catherine Stimpson, and Stephen Greenblatt that followed a four-page spread, "Great Moments in Lit Crit: A Cartoon History from the Stone Age to the Space Age," drawn by S. B. Whitehead, whose previous work included contributions to *Corporate Crime Comics.* The final page of this satiric tour (figure 3) presents the major theoretical movements of the 1970s and 1980s as a carnival of competing freak shows and sideshows.

Tiresome wheel-spinning is, in fact, shown in the foreground as the Ferris Wheel of History, operated by Fredric Jameson and Raymond Williams,

FIGURE 3. "Great Moments in Lit Crit," *Voice Literary Supplement*, October 1988. Reproduced by permission of Samuel B. Whitehead.

with glum workers and capitalists reluctantly sharing the ride. French feminists emerge from a tunnel of love, including Julia Kristeva in her Maoist phase and Luce Irigaray in the psychoanalytical mode of her *Speculum de l'autre femme*. Among the other sideshows, Foucault bends gender norms, the Frankfurter School sells hot dogs, and feminists and African-Americanists deploy their alternative canons to launch books by Zora Neale Hurston and Charlotte Perkins Gilman. Are they failing to hit the bull's-eye, or are they deliberately aiming for the margins?

Next to them is the Yale school, with Harold Bloom shown as a belated White Rabbit anxiously consulting his watch, J. Hillis Miller and Geoffrey Hartman as Tweedledum and Tweedledee, and Paul de Man—whose early essays for collaborationist Belgian newspapers had recently come to light—as Doctor Strangelove, struggling to keep his right arm from performing the Nazi salute. Nearby, Roland Barthes is about to be run over by the laundry truck that killed him on a Paris street, while Susan Sontag tries to warn him, or else hastens to take his place on the critical scene. Three displaced ancient Greeks race between the booths, far from the Platonic Academy featured in the first of the cartoon history's four pages. Meanwhile, the whole carnival is being deconstructed by beefy workmen armed with jackhammers, starting with the Yale booth itself and also breaking the frame in the foreground—coming, it seems, for us.

Three decades on, all these movements, and even the individual theorists, remain prominent in literary studies. Some are no longer alive, but none of them has gone away, and by now the fairgrounds would need to be enlarged to make room for postcolonial studies (already burgeoning in the late 1980s) and such newer movements as ecocriticism, diaspora studies, digital humanities, and a congeries of competing theories of globalization and world literature. What had already seemed in the 1980s to be a disorienting range of approaches must strike many current graduate students as a truly daunting mass of challenging materials. The comparatist's toolbox would take some heavy lifting today.

To be sure, no one needs to master every theory, any more than any of us can learn every language or study every literary tradition. "Theory" is not a unified whole or even a stable set of discourses, but it needs to be understood (indeed, theorized) in the contexts in which we receive and employ it. Though we may think of contemporary "literary theory" as a shared international field of discourse, there are pronounced differences in how theory is conceived and practiced around the world. In Japan, influence studies have greater prominence than in many other countries, while in Europe questions of aesthetics and of narratology often take center stage. In a survey of the field in Spain, *Teoría literaria y literatura comparada* (2005), Jordi Llovet and four colleagues delineate the varieties of theory very differently than would scholars in the United States. They present the field of postcolonial studies largely through two figures: Edward Said, as could be expected, but also Armando Gnisci, the Italian comparatist and theorist of *decolonizzazione*, who is little discussed outside Europe. Llovet and his colleagues make no mention of Homi Bhabha, Frantz Fanon, Édouard Glissant, or Gayatri Spivak, figures so central in American postcolonial studies, and they devote far more space to genre theory and to periodization than to poststructuralist approaches. Said receives less space in their survey than either Northrop Frye or the narratologist Gérard Genette.

Very differently, Terry Eagleton has claimed that "there is in fact no 'literary theory,' in the sense of a body of theory which springs from, or is applicable to, literature alone. . . . On the contrary, they all emerged from other areas of the humanities" (*Literary Theory*, vii). So too Jonathan Culler has argued that "theory in literary studies is not an account of the nature of literature or methods for its study" but instead designates a loose set of "writings from outside the field of literary studies that have been taken up by people in literary studies because their analyses of language, or mind, or history, or culture, offer new and persuasive accounts of textual and cultural matters" (*Literary Theory*, 3). In keeping with Culler's extraliterary definition, he gives much more attention to Derrida and Foucault than to Frye and Genette.

A different construction of theory would place greater emphasis on Russian formalism and its influence, an approach often championed by comparatists with a base in Slavic studies. In the United States, Wellek and Warren's *Theory of Literature* drew extensively on the formalist tradition of Wellek's youth in Prague, while in the 1980s Michael Holquist and Caryl Emerson's Bakhtin collection, *The Dialogic Imagination*, had a significant impact on comparative studies. Viktor Shklovsky was a presiding spirit in the work of Svetlana Boym, from *The Future of Nostalgia* (2002) to *Another Freedom* (2012) and *The Off-Modern* (2017). Both Russian formalism and French theory play prominent roles in D. N. Rodowick's *Elegy for Theory* (2015), the central volume in a trilogy in which Rodowick develops the connections between literary theory, philosophy, science, and film studies.

Given the many varieties of theory, what each of us needs to know is not a set theoretical canon but how best to use whichever theories are most suited for the questions we want to ask. Used badly, a theoretical lens may distort as much as it reveals. Benedetto Croce already highlighted this problem in his *Estetica*, in which he deplored the use of *pseudoconcetti* that devolve into infinite subcategories in the face of the diversity of individual works. In marked opposition to the scientism that Northrop Frye and many structuralists would later embrace, Croce argued that "the complications are infinite, because the individuations are infinite," and that categories such as "the comic" are condemned to be construed "in the arbitrary and approximate manner of the natural sciences" (*Aesthetic*, 84). Seventy years later, Edward Said expressed a version of this concern in the introduction to *Orientalism*: "My two fears are distortion and inaccuracy, or rather the kind of inaccuracy produced by too dogmatic a generality and too positivistic a localized force" (8). Throughout his study, he says, he sought "to recognize individuality and to reconcile it with its intelligent, and by no means passive or merely dictatorial, general and hegemonic context" (9).

A classic expression of the fear of dogmatic generalization can be found in Erich Auerbach's *Mimesis: The Representation of Reality in Western Literature*. Despite the Aristotelian abstraction of his title, in his epilogue he denies having had any guiding framework whatever:

> My interpretations are no doubt guided by a specific purpose. Yet this purpose assumed form only as I went along, playing as it were with my texts, and for long stretches of my way I have been guided only by the texts themselves. Furthermore, the great majority of the texts were chosen at random, on the basis of accidental acquaintance and preference rather than in view of a definite purpose. (556)

Yet even Auerbach's pronounced resistance to general schemas wasn't enough for the more committed historicists among his readers. In a review of *Mimesis* in 1950, the classicist Ludwig Edelstein took issue with Auerbach's sharp opposition between Hebraic and Hellenic cultures in his opening chapter. Arguing that "the Pagan and Christian literatures show a tendency to converge rather than to stand in diametric opposition to one another," Edelstein says that Auerbach "looks at antiquity with the eye of the classicistic interpreter, while I am trying to look at it with the eye of the historian. In the classicistic view, the ancient attitude is one and unchangeable," whereas "in the historical view, even the fifth century is not a unity" (Review of *Mimesis*, 429, 431).

Four years later, Auerbach replied that those who claimed he had understated the varieties of ancient realism had failed to understand the particular *kind* of realism he was discussing. "Perhaps I would have done better to have called it 'existential realism,'" he says, "but I hesitated to use this all too contemporary term for phenomena of the distant past" ("Epilegomena to *Mimesis*," 561). He thus both proposes and withholds "existential realism," a term openly reflecting a modern perspective. He returns to the problem a few pages later: "abstract, reductive concepts falsify or destroy the phenomena. The arranging must happen in such a way that it allows the individual phenomena to live and unfold freely. Were it possible, I would not have used any generalizing expressions at all" (572). Yet such a book would have been impossible to write. Not only Auerbach's Greek title but every substantive word in his subtitle is a general term: "Mimesis," "Representation," "Reality," "Western," "Literature." Without these terms, his title would have been left only with "the," "of," and "in."

Since the 1950s an increasing number of comparatists have embraced varieties of literary and cultural theory. As Jordi Llovet has said, the theories that came into prominence in the 1960s and 1970s went beyond positivistic literary history and philological analysis by offering "a far more capacious conception of what language signifies in the dialectical complex that brings the individual, society, and history together face to face" (*Teoría Literaria*, 23). It is a sign of the prestige of theory in comparative studies that Llovet holds the chair in Teoría Literaria y Literatura

Comparada at the University of Barcelona, with pride of place given to literary theory in his department's name.

There were good institutional as well as intellectual reasons why theory came to play such a large role in the discipline's evolution. With modern literature departments established on a national basis during the historicist nineteenth century, course offerings were (and often still are) based on an orderly sequence of periods and movements within a single country or region, and scholarly studies could build on known connections among writers who shared a common literary background, without necessarily needing any more general basis of analysis. Of course, the idea that literary history could proceed free of theory was always dubious. To take just one example, the very title of Ian Watt's influential study *The Rise of the Novel*—published in 1957, the same year as Frye's *Anatomy of Criticism*—announces both an implicit theory of history (it rises) and of genre ("the" novel, a unitary concept that Frye's book was centrally concerned to complicate). Watt's title, furthermore, occludes a whole series of social assumptions: of gender (the three novelists he treats are all men), of class (the middle one), and of a departmental nationalism that locates the novel's rise in England and not in Spain or France, much less in ancient Alexandria or in Heian Japan.

In the nineteenth century, comparatists like Posnett had begun to look for different ways to analyze works beyond the range of direct *rapports de fait* between writers or works. In France, "littérature générale" encompassed questions of genre and the study of movements such as Romanticism and modernism, which could include writers who had never heard of one another. The growth of "East/West" studies in the middle decades of the twentieth century provoked an interest in broader frameworks such as comparative poetics. At the Sorbonne, the redoubtable René Étiemble specialized both in French and in Chinese literature and culture, with forays into many other languages and literatures, and he went from separate studies such as *Le Mythe de Rimbaud* (1952) and *Confucius* (1958) to his three-volume *Questions de poétique comparée* (1960–62) and his *Essais de littérature (vraiment) générale* (1974), with the "truly" in his title ironically suggesting the Eurocentrism of most "general literature" studies of his day. In 1988—when Said was complaining that the energy had gone out of literary theory—Étiemble published *Ouverture(s) sur un comparatisme planétaire*, a pioneering response to globalization. In the United States, Earl Miner earned his BA in Japanese and a PhD in English at the University of Minnesota, then wrote his first book on *The Japanese Tradition in British and American Literature* (1958). In the ensuing years he devoted himself largely to separate studies of English and Japanese poetry before writing his pathbreaking *Comparative Poetics: An Intercultural Essay on Theories of Literature* (1990).[1]

Since then, the need for viable theoretical frameworks has only increased, given the expansion of comparative studies to a much broader engagement with the world's literatures. Yet at the same time, the variety of the world's past and present literary cultures poses enormous problems for any given theoretical framework. Almost all theories have been developed in a particular historical and cultural context, and literary theories usually derive from quite specific archives, whether the premodern English and Japanese poetry that Miner used for his comparative poetics or the British Romantic writers so important to Frye and Bloom. How should we make use of such time-bound and culture-specific theories, even to study later British or Japanese literature? Can we legitimately use them at all when we look farther afield? The comparatists' import-export trade in literary theory may heighten rather than alleviate the problem of studying foreign literatures. If theories developed in Paris or Frankfurt are applied by Chinese and American scholars to Brazilian novels or Sanskrit poetry, how much will be distorted or lost altogether in such a triangular trade?

It has sometimes been argued that it is an outright mistake to employ a theory beyond its home context. Jonathan Culler has remarked that the intertextual nature of meaning "makes literary study essentially, fundamentally comparative, but it also produces a situation in which comparability depends upon a cultural system, a general field that underwrites comparisons." He cautions that "the more sophisticated one's understanding of discourse, the harder it is to compare Western and non-Western texts" ("Comparability," 268). Certainly theory can be poorly or mechanically

---

[1] In addition to serving as president of the International Comparative Literature Association, Miner enjoyed the unique distinction of serving as president of the Milton Society of America and also receiving Japan's Order of the Rising Sun. Like the Japanologist Edward Seidensticker before him and Clint Eastwood after him, he was honored with the third highest of the order's eight classes: Gold Rays and Neck Ribbon.

applied to new materials, but without some theoretical basis of analysis, we are likely to be left with disjointed traditions or even microtraditions, divided and subdivided by nation, period, genre, gender, and class. The novel could no longer be studied as a general phenomenon but would be dispersed within an endless series of discursive formations, yielding a scholarly Library of Babel in which Ian Watt's *Rise of the* [*English*] *Novel* would be shelved a hexagon away from Ina Watt's *Écriture féminine dans l'Ancien Régime*, two floors above Angkor Watt's *History of Cambodian Fiction*, and so on ad infinitum.

In this chapter, I propose three ways of dealing with the problems that arise when theory travels to new times and places. First, we have to resist the impulse to treat theoretical texts as repositories of transcendent ideas that can be understood without close attention to their original literary and cultural-political contexts. If we draw on the dialogism of Mikhail Bakhtin today, we do so in a very different context from the Stalinist Soviet Union in which he formulated his ideas on the subversive force of the carnivalesque. Second, we have to engage theories dialectically with the literatures we read. A theory can genuinely help us understand a new body of material only if the material is allowed to exert real pressure on the theory, modifying it in turn: the theory of "the novel" becomes something different if we put *Tom Jones* together with *Don Quixote* and *The Tale of Genji* rather than with *Moll Flanders* and *Clarissa*. Third, a much wider range of theoretical perspectives needs to be brought into the conversation today, well beyond the Euro-American theories that continue to dominate much critical discourse, both in the West and often elsewhere too. These perspectives can include not only the work of non-Western theorists and aestheticians but also the theoretical viewpoints contained within literature itself, often made explicit by self-reflective writers such as Miguel de Cervantes and Murasaki Shikibu.

Rereading Paul de Man

We can explore many of these issues through the work of Paul de Man, one of the most influential, and unsettling, of modern theorists. More than any other émigré comparatist of the postwar years, de Man established himself at the center of a major theoretical movement, building on his profound knowledge of French, German, and English literature and philosophy from the eighteenth century through the modernist era. He never wrote any autobiographical essays, and indeed he cultivated an attitude of such rigorous impersonality that T. S. Eliot seems winsome by contrast. Yet de Man was among the most charismatic of teachers, and many of his graduate students developed an intense cathexis to their mentor, whose methods they sought to emulate and whose influence they sometimes struggled to escape or simply survive; more has been written about de Man, as a person and as a teacher, than about any other comparatist I know of.

Personal reflections began to appear soon after de Man's death in 1983, starting with *The Lesson of Paul de Man* (1985), a 330-page special issue of *Yale French Studies*, edited by Peter Brooks, Shoshana Felman, and J. Hillis Miller, whose cover features a portrait of de Man at his desk, looking into the camera with an ironic twinkle in his eye. The volume includes a set of tributes from a memorial service held in early 1984, supplemented by de Man's last lecture and eighteen scholarly essays. The editors assembled the collection, as they say, "to bear witness to the legacy of an extraordinary critic, teacher, and colleague" who "never was not teaching," and they concluded the volume with "what we hope is a complete bibliography of Paul de Man's published work," with ninety-four items in all (Brooks et al., "Foreword").

Their hopes were soon dashed. In 1987 a Belgian graduate student, Ortwin de Graef, discovered nearly two hundred essays and reviews that a young de Man had written from 1940 through 1942 for two collaborationist newspapers, *Le Soir* and *Het Vlaamsche Land*. A few of de Man's essays showed elements of anti-Semitism, while several others suggested that French culture could use a dose of German discipline. These revelations produced a further outpouring of writing on de Man's life and work, including a large collection entitled *Responses: On Paul de Man's Wartime Journalism* (Hamacher and Hertz, 1988). Some of the thirty-eight contributors were seriously rethinking their admiration for their mentor or colleague, while others—including the Jewish scholars Jacques Derrida and Geoffrey Hartman—insisted that de Man had never shown any hint of racial bias in their many years of friendship.

FIGURE 4. Paul de Man, before and after 1987. Illustration on right reproduced courtesy of Delphine Lebourgeois, *The New Yorker* © Conde Nast.

The story doesn't end there. Rumors were circulating that de Man hadn't behaved honorably in his personal life during and after the war—bankruptcies, embezzlements, falsified academic records, and even bigamy were hinted at. Two decades later, these charges were exhaustively documented in a prosecutorial biography by Evelyn Barish, *The Double Life of Paul de Man* (2014). Her biography was widely reviewed in the trade press, with not a few reviewers declaring that de Man's early malfeasance showed the hollow core at the heart of his deconstructive theory. The *New York Times* titled its (actually very balanced) review "Revisiting a Scholar Unmasked by Scandal," and the *New Yorker* illustrated a more critical assessment by Louis Menand, "The de Man Case," with a hall-of-mirrors portrait of a now guilt-ridden de Man, very different from his pre-revelation self (figure 4).

Seen in this darkened light, de Man's impersonal essays begin to seem like "fragments of a great confession," as Geoffrey Hartman put it in 1989 ("Looking Back at Paul de Man," 20). Confessional overtones can be found in de Man's *Allegories of Reading* in his dissection of Jean-Jacques Rousseau's *Confessions*, or in the many passages elsewhere in which de Man separates texts from experience. Thus he concludes a late essay on "Reading and History" with a reading of Baudelaire's poem "Spleen (II)," whose speaker describes himself as a graveyard that the moon abhors and an ancient sphinx forgotten by the world. De Man says that the poem displays "the grammatical subject cut off from its consciousness," arguing that the poem is "not the sublimation but the forgetting, by inscription, of terror" (70).

De Man's depersonalizing gesture is remarkable here, as he wrote this essay to introduce the English translation of Hans Robert Jauss's *Toward an Aesthetic of Reception*, which begins with Jauss's manifesto "Literary History as a Challenge [*Provokation*] to Literary Theory." Clearly, de Man was returning the provocation on behalf of theory. Several years later, Jauss replied in an essay cast in the form of a letter to his—now-deceased—friend. He begins by noting that he'd often been asked whether he felt hurt by de Man's having introduced his book by attacking its basic theme of literature's historical and political embeddedness. He replies by emphasizing common ground between their approaches, and slyly suggests that his historically grounded hermeneutical mode "is constantly used in deconstructionist criticism without, as far as I know, having been incorporated in its theory" ("Response to Paul de Man," 204).

In a further turn of the screw, it subsequently emerged that as a young man Jauss had been an officer of the Nazi Waffen-SS. This revelation has produced troubled reassessments comparable to those concerning de Man, such as Ottmar Ette's *Der Fall Jauss* (2016). It would be intriguing to know whether de Man was aware of this suppressed dimension of Jauss's biography when he wrote his antihistoricist introduction. In a recent essay on Jauss, "Memórias de tempos sombrios," the Brazilian scholar Regina Zilberman directly draws the comparison to de Man (10), and she asks, with reference to Jauss's reception theory, whether Jauss's own readers can ever again receive his works as they did before.

The revelations of de Man's seriously misspent youth hardly invalidate his mature theories, and indeed the author of *Blindness and Insight* would scarcely have been surprised if his readers discovered that his theory was founded on an occluded history to which they, if not the theorist himself, were long blind. In a perfect deconstructive reversal, his antihistoricism is validated by the very revelations that appear to invalidate it. To put the matter more positively, it may well be, as Christopher Norris has argued in *Paul de Man: Deconstruction and the Critique of Aesthetic Ideology*, that de Man's mature work represents a deep disenchantment with the ideology that had seduced him in his youth. Deconstruction thus attacks any rhetoric that cloaks itself, as Adorno would have said, in the lie of being truth. Even so, we can't now unlearn what Ortwin de Graef and Evelyn Barish have uncovered, any more than we can forget the Nazi involvements of Jauss or of Heidegger. Over time it is likely that still more uncomfortable histories will be recovered from the war years and their postwar aftermath—a fact underscored by the revelation in 2018 that Julia Kristeva served as an informer for the Bulgarian state security service in the early 1970s, under the code name "Sabina."[2]

In de Man's case (*der Fall de Man*, as Ottmar Ette would say), I actually wish we knew more than we do. Though Barish's biography is over five hundred pages long, it ends in 1960, just as de Man has finally established himself on a solid footing in American academia, moving to Cornell after failing to receive tenure at Harvard. Some of Barish's claims are speculative or overdrawn, but she shows beyond a doubt how deeply disturbed de Man's early life had been. In 1933, when he was fourteen, his troubled older brother Rik—his mother's favorite—raped a twelve-year-old cousin. Three years later, Rik was killed by a train at a road crossing, in what was either a tragic accident or a suicide. The following spring, de Man's mother was missing at dinnertime one evening. Sent upstairs by his father

---

[2] Kristeva indignantly denied the charge and even insisted that the four-hundred-page secret police dossier on her was a work of fiction, created to discredit her. Ironically, an actual work of fiction, Laurent Binet's academic satire *La Septième fonction du langage*, had portrayed her in 2015 as a murderous Bulgarian secret agent, but the reality was less dramatic and more ambiguous. As Martin Dimitrov commented to the *New York Times*, "Was she a spy? State Security thought so; she says otherwise. This raises a question that is more moral than legal: Namely, who is a spy?" (Schuessler and Dzhambazova, "Bulgaria Says French Thinker Was a Secret Agent").

to see what she was doing, de Man found her body hanging in the attic laundry room. Three years later, the Germans invaded Belgium. Little wonder de Man fled into literature, seeking "the forgetting, by inscription, of terror." The more interesting question would be how he managed to rebuild his shattered self in later life, after his chaotic early years in Belgium and then the scramble to make a place for himself in the United States. Yet Barish disclaimed any interest in de Man's theoretical work, and her foreshortened biography allows a hostile critic such as Clive James, in a blurb for the book, to describe de Man as a charlatan who "fooled one high-level American college after another into treating him as a genius."

Reading de Man's later essays in the personal and political contexts of his youth can help us understand and correct for the exaggerations of his flight from history. A number of his former students and colleagues, in fact, were beginning to undertake such a correction well before Ortwin de Graef made his discoveries. An illuminating account of a move beyond pure textuality can be found in Alice Kaplan's 1993 memoir, *French Lessons*. There she recounts how she found her way into French studies at Yale and wrote her dissertation on collaborationists in Vichy France—the very kind of theme that de Man had edited out of his own background and work. Kaplan grew up in the Midwest in a Jewish family within a largely gentile milieu, but her family had strong European connections. Her grandmother still spoke the Yiddish of her native Poland, and her father had been a prosecutor at the Nuremberg war crimes trials; the cover of her book shows a row of weary-looking lawyers, her father among them, listening through headphones at the simultaneous translation of testimony during the trials.

A signal loss marked Kaplan's childhood: her father died of a heart attack when she was eight years old. Throughout the book, she describes her quest for substitute fathers, including a seductive "Mr. D," father of a classmate of hers, who shows her around Paris when she is twelve years old and gives her perfume and her first taste of champagne. This is a resonant gesture, we realize late in the book, when Kaplan reveals that her father had been an alcoholic and, strangely, had nicknamed her Alkie, "a Jewish name. Also Alkie, short for alcoholic" (201). During her adolescence, Kaplan threw herself into the alternative realities of literature and a dreamed-of France, and she writes eloquently of the joy of mastering the French "r." Learning French represented "a chance for growth, for freedom, a liberation from the ugliness of our received ideas and mentalities" (211). And yet, as she says a few pages later: "Learning French did me some harm by giving me a place to hide" (216).

Kaplan earned her BA at Berkeley, where she became active in leftist causes, and then proceeded to Yale in 1975 to do a PhD in French. Like many of her classmates, she became fascinated by deconstruction, which she saw as the most bracing form of close reading, piercing the veil of any sentimentality and getting to the heart of literary experience. In a chapter entitled "Guy, de Man, and Me," Kaplan describes her romance with a fellow student as they both study with de Man. "Guy"—rhyming with "Me"—is short for "Guillaume," her fondly ironic nickname for a francophile American named William. She says that Guy chose de Man as his mentor "because de Man, like Guillaume's absent mother, was impossible to please" (148). She sums up de Man's ambiguous influence: "De Man made literature matter more than anything in the world and then said it was only literature. He had put us all in a bind" (167). Guy slogged through writing a five-hundred-page thesis on irony in the poems of the mentally unbalanced Gérard de Nerval and then left the profession soon after completing his degree.

In a long, troubled chapter of his book *Cultural Capital*, "Literature after Theory: The Lesson of Paul de Man," John Guillory has described de Man as an inaccessible yet irresistible mentor, binding his disciples to him "with the utmost subtlety and effectiveness in the cafés and in the classrooms, in the psycho-pedagogy of everyday life" (190). Alice Kaplan, however, decided against trying to please the formidable Doktorvater. When it came time to write her dissertation, instead of decoding metonymy in Mallarmé or the rhetoric of temporality in Proust, she developed her project on French collaborationists. She was drawn to the topic through the writings of Leo Spitzer's Rabelaisian *bête noir*, Ferdinand Céline, whose prose she found inspiring even as she despised his politics. She decided to look seriously into his milieu, exploring the writings of collaborationist intellectuals such as Robert Brasillach and Pierre Drieu la Rochelle, whose obscure writings no one in her department would have thought to work on.

In her memoir, Kaplan connects her decision to a primal scene of research. After her father's death she explores his desk, finding all sorts of letters and memos dating back to his Nuremberg days. At the back of a drawer she makes a shocking find: a box of photographs from Auschwitz. She takes the box to school, for a show-and-tell that must have been unlike any her third-grade class had ever experienced. Her mother wanted to remove the most gruesome photographs of naked corpses and emaciated survivors, but little Alice insisted on showing them all: "I believed in facts. I believed that my friends had no right to live without knowing about these pictures, how could they look so pleased when they were so ignorant. None of them knew what I knew, I thought. I hated them for it" (30–31). In graduate school, revisiting her lost father's career in her dissertation, she found her own career path. On completing her first book, "I understood how much I owed to his death, his absence a force field within which I had become an intellectual; his image, silent and distant with headphones over his ears, a founding image for my own work. Headphones were also an emblem for loneliness and isolation: they transmitted voices, they absorbed testimony; but they had no voice to give back" (197).

"Maybe I could have it both ways," Kaplan writes; "I could deconstruct fascism, and I could show that intellectuals were just as subject as anyone else to fascist longings" (159). Yet it didn't occur to her that de Man could have been such an intellectual, even though she knew that de Man's uncle Hendrik de Man, a leading Belgian socialist, had welcomed the German victory. Thinking of de Man as "the disinterested rhetorician, cleansed of his family's historical improprieties" (161), she never discussed her topic with him, and instead sought out an assistant professor to direct her dissertation. "De Man had failed me," she writes in her memoir, "only it was a failure that I wasn't aware of. I didn't go to talk to him, because I had no idea that he had given a minute's thought to the problem that interested me most—the problem of the fascist intellectual" (173–74). As she says, de Man "would have been a better teacher if he had given more of his game away" (172).

The Two Barbara Johnsons

Alice Kaplan turned to the very theme that de Man had repressed, but she was still applying deconstructive principles to French intellectuals of de Man's era. The challenge becomes greater when comparatists seek to extend a theory beyond its original cultural milieu. It could be a stretch to bring Continental theory to bear even on American literature, as we can see from the example of one of de Man's most brilliant and creative intellectual heirs, Barbara Johnson. After completing her dissertation under his direction in 1977, Johnson began her career with deconstructions of French writers and theorists, but she soon expanded her analyses to questions of race, gender, and sexuality. In his contribution to the ACLA's 1995 disciplinary report, Roland Greene reports that "I remember standing on Broadway and Ninety-eighth Street in Manhattan in about 1983 and hearing a graduate student at Columbia tell me emphatically that there were two scholars named Barbara Johnson: the well-known deconstructionist at Yale, and another one who was publishing essays on African American women's literature." Greene says that he was struck "that the field's view of itself simply could not contain the possibility that one of its paragons might already be restless with the theory that was being sold to everyone else," and that Johnson, like Gayatri Spivak, could be "successfully negotiating between deconstruction, historicism, feminism, and interpretation" ("Their Generation," 150).

Barbara Johnson's trajectory can be illustrated by two essays she published four years apart in the deconstructionist journal *Diacritics*. In "The Critical Difference: BartheS/BalZac" (1978), she performed a deconstructive reading of Roland Barthes's structuralist tour de force, *S/Z*. Drawing on Saussurean linguistics, Barthes had advanced a binary opposition between the classic "readerly" text, whose meaning has been established by the writer, versus the much greater variability of contemporary "writerly" works, such as the *nouveau roman*, that require the reader's equal participation in making meaning. Barthes illustrated the norms of the "readerly" text through a sentence-by-sentence analysis of the network of narrative and cultural codes that he saw as structuring Balzac's short story "Sarrasine." In the story, Balzac's protagonist falls in love with an elusive opera singer, La Zambinella, who turns out to be a castrato rather than a woman, a revelation that solves the mystery of her (or "her") unavailability. Balzac has thus set up a situation of seemingly radical ambiguity that is resolved at the story's end.

Johnson turns Barthes's structuralist reading on its head. She argues that Barthes himself was imposing uniformity on Balzac, who was already deconstructing the binary oppositions of male versus female and of reader versus writer. More precisely, Balzac's *text* is performing this deconstruction, whatever the actual author may have thought. For Johnson, "Balzac's text has already worked out the same type of deconstruction of the readerly ideal as that which Barthes is trying to accomplish as if it stood in opposition to the classic text. In other words, Balzac's text already 'knows' the limits and blindnesses of the readerly," and thus "the readerly text is itself nothing other than a deconstruction of the readerly text" (11).

Johnson published "The Critical Difference" soon after completing her dissertation, and both her method and her choice of material were thoroughly de Manian. Yet she soon began to apply and adapt deconstruction to very different kinds of texts, as in "My Monster / My Self," which she published in *Diacritics* in 1982, the year before Roland Greene's interlocutor invented her theoretical doppelgänger. There she discusses Mary Shelley's *Frankenstein*, framing her analysis in terms of questions of motherhood raised by two works of American feminist social analysis, Nancy Friday's *My Mother / My Self* (1977) and Dorothy Dinnerstein's *The Mermaid and the Minotaur* (1976). Both Friday and Dinnerstein discuss the troubled intensity of the mother/child bond. Friday emphasizes the challenge for girls to gain their independence from powerful maternal figures, while Dinnerstein argues that since society has placed the burdens of parenting primarily on mothers, children are led to direct their resentments disproportionately toward the women in their lives.

Johnson argues that Mary Shelley was already exploring the troubled dynamics of parenthood in *Frankenstein* and was actually taking a more radical stance than Friday or Dinnerstein, as her novel doesn't portray a unified self playing a single role. As in Johnson's Balzac article, the fiction knows (or "knows") more than the critics do, complicating Friday's and Dinnerstein's well-meaning messages. Johnson discusses the fraught relations of Victor Frankenstein and of Mary Shelley to their parents and also to their progeny—Frankenstein's monster, Shelley's children and her own book. Johnson thus brings a deconstructive perspective to materials that de Man never seriously treated, counterpointing a gothic novel written by a woman against popular American social psychology. Friday's and Dinnerstein's best-selling books were rallying points for second-wave feminism, but Johnson unsettles both writers' pleas for women's empowerment by revealing an undercurrent of "the monstrousness of selfhood itself" in their books (189).

In contrast to de Man's rhetoric of impersonality, Johnson proposes that all three books are covert autobiographies. She probes the psychic investments hinted at by Friday and by Dinnerstein in their books, and she describes the self-justifying accounts presented by Victor Frankenstein and by his monster in terms that echo de Man on Rousseau's *Confessions*: "Simultaneously a revelation and a cover-up, autobiography would appear to constitute itself as in some way a repression of autobiography" (182). Johnson then moves beyond de Man's perspective, noting that such revelatory cover-ups have traditionally been a male privilege: "the very notion of a self, the very shape of human life stories, has always, from Saint Augustine to Freud, been modeled on the man" (189). She shows how Mary Shelley's preface to her book at once advances and disclaims her writerly authority, and she connects Shelley's ambivalence toward writing with Victor Frankenstein's ambivalence toward his monstrous creation. Johnson also unfolds Shelley's traumatic experience of motherhood, first as a daughter whose birth had killed her mother and then as a mother who lost a child shortly before she wrote her novel. Rousseau comes directly into view at the end of Johnson's essay, but as a model that women must leave behind:

> Rousseau's—or any man's—autobiography consists in the story of the difficulty of conforming to the standard of what a *man* should be. The problem for the female autobiographer is, on the one hand, to resist the pressure of masculine autobiography as the only literary genre available for her enterprise, and, on the other, to describe

a difficulty in conforming to a female ideal which is largely a fantasy of the masculine, not the feminine, imagination. (189)

In Johnson's essays there are more gender positions, and more kinds of literature, than were dreamt of in her mentor's philosophy.

In 1990 Johnson wrote a probing essay, "Poison or Remedy? Paul de Man as Pharmakon." Building on Derrida's discussion of the Greek term as meaning both remedy and poison, she ruefully remarks that "in our current inability either to excuse or to take leave of de Man, we are now getting a taste of our own *pharmakon*" (357). Assessing his work in light of Ortwin de Graef's discoveries, she describes de Man as having "a deep suspicion of false images of harmony and enlightenment," and she proposes that "the ideological aberrations he is unmasking were once his own" (360). Yet she doesn't let de Man off the hook; she argues that he continued to indulge in an understated but pervasive authoritarianism, which we might describe as the mirror image of a fascist cult of personality: a cult of impersonality. His seductive impersonality became part of his appeal to the disciples he simultaneously attracted and rebuffed: "that person was always there, idealized as impersonal. In other words, it was not *despite* but rather *because* of his self-effacement that students and colleagues were led to substantialize and idealize him" (367).[3]

As examples of such idealization, she gives two quotations from the 1984 memorial for de Man. The first is from Shoshana Felman, who claimed that "Paul disclaimed his own authority, yet none had more authority than him" (367). Johnson then quotes, without comment, her own similarly mystified assertion that "the last thing he probably would have wanted to be was a moral and pedagogical—rather than merely intellectual—example for generations of students and colleagues, yet it was precisely his way of not seeking those roles that made him so irreplaceably an exception, and such an inspiration" (367). She concludes her essay by arguing

---

[3] This dynamic could be very near the surface in his teaching. In a seminar I took with him in 1976, on the overdetermined topic "Theory of Irony," a memorable session was devoted to Plato's *Symposium*, in which de Man argued that Socrates seduced the traitorous Alcibiades precisely by *refusing* to seduce him. Could de Man have been the only person in the room unaware of the direct applicability of his interpretation?

that de Man's attempts to efface history and even himself were destined to fail and limited the force of his theory. But rather than cordon de Man off as an exception to proper critical practice, she sees his stance as part of a larger and problematic pattern:

> It is no accident that few students ever asked de Man what he had done during the war. De Man's subversive teaching unsettled many of the assumptions that have accompanied the humanist under-standing of the canon, but he did nothing to unseat the traditional white male author from his hiding place behind the impersonality of the universal subject, the subject supposed to be without gender, race, or history. (369)

Instead, Johnson says, de Man "created a slightly idiosyncratic canon of his own" within "a traditional understanding of canonical texts and questions." She closes with a challenge to her readers, and to herself: "It is up to us to open the subversiveness of teaching further—*without* losing the materialist conception of language that remains de Man's truly radical contribution" (369).

Relocating Theory

When a theory circulates beyond its immediate milieu, it is liable to trace a trajectory "From Rags to Riches to Routine," as Gerald Graff titled the penultimate chapter of *Professing Literature*. This declension can already begin in the theorist's home country. In *Roland Barthes par Roland Barthes*, Barthes illustrates the concept of "Récupération" with a page that he iron-ically reproduces from an assignment in a girls' lycée. The assignment is based on a paragraph from his book *Le degré zéro de l'écriture*, in which he describes style as the most private, even secret, feature of a work. The students are instructed to summarize the passage in their own words, to extract its principal points, and then "d'apprécier librement cette concep-tion" (155). At the bottom of the page is a typed comment from their teacher, instructing the class to repeat the assignment, as their first attempt was unsatisfactory: "A large number of the students having seemed to be thrown off [*déroutées*] by the analysis, we will insist upon this exercise, and we will indicate the principal directions in which the discussion could be carried out," based on "certain essential rules for how to read a text." Barthes makes no comment on this assignment.

In "Travelling Theory" (1982), Edward Said outlines the stages of a theory's circulation from its point of origin to "a passage through the pressure of various contexts as the idea moves from an earlier point to another time and place," then a phase of resistance that the idea encounters in its new environment, and finally a fourth stage in which the idea "is to some extent transformed by its new uses, its new position in a new time and place" (227). Though Said doesn't reference translation theory—still typically neglected by comparatists in the early 1980s—his stages of a theory's transmission closely track those of literary translation. As with translation, a central question is what is gained or lost in the process; Said argues that a radical or insurrectionary theory often loses its edge as it becomes domesticated in a new cultural discourse. For example, he traces the progressive muffling of Georg Lukács's concept of reification as it moved from Lukács's urgent political moment in Hungary to Lucien Goldmann in Paris and then to Raymond Williams, for whom the theory became "reduced, codified and institutionalized," even "an ideological trap" (239, 241).

Said's dyspeptic account of theory's loss in translation suited his polemic at the time against depoliticized literary criticism. He took a more positive view twelve years later, amid the upsurge in political criticism that he had helped inspire. In "Travelling Theory Reconsidered" (1994), he allows that his earlier essay had shown a bias in favor of a theory's organic connection to its moment of origin, and he now proposes that "transgressive theory" can gain in force as it moves into new circumstances. He discusses the ways in which Adorno and then Fanon had revitalized Lukács's theory of class struggle, freeing it from the limitations of Lukács's redemptive progressivism. Thus "Lukács's dialectic is grounded in *The Wretched of the Earth*, actualized, given a kind of harsh presence nowhere to be found in his agonized rethinking of the classical philosophical antinomies" (260).

Like literature, then, a theory can gain or lose in translation, and in either event we do well to pay close attention to the circumstances of its origin, its transmission, and its adaptation or co-optation in new times and places. Not only the muffling but also the heightening of a theoretical formulation can become routinized in a new context. Haun Saussy has observed that Derrida's passing comment in *De la grammatologie* that "il n'y a pas de hors-texte" became a rallying cry for (and against) deconstruction in the United States after Gayatri Spivak dramatically translated it as "there is nothing outside the text." This formulation suggested a radical disconnection of textuality from reality, yet Saussy argues that this was a mistranslation; Derrida's claim "was rather that 'there is no extra-textual, tipped-in illustration (*planche hors-texte*) that I can send you to, no stone I can tell you to kick, that would not obey a textual logic or testify to the textual condition,' a claim as modest as the usual translation is exorbitant" ("Exquisite Cadavers," 33). He adds in a note: "The misunderstanding owes as much to reception and circulation as it does to translation: if a (U.S.) public had not been ready and willing to see in deconstruction a text-based solipsism, these few words would never have embarked on their career of endless reiteration" (41n.85).[4]

The problems of translation and reception increase when a theory travels not just from Paris to New York but out into very different cultural spheres. At the same time, new bodies of literature, and different material circumstances, provide opportunities to refine and revitalize a theory, testing its propositions and moving beyond its limits. Said shows movement of this sort in "Fanon's crucial reworking and critique of Lukács, in which the *national* element missing in *History and Class Consciousness*—the setting of the work, like Marx's, is entirely European—is given an absolute prominence by Fanon" ("Travelling Theory Reconsidered," 261). Here Said is discussing a traveling theorist as well as a traveling theory, as Fanon had spent most of his adult life in France and in Algeria. He dictated *The Wretched of the Earth* in Tunis, where he was

---

[4] In her revised translation of *Of Grammatology* in 2016, Spivak obliquely responds to criticisms of her rendering of the phrase. She retains her original wording but adds a rather overliteral alternative in brackets, followed by the French: "there is nothing outside the text [there is no outside-text; *il n'y a pas de hors-texte*]" (172). There is no "outside-text" in the English language, at any rate; the usual translation of *hors-texte* is simply "an inset," just as Saussy proposes.

dying of leukemia; perhaps not coincidentally, Said himself was struggling with the same disease when he wrote his essay.

Inspired by postcolonial studies, the opening of theory to the world beyond the West has now been underway for several decades, but it is still an incomplete project, not least because "theory" remains a discourse of largely European and North American provenance. A canon—or hypercanon—of works by theorists based in western Europe and the United States circulates widely around the world, even among critics who reject the canonicity of "Great Books" in literature itself. As Revathi Krishnaswamy has argued, "politically engaged comparatists have often been rightly skeptical of grand sweeping metanarratives theorizing literary productions across the (third) world," such as those advanced by Jameson and Moretti, "but few, even among the skeptics, have called for redefining theory itself as a way out of comparative literature's Eurocentrism. The result is what we have today: world lit without world lit crit" ("Toward World Literary Knowledges," 136). She argues that the hegemony of Euro-American theory will only be broken when comparatists start attending seriously to a wider range of theoretical discourses elsewhere, and she gives the example of Tamil as a language with a long tradition of poetry and poetic reflection that has been neglected within India as well as abroad.

Major theoretical traditions go back many centuries in Asia and the Middle East, and a substantial number of contemporary literary and cultural theorists are working there and elsewhere in the world. Yet they rarely achieve the broad currency of Western-based scholars, if they are read at all beyond their home country or region. Like the older canon of Great Books, the theory canon privileges Euro-American theory as globally applicable, while non-Western theories have primarily been used in discussions of their culture of origin. This ghettoization has often been reinforced by area specialists themselves. Working with the originals and talking mostly to others in their area, they have often been slow to produce translations and commentaries for people outside the field. As the Arabist Alexander Key has said,

> the problem that comparativists usually face in the European and
> Anglophone academy is that our conversations stall on the thinness

of our knowledge of each other's traditions outside Europe. Absent a sense of how a language culture's conceptual vocabulary works and has developed, absent an orientation to the genres and disciplinary conventions of that language culture, absent a comprehension of the depth, complexity, and historical weight of ideas that have no analogue in the traditions with which one is familiar, comparative conversations tend to stumble. ("Kavya," 163)

Key's essay is part of an interesting forum in the journal *Comparative Studies of South Asia, Africa and the Middle East*, organized by Sheldon Pollock to discuss an ambitious history of Sanskrit court poetry, *Innovations and Turning Points: Toward a History of Kāvya Literature* (Bronner et al., 2014). Pollock invited several specialists in classical Arabic, Persian, Chinese, and Japanese literatures to reflect on the collection's potential as a starting point for comparison with the poetics of their own traditions.

A recurrent theme among the responses he received is regret that the volume's contributors hadn't done more to make their eight-hundred-page history fully understandable to outsiders. Thus Karla Mallette: "reading the essays in this book feels a bit like turning the pages of another family's photo album. Individuals, relationships, and the history in which they are entangled come into focus briefly, then blur and recede, leaving behind a sense of vague but urgent affection, like the smoke skeleton of fireworks" ("Sanskrit Snapshots," 127). As Pollock says in introducing the forum, "We need to do more to ensure that those located outside our specialism but eager to help construct a truly global (and no longer peripheralized) object of study will not find the entryway blocked by unfiltered particularist knowledge" ("Small Philology," 125).[5]

The already serious imbalance between accessible materials from the West versus other regions is redoubled by a lingering linguistic imperialism: English, French, and (to a diminishing degree) German are the privileged languages of international theory. If you think of prominent theorists from the global South today, almost all of them write in English or

---

[5] Pollock himself has created a wide-ranging collection accessible to nonspecialists, *A Rasa Reader: Classical Indian Aesthetics* (2016), the inaugural volume in a series he is editing for Columbia University Press, Historical Sourcebooks in Classical Indian Thought.

French. People writing in Chinese or Hindi, or even in the global languages of Spanish or Portuguese, are far less prominent. They are usually encountered only in one or two of their works, often translated decades after they were published, in contrast to the speed with which almost any work by Spivak or Kristeva will be translated into their language.

The limited reach available to most peripheral intellectuals can be illustrated by the examples of two leading Brazilian comparatists, Antonio Candido (1918–2017) and Roberto Schwarz (b. 1938). Both of them made their careers in São Paulo, where Schwarz developed his influential conception of belated peripheral modernity in the context of a discussion group led by Candido, his long-lived mentor and senior colleague. The two figures have major status in Brazil, as seen in Paulo Eduardo Arantes' *Sentimento da dialética na experiência intelectual brasileira: Dialética e dualidade segundo Antonio Candido e Roberto Schwarz* (1992). Yet it is only Schwarz who has achieved a measure of global currency, chiefly for his book on Joaquim Maria Machado de Assis, *A Master on the Periphery of Capitalism*, and for a collection that appeared in English in 1992 under the title *Misplaced Ideas: Essays on Brazilian Culture*. None of his many other works has been translated into English, apart from another essay collection in 2013. I've found no translations of his books into French or German, but at least he has some presence in the critical anglosphere.

Antonio Candido hasn't found the same response, despite his theoretical originality and his manifold contributions to Brazilian scholarship and society. Both a scholar and a public intellectual, he founded a cultural journal in 1942 while he was still an undergraduate in sociology at the University of São Paulo. He developed a lifelong interest in Marxist theory and became closely involved in political struggles; co-edited a clandestine political journal, *Resistência*; and co-founded the Brazilian Worker's Party (Partido dos Trabalhadores). After earning his PhD, he shifted from teaching sociology and became a professor of literary theory and comparative literature in São Paulo. Apart from two years in Paris, he taught in São Paulo for the rest of his life, becoming his country's leading literary critic. Even today, Carolina Correira dos Santos has remarked, "any scholar working on Brazilian literature has to reckon with his influence" ("Brazilian Literary Theory's Challenge," 336). Candido is notable for his ability to combine broad sociological insights with close analysis of individual texts, and rather than simply identify social themes in literary works, he looked for deeper connections between literary form and social concern. Decades before Bourdieu and Casanova, he understood Brazilian literature not as a canon of works but as a dynamic system that evolved in the shifting interactions of a range of agents in the literary field, as they responded both to internal and external events and pressures, at once belated in terms of Europe and utopian in creating a new national culture.

Candido achieved a broad reputation in Latin America, and in 2005 he was awarded Mexico's Premio Alfonso Reyes, a prize previously given to Jorge Luis Borges, André Malraux, and Octavio Paz. He published nineteen books over the course of nearly sixty years, but outside Latin America he is known only to specialists in Latin American studies. At the tender age of ninety-five, Candido did live to see a selection of his essays published by Princeton (*On Literature and Society*, 2014), but no other book of his has ever appeared in English. Of course, translation into English shouldn't be a precondition for international recognition, particularly among scholars opposed to neoliberal Anglo-globalism. Even for those who don't work on Lusophone literature, it really isn't difficult to gain enough grounding in Portuguese to read scholarship if one knows Spanish or French, as many comparatists do. Yet to judge from his invisibility outside Latin America, Antonio Candido might as well have been writing in Tamil.

Though he has also written only in Portuguese, Roberto Schwarz has achieved a significantly greater reach, albeit not nearly to the extent of such Anglophone and Francophone theorists as Ngũgĩ, Fanon, and Glissant. His relative success has as much to do with his upbringing and formation as with the ideas that he developed in dialogue with his mentor. Born in Vienna in 1938, he was only a year old when his family fled Nazi-occupied Europe, but he grew up with a sense of connection to German culture, and he looked outward for his higher education. Following his graduation from the University of São Paulo in 1960, he earned an MA in comparative literature at Yale and then moved to Paris, where he earned a PhD from the Sorbonne Nouvelle before going back to São Paulo to teach. He returned to France in 1969 for what turned out to be an eight-year period of exile, during which he elaborated his ideas on peripherality. In the preface to his book on Machado, Schwarz says that "I owe a special note of gratitude to Antonio Candido, whose books and points of view have had a pervasive influence on me," but he continues: "My work would also be unthinkable without the—contradictory—tradition formed by Lukács, Benjamin, Brecht, and Adorno, and without the inspiration of Marx" (*A Master on the Periphery of Capitalism*, 4).

Schwarz's very title indicates his geopolitical emphasis; in English as in Portuguese, the specific author discussed is named only in the subtitle, following the statement of a global theme: *Um mestre na periferia do capitalismo: Machado de Assis*. Antonio Candido was fluent in five languages and was equally in dialogue with Marxism, but he focused his attention largely on writers not known outside Brazil. Most notably, his seminal *Formação da literatura brasileira* (1959) treats Brazilian literature from 1750 to 1870, ending just before Machado began his literary career. Howard Becker, the editor of the Princeton collection of Candido's essays, opens his volume by saying that he'd reluctantly decided against including selections from the *Formação*, focused as it is on "a literature almost all of which would be totally unfamiliar to readers of this volume" (*On Literature and Society*, vii). Instead, Becker translated essays dealing with better-known writers, particularly Europeans. The collection begins with essays on Dumas and on Conrad, followed by a comparative discussion of the theme of "waiting for the barbarians" in writers including Cavafy, Kafka, and Dino Buzzati. Becker did include some of Candido's essays on Brazilian themes, yet it is in fact Candido's two-volume *Formação da literatura brasileira* that offers his richest contribution to postcolonial and world literary studies. There he explores in depth how a peripheral literature achieves a distinct national identity vis-à-vis a foreign cultural center, in Brazil's case involving the dual foci of Portugal and Paris.

Brazilian culture is further distinguished by the complex mix of races and classes at home and the transformation of European literary values in a country surrounded by a different, competing ex-colonial language, Spanish. Taking these varied factors into account, Candido's *Formação* unfolds a very different literary system than is found in colonial/decolonial circumstances elsewhere. As Stefan Helgesson has recently observed, in one of the few articles yet written in English on his work,

> If a cluster of insistent questions in literary studies today revolve around the enabling potential (or lack thereof) of "world literature," then Candido can help us to see why those questions require constantly new answers that refrain from skirting the density of local literary histories but, on the contrary, understand this density to be the very substance through which world literature can be thought. ("Literature," 156–57)

The primary substance through which literature is read and thought is language, and this is a crucial arena in which comparatists have to work against old patterns that have long marginalized most of the world's critical and theoretical perspectives. This problem extends beyond Arabic, Hindi, or Brazilian Portuguese; scholarship in many languages within Europe itself has been subjected to an ongoing subalternity in theoretical discourse. This fact is close to home for Jordi Llovet and his coauthors in Barcelona. In the concluding chapter of their *Teoría literaria y literatura comparada*, Antoni Martí Monterde argues that in order to complete the postcolonial project, it is necessary "descolonizarnos de nosotros mismos, los europeos" (to decolonize ourselves from ourselves, the Europeans [397, citing Armando Gnisci]). Though Martí Monterde wrote this plea in the hegemonic language of Spanish, six years later he took a significant step toward disciplinary decolonization, publishing a probing four-hundred-page history in Catalan, *Un somni europeu: Història intel·lectual de la Literatura Comparada* (2011)—the best account yet written, in any language known to me, of the intertwined growth of comparative and world literary studies in the nineteenth century.

It is certainly good to read theorists from Barcelona or Brazil who are in active dialogue with their counterparts abroad and who treat internationally known writers, but our perspectives will be considerably enlarged when we go beyond such cosmopolitan traveling theorists as Fanon and Schwarz and begin to read seriously the more locally rooted thinkers such as Antonio Candido and Antoni Martí Monterde whose work has broad implications elsewhere as well.

Literature's Theories

In addition to reading more widely in theory per se, we can take fuller account of the theoretical perspectives embedded in literature itself. In "Toward World Literary Knowledges," Revathi Krishnaswamy proposes that our limited canon of theory should be opened out by incorporating the theoretical dimensions of much literary writing, including subaltern and Dalit works. Her argument can be compared to the debates over the existence or nonexistence of "Chinese philosophy" that have led to the opening up of the category of philosophy to include such works as the *Zhuangzi* and the *Dao De Jing* that traditionally weren't included in the curricula of Western philosophy departments.[6] Theory has much to gain from the critical reflections already present in self-aware literary works, as Djelal Kadir has also argued ("To World, to Globalize"). Paul de Man was explicit on this point. In a late interview, he emphasized that his starting point was "not philosophical but basically philological," and he somewhat self-mockingly distinguished his dependence on primary texts from Derrida's self-generated approach:

> The difference is that Derrida's text is so brilliant, so incisive, so strong that whatever happens in Derrida, it happens between him and his own text. He doesn't need Rousseau, he doesn't need anybody else; I do need them very badly because I never had an idea of my own, it was always through a text, through the critical examination of a text. I am a philologist and not a philosopher. (Rosso, "An Interview," 118)

Identifying himself as a philologist, de Man here comes close to Erich Auerbach's having derived his understanding of mimesis from "playing" with his literary texts.

Literary historians have always sought to tease out writers' principles from their works, and theorists have often derived broad conceptions from close examination of a select group of writers, as when Harold Bloom identified "the anxiety of influence" in his favorite British Romantics. Even a

---

[6] For a cogent account of these debates and the canon of Masters texts, see Wiebke Denecke, *The Dynamics of Masters Literature*.

single work can inspire theoretical reflection, as in Barthes's exploration in *S/Z* of the codes structuring Balzac's "Sarrasine," or Gérard Genette's Proust-based narratology in *Figures I–III*. Non-Western writers are just as likely to include theoretically significant moments of definition or self-reflective commentary. Even if we didn't have the great tradition of aesthetic theory in Sanskrit, we could find the poetics of a foundational work such as the *Rāmāyaṇa* signaled in the epic itself. In a striking metapoetic scene, the sage Vālmīki—the epic's supposed author—surprises himself by inventing poetry at the beginning of his own work. Master of a forest ashram, he is on his way to take a ritual bath when he is brought up short by a distressing scene of violence: a forest hunter has cruelly shot a bird in the act of mating.

> Seeing him struck down and writhing on the ground, his body covered with blood, his mate uttered a piteous cry.
>
> And the pious seer, seeing the bird struck down in this fashion by the hunter, was filled with pity.
>
> Then, in the intensity of this feeling of compassion, the Brahman thought, "This is wrong." Hearing the *krauñca* hen wailing, he uttered these words:
>
> "Since, Nisada, you killed one of this pair of *krauñca*, distracted at the height of passion, you shall not live for very long."
>
> And even as he stood watching and spoke in this way, this thought arose in his heart: "Stricken with grief for this bird, what is this I have uttered?"
>
> But upon reflection, that wise and thoughtful man came to a conclusion. Then that bull among sages spoke these words to his disciple:
>
> "Fixed in metrical quarters, each with the same number of syllables, and fit for the accompaniment of stringed and percussion instruments, the utterance that I produced in this welling-up of grief, *shoka,* shall be called *shloka,* poetry, and nothing else."
>
> But the delighted disciple had memorized that unsurpassed utterance even as the sage was making it, so that his guru was pleased with him.
>
> (Vālmīki, *Rāmāyaṇa,* 1:2)

Several features in this scene resonate with poetry as it is still understood today, and these can tell us much about early Sanskrit poetics. Vālmīki's *shloka* is made up of artful language, surprising the poet himself by its difference from an ordinary utterance; it presents an experience in symbolically charged terms that give human meaning to the birds' suffering; and it is received and transmitted through an incipient literary institution or network.

These formal, symbolic, and sociological features are what distinguish Vālmīki's verse from the cry of the bereaved bird. Though poets throughout the ages have loved to compare themselves to tuneful birds, the wailing of the *krauñca* hen is anything but artful; its despairing cry could only delight the heart of the hunter who had shot her mate. By contrast, Vālmīki's grief-stricken utterance is "fixed in metrical quarters, each with the same number of syllables, and fit for the accompaniment of stringed and percussion instruments"—a succinct definition of the term *shloka*. The most common of all Sanskrit metrical forms, often standing for "song" or "poetry" in general, the *shloka* is typically a couplet composed of two sixteen-syllable lines, often in four groups of four syllables each. This wasn't actually the only possible form for a *shloka*; much like Aristotle's definitions in his *Poetics*, Vālmīki's supposedly spontaneous definition seeks to enshrine *a* poetics among the possibilities current in his culture.

Thus far, we have a fair degree of commonality with aspects we would know from the European context. Yet the passage differs from much Western thought in its emphasis on poetic creation as an intensely social act. Vālmīki isn't recollecting an overflow of emotion months later in Wordsworthian tranquility, nor is he offering a Petrarchan apostrophe to a distant or deceased lover; his couplet is an immediate ethical response to an encounter with suffering. Crucially, the newborn verse is communicated to the sage's delighted disciple. The *Rāmāyaṇa* was the product of a long oral tradition, and the prologue doesn't represent the couplet as being preserved through writing. It could fade away once Vālmīki begins thinking of something else, and it would certainly die with the poet unless it was preserved in a repeatable form and then transmitted to an audience. So Vālmīki is accompanied by a disciple who instantly memorizes the *shloka*, "even as the sage was making it, so that his guru was pleased with him."

Thus preserved, the poem must be transmitted to a wider audience, the ongoing community of hearers at Vālmīki's ashram, in an early instance of what Germaine de Staël would call literature's "rapport avec les institutions sociales." Vālmīki takes his ritual bath and returns to his ashram, at which point his disciple teaches the couplet to the guru's assembled devotees. "Then all his disciples chanted that *shloka* again. Delighted and filled with wonder, they said over and over again: / 'The *shoka*, grief, that the great seer sang out in four metrical quarters, all equal in syllables, has, by virtue of being repeated after him, become *shloka*, poetry'" (1.2). The utterance becomes poetry by virtue of being repeated over and over again by the entire community: in the Sanskrit tradition, poetry is not an artifact but an activity.

As in India, poetic theory in Japan was developed over the course of centuries, providing the rich fund of theoretical statements on which Earl Miner drew for his *Comparative Poetics*. Prose fiction, on the other hand, traditionally had far lower status, and there was less formal discussion of prose during its first flowering in the Heian period. Even so, in *The Bridge of Dreams: A Poetics of "The Tale of Genji,"* Haruo Shirane was able to derive Murasaki Shikibu's narrative poetics through close examination of her practice, supplemented by statements from her contemporaries and by early commentators on her masterpiece. As Shirane says, Murasaki was well aware that she was revolutionizing the genre of the monogatari as she built up her tale from chapter to chapter through "a process of self-reflection and self-scrutiny" (xxii).

Murasaki's work also includes frequent reflections on poetry, as she comments directly on many of the nearly eight hundred poems that appear throughout her text. To give just one aspect of Murasaki's differential poetics, she not only remarks on themes and images in the poems, as we might expect, but she places equal weight on an aspect we might not anticipate: her characters' *handwriting*. One poem is written—by an aging nun—"in a casual hand remarkable for its character and distinction" (*Tale of Genji*, 93), while a woman whom Genji has neglected sends him a poem written "on heavily perfumed paper, in ink now black, now vanishingly pale" (266). A Heian poem's meaning is conveyed as much through a host of carefully considered material effects as through the actual words on the rice paper. If we follow Barbara Johnson in considering that Paul de Man's major contribution was his materialist conception of language, Murasaki Shikibu can help us extend our attention—in Japanese literature and beyond—to the materiality of writing itself.

In opening up theory to a wider range of perspectives, comparatists need to attend to the critical difference of texts from outside the modern Euro-American world. Too often, metropolitan theorists find in non-Western material a confirmation of what they already know, and this tendency can be seen even in Revathi Krishnaswamy's essay. She makes a strong case for studying *bhakti* poetry and poetics as an alternative to the elite Sanskrit tradition: "Composed by cobblers, weavers, cowherds, shepherds, untouchables, and women (among others), *bhakti* poetry drew on the oral traditions of folksong and epigram to articulate an incandescent iconoclastic vision of spiritual liberation" (146). Yet when she gives the example of the twelfth-century woman poet Mahadeviakka, she emphasizes elements that closely track the interests of modern secular feminism. Mahadeviakka, she says, "repeatedly complains of the restrictions placed on women both by the stifling demands of parents, husbands, and in-laws and by the fierce opposition from pundits and priests." The Sanskrit tradition's "conventional structure of love—longing, separation, and union between devotee and divine . . . becomes, in effect, nothing more than a flimsy veil for a more subversive message about social transgression and spiritual transformation" (146). The critical difference of *bhakti* poetry from Sanskrit tradition is almost too clear, but it doesn't look so different after all from contemporary Western concerns.

Reading Kālidāsa, Contrapuntally

Whether embedded in literary texts or elaborated in aesthetic treatises, culturally specific theories provide an essential check against vague universalism and imperialist exoticism. They can keep us from declarations that, say, a Lacanian perspective on *The Story of the Stone* has revealed its long-hidden meaning, invisible to readers in the Qing Dynasty. Yet anyone using a broad theoretical perspective will be assessing a work to some degree in terms derived elsewhere than within the work itself, and even scholars deeply immersed in their home culture are rarely stewards of unmediated local traditions. Whether they are based in Beijing or Karachi, scholars of Qing Dynasty fiction or Urdu poetry rarely read their materials without some contemporary critical or theoretical framework, often one that has largely been developed elsewhere and on the basis of a very different archive, as we've seen in the importance of Marx for Antonio Candido and Roberto Schwarz.

The problem is particularly acute when we deal with premodern literature. For all of us today, "the past is a foreign country; they do things differently there." Appropriately for the theme of cultural transmission, academic readers have most likely encountered this line at the start of Salman Rushdie's "Imaginary Homelands" essay rather than in its source, L. P. Hartley's 1953 novel *The Go-Between*. Hartley set his novel in 1900; if just half a century had turned his own country into a foreign land, how much greater is the distance when we look centuries farther back? We can hardly erase all knowledge of the modernity in which we have grown up and have been trained, despite our best efforts to recover a work's premodern values. Today's dominant theoretical discourses are of modern or even contemporary origin, and they are based primarily on literature of the last one or two hundred years. How successfully can we employ a theory formulated by Derrida in Paris or by Partha Chatterjee in Kolkata—following his PhD studies in Rochester, New York—to analyze a poem composed in China or India a millennium or more ago?

The challenge is to employ our modern theories in dialogue with the theoretical knowledges found in the traditions we explore. My test case for pursuing this question will be Kālidāsa's narrative poem *Meghadūta* ("The Cloud Messenger"), written sometime around 400 CE. One of the first Asian writers to be widely appreciated in Europe, Kālidāsa was a key figure in the South Asian contribution to the early development of both comparative and world literature. The pioneering Orientalist Sir William Jones translated his play *Shakuntala* in 1789, and Jones's disciple Horace Hayman Wilson translated the *Meghadūta* in 1814. The poem takes distant communication as its theme. It is built around the separation of a Yaksha, a minor heavenly figure, from his beloved; the Yaksha has been banished for months from the Himalayan court of Kubera, god of wealth, and is languishing far to the south. Desperate to send a message to his beloved, he implores a cloud to travel across India and assure her of his undying devotion. The Yaksha then spends most of the poem's 111 stanzas sketching out the route the cloud must take, presenting a gorgeous panorama of a sensually charged landscape, before he finally pictures the cloud's meeting with his beloved.

The *Meghadūta* deals with universal themes of love and longing, but from the time Wilson first translated it into English, Western scholars have recognized the importance of local knowledge, given Kālidāsa's blizzard of references to place-names, divinities, plants, birds, and epic traditions. Equally valuable are Sanskrit theories of poetry. Starting with Bharata's *Nātyaśāstra* ("Rules for Representation") two millennia ago, a host of Sanskrit poets and intellectuals discussed issues of poetics and poetic language. Yet in 1814 Wilson had to rely on classical and neoclassical conceptions of poetry in framing his translation, as Western scholars had barely begun to gain access to Sanskrit poetics. It is possible today to approach the *Meghadūta* by counterpointing classical Sanskrit and modern Western theoretical perspectives, gaining a fuller understanding of Kālidāsa's poem than we can achieve from either vantage point alone.

In 1976 the American poet and translator Leonard Nathan published an eloquent translation of the *Meghadūta* under the punning title *The Transport of Love*. Nathan makes a sustained effort to stay close to the sense of the Sanskrit original, which is even printed on facing pages next to the translation. Both in his introduction and in his endnotes, Nathan offers a wealth of historical and cultural information, doing his best to bridge the gaps between Asia and the United States and between antiquity and the present. He also allows the text to preserve a measure of the untranslatable, retaining dozens of foreign terms, with a glossary at the end of the volume. Even so—in a pattern that wouldn't have surprised Said in the least—Nathan gives his translation a largely Eurocentric interpretive framing. Despite his extensive cultural references, he often reads Kālidāsa with the eye of an American New Critic, while he assimilates Kālidāsa philosophically to his counterparts in the ancient Mediterranean world, in a more sophisticated version of what Horace Wilson was already doing in comparing Kālidāsa to Ovid and Horace ("the elegant FLACCUS," as Wilson calls him [145]). Nathan's Neoplatonist emphasis emerges early in his introduction, just when he claims to be showing Kālidāsa's stark difference from Western assumptions: "Behind Indian poetic expectation and the poems addressed to it were two major assumptions that we do not share. First, that reality was not to be sought through personal sensory apprehension of our changing empirical world, but beyond it to one that is permanent and ideal. . . . Poems, then, were a way of experiencing the reality beyond appearance" (3). India is not like the West, which "has largely treated the phenomenal world as a real one, no matter what lay beyond it" (4).

Instead of physical reality, according to Nathan, what Kālidāsa's poem conveys is a changeless social and religious world, virtually the timeless East that Hegel or Sir Richard Burton would readily have recognized. Within this immemorial order, Nathan invites us to relish the harmonies of "the ideal world, whose beauties are interchangeable or related through a profound correspondence of great to small, high to low, supernatural to natural" (9). In his commentary Nathan develops a New Critical reading of the poem as a balanced structure of ironies, with each image contributing to a well-wrought whole, elegantly playful and socially ordered. Though the opening stanzas describe the Yaksha as desolate, impotent, aching for love, shaken, and heartbroken, we are not to take his intense unhappiness too seriously, as he isn't a real character in any Western sense. In Nathan's reading, the Yaksha is an excuse for erotic reverie rather than a suffering individual. Instead, it is the most abstract entity in the poem, the cloud itself, that is the poem's true hero: "if there is any real character in the *Meghadūta*, it is the cloud, who, through the Yaksha's erotic imaginings, becomes a sort of magnetic center for the complex associations of all things in the world" (7–8).

The powers of love and of language join together in the message that the Yaksha dictates to the cloud starting in stanza 99, which Nathan calls "the tonal climax of the poem." The Yaksha's message expresses the classic Sanskrit trope of love in separation, a union that survives absence and is even intensified by it. "You should say this to her," the Yaksha declares:

> He, far off, a hostile fate blocking
> his way, by mere wish joins his body
> with your body, his thinness with your thinness,
> his pain with your intense pain, his tears
> with your tears, his endless longing
> with your longing, his deep sigh with your sigh. (81)

Nathan's framing prepares us well for this stanza but accounts less well for the rest of the message, which goes on to stress the *failure* of metaphor to embody a satisfying correspondence. Now the image of a cloud suggests loss of vision:

> With red rock I've drawn you on a stone slab,
> feigning anger, but however much I want
> to portray myself fallen at your feet,
> my eyes are clouded with tears that
> well up over and over. So hard is this fate
> that won't permit even our pictured union. (83)

Throughout the *Meghadūta*, moments of order and harmony are disrupted by images of radical instability and uncertainty. While the poem often evokes the joys of love and fulfillment, it speaks as much about anguish, violence, and emptiness. At the very beginning, the Yaksha's nebulous messenger is introduced not as a "magnetic center" of meaning and communication but as a figure of transience and of incomprehension:

> What does a cloud—a mix of vapor,
> flame, water, and wind—have to do with messages
> made to be sent by beings fit to bear them?
> But still the Yaksha implored it. Those
> sick with desire can no longer tell
> what will answer and what is dumb. (19)

In this stanza, the cloud sounds less like a Platonic Form than like a floating signifier.

A reader of Derrida will find many passages that seem tailor-made to illustrate deconstructive themes of the deferral and self-cancellation of meaning. Far from directly conveying the Yaksha's correspondence to (and with) his beloved, the cloud's journey becomes an experience of endless deferral:

> I foresee, friend, that though you want to hurry
> my message, there will be pause after pause
> on each peak that blossoms with fragrant kakubhas,
> and though peacocks, eyes moist with gladness,
> make you welcome, their cries risen to meet you, I pray
> you somehow find the will to move quickly on. (31)

Here the Yaksha envisions a tantalizing double deferral: the cloud will continually pause on the fragrant peaks, only to deny the peacocks' satisfaction by moving on to the next peak, where it will once again pause, postponing the delivery of the ever-more-deferred message. This is a letter carrier's *différance* a millennium and a half before Derrida sent *La Carte postale* to his publisher.

The cloud passes over a landscape charged with violence. In one stanza, the Yaksha tells the cloud to "offer yourself / to Shiva for the elephant's bloody hide / he wears in his dance" (39). Such moments are typically discounted in Nathan's balanced, harmonious reading. In stanza 48, for instance, the cloud passes the field of the Kurus, "renowned as the battleground where Arjuna / showered his sharp arrows on princely chests, / as you pour jets of water on the lotus" (47). In his notes, Nathan discusses this evocation of epic violence only to deny that it signifies violence at all:

> Kālidāsa's ability to bring everything into the complex of relations that make up the poem is tested severely in 48, when the cloud crosses the field of the Kurus; this is the battleground on which, in the epic *Mahābhārata*, vast armies slaughtered each other, leaving only a few heroes alive. So massive is the lore suggested by this allusion to the great epic and so well-known to his audience, that, had

the poet brought it too far forward, he could have upset the poise of the established tone, which is not heroic. In fact, the heroic here, embodied in the deeds of Arjuna, the greatest warrior in the epic, is kept in the background, serving merely as a comparison for the impact of the cloud's downpour on vulnerable lotus blossoms. (100)

Possibly this scene of apocalyptic violence serves only to establish a delicate metaphor, yet it may be Nathan's insistence on harmonious poise, rather than Kālidāsa's poetic ability, that is being "severely tested here."

The social and the personal come together in the poem's conclusion, in which the cloud is supposed to reassure the beloved that the Yaksha is well and is pining away for her. The Yaksha tells the cloud to demonstrate his good faith as a messenger by citing a private story from the lovers' past. This is well and good, and yet the Yaksha chooses an odd anecdote for the proof:

> And tell her I said this: "once
> in bed, though clinging in sleep to my neck,
> for some reason you woke crying aloud,
> and when I asked why again and again, answered
> with an inward smile: *You cheat, I saw you*
> *playing with another woman in my sleep!*" (87)

Is infidelity really a good theme to bring to the distant beloved's mind? This anecdote threatens to cancel itself out, as de Man might say, producing precisely the anxiety that the message is supposed to allay. Here again, Nathan's harmonious interpretation is severely tested, but he rises to the challenge: "the Yaksha adds a token of authenticity to the message by reminding his mate of an incident only the two could know. With superb tact he chooses a humorous one that might help in cheering her up" (110). Superb *tact*?

Having undercut his stance of fidelity in his very profession of faithfulness, the Yaksha reveals that the cloud may not actually be inclined to deliver this ambiguous message at all:

> I trust, friend, that you'll do this for me
> and am certain your grave look does not

forebode refusal. You silently grant
the chātakas the rain they crave.
For the answer of good men to those
who ask their help is simply to do what's desired. (89)

Nathan has provided us a wealth of contextual information, but his undertheorized reading is far from theory-free, as he has given a Sanskritized inflection to the New Critical principles in which he had been trained. All in all, it is hard to feel that Nathan has really accounted for the poem's uncanny power, and an infusion of deconstructive insights can help us attend to important elements that escape Nathan's reading. Yet we should be wary of claiming that a naïve New Critical reading has now been superseded by a rigorous deconstructive perspective, revealing Kālidāsa's secret preference (hidden in plain sight) for violence over order, infidelity over devotion, and deferral over consummation. If Jacques Derrida rushes in where William K. Wimsatt would fear to tread, the result may be an anachronistically alienated reading.

For a more grounded understanding of the *Meghadūta*, we can draw on a classic work of Sanskrit poetic theory, the *Dhvanyaloka* ("Light on Suggestion") of the ninth-century scholar Anandavardhana, which is folded within an extended commentary, the *Locana*, by his follower Abhinavagupta. This dual work several times draws examples from Kālidāsa, and it gives a wealth of insight into how Sanskrit poetry was being read a thousand years ago. As in the *Rāmāyaṇa*, poetry is seen as an interpersonal experience. Rarely do Anandavardhana and Abhinavagupta suggest that the lyrics they discuss show a solitary individual, speaking in soliloquy to an absent lover or to no one at all. Anandavardhana and Abhinavagupta envision a crowded social landscape when they interpret poems, and their overriding interest is in the speaker's ethical engagement with the surrounding social and natural world.

Anandavardhana's and Abhinavagupta's eminently social poetics, derived from a thousand years of Sanskrit tradition, enable us to consider the *Meghadūta* in a very different light from what we would expect in a Western poem. The Yaksha and his beloved are joined in their separation by the continuous chain of people and other beings whom the cloud will

encounter on its way, and we as readers can identify with these interme-
diary figures as much as with the lovers at the two ends of the signifying
chain. As the cloud sets out,

> Women whose men travel far roads will look up,
> brushing hair from their eyes to see you crossing
> the sky, their hearts lifted remembering what
> you bring. (21)

Memory is a crucial term here, according well with Anandavardhana's and
Abhinavagupta's poetics. Their immensely influential theory of *rasadhvani*
or "relished suggestion" explains, among other things, how audiences can
enjoy representations of painful events without becoming overwhelmed
by them. When the poem's speaker suffers grief at loss or separation, this
grief will stimulate memories of similar events in our own past. Experiencing these remembered traumas in conjunction with the poetic scene,
we listeners will feel compassion for the speaker, and our own memories
will be purified and freed from self-obsession. Through this process, self-
regarding sorrow "becomes the flavor of compassion," as Abhinavagupta
comments, "which differs from ordinary grief by its being experienced
primarily as a melting of one's thoughts" (Ingalls et al., *Dhvanyaloka*, 115).
The intense sociality of Sanskrit poetry yields at once an ethics and a poetics of compassion.

On this understanding, we can turn to the final stanza of the *Meghadūta*,
in which the key term "compassion" appropriately appears in Nathan's
translation:

> Having done this favor for me (who asked more
> than I should have asked), whether from friendship or compassion
> for my lonely state, now wander, Cloud,
> wherever you will, your glory swelled by rain.
> And may you never—even for an instant—be
> parted, like me, from your lightning. (89)

Kālidāsa's floating signifier shouldn't be understood as revealing a de
Manian aporia, as though the cloud can never carry out a metaphoric
transfer of meaning but is doomed to suffer a metonymic effacement as it

wanders across India. Yet it would be a mistake to conclude that an externally derived deconstructionist reading has now been falsified by an authoritative Indian poetics. Anandavardhana and Abhinavagupta lived half a millennium after Kālidāsa, and they were great systematizers of a varied and even unruly poetic tradition. They were also theologians as well as rhetoricians. They had agendas of their own, not unlike the Confucian commentators who allegorized the erotic poems in the Chinese *Book of Songs,* or the biblical tradition that softened the radicalism of Ecclesiastes. Anandavardhana and Abhinavagupta downplay the tendency of passion to escape the boundaries of compassion, unlike Kālidāsa, who was complicating the ethical framework within which he was nonetheless still writing. Derrida—and indeed Wimsatt—can help us understand dimensions of the *Meghadūta* not accounted for in *rasadhvani* theory, even as Sanskrit poetics provides a crucial check against a too direct application of contemporary theory to the dilatory drifting of a compassionate cloud.

The challenge for comparatists today is to develop what Sheldon Pollock has called "Comparison without Hegemony." This is a subject with a variety of dimensions, to which we will return in the final chapter, but a prerequisite for such comparison will be an opening out of "Theory" beyond its Euro-translation-zone. If we work against the great-power dynamics still prevalent in much theoretical discussion, we can mitigate the hegemonic tendencies long baked into comparative studies. Both in theory and in practice, we have a long way to go if we want to have a world literary theory worth the name.

5

Languages

In the months leading up to his fourth birthday, René Étiemble lost his father and discovered world literature. Though he was a precocious reader, a literary life was hardly in the cards for him. He was born in 1909 to working-class parents in Mayenne, a rural town in northwest France, where his parents had left school by age thirteen. His mother became a milliner; his father was a salesman before succumbing at age twenty-seven to tuberculosis, leaving his widow to support herself and their seven children with the hats she sold to a local clientele. As often as possible, Étiemble escaped the tiny apartment where the family shared a single bedroom and ensconced himself in the building's attic. There he found a trove of old books, together with back issues of the *Mayenne-Journal*, which was published on the ground floor. He fell in love with an illustrated edition of *Don Quixote* and discovered many more tales of travel and adventure. As he says in the opening chapter of his *Ouverture(s) sur un comparatisme planétaire*, "thanks to the attic where I spent as much time as I could from the time I knew how to read and write—that is, at three years and a half—unawares I discovered comparatism: I was unwittingly impregnated with it" (20–21). The chapter is titled "Le Tour du monde dans un grenier: ou, Naissance d'un comparatiste" (Around the world in an attic: or, Birth of a comparatist).

The future novelist and Sorbonne professor was reading only in French, and he might well have focused his exceptional energies on French literature, but he was fascinated by the foreign phrases that kept cropping up in his reading: a Russian prisoner who sighed that *doucha bolit*, "the soul hurts," an Algonquin *squaw* in her *wigwam*. Amid the often racist portrayals of primitive or malevolent Sioux, Iroquois, and Hurons, "it was the words of their languages that I fervently recorded" (25). Reading an African travelogue, he was transfixed by an untranslated phrase: "*La allah il-allah, Mohammed rasoul oullahi*, according to the transcription that I have verified in the recent republication of the famous *Voyage à Tombouctou*" (22). Though he didn't know he was encountering the Muslim profession of faith, "it was Arabic, there, before my eyes, in my attic where the 'mother' of vinegar [*mère du vinaigre*] did its work in an enormous bottle much taller than me!" (23).[1]

By age six he was reading the *Petit Larousse illustré* from A to Z. "The foreign alphabets that were shown there plunged me into a joy at once intense and uneasy. Though I could recognize fourteen of the capital letters in the Russian alphabet, I couldn't understand why the B had to be pronounced *v*, why the H became an *n*, the P an *r*, and the C an *s*; but who could I ask?" (25). He appealed to the printer of the *Mayenne-Journal*, but the printer had never even heard of Cyrillic. Equally enticing was his first encounter with the Mexican salamander: "The word *axolotl* seemed mysterious to me: perhaps because of these tiny creatures' mode of existence, but above all, above all, because of the ending in *-tl*. That was familiar to me in medial position, a*tl*as, A*tl*antic, there it seemed self-evident. But in final position? Who ever heard of that?" (30).

Étiemble was as precocious in writing as in reading. In his 1988 memoir *Lignes d'une vie*, he includes a photocopy of what he describes as "mon premier 'oeuvre,'" a New Year's letter he'd written to his mother seventy-five years earlier, a month before his fifth birthday (figure 5). Already his sentences are perfectly formed in elegant handwriting, as he tells his mother that he loves her with all his heart, and he hopes that his letter will help "à faire un peu oublier la grande peine de petit Père"—to forget

---

[1] Étiemble's fascination with the *Voyage à Tombouctou* can hardly have been random. Its author, René Caillié (1799–1838), was an adventurer and linguist who not only shared Étiemble's first name but had also been born in poverty and had lost his parents as a child. Having left his village to seek his fortune, he learned Arabic in order to visit Timbuktu (then closed to Europeans) disguised as a Muslim pilgrim. He published his wildly popular three-volume travelogue in 1830, then died eight years later—like Étiemble's father, of tuberculosis.

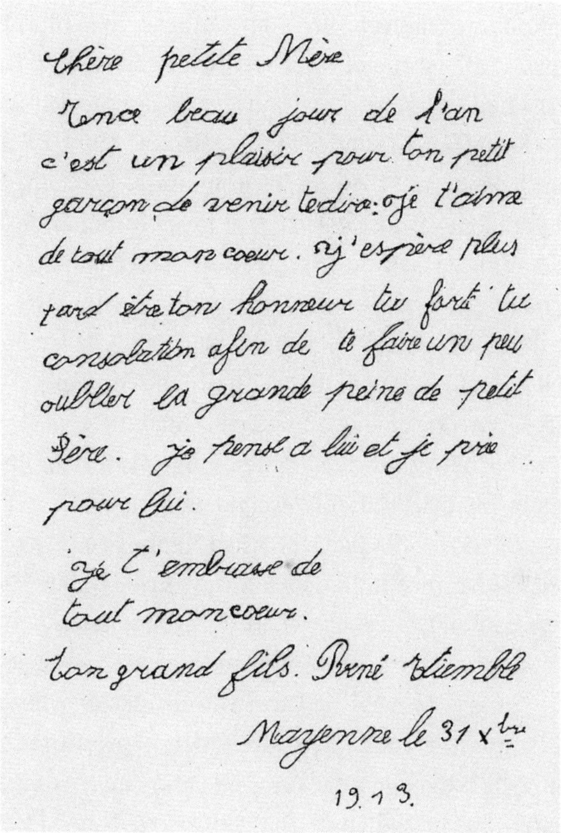

Chère petite Mère
bonne beau jour de l'an
c'est un plaisir pour ton petit
garçon de venir te dire: je t'aime
de tout mon coeur. j'espère plus
tard être ton honneur tu fort tu
consolation afin de te faire un peu
oublier la grande peine de petit
Père. je pense a lui et je prie
pour lui.

je t'embrase de
tout mon coeur.
ton grand fils. René Etiemble
Mayenne le 31 Xbre
1913.

FIGURE 5. René Étiemble, letter to his mother, December 31, 1913. Courtesy of Sylvie Étiemble.

a little the great sorrow of the loss of his dear father. After saying that he thinks of his father and prays for him, he ends with a formal flourish: "Je t'embrasse de tout mon coeur. Ton grand fils, René Étiemble" (I embrace you with all my heart. Your big boy, René Étiemble [89]).

At the end of World War I, his mother found a practical use for her eight-year-old's linguistic abilities: she had him given English lessons, so that he could help her sell hats and chemises to the American G.I.s in town, as presents to their new French girlfriends. Three years later, he so impressed his schoolteachers that he was awarded a scholarship to attend secondary school in Laval, the district capital, where he learned Latin, Greek, and German. Many more languages were to come, first at the École

Normale Supérieure, where he took up Chinese, and then in worldwide travels far beyond the scope of René Caillié's African adventures.

Étiemble studied an exceptional variety of languages, including Arabic, Chinese, Egyptian hieroglyphics, German, Hungarian, Japanese, Malay, Nahuatl, Persian, Portuguese, Romanian, Russian, Spanish, and Turkish, and yet he never lost his visceral love of French. In 1964 he published a best-selling attack on the creeping Americanization of French, *Parlez-vous franglais?*, and he later affirmed to an interviewer that "ma langue, c'est donc, ma patrie" (Karátson, "Étiemble et les langues," 132). Asked why he hadn't rested content with French, he replied that as a boy he was painfully aware of the limited circumstances of his upbringing, an awareness sharpened by the higher vulgarity of his mother's well-to-do customers, who would condescend to him while refusing to pay the bills he'd deliver on his bicycle. Alice Kaplan could escape the constraints of her Midwestern milieu by learning French, but Étiemble's mastery of French couldn't erase the class difference from people to whom such phrases as "je t'embrasse de tout mon coeur" were second nature. As he told his interviewer, "I had to flee, no matter where, 'out of the world' that was mine, through the 'foreignizing' privilege of foreign languages." Learning languages, he says, became "my revenge against the other vulgarity, that of the caste that imprisoned me" (127). What the French *r* would be for Alice Kaplan half a century later, the Nahuatl *tl* became for him.

Étiemble deployed his exuberant linguistic range in many of his works. To take an example from his *Essais de littérature (vraiment) générale*, in "Sur quelques adaptations et imitations de *haiku*" he quotes poems in Japanese, French, English, Italian, Spanish, Russian, Croatian, German, and modern Greek. Yet he was well aware that he could only access a fraction of the world's languages, and he became a fierce advocate for translation. Always an activist, in 1958 he founded a major series of works in translation, Connaissance de l'Orient, published by Gallimard in collaboration with UNESCO. To date 120 volumes have been published in the series, which has sections devoted to China, India, Japan, Korea, Vietnam, Persia, Central Asia, ancient Egypt, and Arabic literature.

In his edgy survey of the discipline in 1963, *Comparaison n'est pas raison* (*The Crisis in Comparative Literature*), Étiemble highlighted the importance of translation for the next generation of comparatists. "How many years will it take," he asks, "to prepare the comparatist who will be capable of practicing and teaching his discipline around 1990 or 2000?" (20). He observes that in France (as in the United States), few people grow up with the fluency in several languages possessed by central European émigrés such as René Wellek, then adds: "If one must rely on tyrannies and revolutions, and on émigrés alone to recruit comparatists, it will be a long time indeed before we have competent masters in sufficient numbers" (20). He remarks that the only practical solution even for a polyglot like himself is to make regular use of translations:

> To the extent that my dual capacity of professor and novelist forces me to be interested in the theory of the literary genre I practice, I know all the benefits I drew from reading the *Genji Monogatari* in Waley's English version, or the *Shilappadikaram* translated from Tamil into French, or furthermore the Vietnamese novel *Kim Van Kiêu* in the version recently produced by Dr. Nguyen Tran Huan. If he has not read the *Hizakurige*, even in an English translation, or the *Si Yeou Ki*, even in a French version, or Tolstoi and Dostoievski, even in German translation, what European will dare to speak of the novel in general? (23)

Three decades before Lawrence Venuti published *The Translator's Invisibility*, Étiemble noted that translators were rarely paid a living wage; translation was often a hobby of men of leisure or a poorly compensated form of women's work. He argued that comparative literature programs should begin to treat translation "not as an occupation for ladies or dilettantes but with respect and as one of the essential tasks of our discipline" (25). He advocated greatly expanding comparatists' linguistic preparation: "Let us train, as quickly as possible, translators capable of handling, without distorting them, Hungarian, Bengali, Finnish, Tamil, Chinese, Tibetan, Malagasy" (25). Driving his point home with polemical brio, he declared: "Provided that he pretends to be engaged in 'research,' any imbecile with an index file will be able to obtain a fellowship, funds, an Institute of his own, and will have no difficulty in publishing junk, scraps of garbage, whereas translators, in whom comparative literature is interested only as 'intermediaries,' seem to him quite unfit to live" (25).

The challenge of language has only increased in the half-century since Étiemble wrote these sardonic words. Even imbeciles with their own institutes—myself included—must now be engaged with translation to an extent that Étiemble himself might not have anticipated. This is not only a result of the expansion of the field to areas not previously studied. Programs can no longer assume that every student comes to graduate school knowing French and German and probably Latin as well as English; still less can such common linguistic knowledge be assumed for the many students from other departments who enroll in our courses. "National" literature departments themselves now teach a substantial proportion of courses in translation, and translations play a key role in most comparative literature courses today, even when the instructor and some of the students can read the originals.

Fortunately, the quality of literary translation has steadily grown during the past several decades. In 1988 Étiemble complained that "whoever has read Mishima in the French translations concocted from the English versions has read no more than a spin-off of the real Mishima, a thousandfold more deadened than by his *seppuku*" (*Ouverture(s)*, 167). Today, Mishima's works are translated into French by Japanologists such as Gérard Siary, who lived in Japan for eight years before becoming a professor of comparative literature in Montpellier. The quality of translations has grown considerably, and their sheer quantity has increased exponentially. New translations of Homer and of Dante appear almost annually, and major non-Western works are often freshly retranslated as well. Though Étiemble had a working knowledge of Japanese, he read the *Genji Monogatari* in Arthur Waley's classic English translation. In the 1960s his only option in French would have been a 1928 translation—heavily indebted to Waley—of just nine of Murasaki's fifty-four chapters. But since then, a full French translation has appeared (René Sieffert's *Le Dit du Genji*, 1988), as have no fewer than three new English translations, by Edward Seidensticker (1976), Royall Tyler (2001), and Dennis Washburn (2016), and all have been widely reviewed in the general press.[2] The *Genji* is now available in many smaller-market languages as well, often translated directly from Japanese, as with the Romanian *Povestea lui Genji* (2017), which appeared in a deluxe illustrated edition underwritten by the Japan Foundation; it sold out within a year.

Excellent translations have also been made of many modern works, including from the rarely studied languages listed by Étiemble. A Hungarian example is the great novelist Sándor Márai, who spent four decades writing in isolation after he fled Hungary in 1948. He settled in the United States, working for Radio Free Europe, and published his postwar books in limited editions for the exile community. Unknown in his adopted country and largely forgotten at home, he committed suicide in 1989. His work seemed destined to vanish forever, until the Italian writer and publisher Roberto Calasso chanced upon his novel *Embers* in 1998 in a French translation and realized that he'd discovered a major writer. *Embers* became a posthumous international best seller, and English translations are now available in paperback of several of his works, including his darkly ironic *Casanova in Bolzano* and his moving, fractured *Portraits of a Marriage*. By now he has been translated into many other languages as well, including Catalan, Dutch, Icelandic, Korean, Polish, and Urdu.

To take the example of Tamil, no fewer than seven anthologies of Tamil poetry have appeared in English just since 2010. Western readers long favored premodern Asian works, such as the epic *Shilappadikaram* that Étiemble mentions, which he had published in his Connaissance de l'Orient series (*Le Roman de l'anneau*, 1961, published in English as *The Ankle Bracelet* in a retranslation from the French). But modern Tamil literature is now also readily available, and the prolific Perumal Murugan is translated almost as quickly as a major French or German writer would be. His controversial novel *Madhorubhagan* (2010), which features a woman

---

[2] The vogue for Homer translations has directly benefited the *Genji*. As Royall Tyler's translation went to press, Penguin increased its budget and produced an elegant two-volume edition graced with woodcuts. "Eventually," Tyler says, "I asked Penguin in New York why they had treated so grandly a massive novel written a thousand years ago in Japan. They told me the deciding factor had been the commercial success of Robert Fagles' translations of the *Iliad* and the *Odyssey*" ("Translating *The Tale of Genji*").

seeking to become pregnant through a sexual encounter at a temple dedicated to a hermaphrodite deity, won a translation prize when it appeared from Penguin India in 2013 under the title *One Part Woman* and was then brought out in England the next year. Clearly sensing an opportunity, Penguin published four more of his books in 2017.

The situation is a good deal better than it was in the 1960s, but the question of language remains crucial and highly problematic. The rise of global English leaves many literary scholars all too comfortably ensconced within the imperium of English. Meanwhile, the steady decline in humanities enrollments puts language instruction at risk in many places. Though many more works are now being brought into English with considerable success, translators themselves are always aware of how much they have been unable to convey of the beauty of the originals and of the cultural contexts that the works embody or presuppose. It is always the responsibility of a teacher or interpreter to determine how much contextual information, and of what sort, is needed in order to understand and appreciate a work "on its own terms," or more precisely, in terms of the particular approach and understanding that the teacher or critic wishes to impart. That said, the challenge of contextualization is all the greater with works read in translation, as language carries literary, historical, and cultural references that often aren't easy to convey in a new idiom. Introductions and footnotes can do a good deal, but translators always have to pick their battles, especially when confronted with meanings that are closely tied to wordplay and stylistic nuances.

Étiemble rightly stressed the pressing need for translators who can produce versions of real literary value, but the problems of translation aren't resolved simply by a translator's fluency and poetic sensitivity. Étiemble's advocacy for translation was itself phrased in terms that can't be directly translated into English. In the original French, he plays on the classic Italian formulation of untranslatability, *traduttore traditore* ("the translator, a traitor"), when he urges programs to train "traducteurs capables de ne trahir" their sources. Étiemble is clearly echoing the Italian adage, but his translators, Herbert Weisinger and Georges Joyaux, couldn't find an English equivalent. They opted for the milder "translators capable of handling, without distorting" the originals—thereby distorting Étiemble's own prose even as they handled it as best they could.

The very title of Étiemble's book, *Comparaison n'est pas raison,* involves an untranslatable play between comparison and error or unreasonability ("n'est pas raison"). Unable to reproduce this in English, Weisinger and Joyaux dropped it altogether and took their title from Étiemble's subtitle, *La crise de la littérature comparée.* Yet this change shouldn't be seen simply in negative terms. Most forcefully in *Contra Instrumentalism* (2019), Lawrence Venuti has argued that the entire language of loss and gain should be abandoned, as it implies an essentialist view of an invariant original, seen in such "proverbs of untranslatability" (83) as "traduttore traditore." He advocates a hermeneutic understanding that sees translations, like all interpretations, as activating some but not other aspects of the original, as a work becomes reoriented toward the needs and interests of a new audience or interpretive community. That said, there are more and less effective translations, just as there are more and less persuasive interpretations. Even apart from outright blunders, run-of-the-mill translations often lose important aspects of the original without achieving any significant hermeneutic insight, whereas the best translations resituate works in effective ways. Weisinger and Joyaux had to forgo the oxymoronic wit of Étiemble's original title, but their choice of *The Crisis in Comparative Literature* highlights the urgency of the subject, and it resonated with René Wellek's 1960 essay "The Crisis of Comparative Literature," which Étiemble evokes on his first page. In this respect, the English title effectively represents what Venuti would call an interpretive inscription of the text into a new context (*Translation Changes Everything,* 101).[3]

In the realm of language, what we need to know in order to undertake comparative studies isn't a common set of three or four languages, western European or otherwise, nor do we need to achieve near-native fluency in every language we study in order to be able to use them at all. But each

---

[3] Sometimes such changes do actually improve on the original. When my book *How to Read World Literature* was translated into Turkish, I found that my can-do English title had become a pleasingly optative interrogative, *Dünya Edebiyatı Nasıl Okunmalı?* (How Should World Literature Be Read?).

of us does need to know whichever languages are most important for our teaching and research, and we need to decide just how well we need to know each of them for our purposes. We also need to know how to work intelligently with translations when necessary, and for this purpose it is important to gain a good grounding in the field of translation studies. Most fundamentally, we need to use originals and translations alike in active awareness of the deeply intertwined problems of language and of politics that confront every use of language today.

"His French Really Isn't That Good"

In my student days in the 1970s, the ideal for an American comparatist was to have a really good *accent* in French and German. You might be a Romanticist or a modernist, a humanist or a deconstructionist, and you might also work in other languages, but French and German were the price of admission to the discipline. A good accent was a prime signifier of seriousness and sophistication, though if you were an émigré there could actually be a certain cachet in speaking English with a heavy accent. But the ability to speak "good" or "pure" French or German was a means of self-affirmation if all else failed. Coming out of a class of Paul de Man's one day, after a dense session on figural language in Rousseau or Proust, one of my classmates shook her head and remarked, "But you know, his French really isn't that good." What she meant was that his French really wasn't very Parisian. De Man grew up speaking French at home, but he spent little time in France and never lost his Belgian accent. My classmate could comfort herself on a superior accent even if she, like me, was having trouble following his theories.

The stress on mastering two or three foreign languages partly reflected comparative literature's philological roots, but it equally had to do with the discipline's strategies for positioning itself within the academic ecosystem. As comparatists began to elbow their way into American colleges and universities, the less sympathetic souls in the national literature departments responded with charges of amateurism and superficiality, to which the ambitious comparatist could reply by proposing a mutually productive symbiosis. Far from denying the value of the national traditions, comparative literature would set them in a glittering international frame, while meeting the national specialists on the common ground of fluency in the languages needed for the comparison. Language was key to this line of defense, not only to justify the existence of comparative literature as a discipline but also as the basis for a territorial accommodation with the national literature departments.

Fortified with their cosmopolitan multilingualism, comparatists could make connections across linguistic borders far better than could the typical professor of French or Italian, who might have a shaky grasp of German and none at all of Russian. At the same time, however, the practitioners of the new discipline tacitly agreed to avoid trespassing unduly on their rivals' linguistic home turf. They themselves might hold a joint appointment in English or French, and they could periodically work on English or French writers alone, but they would do so with their bowler or beret firmly in place for the occasion. The essays they would publish in *English Literary History* or *Yale French Studies* would be clearly distinct from the ones they would publish in *Comparative Literature* or the *Revue de littérature comparée*.

This division of academic territory meant that comparative studies were almost always conducted across linguistic as well as national borders, ceding to national literature specialists their long-held primacy in their "national language" of choice, even when the language in question was distributed across a variety of countries. So a dissertation in comparative literature could be written on Mann, Proust, and Joyce, but not on Mann, Kafka, and Hesse, a grouping that would be left within the purview of the "national" literature specialists despite the equally international quality of the comparison between works written by Mann in Germany, Kafka in Prague, and Hesse in Switzerland. When it came to multilingual societies, on the other hand, the focus shifted from the national language to the national borders, leaving American literature to Americanists and the vernacular literatures of India to South Asianists, no matter how many Americans might speak Spanish or Navajo, or how much literature has been written in the two dozen languages recognized by the Sahitya Akademi.

The time has come to abandon this all too neat division of territory. The one-to-one identification of nation and language was almost always a fiction, and it is becoming more and more tenuous today, even in the case of many small countries with a national language rarely spoken beyond their borders. A full view of contemporary Israeli literature should include writing in Arabic, Russian, and Yiddish as well as Hebrew, and Romanian literature includes the work of the Nobel Prize winners Eugène Ionesco in French and Herta Müller in German as well as Andrei Codrescu and Norman Manea in America, writing in English and Romanian, respectively. On this perspective, a multilingual comparative study can well concern writers from a single country, and with a widespread language such as Arabic, English, or Portuguese, a comparative study can encompass works written not just in three neighboring countries but on three different continents.

Throughout the twentieth century, comparatists staked out their linguistic high ground at a defensible middle range. Comparatists would work in more languages than national literature specialists would—but not *too many* more. Only as many foreign languages as an individual could more or less master would be required, three being the norm, usually selected from the largest of the "NATO-literatures." By 1975, however, the ACLA's Greene Report was aware of the challenge posed by the rising tide of globalization: if the discipline's high goal really was to seek broader perspectives and more general understandings, why stop at the borders of Europe? As Greene noted with evident unease,

> There has also arisen widespread and growing interest in the non-European literatures–Chinese, Japanese, Sanskrit, Arabic, and many others less familiar. . . . A new vision of *global* literature is emerging, embracing all the verbal creativity during the history of our planet, a vision which will soon begin to make our comfortable European perspectives parochial. Few Comparatists, few scholars anywhere, are prepared for the dizzying implications of this widening of horizons, but they cannot be ignored. (30)

Hoisted by its own petard, the discipline was finding itself vulnerable to the very charges of narrowness and parochialism that it had formerly leveled against its rivals in the national literatures. The novelty of this situation is signaled by Greene's use of italics to designate the new vision of "*global* literature," and yet Greene wasn't questioning the value of embracing the creativity of writers around the globe; he simply couldn't reconcile such a project with his commitment to deep engagement with works in the original languages and to studying literary relations within a common cultural tradition. His readings of Renaissance *imitatio* depended on many years spent reading Petrarch, Ronsard, Wyatt, and their Latin forebears, line by line and word by word. Working in the four languages he knew well, Greene entered as fully into his poets' world as any national literature specialist could require.

As the purview of comparative literature expands, language becomes a severe challenge. Not just individual scholars but entire departments can't hope to embrace the dozens of languages represented in today's world literature anthologies. What role can classic, philologically based comparison have in the brave new world of world literature today? Too often, the answer appears to be: none. Not only many introductory survey courses but also Franco Moretti's scholarly program of "distant reading" presuppose a substantial if not entire reliance on translation. In "Conjectures on World Literature" (2000), Moretti recommends that we rely on literary histories and publication statistics to chart the global flow of the novel. He advances this program as the way to break through the philological impasse: "Many people have read more and better than I have, of course, but still, we are talking of hundreds of languages and literatures here. . . . But I actually think that it's our greatest chance, because the sheer enormity of the task makes it clear that world literature cannot be literature, bigger; what we are already doing, just more of it. It has to be different" (45–46). Yet the differential nature of a global perspective shouldn't entail abandoning the philological grounding of classic comparative studies; we need to develop better ways of working both with original texts and in translation. More languages, then, as well as more use of translation. But is translation even possible without severe linguistic distortions, ethical compromises, and negative political effects?

Translating the Untranslatable

Attitudes toward translation have long oscillated between the extremes of ubiquity and impossibility. These are well captured in the set of twenty "Theses on Translation" with which Emily Apter opens *The Translation*

Zone (2006). The first of these is "Nothing is translatable"; the last is "Everything is translatable" (xi–xii). Assumptions of untranslatability are often as much ideological as linguistic, as when an ineffable sacred language is held to be the only medium in which the divine message can be fully conveyed. Thus the Qur'an is widely considered to be untranslatable— a stance that hasn't at all impeded its worldwide dissemination, both in Arabic and in what a nonbeliever might think are translations. These have traditionally been presented as interpretations, as with Muhammad Muhsin Khan's bilingual edition, *Interpretation of the Meanings of the Noble Qur'an in the English Language* (2011). In a way, this stance dovetails with the hermeneutic theories of George Steiner and Lawrence Venuti, though the Qur'anic view presupposes a resolutely invariant original that retains absolute priority over any "interpretation" into another language. Though this understanding is theologically grounded, it isn't necessary to be a Muslim to agree that the Qur'an's Arabic carries a spiritual value independent of verbal comprehension, as anyone can attest who has heard verses performed by a devout reciter imbued with a poetic sensibility. So strong is the attraction of the original that Muslims in Turkey, Iran, and Indonesia have often memorized the entire Arabic text even if they know no Arabic themselves.

At the other extreme, the story of Pentecost celebrates a kind of hypertranslatability. As "divided tongues" settle upon the heads of the apostles, each of them receives the ability to speak "in other languages, as the Spirit gave them ability" (Acts 2:4, New Revised Standard Version). Pentecostals today trace their practice of glossolalia to this event, a practice that Apter (following Daniel Heller-Roazen) presents in *Against World Literature* as the epitome of untranslatability. Saint Paul discusses the incomprehensibility of glossolalia elsewhere (1 Corinthians 14), but what the passage in Acts describes is the apostles' God-given ability to communicate with the entire crowd of foreigners gathering around them in Jerusalem. The amazed listeners ask themselves:

Are not all these who are speaking Galileans? And how is it that we hear, each of us, in our own native language? Parthians, Medes, Elamites, and residents of Mesopotamia, Judea and Cappadocia,

Pontus and Asia, Phrygia and Pamphylia, Egypt and the parts of Libya belonging to Cyrene, and visitors from Rome, both Jews and proselytes, Cretans and Arabs—in our own languages we hear them speaking about God's deeds of power. (Acts 2:7–11)

The passage implies that each of the fifteen groups has its own native language; as there are only twelve apostles speaking, the translation may be taking place in the listeners' ears rather than in the speakers' mouths. In either event, the result is an outpouring of simultaneous translation on a scale not again seen until the invention of Google Translate. The story of Pentecost thus advances a pragmatics of full translatability, highly appropriate to a work focused on the "acts" (*práxeis*) of the apostles.

Occupying a middle ground are understandings of translation as possible but undesirable, as when a minority group resists having its secrets conveyed to outsiders or refuses to allow a hegemonic language to swamp the local language and its traditions. This is the "militant semiotic intransigence" that Apter describes in *Against World Literature* (34). Though this need can be felt with particular urgency by oppressed or minority populations, George Steiner has argued that this self-protective drive is fundamental to all linguistic communities. "The outwardly communicative, extrovert thrust of language is secondary," he says;

the primary drive is inward and domestic. Each tongue hoards the resources of consciousness, the word-pictures of the clan. . . . [A] language builds a wall around the "middle kingdom" of the group's identity. It is secret towards the outsider and inventive of its own world. There have been so many thousands of human tongues, there still are, because there have been, particularly in the archaic stages of social history, so many distinct groups intent on keeping from one another the inherited, singular springs of their identity, and engaged in creating their own semantic worlds, their "alternities." (*After Babel*, 212–13)

Very differently, untranslatability can be enforced, as when Church authorities took away Rabelais's Greek New Testament, not wanting him to have a linguistic basis to challenge the authority of the Latin Vulgate and its orthodox interpreters. Appropriately in this context, the biblical description of the apostles' "divided tongues" (*diamerizómenai glōssai*) is based on the verb *diamerízō*, which means "to divide" but also "to cause dissension."

Ideas of untranslatability were heightened during the modernist period, when writers were praised for writing difficult works in a style uniquely their own. In 1902 Benedetto Croce emphasized "the irreducible individuality of the aesthetic fact" and argued that literary language is inherently untranslatable (*Aesthetic*, 146). The challenge of translation was especially great in the case of works such as Marinetti's sound poem "Zang Tumb Tumb" or Eliot's *The Waste Land*, but the modernists often regarded far more accessible works as untranslatable as well. Robert Frost famously declared that "poetry is what is lost in translation," a statement that critics of translation have often cited as a general truth. Yet, as Venuti has shown, Frost's view rested on a very particular—and debatable—poetics, grounded in a quasimystical belief in the inseparability of poetry and prose alike from the "sentence-sounds" of the author's language (*Contra Instrumentalism*, 109–18). People who quote Frost's dictum, moreover, rarely give his full statement, which he made to his friend Louis Untermeyer concerning possible interpretations of his poem "Stopping by Woods on a Snowy Evening." As he remarked, "You've often heard me say—perhaps too often—that poetry is what is lost in translation. It is also what is lost in interpretation. That little poem means just what it says it means, nothing less but nothing more" (Untermeyer, *Robert Frost*, 18). Any scholar who endorses Frost on untranslatability should give up writing literary criticism as well.

In *Against World Literature: On the Politics of Untranslatability* (2013), Apter doubled down on untranslatability, elevating it from a section of *The Translation Zone* to become the theme of the new book. Along with glossolalia, Arabic serves as a prime testing-ground for untranslatability. Apter has a chapter centered on Abdelfattah Kilito's *Lan tatakalama lughati* (2002), elegantly translated into English by Waïl Hassan as *Thou Shalt Not Speak My Language*, in which the Moroccan writer and theorist declares, "I used to think it my duty to endeavor as best I could to make my language radiate its brilliance, to increase the number of its learners, and so forth. But that noble goal disappeared when I realized that I dislike having foreigners speak my language" (87). He had this realization when an American woman used the colloquial phrase *wallahila* as a general expression of surprise, without realizing that it contains the name of Allah. As Apter says, Kilito's discomfort involves "the problem of sacred language used in ignorance as well as the issue of broken trust among native speakers in the face of foreign entry into their language world," leading him to formulate "something like a divine right to untranslatability" (254).

Yet Kilito's resistance isn't based on any sacral essence of Arabic but is a cultural-political stance, and other members of the same community may not share his view. Kilito himself had no objection to the translation of his attack on translation, which appeared in French in the year of its initial publication in 2002 and in Waïl Hassan's lucid English translation in 2008. In 2013 Kilito published a countervailing volume, in French, under the title *Je parle toutes les langues, mais en arabe* (I speak every language, but in Arabic). In this (as yet untranslated) collection of essays and reviews, he offers judicious assessments of translations of Arabic works and resumes helping Moroccan literature "radiate its brilliance" abroad as well as at home. Like many Moroccan intellectuals, he writes both in Arabic and in French, and in *La Langue d'Adam* (1996; *The Tongue of Adam*, 2016) he affirms multilingualism as the original human condition, not in terms of the "divided tongues" of Pentecost but by identifying ironically with the forked tongue of the serpent in Eden.

We saw in the last chapter that Roland Greene's friend was mistaken in supposing that there were two Barbara Johnsons, the deconstructionist and the African-Americanist, but we might well say that there are two Abdelfattah Kilitos: the Arabic essayist-novelist and the French professor and theorist, holder of a PhD from the Sorbonne, who in the year he published *La Langue d'Adam* actually received the "Prix du rayonnement de la langue française" from the Académie Française. Even in *Thou Shall Not Speak My Language*, as Shaden Tageldin has said, "the 'untranslatability' of Arabic unfurls, for Kilito, along a Möbius strip that ever twists it toward translatability" ("Untranslatability," 235). Taken together, Kilito's books more fully illustrate both sides of Emily Apter's 2006 theses on translation than she suggests in *Against World Literature*: nothing is translatable, and everything is translatable.

Writing between Languages

Disparate and often conflicting languages intertwine in the lives of exiles and emigrants. This theme goes back at least as far as Ovid's *Tristia*, in which he movingly describes his struggle to retain his poetic fluency in Latin during his unending exile on the shores of the Black Sea:

> Verba mihi desunt dedicique loci.
> Threicio Scythicoque fere circumsonor ore,
> et videor Geticis scribere posse modis.
> Crede mihi, timeo ne sint inmixta Latinis
> inqua meis scriptis Pontica verba legas.
> (*Tristia* III.xiv.46–50)

> I've unlearnt the art of speech.
> Around me Thracian and Scythian voices resound,
> and I think I could write verse in Getic style.
> Believe me, I fear you may find Pontic terms
> in my Latin writings, all mixed in.
> (*Poems of Exile*, 63)

Osip Mandelstam evoked Ovid in his poem "Tristia," and the British poet Geoffrey Hill evoked both of them in "Tristia 1891–1938," subtitled "A Valediction to Osip Mandelstam": "Difficult friend, I would have preferred / You to them. The dead keep their sealed lives / And again I am too late. / . . . Images rear from desolation / like ruins upon a plain" (*Selected Poems*, 43). Neither Mandelstam's Russian nor Ovid's Latin appears in this landscape of loss, but the next poem in Hill's collection, "The Imaginative Life," recalls "Evasive souls, of whom we lose track," and ends with a single, resonant Latin word in its final line: "As though the dead had *Finis* on their brows" (44).

A growing body of literature probes the losses and the new possibilities of writing as a stranger in a strange language, and a number of writers have taken displaced translators as their protagonists. Sammar, the heroine of Leila Aboulela's *The Translator* (2006), is a Sudanese immigrant who works as an Arabic translator in wintry Aberdeen, providing translations for Rae Isles, a leftist Orientalist who has books by Fanon and Said on his shelves. A romance begins to grow up between them, but Sammar is shocked when a friend tells her that Rae is "an agnostic"—a word she has never heard before—or even an atheist. When she responds that Rae has spoken of the Qur'an as "a sacred text," her friend replies: "That's the way they do research nowadays. It's a modern thing. Something to do with not being Eurocentric" (93–94).

Though Sammar (like her author) had been schooled in English in Khartoum, she struggles in Scotland to find a place for herself in a world of unknown words, from "Sixties scene" to "Wonderbra." She wants to find her favorite spice, *habbahan*, but the word isn't included in her Arabic-English dictionaries. "She must walk around the supermarket, frantically searching for something she could not ask about, and she was a translator, she should know. . . . At last she found the *habbahan*. It existed, it had a name: whole green cardamom" (97). Unable to feel at home in Aberdeen and unwilling to become involved with an unbeliever, Sammar returns to Khartoum. Months later, she receives a letter in Arabic from a mutual friend, who says that Rae has converted and hopes that Sammar would be willing to have him visit. "He was cautious like that. And now asking . . . It made her smile. She had an airmail letter pad with her, a ball-point pen, two envelopes. She was going to write two letters in two languages. They would say the same thing but not be a translation" (190).

Perhaps no novel has more fully embodied the complexities of a life in translation than Christine Brooke-Rose's comic, melancholic novel *Between* (1968). Her unnamed heroine is a simultaneous translator who spends much of her time in the air, flying from one conference to another, "as if inside a giant centipede. Or else inside the whale, who knows, three hours, three days of maybe hell. Between doing and not doing the body floats" (395). Brooke-Rose was born in Geneva to an English father and an American-Swiss mother, then educated in Brussels and in England. She began her career writing experimental novels in England, then moved to France in 1968, the year she published *Between*. A friend of Alain Robbe-Grillet and other practitioners of the *nouveau roman*, she used grammatical constraints in a number of her works. In *Between*, silently expressing her heroine's lack of a stable identity, neither the pronoun "I" nor any form of the verb "to be" ever appears.

The novel includes scenes in England, France, Spain, Italy, Germany, Poland, Yugoslavia, Greece, Turkey, and the United States. The pace of the heroine's multinational life is such that actions keep repeating themselves, in language after language, and one hotel room merges into another:

> At any minute now some bright or elderly or sour no young and buxom chambermaid in black and white will come in with a breakfast-tray, put it down on the table in the dark and draw back the curtains unless open the shutters and say Buenos días, Morgen or kalimera who knows, it all depends where the sleeping has occurred out of what dream shaken up with non merci nein danke no thank you in a long-lost terror of someone offering etwas anderes, not ordered. (396)

Brooke-Rose's heroine suffers less from untranslatability than from a decidedly non-Pentecostal hypertranslatability, as her thoughts are continually battered about in a blizzard of languages. In his book *In Babel's Shadow* (2010), Brian Lennon presents translation "as a victory and a threat, a necessity and a violation" (1). He discusses *Between* as a prime example of "strong multilingualism" that probes the limits of translation and of language itself.

Lennon begins his book with an epigraph from the Japanese-German writer Yoko Tawada, in which she expresses impatience with people who speak their mother tongue so fluently "daß sie nichts anderes denken und spüren konnten als das, was ihre Sprache ihnen so schnell und bereitwillig anbietet"—that they couldn't think and feel anything but what their language so quickly and readily offers them (1). For Tawada, a reflective semifluency may have advantages over naïve native fluency, as it does for Brooke-Rose's heroine, who gradually comes to terms with her life of dislocations and escapes the pre-set social roles of office girl, mistress, wife, and interpreter for men. Brooke-Rose has described her own life in terms that could be used of Tawada. In an article on literary exiles, she wrote that "I too am astride two languages and cultures," and she expressed a deep understanding of the mixed blessings of exile:

> exile is an immense force for liberation, for extra distance, for automatically developing contrasting structures in one's head, not just syntactic and lexical but social and psychological; it is, in other words, undoubtedly a leaping forth. But there is a price to pay. The distance can become too great, the loss of identity as writer in the alien society . . . can be burdensome; the new live language can feel more and more remote. So one has to fight all that as an extra effort, although that effort can also result in escaping the familiar phrase, the expected word, simply because it no longer comes into one's head, so even here there is advantage. ("Exsul," 299–300)

A particularly apt comparison for *Between* is Tawada's *Überseezungen: Literarische Essays* (2002). Her title is an ironically untranslatable pun on "translations," *Übersetzungen*, changed by a single letter to become "Overseas-tongues." The title could also be read as *Über Seezungen*, "About Soles" (the fish); in Tawada's world, we swim in a sea of language. The essays in *Überseezungen* appear to be loosely fictionalized accounts of real-life encounters. Journeys, conferences, and readings melt into dreams or crystallize in poems, and scenes are described with a novelist's eye. Critics typically speak of "the narrator" rather than "Yoko Tawada," whose name never appears within the book. As the cover of her 2016 collection *Akzentfrei* says, Tawada's essays are "imaginäre Reisen in eine 'Zwischenwelt,'" imaginary journeys in a "between-world." As Homi Bhabha has said, "the 'foreign' element that reveals the interstitial . . . becomes the unstable element of linkage, the indeterminate temporality of the in-between, that has to be engaged in creating the conditions through which newness comes into the world" (*The Location of Culture*, 326). The *Zwischenwelt* is both a place of loss and a space of creativity.

Überseezungen is structured in terms of three linguistic geographies: "Euro-asiatische Zungen," "Südafrikanische Zungen," and "Nordamerikanische Zungen." The first section doesn't separate Europe from Asia but presents a single landmass, while the other sections feature multilingualism in a specific locale. With all its freedoms of travel and of identity, Tawada's globalized world is no cozy global village. In South Africa she studies Afrikaans, which she thinks of as "die deutsche Sprache, jedoch völlig deformiert"—the German language, but completely deformed (66). Deformation and loss are recurrent experiences for the narrator as well. She spends a semester at MIT as a writer in residence, and while there she reflects on what is lost in translation and in transit:

> Can a language fly across an ocean? I often received emails with gaps. A friend from Hamburg writes me that on their way to America, the German umlauts often fall into the Atlantic and disappear. Japanese characters on the other hand fall into the Pacific and also don't arrive. The oceans must already be overflowing with umlauts and ideograms. What will MIT's "marine engineers" make of all the letters? Do whales eat umlauts? (109)

Tawada's world is always on the brink of "Anarchie im Mundbereich" (13)—anarchy in the region (or realm) of the mouth, a phrase that Christina Szentivanyi has taken as the title for a perceptive essay on *Überseezungen*. Multilingualism estranges languages, at once confusing and pleasing the narrator by the surreal images that result. Thus the name "Heidelberg" (Blueberry Mountain) takes on a new meaning when she understands the middle syllable, *del*, as its Japanese homophone, which means "to surface." If the first syllable is heard as German *Hai* ("shark"), "Blueberry Mountain" becomes "The mountain where a shark surfaces" (46). As Bernard Banoun has observed, the Babel of languages in *Überseezungen* embodies "l'intraduisibilité, les décalages et les ruptures" ("Notes," 421).

Throughout the book, the narrator and her friends struggle to find their bearings in a world of dislocations and dislocutions. In one tale, "Die Botin" (The Messenger), a woman named Mika has returned to Japan after suddenly abandoning her musical studies in Munich. Learning that a friend will be visiting Munich, Mika asks her to convey a private message to her former music professor, to explain her abrupt departure. She doesn't want to send a letter, or to have the professor's wife overhear her reason. Instead, she wants her friend to whisper the message into the professor's ear. Mika's friend, however, doesn't speak German, and the professor doesn't speak Japanese, and so Mika devises a complicated solution: she writes a message for her friend to memorize, but uses Japanese words that have German homophones. Her friend can recite this seemingly random set of Japanese words so that the professor will understand the German message that she herself cannot comprehend.

A traumatic backstory is hinted at but never explained, unless bilingual readers can decode the page-long message. The challenge of doing so is complicated by the fact that Tawada doesn't give the message in Japanese characters but transliterates them, as if to aid her German readers. But Tawada's transcription yields a nonsensical string of words: "ein faden der schlange neu befestigte küste welche schule welche richtung der brunnen des jahres wurde zweimal gemalt das bild brechen . . ." (a thread of the snake new fastened kissed which school which direction the stream of the year was twice painted the picture to break [52–53]). To make anything out of this, we would have to retranscribe these words back into hiragana (or kanji? katakana?) and then read the result as though it were written in German. Yet as Arne Klawitter has remarked, there would be more than one way to write many of these words, quite apart from the fact that German is pronounced so differently from Japanese that we would also have to guess what German phrases might be loosely suggested by the Japanese. He concludes that "the encoded message is inscribed in the text as a secret, one that really can never be unlocked" ("Ideofonografie," 341).[4]

An undercurrent of melancholy runs through *Überseezungen*, culminating in the long final essay/story, "Porträt einer Zunge," which circles around the narrator's relationship with a woman she identifies only as P. When the narrator arrives for her semester as artist in residence at MIT, her friend P meets her at the airport, and they spend a great deal of time together in the ensuing months. Their relationship centers on language, which they continually discuss, but an unrequited passion hovers just

---

[4] In Tokyo in July 2018, I asked Tawada whether she had in fact made her German transcription from a Japanese original. "I must have," she replied, but she said (or claimed) that she can no longer find the draft.

beneath expression. "I loved how P would stand under the shower after swimming and would stick her curious, glowing face through the veil of the water, to ask me something. . . . Eagerly I'd wait for her voice, which came to me through the sound of the rushing water" (144). When P remarks that the narrator's lips are always dry, "I was surprised, and was privately glad that she'd thought about my lips" (145). The narrator says that "a swimming body is strangely naked, and embodies nothing," then adds: "I don't want to embody anything, let alone take anyone's place. But what am I to her? I don't have a family or a job, I'm nothing more than a living being with sense organs, a collector of words, someone who keeps writing things down" (148).

We never know whether P would like the relationship to become something more, and the book ends with two short paragraphs:

> P pronounced the word "heart" [*Herz*] in a particular way. The middle of the heart, an Er, got swallowed up in her throat, and the sibilant at the end lingered a long time on her tongue.
>
> "Yes, dear heart," she sometimes said to me. I was embarrassed when I heard the word "heart." It was too warm for me, and too vulnerable. The word "artichoke heart," though, always made me happy. (152)

The narrator is returning to Germany and to life in her perpetual *Zwischenwelt*, but she takes pleasure from the words that she visualizes with surreal intensity, and her intimacy with P can live on in language. As she reflects when P sees her off at the airport: "Maybe I'd been afraid of a rupture in our feelings. But now she was sitting there like always, and I had the feeling that I couldn't ever lose anything, because we live in a net of languages" (150). In *Überseezungen*, Yoko Tawada has caught the untranslatable in the net of her multiple languages.

Languages on a Sliding Scale

Whereas comparatists traditionally made as little use of translation as possible, we now see an increasing focus on the global circulation of works in translation. All the same, this should by no means require a

thoughtless surrender to the hegemony of global English. Harald Weinrich has noted the irony that in a special issue of *PMLA* devoted to
"Globalizing Literary Studies" in 2002, despite several contributors' critiques of Anglo-globalism, hardly any works were cited in any language
other than English—just 16 out of 687 titles cited. As Weinrich observes,
"even among authors who remain comparatively skeptical about globalization, multilingualism has been for all intents and purposes abolished"
("Chamisso, Chamisso Authors, and Globalization," 1343). The best scholarship in comparative and world literature today resists such critical
monolingualism and involves extensive work with texts in the original,
supplemented with a measured use of translations, critically informed by
translation studies.

To return to the case of Arabic, a flexible multilingual approach can be
seen in Ronit Ricci's *Islam Translated: Literature, Conversion, and the Arabic Cosmopolis of South and Southeast Asia* (2011). There she traces the
fortunes of a tenth-century conversion narrative, the *Kitāb Masā'il 'Abdullāh
Bin Salām* (the *Book of One Thousand Questions*), as it was translated and
adapted from Arabic into Tamil, Malay, and Javanese. Repurposing Sheldon Pollock's conception of a "Sanskrit cosmopolis," Ricci offers a global
view of premodern world literature, rooted not in European imperialism
or in the modern economic world system but in the Islamic *ummah*. Alive
to the challenge of untranslatability, Ricci begins her study with a chapter "On 'Translation' and its Untranslatability," noting that the very term
"translation" has no direct translation in the Southeast Asian languages
at the heart of her study. Ricci uses primary or secondary sources in Arabic, Dutch, English, French, German, Hebrew, Indonesian, Javanese,
Malay, Persian, Portuguese, and Tamil, but she probably doesn't possess
near-native fluency in all twelve languages. This likelihood points us to
another aspect of comparative studies today: we need to study more languages than ever, but we don't have to match the fluency of the national
or area specialist in them all.

Even the polyglot Étiemble never mastered most of the languages he
studied, and he didn't expect every comparatist to learn dozens of
languages. More modestly, but importantly, he required that each of his
students "must know at least passively, to exercise his profession and do

a minimum of research, one or two of the languages less commonly studied in France" (*The Crisis in Comparative Literature*, 22). He regularly worked with translations even when he had an ability to read in the original, and his *Comment lire un roman japonais* (1980) centers on a Kawabata novel that he discusses only in its French translation. He could certainly have cited Kawabata in Japanese, but his intention was to demonstrate how works can be intelligently read in translation.

As Muriel Détrie has commented, despite the idea "that Étiemble exercised a sort of terrorism in requiring every comparatist to learn Arabic, Russian, Chinese, Japanese, etc.," this book shows that "he vindicated the contrary right of non-specialists to speak about literatures whose languages they do not know" ("Connaissons-nous Étiemble?" 419n). In many of his books and essays, Étiemble discusses poems and novels that he had read in the original along with ones he read in translation. Thus in one essay he surveys a range of European accounts of the novel's origins, and he concludes that "all of them were falsified by Eurocentrism" (*Ouverture(s)*, 251). He goes on to discuss the European novel together with fiction written in Sanskrit, Chinese, Japanese, and Vietnamese. His comments on Nguyen Du's *The Tale of Kieu*, which he could read only in translation, are as pertinent as his remarks on his countryman Diderot, as he surveys key features of novelistic narrative (structure, characterization, social setting, audience, and other determinants) that are readily visible in translation.

The ideology of original-language work has been so strong among comparatists that it can lead them to think they're reading scholarship based on original texts even when translations alone are being discussed. This assumption appears on the back cover of my own book *What Is World Literature?*, where Wlad Godzich generously says that it treats "cuneiform-inscribed shards, Egyptian hieroglyphics, medieval German female mystics, Inca Chronicles, Kafka translations and contemporary Native protest literature with equal philological attention, poise, and erudition." I did make use of the originals in most of my case studies, but not for my chapter on Milorad Pavić's born-to-be-translated *Dictionary of the Khazars* or for a chapter on *The Epic of Gilgamesh*, where my focus was on the imperial and class politics of the epic's recovery in the nineteenth century. In both chapters I discuss various passages in translation, but I don't quote a single sentence from Pavić in Serbo-Croatian, which I can't read, nor a single line from *Gilgamesh* in Akkadian, a language that at that time I had never studied.[5] It has crossed my mind that in describing the book as displaying "equal" philological attention throughout, Godzich might have been casting an ironic glance at my German, Spanish, Nahuatl, and Middle Egyptian, suggesting an overall competence little better than my nonexistent Serbo-Croatian. Yet it seems likelier that Godzich simply assumed that I was reading originals that I never used.

A major theme of Gayatri Spivak's *Death of a Discipline* (2003) is the need for American comparatists to learn languages traditionally studied only in area studies programs, and she makes a compelling case for the rigorous acquisition of non-Western languages. Yet when I raised with her the idea of a sliding scale of language learning, she readily agreed, and with characteristic directness she gave herself as an example: "my classical Greek is awful and I often hit my head against it, and my students know this, yet I can use it to ask questions. Even my French and German are not good," she went on; "I've never made a secret of it." Having had limited opportunities to study French and German in Calcutta, and lacking time for extended language study while in graduate school at Cornell, she determined that "one should really try to proceed with what one has rather than try to be as good as one can be in a single language."[6] As she has recently affirmed, comparative literature

> begins to insist on the irreducibility of idiom, even as it insists on translation as commonly understood. When we rethink comparativism,

---

[5] I did work my way through Huehnergard's six-hundred-page Akkadian grammar before I wrote a full book on the epic's history, *The Buried Book*. Even then, I decided not to attempt Sumerian, the notoriously difficult language in which the first poems about Gilgamesh had been written, and so I relied on translations of precursor poems such as "The Death of Bilgames." The afterlife is just too short for eternal language study.

[6] From Damrosch and Spivak, "Comparative Literature / World Literature" (467–68), based on a discussion at ACLA's 2011 annual meeting in Vancouver. We aren't the only comparatists for whom a full mastery of both French and German has been more theoretical than actual. I recall that when Jonathan Culler was hired as an assistant professor in Cornell's English Department, he remarked, "Now I can be proud of my French instead of embarrassed about my German."

we think of translation as an active rather than a prosthetic practice. I have often said that translation is the most intimate act of reading. Thus translation comes to inhabit the new politics of comparativism as reading itself, in the broadest possible sense. ("Rethinking Comparativism," 472)

Both for intellectual purposes and for the academic job market, every formally trained comparatist should have an excellent knowledge of at least one language beyond their "native" language (if they don't already grow up with two or three), and some will need an equally good knowledge of at least one more. But an intermediate level of skill can be very valuable even when we haven't acquired near-native fluency, enabling us to read scholarship in other languages and to work our way through literary texts in a bilingual edition or with a translation at hand. The bilingual editions in the Loeb Classical Library have long been gratefully used by many comparatists as well as by many professors of English—and probably by not a few Latinists (and Hellenists) whose Greek (or Latin, respectively) is rustier than they'd care to admit. Comparatists who answer Gayatri Spivak's call and who work on South Asia now have available over fifty bilingual volumes in the Clay Sanskrit Library, modeled on the Loeb series, as well as a growing set of bilingual volumes in the Murty Classical Library of India, which features works in Bengali, Malayalam, Tamil, Urdu, and other languages.

Even without an intermediate knowledge of a language, a basic reading ability allows us to check key passages and not be prisoners of whatever translation we may have available. To be sure, not every topic can be approached in this way. When we have to rely partially or entirely on translations, we can only work successfully if we have the discernment to pursue topics for which our level of knowledge is sufficient, or to shape the topics appropriately for our abilities. If we need to know more, then it is time to get back into language class—a worthwhile endeavor at any age—or to collaborate with someone who has the language we lack. If neither is an option, the topic is best left for someone else.

A driving force behind Franco Moretti's proposal for "distant reading" is that no one can learn hundreds of languages, but the situation is greatly improved if we can allow ourselves to do serious work in translation. This doesn't mean that we should cheerfully succumb to the enticing convenience of English (or French or Mandarin if those are our primary languages), without asking ourselves whether our topic should entail dealing with the texts in the original. An example of this problem can be seen in *Combined and Uneven Development: Towards a New Theory of World-Literature* (2015), collaboratively written by the Warwick Research Collective (WReC). Their ambitious study has much to recommend it. The seven contributors look both in and beyond the Anglophone world, combining postcolonial critique and world-systems analysis in extended discussions of a very interesting selection of novelists, from Tayeb Salih to the Russian postmodernist Victor Pelevin, Slovakia's Peter Pišťanek, the Spanish modernist Pío Bareta, the South African Ivan Vladislavić, and Glasgow's James Kelman. Adapting Leon Trotsky's economic theory of combined and uneven development, they present modern literature as part of a capitalist world system built on center-periphery relations of growing inequality. They clearly feel a rhetorical as well as ideological affinity for Moretti's "firecracker of an article 'Conjectures on World Literature,'" which they praise as "witty, down-to-earth, erudite, and terrifically 'good to think'" (7), but unlike Moretti they combine global theory with selected close readings, rather than reading at second or third hand.

Coming primarily from backgrounds in English, American, or postcolonial Anglophone studies, the collective employs a wide field of reference, extending from Cervantes and Dostoevsky to Ahmet Hamdi Tanpınar and Haruki Murakami and involving many critical and theoretical works; their bibliography runs to nearly five hundred entries. Yet, remarkably, they don't list a single work in any language other than English, and they never refer to the originals when discussing their foreign-language novels. The neglect of Salih's Arabic, Pelevin's Russian, Pišťanek's Slovak, and Bareta's Spanish represents a set of missed opportunities, limiting the group's ability to develop their analysis or to fully situate their writers in their material circumstances, starting with the materiality of language itself. Symptomatic here is that the names of three of their seven key writers are spelled with diacritics, but they invariably cite Pišťanek, Pío Bareta, and Vladislavić without the accents that belong on their names. Materialist critics without diacritics?

In their chapter on Salih's *Season of Migration to the North*, the authors say that they will discuss the novel in terms of "both 'story' and stylistics" (83), but lacking Arabic they are unable to offer any substantial stylistic analysis. They note that Salih's tale builds on oral traditions, and they express a passing regret for all they are missing in translation (82), but they made no effort to bring an Arabist into their group to see how orality is echoed in Salih's prose. While it is refreshing to find a reading of *Season of Migration to the North* that doesn't see it simply as rewriting Conrad's *Heart of Darkness*, the authors do nothing with Salih's Arabic intertexts, whether North African storytelling, *The Thousand and One Nights*, or the agonized love poetry of Salih's friend Tawfiq Sayigh, whose sadomasochistic love affair with an English woman was an inspiration for the novel.

In their most extended comments on translation, the authors criticize comparatists for insufficient attention to the inequalities between hegemonic and subordinated languages. After giving a cogent critique of Emily Apter's assertion in *The Translation Zone* of an always-already global comparative literature, they go so far as to deny that original-language work usually yields any genuine understanding at all. "Comparative literature's insistence on multilinguisticality," they claim, "is more often the leading edge of an unambiguous fetishism of language (and hence of the authority of professional experience) than of any commitment to cultural dialogue or social mutuality" (27).

They may have a point with Apter. Though she is certainly committed to cultural dialogue, she sprinkles her prose with French terms (*en soi, décalage, forçage*) that seem to have more to do with banking on the cultural capital of French than with any lack of English equivalents for phrases that add—what shall I say?—a certain *je ne sais quoi* to her upmarket style. Yet the Warwick group's lofty rejection of multilingualism has led them to renounce the use of languages that would be directly useful for their analysis. Some of these are languages that members of their collective actually possess, including Spanish, and they could have added people to their working group to mobilize other relevant languages, whether for analyzing their primary texts or for reading secondary literature. Most of what has been published to date on Victor Pelevin, for instance, is in Russian, and there are useful articles on him in French and German, but the Warwick collective uses none of them. Excluding every language but English from their book, they reinforce in practice the Anglo-imperialism that they combat in theory.

The Language(s) of Scholarship

Specialists even in a single literature will often benefit by reading scholarship written elsewhere, and it is all the more important for comparatists to look beyond the boundaries of their local scholarly discourse. In *The Crisis in Comparative Literature*, Étiemble closes his chapter on "Crucial Questions" with a section entitled "A Universal Working Language?" He argues that scholars need to share a common language or a small set of languages, but he knows that the time has passed when comparatists could assume that English, French, and German would suffice for the purpose. In a world of warring linguistic imperialisms, the problem is political as well as linguistic. He observes that the Soviet bloc (still firmly in place in 1963) would never accept English, the language of their American "rival, and at times slanderer," as a scholarly lingua franca (27). Yet German isn't a language of global reach, and by midcentury French had lost its place as the supposedly universal language of culture. Devoted though he was to his linguistic *patrie*, Étiemble considered it unlikely "that the course of history could be reversed and to presume that French could ever become, by virtue of its past merits, the future language of mankind" (28).

But if not French or English, then which language could be acceptable worldwide? Étiemble rejects both Esperanto (too artificial) and Latin (too tied to Catholicism, a deal-breaker for militant atheists such as himself). Looking ahead, he foresees machine translation becoming viable for papers in the natural sciences, but he describes the technology as far too crude for humanistic scholarship, "where the quality of the language counts, no matter how little" (27). Instead, he boldly proposes Chinese—not the language itself, but its script. He argues that people anywhere could learn the characters but then pronounce them as they please, as premodern Japanese, Korean, and Vietnamese literati had done. He admits that this solution is unlikely to find acceptance, though interestingly he doesn't allude to the difficulty of persuading scholars everywhere to learn thousands of Chinese characters, or the major problem of adapting Chinese characters to the syntax of many different languages. Rather, his chief concern is again political. "Unfortunately," he remarks, "national pride and the present situation of China, isolated within the socialist camp and banned from the United Nations, do not exactly favour this solution, which nevertheless seems the wisest" (28). He closes the chapter without any resolution: "So here we are, in the middle of an unsolved problem!" (30).

In 1988 Étiemble returned to the problem in "La littérature comparée vingt ans après" (*Ouverture(s)*, 147–98). There he observes that comparative studies were moving far beyond even Hugo Meltzl's "decaglottism." He cites two new Japanese journals of comparative literature as well as scholarship being written in Arabic, Bengali, Chinese, Polish, Romanian, Russian, and Serbo-Croatian. As he says, all of these languages "have entered into the grand *farandole* of the languages of scholarly work and of delectation" (162). A nice Herderian touch, to take the Provençal folk dance as his image for scholarly interchange; we can imagine the field of comparative literature as bordered with olive trees and filled with fragrant lavender.

Yet he sees comparative scholarship as blossoming in a world going rapidly to hell. Anticipating the "planetary dysphoria" with which Apter concludes *Against World Literature*, he combines his plea for languages with a sharply dystopian view of the contemporary world:

> It is necessary for Europeans, for North Americans, to finally understand that despite the imperialism of the Anglo-American language, the time has come for them, if they want to have comparatists worthy of the name and of the future of humanity, so far as one can predict it—always supposing that our miserable species, threatened on all sides with extinction, manages to survive (nuclear wars, pollution of the air and of the oceans, overpopulation that can only be resolved by cannibalism, or by enforced homosexuality of men and of women, with the reproduction of the species confined to breeding-

convents)—the time has come, I say, to consider seriously what the agonizing problem of working languages requires. (162)

In this urgent series of cascading clauses, Étiemble unleashes his novelistic imagination in an apocalyptic scenario more attuned to Margaret Atwood's 1985 novel *The Handmaid's Tale* than to ordinary scholarly analysis. Yet his concern is precisely to show how intimately our scholarly pursuits are bound up with the problems of our wider world, and it is this indissoluble linkage that renders the practical question of working languages a genuinely agonizing problem.

Language is at once the medium of international communication and a worldwide battleground. Étiemble sees that far from creating a harmonious world, globalization is heightening "the intense, often brutal, sometimes forcible contact among languages" (162). Major and minor languages alike are becoming increasingly infected with a leveling global argot that he sarcastically labels "Babélian," which threatens "to massacre all literatures, and to render pointless, or impossible, all teaching of comparative and general literature" (166). In 1952 Erich Auerbach had gloomily prophesied that soon "only a single literary culture may survive in this homogenized world. It may even happen that, within a comparatively short period of time, only a limited number of literary languages will continue to exist, soon perhaps only one. If this were to come to pass, the idea of world literature would simultaneously be realized and destroyed" ("Philology of World Literature," 254). In 1988 Étiemble saw this cultural and linguistic implosion accelerating.

Neither he nor Auerbach had any intention, however, of simply giving in to the hegemony of global English, much less surrendering to a dumbed-down "globish" or *franglais*. Auerbach's vision of the impending unification of world culture is sometimes quoted as though this was his final judgment on the eclipse of world literature as a viable idea. Yet his gloomy prophecy is not the essay's conclusion but the opening statement of the problem he wants to address. It is through world literature, properly— that is, philologically—understood, that he proposes to counter the effects of modern massification. He argues that our increasing access to the world's literatures may finally make it possible to create "a unified vision of the human race in all its variety," which he says "was the actual purpose of philology, beginning with Vico and Herder" (254). As pessimistic as he is about the state of the world, he is guardedly optimistic about the rising generation of scholars: "there is a small number of intensely committed young people, distinguished by their talent and originality, and interested in pursuing philology and intellectual history, who give grounds for hope" (255). Together, they can preserve "an awareness of the abundance and depth of intellectual and spiritual developments over the past millennia" (257).

But how will a worldwide band of scholars communicate their awareness to one another? For his part, having evoked the spectre of a Babelian dystopia, Étiemble returns in "La littérature comparée vingt ans après" to the problem of working languages that he had broached in 1963. The more global scholarship becomes, and the more literatures scholars bring into conversation, the greater is the need for a common language of scholarly exchange. Yet any resolution to this problem seemed farther away than ever. China had been admitted to the United Nations and was a rapidly rising global power, but its advancement on the world stage was leading to the same drawbacks as Anglo-globalism: scholars need "to avoid all linguistic imperialism, but as China will doubtless be the leading power of the 21st century, it will succumb to the same temptations as the Anglo-Saxon world does today," Étiemble says, forecasting the growth of a self-centered Sinophone imperialism (165). As a compromise between the dystopias of global English or Chinese and the utopia of everyone learning twenty languages, Étiemble proposes that scholarship, and as much literature as possible, should be translated into "three or four judiciously chosen working languages" (166). He doesn't specify who would be appointed to make this judicious selection, and if English, French, and Chinese are off the table, what choices would his notional transnational jurists make? Étiemble allows that practitioners of hegemonic languages would be unlikely to opt for his preferred solution, which would be to employ languages of small countries that have never wielded an empire, and he leaves the problem once again unresolved.

In the three decades since then, the situation has gotten both better and worse. The hegemony of global English has increased to the point that even committed postcolonialists such as the Warwick group can fail to cite any scholarship in the other languages that their members can actually read, let alone feeling a need to learn any new ones. It is more necessary than ever for scholars to move beyond the translational comfort zones of global English and of Parisian French and to encompass scholarship written in other languages. But language study is under threat in many areas, and we can no longer assume that students come into their graduate programs already knowing all the languages they'll need for their PhD. In an era of shrinking resources and reduced time to degree, programs need to make language study a core aspect of our students' training, not just something students somehow have to do on their own, off to the side of their course requirements.

We confronted this issue in my own department a decade ago, as we found an increasing number of students wanting to learn a new language or to advance their knowledge of ones they hadn't yet mastered. In fact, our graduate students had always been allowed to receive credit for language courses, but only if those courses were offered at the graduate level, as is often the case for less-taught languages. This meant that, oddly, a student could receive course credit for first-year Welsh but not for third-year French. When I proposed opening up the rules to allow credit for undergraduate language courses, one of my senior colleagues—a distinguished professor of French and comparative literature—grumbled, "I don't see why we should give graduate students credit for doing baby French!" She did end up supporting the change, and in recent years we've had many students improve their languages, including Chinese students learning French, Czech, and Old Church Slavonic, a Hispanist from Poland learning Basque and Mayan, and Americans learning Norwegian, Turkish, and Wolof.

Even as we need to foster more and better language study, we need translation more than ever, and our programs need to include translation studies, both in theory and practice. There have always been comparatists, such as Robert Fagles, who were active translators, but translation has often been considered an after-hours activity, secondary to the scholarship that would lead to job offers and tenure. Fagles himself was trained in English, not classics, and he was largely self-taught in Greek and Latin; he began translating for pleasure after completing a dissertation on

Alexander Pope's translation of the *Iliad*. He soon devoted himself primarily to translation, and his eloquent translations of Homer and Virgil sold in the millions, but he eschewed scholarship in translation studies, or indeed in literature. Remarkably, the *MLA Bibliography* doesn't list a single entry for him—an indication of the direction his interests took soon after he completed his dissertation, but also a sign of the long-standing neglect of translation in American scholarship.

In particular, comparatists should engage with the work that builds on the "cultural turn" in translation studies inaugurated by Susan Bassnett, Itamar Even-Zohar, André Lefevere, and Gideon Toury in the 1980s, which revolutionized a previously formalist field to address issues of power, inequality, and the politics of language. Lawrence Venuti's capacious *Translation Studies Reader* and Sandra Bermann and Catherine Porter's *Companion to Translation Studies* should be on the reading list of anyone interested in doing comparative work. In a growing number of comparative literature programs, translation is becoming a central area of scholarship and practice. It is now common for faculty and also graduate students to win prizes in translation (of which there are now many) and to contribute actively to translation scholarship as well.

Lawrence Venuti has noted that it was only in 2012 that the first department of comparative literature in the United States, at the University of Oregon, appointed a tenure-track assistant professor who was "qualified specifically to teach and to conduct and supervise research in translation studies" (*Translation Changes Everything*, 62). This was Karen Emmerich, who is a prizewinning translator of modern Greek literature and also a translation theorist (*Literary Translation and the Making of Originals*). She moved on from Oregon to Princeton, where she received tenure in 2018 in the department that Fagles had founded. There she is part of a group active in translation studies, including Sandra Bermann, Lital Levy, and Wendy Belcher, co-translator of *The Life and Struggles of Our Mother Wallata Petros*. Written in Gə'əz in 1672, this life of an Ethiopian saint is the earliest known biography of an African woman. With the Gə'əz "ə" joining the French *r* and the Nahuatl *tl*, the audioscape of comparative studies is sounding a good deal more various than it did in the era of the Levin and Greene reports.

Going with Google

Along with print publication, the internet offers new possibilities for scholarly translation. Machine translation has advanced enormously since Étiemble regretted its limited success in 1963, and while computers may never create excellent translations of literary works, the best translation programs can now do surprisingly well with scholarly prose. As an experiment, I asked Google to translate Étiemble's plea for more translation from less-studied languages:

> Formons donc, et le plus vite possible, des traducteurs capables de ne trahir ni le hongrois ni le bengali, ni le finnois ni le japonais, ni le tamoul ni le chinois, ni le tibétain ni le malgache. C'est faire admettre aux enseignants férus de *recherche* que la traduction . . . devrait être considérée non pas comme ouvrage de dames, occupation de dilettante, mais avec respect, et comme une des tâches essentielles de notre discipline. (*Comparaison n'est pas raison*, 50)

Within two seconds, Google Translate rendered this passage as:

> Let us train, and as quickly as possible, translators capable of betraying neither Hungarian nor Bengali, nor Finnish nor Japanese, nor Tamil nor Chinese, nor Tibetan nor Malagasy. It is to admit to teachers who are interested in research that translation . . . should be considered not as a work of ladies, dilettante occupation, but with respect, and as one of the essential tasks of our discipline.[7]

Not only did Google Translate instantly produce this English version; it can also render the passage into a hundred other languages, and it performed with equal facility in the several ones I tried. Google offers almost all of Étiemble's examples of neglected languages: Bengali, Chinese, Japanese, Finnish, Hungarian, Malagasy, and Tamil. Tibetan alone isn't represented, for reasons perhaps not unrelated to China's growing presence in the world and on the internet.

---

[7] https://translate.google.com/#fr/en (accessed May 30, 2018).

Google's algorithm is hardly perfect. It does poorly with "faire admettre aux enseignants," which should be "to make teachers admit," not "to admit to teachers," and it misses the nuance—and the ironic italics—of Étiemble's description of scholars who are "férus de *recherche*" as though they are lovesick (*férus d'amour*). The phrase would be better translated as "smitten with *research*," instead of the colorless "interested in research" offered by heartless Google, which gives similarly sober equivalents in German ("an der Forschung interessiert"), Catalan ("interessats en la recerca"), and Icelandic ("áhuga á rannsóknum"). So Google produced an error and some loss in nuance—but the same is true of the published English translation as well, even though it was made by two comparatists, one of whom was a professor of English and the other a native speaker of French. Together Weisinger and Joyaux made a careful and readable translation, introduced with a foreword in which they stress the importance of Étiemble's plea for high-quality translations (xiv). One could hardly have found a better pair of translators for the purpose, and yet they too underplayed Étiemble's "férus de *recherche*," settling for the anodyne "devoted to research," which suggests a purely intellectual commitment, without his ironic italics or the intimation of physical or romantic attraction.

Further, in translating Étiemble's list of neglected languages, they not only flattened his style but made an outright error of their own. In the original, Étiemble has a balanced set of four incongruous pairings ("ni le hongrois ni le bengali, ni le finnois ni le japonais, ni le tamoul ni le chinois, ni le tibétain ni le malgache"), but Weisinger and Joyaux replace his neither/nor clauses with a bald list: "Hungarian, Bengali, Finnish, Tamil, Chinese, Tibetan, Malagasy." Apparently inadvertently, they leave Japanese off the list—a mistake they wouldn't have made if they had taken care to preserve Étiemble's elegantly balanced pairings. All in all, Google Translate is already doing as well with Étiemble as his human translators have done, at least in languages for which it has a good database, and the program is likely to improve further in the near future. Even now it has provided a solid translation of Étiemble's plea for translation, capable of getting his point across without betraying it, in English and in scores of other languages as well.

The Two Frances W. Pritchetts

Scholarly prose is all very well, but what of poetry? Poetry too can seem inherently translatable to those, like Hegel, who locate the essence of poetry in its "idea" rather than in the specifics of its verbal texture. Anna Balakian's hero André Breton refused to allow that poetry could be detained at the borders of any language. As he declared in Prague in 1935, the surrealist principle that poetry should be created by everyone "implies an indispensable counterpart: *poetry must be understood by everyone.* For the love of heaven let us not work toward the raising of the barrier between languages." He bolstered his claim with a quotation from Hegel that poems can be translated "without essential alteration," even though "the relationships between sounds may also be totally changed" ("The Surrealist Situation," 262). For many readers, though, poetry is very much bound up with the relationships between sounds, and however greatly we appreciate a translator's ability to reinvent works in a new language, there is no question that poetry poses special challenges.

An excellent translation possesses poetic power in its own right, yet we remain aware that a very different, and often richer, poetic experience lies behind the translations we read. Even when we don't know a poem's original language, it adds an important dimension if we can experience its aural force, much as with recitations of the Qur'an. Bilingual editions can suggest this effect, but the Greek pages of the Loeb *Iliad* won't be very meaningful to a reader who doesn't know the alphabet and the principles of Greek scansion. Readers who haven't learned the Devanagari script won't be able to make anything at all out of the Sanskrit that faces the translations in the Clay Library.

Recognizing the complexities of poetic translation, in his *Ouverture(s) sur un comparatisme planétaire* Étiemble proposed a multilayered process, beginning with "a precise phonetic transcription of the original text, and if possible a recording on a disk or a minicassette," followed by a meticulous literal translation "taking account of the semantic and syntactic design" (170). Then should come a variety of freer poetic versions, each displaying some of the original's poetic effects, as no one translation could convey them all. Finally, the whole should be enriched with "all the annotations necessary to the understanding of the poem" (170). In 1988 this must have seemed like yet another of Étiemble's impossible schemes, but it has become a live option in the internet age.

A prime example is *A Desertful of Roses*, a website that Columbia's Frances W. Pritchett has created for the Urdu ghazals of the great Mughal poet Ghalib (1797–1869). As she describes the project's genesis, she began working in 1999 on a three-volume scholarly edition and commentary. But then came the attacks of 9/11, and she decided that the wider world needed to have access to this cosmopolitan Mughal poet. The result, she writes, is "by far the largest piece of academic work I've ever undertaken" ("About This Project"). She has continued working on the site ever since, and it has evolved into an immense compendium that meets and even exceeds all of Étiemble's goals for rigorous translation of poetry. Ghalib's 234 Urdu ghazals can all be seen on the site, not only in the original Perso-Arabic script but also phonetically transcribed, both into the Latin alphabet and into Devanagari. Each ghazal is given a literal word-for-word translation, and links are provided to performances of many of them. Each couplet in every poem has a hyperlinked page giving grammatical notes and excerpts from the Urdu commentarial tradition. Other sections of the site present Ghalib's life, Urdu language and poetics, and an extensive bibliography for further reading. Images of manuscripts and of Ghalib's Agra and Delhi are incorporated throughout the site—a visual dimension that Étiemble hadn't even contemplated.

On a page "About the Ghazals," Pritchett says that translating them "in a serious literary way is a doomed mission" and "basically impossible." Even so, she has collected translations of two of Ghalib's most famous ghazals (numbers 20 and 111), with some fifty translations into English of each one, from 1940 to the present. Many are fairly pedestrian, but the best translators achieve beautiful results, as can be seen from the very different renderings of the opening couplet of number 111 by the poet-translators Adrienne Rich and W. S. Merwin. Rich renders the couplet as:

Not all, only a few, return as the rose or the tulip;
what faces there must be still veiled by the dust!

By contrast, Merwin expands each line into its own brief, unpunctuated stanza:

> Here and there in a rose or a tulip
> a few of the faces
>
> only a few
> but think of those that the dust
> keeps to itself

Pritchett wants to lead us into the originals, and she doesn't provide poetic translations for the other ghazals, but her literal translations and commentaries make an ideal companion to whichever Ghalib collection we may choose to buy, and you can lose yourself in *A Desertful of Roses* for hours at a time.

In addition, Pritchett has developed *A Garden of Kashmir*, a site devoted to another great ghazal poet, Mir Muhammad Taqi Mir, and she has also posted a variety of aids for Urdu studies. Nor is this all. A link on her home page takes us to a very different project: *Igbo Language and Literature: Resources for Study*. This site contains a wealth of information about Igbo culture, together with a set of translations, all by Frances Pritchett. These include an early novel, Pita Nwana's *Omenuko* (1933), as well as three plays and a 1980 novella, *Night Has Fallen in the Afternoon,* all presented both in the original and in translation. Once again, we might almost say that there are two Frances W. Pritchetts, the well-known Indologist and the amateur Africanist. Yet we would be wrong to say "almost," for these websites are in fact the work of two different Pritchetts, mother and daughter.

Born on Staten Island, New York, the elder Frances W. Pritchett (1922–2012) was a child prodigy who loved languages and math. According to a local newspaper report posted on the site, she graduated from high school at age fifteen, intending to become a surgeon. In the end, bowing to social norms and economic pressures, she went to a local college and became a legal secretary. She married and then moved with her husband to Little Rock, Arkansas, where her daughter grew up before going on to pursue the professional career that her mother never had. There matters might have rested, but in the early 1970s the elder Frances Pritchett took part in protests against the Vietnam War and became active in the civil rights movement in racially divided Little Rock. She also hosted a pair of college students from Nigeria, and hearing them conversing together in Igbo, she was shocked to realize how little she knew of any African culture. She determined to learn the language, and after several years of studying on her own and with tutors, she made the first of three trips to Nigeria. In a page on the site describing "How I Became an Igbophile," she says: "Why not, I thought, have the tables turned against me and find out what it was like to be the only white face in a sea of black ones." She adds that "I also wanted to practice my new-found language skill in a place where many people knew no English at all." She closes with a plea—far too timely today—for Americans to welcome visitors and immigrants.

Pritchett continued her work to the end of her long life; a photograph from 2010 shows the eighty-eight-year-old studying a new language, Ga, with an African tutor. While she never had the opportunity to make a career in African studies, her lucid translations now reach a worldwide audience thanks to her website, which her daughter helped assemble. Typing "Igbo literature" into a search engine yields nearly five thousand results; her site comes up as the very first item. Though Étiemble regretted that translation was considered an avocation for "ladies and dilettantes," the amateur Africanist gave the world a series of works that no professionals were translating and that few if any publishers would have taken on in the 1980s and 1990s. For her part, the tenured Indologist Frances Pritchett is a dilettante too, in the root sense of someone motivated by *diletto* or delight. Her website is infused with her love for Ghalib and his world, and instead of reaching a few hundred readers in print, it receives upward of fourteen thousand visits *per week*—a million views every sixteen months. Together, the mother-daughter duo of Frances W. Pritchett and Frances W. Pritchett has shown what creative linguistic activists can do to open out the world for a genuinely planetary comparatism today.

6

Literatures

In comparing the literatures, we not only need to have a good understanding of what we mean by "literature"; we also need to consider what is *a* literature—the assemblage of works that make up a literary culture, its canon, and its historical tradition. This is no obvious question, especially with the many traditions created outside the Western world, or within the West itself in periods before the general adoption of the belletristic conception of literature formulated in eighteenth-century France. These matters have been the purview of the national literature departments, which have typically organized their studies in terms of a literary history divided into broad periods, subdivided into movements within periods. Each period and movement would have its particular canon of major and minor figures, who with few exceptions would have written in the national language, contributing to its refinement and to the prestige of the nation itself. Comparatists have often had an uneasy relation to national literatures conceived in these terms, whether through an ideological opposition to nationalism or through their impatience with the parochialism of national traditions seen as essentially self-contained entities, and yet national literatures remain a major force even in a transnational age.

A classic expression of impatience with the very idea of comparing national literatures is a 1958 article by Albert Guérard entitled "Comparative Literature?" Making an analogy to Europe's impending economic unification, Guérard predicted that "Comparative Literature will disappear in its very victory; just as 'foreign trade' between France and Germany will disappear in the Common Market; just as the 'foreign relations' between these two countries will be absorbed by a common parliament" (4).

Unable to anticipate the wrenching tensions of today's Eurozone, Guérard considered that the overriding question for comparatists was "How and When Shall We Commit Suicide?" His answer: "Not just yet: we are needed so long as the nationalistic heresy has not been extirpated" (5). Such dismissive views of national traditions may have had more justification in the 1950s than they have today. More and more specialists in national literatures are exploring transnational and international questions, and as Haun Saussy noted in his introduction to the ACLA report of 2006, broad theoretical perspectives have by now infused many national literature departments, to the point that comparatists can no longer claim ownership of "Theory." Even so, we sometimes still find prominent comparatists speaking of national traditions in oppositional terms. Thus in 2000 Franco Moretti declared that

> you become a comparatist for a very simple reason: *because you are convinced that that viewpoint is better.* It has greater explanatory power; it's conceptually more elegant; it avoids that ugly "one-sidedness and narrow-mindedness"; whatever. The point is that there is no other justification for the study of world literature (and for the existence of departments of comparative literature) but this: to be a thorn in the side, a permanent intellectual challenge to national literatures— especially the local literature. If comparative literature is not this, it's nothing. Nothing. ("Conjectures on World Literature," 68)

Such statements can have a progressive force within an American context, opposing the isolationist nationalism that leads to the demonization of immigrants and to neglect of the wider world, including its literatures. Yet it is the privilege of critics writing within a hegemonic power to mock "the nationalistic heresy" or to be a thorn in the side of the national literatures. Among colonized or otherwise dominated populations, literature has long been a prime force for fostering national identity and rallying opposition to imperial or hegemonic powers, and as we've seen with Hu Shih, literary nation-building has often had a significant comparative and international dimension. A dismissively antinationalistic stance can't do justice to the internationalism of many national literatures.

In major as well as minor literatures, moreover, local traditions exert a shaping force even on works dealing with transnational processes. Jenny Erpenbeck's eloquent novel *Gehen, Ging, Gegangen* (2015; *Go, Went, Gone,* 2017) presents the painful dislocation of North African immigrants in Berlin through the eyes of a retired classicist who (like the author) is a former East Berliner; he now feels like a foreigner in his own city. In the eminently global genre of the detective novel, Boris Akunin's tales of his Holmesian sleuth Erast Petrovich Fandorin, set in the waning years of the Russian Empire, are in dialogue with Pushkin and Dostoevsky as much as with Conan Doyle and Agatha Christie. As Elizabeth Richmond-Garza has shown, the series offers oblique reflections on the corruptions of the Putin era and on the politics of gender identity ("Detecting Conspiracy"). Erpenbeck and Akunin aren't engaged only with their national traditions, yet neither writer can be properly understood without them. If we now seek to move beyond the mutual disregard of comparatists and people working in a single literature, it is not only important that postcolonialists and specialists in national literatures should learn more languages; equally, everyone doing comparative work needs to think more creatively about the vitality of the national traditions with which—and against which—we engage.

A Tale of Two *Knjižnici*

A good place to begin is in Ljubljana. Slovenia's literary tradition dates back hundreds of years, and the capital preserves its rich variety in two major libraries (*knjižnici,* from the common Slavic term for "books"): the eighteenth-century Seminary Library (figure 6, top) and the twentieth-century National and University Library (figure 6, bottom). Attending to the material history of such collections can tell us much about the complex histories of national traditions even in very small countries (Slovenia's entire population is just two million): their inclusions, their exclusions, and the competing currents that continually reform national canons, library collections, and those who frequent them.

Designed by the Vienna-trained Slovenian architect Jože Plečnik and built between 1936 and 1941, the massive National and University Library

FIGURE 6. The Seminary Library (1701–24) and the National and University Library (1936–41), Ljubljana. Top illustration photographed by Steve Outram / Alamy Stock Photo; bottom photographed by Kipperpig / Alamy Stock Photo.

was intended as an expression of Slovene cultural identity in the era of Slovenia's awkward alliance with Serbia and Croatia in the interwar Kingdom of Yugoslavia. Ascending the somber central staircase, you arrive at the high-ceilinged reading room, bathed in light from clerestory windows and side walls of glass and from geometric chandeliers above you; your ascent embodies Plečnik's conception of the progress "from the twilight of ignorance to the light of knowledge and enlightenment" ("Jože Plečnik").

As significant as the drama of the upper floors is the archive of manuscripts and rare books, kept in a vault deep beneath the reading room. A visiting scholar can gain admission by appointment, once the archivist opens the vault's original lock with its massive iron key, then a midcentury deadbolt, and finally punches in a code on a keypad—the door is a veritable exhibit of the history of locking technologies. You may then see important early examples of writing in Slovene, including the Stična Manuscript (1428). You can also peruse manuscripts by modern writers such as France Prešeren (1800–1849), the Slovenian national poet, whose statue dominates Prešeren Square in the city center. In his own faded handwriting, you can read his poem "Zdravljica" (A Toast), which became the text of the Slovene national anthem, having survived the disapproval of an Austrian censor who had deleted a stanza that seemed too Pan-Slavic. More romantically inclined visitors can peruse the sonnets that Prešeren addressed to his muse, Julija Primic, whose bust will have been pointed out to you in Prešeren Square. From her perch on a wall across from the poet's statue, Julija eternally gazes at the would-be lover too early lost to her, first by her marriage to a wealthy businessman and then by the poet's alcohol-induced death.

A very different image of Slovene culture is found in the Seminary Library, the first library ever opened to the public in the country. The ecclesiastics who founded it in 1701, including Janez Krstnik Prešeren— not another poet but the provost of the cathedral—were as concerned with heavenly as with earthly muses. In the central dome of the vaulted ceiling, painted by an Italian artist in 1721, an angel holds open a copy of the Vulgate. Here books lead one to reverence for God, whereas the National and University Library instills reverence for books. Yet Provost Prešeren and his colleagues were true Enlightenment humanists, and their goal was to foster a Slovene intelligentsia that could blend their classical and religious heritage with the latest in European philosophy and the arts. They stocked the library with classical and modern works in several languages, together with an important collection of opera libretti, and their holdings even included many books banned by the papacy. Provost Prešeren personally acquired works by Machiavelli and by Protestant theologians, and he had a particular taste for French erotica, including such agreeable titles as *La belle sans chemise, ou Ève ressuscitée* (Vidmar, *And Yet They Read Them*, 50).

In a retreat from the broad humanism of the library's founders, many of the banned books were rejected as inappropriate in the nineteenth century and were sold off or pulped to make rag stock. The Seminary Library retains its original cosmopolitan character today. In the National and University Library, by contrast, internationalism takes second place to the promotion of Slovene cultural identity. Yet France Prešeren, posthumously honored as the national poet, was a voracious reader in several languages, and he wrote in German as well as Slovenian. His poetry is in dialogue with Lord Byron and Adam Mickiewicz, and with Petrarch before them. He also identified closely with Ovid, both as the poet of the *Ars Amatoria* and as the political outcast writing his *Tristia* on the shores of the Black Sea.

Nationalism and internationalism have been interwoven throughout the country's history, and Prešeren's "A Toast" itself has a pronounced internationalist emphasis:

> God's blessing on all nations
> Who long and work for that bright day
> When o'er earth's habitations
> No war, no strife shall hold its sway
> Who long to see
> That all men free
> No more shall foes, but neighbours be![1]

---

[1] Translation from the Republic of Slovenia's website, www.vlada.si, which also gives versions in Hungarian, Italian, German, French, Spanish, and Croatian, though, interestingly, not in Serbian.

This sentiment is no mere holdover from an earlier era. "A Toast" was set to music in 1905, but it was only designated the national anthem in 1989, as Slovenia agitated for autonomy within the Socialist Federal Republic of Yugoslavia. The nation finally achieved its independence two years later, after a millennium of subordinated existence within the Holy Roman Empire, five centuries of Habsburg rule, and decades of domination by Serbia within Yugoslavia. The anthem is now a carefully guarded symbol of national identity, its usage protected by the 1994 "Act Regulating the Coat-of-Arms, Flag and Anthem of the Republic of Slovenia and the Flag of the Slovene Nation." At the same time, Slovenia's national independence has enabled the country to develop its international posture, and Prešeren's portrait appears on the Slovene two-euro coin. This is a nation that treasures, and banks on, its national literature.

From National Literatures to National Markets

The Prešeren coin raises the question of literary markets, and these have rarely been limited to locally sourced products: national traditions were never as watertight as nationalistic literary histories have often supposed. Émigrés and heritage populations have frequently written in languages other than the predominant national language, but until recently American poets who wrote in Spanish or Yiddish were rarely included in survey courses or anthologies of American literature, while Irish and Welsh were banished outright from the curriculum in nineteenth-century England. Even in the case of a major canonical writer such as Milton, only his English-language poetry is commonly taught: no survey anthology of English literature that I know of includes any of Milton's Latin poems. Though Milton was fluent in Latin and proud of his poetic ability in the language of diplomacy and of humanistic inquiry, we take it for granted that his Latin poems aren't worth our while—a judgment that most of us have made without ever having read any of them. Similarly, Ghalib, who wrote both in Persian and in Urdu, is beloved in India as an Urdu poet and ignored as a Persian poet—even though Ghalib himself preferred his Persian poems to his Urdu ones.

Along with understanding the importance of multilingualism within national cultures, we need to give greater weight to translated works, not only as distant sources or influences from which we can plot the greatness of our great national writers, but also in many cases as works that genuinely become part of the literary culture into which they are translated. If we attend to what is being published and read in a given time and place, we will often find that the national literary space includes a far higher proportion of translated works than our survey courses and our literary histories allow. Tracing the growth of English fiction, for instance, English departments have typically offered surveys that move from *Beowulf* to *The Canterbury Tales* and on to Defoe, Richardson, Fielding, and Sterne. Yet such a parochial evolution would have surprised Henry Fielding, who wrote *Tom Jones* (1749) in comic dialogue with his epic master Virgil rather than with Chaucer. He had never even heard of *Beowulf*, whose sole surviving manuscript had yet to be discovered by Grímur Jónsson Thorkelin, who visited England in 1786 seeking Scandinavian material. And when Laurence Sterne's opinionated hero Tristram Shandy discusses his favorite authors, neither Chaucer nor Defoe makes the grade. His great inspirations, he says, are "my dear Rabelais, and dearer Cervantes" (*Tristram Shandy*, 169). He would have read Cervantes in Charles Jervis's translation of 1742, and he likely read Rabelais in the rollicking translation begun by Thomas Urquhart in 1653 and completed by Peter Motteux in 1708.

It is little wonder that Tristram preferred *Don Quixote* to works such as *The Canterbury Tales*. Cervantes was widely read in eighteenth-century England, and he was far from the only influential foreign author on the scene. "Translations," as one translator had already noted in 1654, "swarm more . . . then ever" (Sauer, "Toleration and Translation," 276). From the sixteenth century until Sterne's day, Spanish and French works would often have outnumbered homegrown productions in London booksellers' shops. Their plots, themes, and imagery made their way into English writing in much the same way as local material would do, adopted by writers who didn't cordon off translated works in some separate mental folder from English-language originals. Nor were major English works always published in England, or even in English. Sir Thomas More's *Utopia*— written in Latin and published in Holland in 1516—was never published in England during More's lifetime; it only became part of "English" literature (narrowly defined) in 1551, when it was finally published in London in an English translation.

Scholars in semiperipheral cultures have long been well aware of the active presence of translated works as constitutive parts of national traditions, though these insights have rarely been developed by literary historians in more hegemonic cultures. Thus in 1894, the Mexican essayist Manuel Gutiérrez Nájera disputed the Spanish-centered perspective of the Peninsular scholars of his day. He asserted that Spanish novelists had become excellent writers less by reading their direct predecessors than by reading foreign works, and he emphasized that national literatures are import-export markets:

> The more prose and poetry Spanish literature imports from Germany, France, England, Italy, Russia, North and South America, etc., the more it will produce, and its exports will be all the richer and more numerous. It seems improper for me to apply such plebeian commercial terms to literature, but I do not find other terms that translate my thought as well. . . . The rebirth of the novel in Spain has coincided— and had to coincide—with the abundance of published translations. Today the Spanish read a lot of Zola, a lot of Daudet, a lot of Bourget, a lot of Goncourt. . . . In other words: the Spanish novel has traveled, and it has learned quite a bit from its travels. (Siskind, *Cosmopolitan Desires*, 138)

Mariano Siskind comments that Gutiérrez Nájera is giving a positive valence to the peripheral writer as importer of goods from the cultural center: "Even before Spain or Mexico or Latin American countries generally engage the world, their marginal situation determines their role as cultural importers. But through importation, they modify the sign of their marginality and become importing/exporting cultures" (138). This is an ideological stance that the Slovene comparatist Marko Juvan has labelled "peripherocentrism," a means by which peripheral cultures negotiate a mode of locally grounded cosmopolitanism (Juvan, "Peripherocentrism").

National literary cultures have regularly become homes away from home for many foreign works. This internationalism isn't only found among peripheral literatures but is an important feature of the metropolitan literatures as well. From this perspective, an internationally influential author such as Bartolomé de Las Casas should rightfully be seen as part of British as well as of colonial Spanish literature. His *Brevíssima relación de la destrucción de las Indias* (1552) is a major critique of Spanish rule in Mexico and the Caribbean, and it circulated in translation in England during the seventeenth century with literary as well as political results. Of particular interest is the second English translation, published in London in 1656. The translator, John Phillips—who was also an early translator of *Don Quixote*—evidently undertook the translation at the request of his uncle, John Milton, who treated him almost as an adopted son. The *Brevíssima relación* had been translated several decades before, but as Elizabeth Sauer has argued in a probing essay, "Toleration and Tradition: The Case of Las Casas, Phillips, and Milton," a new version would be useful to Oliver Cromwell as he sought to counter Spanish hegemony in the New World. He had failed to do so by direct action; the Spanish had soundly defeated a fleet he sent to the Caribbean in 1654. And so Cromwell turned to textual means. In 1655 he published *A Declaration of His Highness, by the Advice of His Council; Setting Forth . . . the Justice of Their Cause against Spain,* a tract that Milton translated into Latin for foreign consumption. Soon afterward, John Phillips was commissioned to translate Las Casas as part of the propaganda effort to highlight the evils of Spanish misrule.

In the introduction to his translation, addressed "To all true English-men," Phillips echoes language that his uncle had employed in his *Observations on the Articles of Peace with the Irish Rebels,* a tract that Milton had written in support of Cromwell's violent suppression of the Irish rebellion of 1649. To a modern eye, England's Irish subjects might seem more like colonized Amerindians than like conquistadors, but to Milton and to Cromwell the common term was Catholicism, and they sought to combat the spreading power of the papacy and the Holy Roman Empire then governed by Spain's monarchs. In translating the *Brevíssima relación,* Phillips played up the human drama of the Spanish practices denounced by Las Casas. "The destruction of the Indies"—*las Indias,* the region—becomes "*The Tears of the* INDIANS," personified victims of oppression. An expansive subtitle mounts a wholesale attack on Spanish imperialism, typographically weighted toward the West Indies, the primary arena of British-Spanish imperial conflict (figure 7).

FIGURE 7. Bartolomé de Las Casas and John Phillips, *Tears of the Indians* (1656). Courtesy of the Huntington Library.

The frontispiece created for the English edition furthers the redirection of the text, with lurid images giving a pornography of violence. The caption makes explicit the link between politics and religion, as the conquistadors are shown conducting an "inquisition for Bloud." The hapless natives in the lower-left panel sink under the weight of a great anchor, at once an image of Spanish naval power and a religious *ancora spei*. The anchorbearing natives are lashed by a demonic Spaniard, as though they are Jesus struggling to carry his cross to Golgotha. Flames shown in all four panels strengthen the identification of the conquistadors as the Devil's henchmen, visually echoing Phillips's preface, which declares that "doubtless it hath been the Satanical Scope of this Tyrant, To set all the European Princes at Variance, and to keep them busie at home, that they might not have leasure to bend their Forces against his Golden Regions" (25).

Furthering the satanic theme, strung-up body parts associate the Spanish with the cannibalistic Aztec priests, widely viewed as minions of the

Devil in his Mexican guise of Huitzilopochtli, god of war. One Spaniard is even shown cutting the heart out of his dismembered victim. Phillips's presentation is thus very different from the Spanish original. For all the severity of Las Casas's critique of the conquistadors' excesses, he was pleading for reform within the imperial project. In John Phillips's hands, his book became a wholesale denunciation of Spanish rule, even an attack on Catholic culture at large—a radical revision that would have shocked Las Casas.

If John Phillips drew on his uncle's tracts in framing his translation, *The Tears of the Indians* became a resource for Milton in turn, inflecting his portrayal of Satan in *Paradise Lost*. Traditionally seen in terms of classical paganism, Milton's Satan is also closely associated with Catholic imperialism, as Miltonists have underscored in recent years. In book 4 of *Paradise Lost*, Satan voyages from Hell to the "boundless Continent" of Earth, where he hopes to increase his "Honor and Empire with revenge enlarg'd, / By conquering this new World" (4.390–91). The tears of the Indians come to the fore as Adam and Eve contemplate their fallen bodies in their newly sewn clothing:

> O how unlike
> To that first naked Glory. Such of late
> *Columbus* found th' *American* so girt
> With feather'd Cincture, naked else and wild
> Among the Trees on Isles and woody Shores.
> Thus fenc'd, and as they thought, thir shame in part
> Cover'd, but not at rest or ease of Mind,
> They sat them down to weep, nor only Tears
> Rain'd at thir Eyes, but high Winds worse within
> Began to rise, high Passions, Anger, Hate,
> Mistrust, Suspicion, Discord, and shook sore
> Thir inward State of Mind, calm Region once
> And full of Peace, now toss't and turbulent . . .
> (9.1114–26)

The tears of Adam and Eve, brought about by a Hispanized Satan, are the mirror image of the tears of the Indians caused by Phillips's satanic Spanish monarch, who foments discord in Europe in order to keep rivals away from his New World possessions. As Elizabeth Sauer has observed, "The dialectical process of England's identity formation was decisively shaped through its religious, cultural, political and economic relations with Spain" ("Toleration and Translation," 272). She concludes that "textual representation, appropriation, and translation serve in turn as vital but neglected 'forms of nationhood,' thus demonstrating the role of literature in the fraught history of English identity formation" (286). *The Tears of the Indians* is as much an English as a Spanish work, significantly reframed by John Phillips for its English audience. Indeed, his title page puts the matter very aptly: the Spanish original has been "made English" by J. P.

Writers as well as their works can be located on a broad spectrum of national and linguistic belonging, and many important writers have had transnational identities. We have always recognized the presence of a favored few migrant authors within national literary space: T. S. Eliot is regularly included in anthologies of British literature, even as Americanists justifiably continue to claim him as one of their own. Though he was raised in Saint Louis and educated at Harvard, he made his career in England and became a British citizen, exerting a tremendous influence on British literary life through his poetry, his criticism, and his editorial work for Faber and Faber. Yet what of Marie de France? Although this major medieval writer also made her career in London, and though she drew heavily on Arthurian themes in her *lais*, until recently she remained a wholly owned subsidiary of French departments, simply because she wrote in Anglo-Norman and not Anglo-Saxon or Middle English. And this despite the fact that her very name means Marie *from* France—a name that no writer active in France would ever have had. Marie would long since have been taken up by English departments if she had abandoned her cultured French to begin writing in the language of the London streets.

A similar linguistic myopia limits our view of American literature today. From the time *Lolita* hit the best-seller lists, Vladimir Nabokov has been recognized as a major American writer. American studies of Nabokov also regularly take into account his earlier Russian-language works, which entered American literary culture once they were translated by Dmitri Nabokov under his father's watchful eye. Yet what of Marguerite Yourcenar? Like Nabokov, she emigrated to the United States relatively early in her adulthood, and she spent most of her working life in her adopted country. Yet she never shifted from French to English. She continued to set her novels and memoirs in Europe, and in 1980 she became the first woman ever elected to the Académie Française. Though she is certainly a major Belgian-French writer, we misrepresent her work, and the American literary culture of her era, if we consider her exclusively as an eternal European.

Yourcenar moved to the United States in 1939 at age thirty-six. She lived in New England for the dozen years preceding the publication of her masterwork *Mémoires d'Hadrien* (1951), a book she'd begun in France but then set aside, returning to it in 1949. She became a U.S. citizen in 1947, and so she was indeed an American writer, legally speaking, when she composed her most famous novel. Until her death in 1987 she lived in Northeast Harbor, Maine, where "Petite Plaisance," the home she shared with her American partner Grace Frick, is now a museum of her life and work. Like Marie de France before her, however, Yourcenar has been discussed almost exclusively by French scholars, who tend to treat her American sojourn as a long exile in a cultural wasteland, "un pays qu'elle n'aimait guère"—a country she didn't much like (Schurr, "Marguerite Yourcenar," 28). This perspective pervades the 1993 biography by Josyane Savigneau, in which the principal index entry for the United States is "American language and culture, Yourcenar's resistance to" (*Marguerite Yourcenar*, 506). Savigneau portrays Grace Frick as a manipulative seductress who "snatched" Yourcenar away from France and exerted a "tyranny" over their everyday life (149, 154)—a skewed portrayal that has now been corrected by Joan Howard's excellent biography of Frick, *We Met in Paris* (2018), which gives a nuanced account of Yourcenar's relationship to America and her complex, loving relationship with her partner.

Yourcenar was a woman of iron will, and she made a deliberate choice to distance herself from Paris. She and Grace Frick made their life together for four decades, and they traveled widely in the United States, whose expansive breadth Yourcenar praised. "If I were you I would start by hitchhiking to San Antonio or San Francisco," she wrote to one friend. "It takes time to get to know this great country, at once so spread out and so secret" (Savigneau, 197). Deeply if selectively interested in American culture, she collected African American spirituals in the South and translated a volume's worth of them, published under the title *Fleuve profond, sombre rivière* (1964). She published a French translation of Henry James's *What Maisie Knew* in 1947, two years before resuming her work on Hadrian, and later translated James Baldwin.

Yourcenar's active relations to American literature and culture go largely undiscussed by French scholars and are equally neglected by Americanists, who have hardly ever written about her at all.[2] Yet it is likely that her American experiences enriched her meditations on Hadrian's far-flung empire and informed her hero's bemused tolerance of minority populations such as the Jews in Roman Judea. Living in Connecticut and teaching at Sarah Lawrence College as she worked on *Mémoires d'Hadrien*, Yourcenar was surely gathering impressions from her students as well as information from the Yale library, where she conducted much of the extensive research that underlies her novel. Even her disengagement from American popular culture can be seen as contributing to her Olympian portrayal of the Roman emperor. As Edmund White shrewdly noted in a review of Savigneau's biography, "Yourcenar's aloofness at Sarah Lawrence sounds remarkably like Vladimir Nabokov's at Cornell" (White, Review). Both novelists lectured on comparative literature at their respective colleges, and in the very years that Nabokov was gathering local color for *Lolita* at Cornell, Yourcenar was plotting out her universalized portrait of Hadrian in Connecticut and Maine.

Her choice to settle in the United States, she later said, "is not that of America against France. It translates a taste for a world stripped of all

---

[2] As of May 2019, of the 141 entries in the *MLA Bibliography* that discuss Yourcenar's novel, a grand total of three are by Americanists. Among French scholars, a rare exception is Stéphanie Durrans's "The Translation in the Closet" (2015), which outlines significant parallels between *Mémoires d'Hadrien* and Willa Cather's *Death Comes for the Archbishop*, which Yourcenar had unsuccessfully tried to translate not long before resuming work on her novel.

borders" (Savigneau, 197)—a rather American take on life at the time of such works as Jack Kerouac's *On the Road*. In an afterword to *Memoirs of Hadrian*, Yourcenar wrote of the intense pleasure of resuming her long-abandoned novel while she was on an extended road trip of her own, by train, in February 1949:

> Closed inside my compartment as if in a cubicle of some Egyptian tomb, I worked late into the night between New York and Chicago; then all the next day, in the restaurant of a Chicago station where I awaited a train blocked by storms and snow; then again until dawn, alone in the observation car of a Santa Fé Limited, surrounded by black spurs of the Colorado mountains, and by the eternal pattern of the stars. Thus were written at a single impulsion the passages on food, love, sleep, and the knowledge of men. I can hardly recall a day spent with more ardor, or more lucid nights. (328)

Yourcenar was always sensitive to place—she and Grace Frick became environmental activists in their later years—and she drew inspiration from the expansive American landscape, at once local and universal (surrounded by the black spurs of the Rockies and the eternal pattern of the stars), both linked to the landscape and separated from it, "alone in the observation car of a Santa Fé Limited."

Published in Paris in 1951, *Mémoires d'Hadrien* entered American literary space in 1954 when Farrar, Straus brought it out in the eloquent translation prepared in Northeast Harbor by Frick in close collaboration with Yourcenar. *Memoirs of Hadrian* received glowing reviews and stayed on the *New York Times* best-seller list for twenty weeks, from December 1954 through May 1955. It was eventually edged off the list by a varied group of American and imported novels, including Françoise Sagan's *Bonjour Tristesse,* Thomas Mann's *Confessions of Felix Krull,* and—very different in provenance and tone—Mac Hyman's military comedy *No Time for Sergeants,* which featured a cover blurb by Bennett Cerf praising it as "a four-star, one hundred per cent wowser." *Lolita* was then in press, and Nabokov was pondering his next fictional move; it seems likely that he was intrigued by his fellow émigré's portrayal of a homosexual philosopher-king. The popular success of Hadrian's fictional memoir certainly helped pave the way for the reception of Nabokov's next novel, the commentary-memoir of the deposed Zemblan monarch Charles X. Kinbote.

Taken together, the examples of France Prešeren, Bartolomé de Las Casas, and Marguerite Yourcenar can suggest something of the international variety that is regularly to be found within a national literary culture. What such cases show is that the national and the global are by no means opposed spheres. If we adopt Gutiérrez Nájera's "plebeian commercial terms" and follow the money, we find that local products share the bookstore shelves with international imports, and that a national literature is most fully understood as the storehouse of all the works that have an effective presence within their national market.

Canon and Hypercanon, Minor and Ultraminor

We can think in terms of literary markets without surrendering to them. Scholars are always seeking to intervene in the academic marketplace and ultimately to influence a wider public, directing attention to neglected authors, texts, and approaches. Comparatists in particular tend to have an oblique, or we might say transversal, relationship to national markets. We often aggregate and value writers differently from their usual ordering within the national canon, and we press our specialist colleagues to open out more fully to the international dimensions within and beyond their borders. Both the national and the international literary canons are constantly shifting, as a result of changing tastes as well as scholarly interventions.

In the United States, the civil rights and feminist movements of the 1960s led to a major opening up of what had been an almost entirely white male canon. These changes soon began to affect literary theory as well, as we saw in chapter 4 in the scholarship of Barbara Johnson and Gayatri Spivak. Today, the six-volume anthologies of English, American, and world literature published by Bedford, Longman, and Norton present as many as five hundred authors in their six thousand pages, often with dozens of countries included in the world anthologies that formerly presented only European writers. It is even possible to consider that the old Eurocentric canon is fading away. As Christopher Braider put it in his contribution to the Saussy Report in 2006, contemporary postcolonial scholars "have not only completed the critical dismantling of the inherited literary canon but have displaced the European metropolis from the traditional center of comparatist attention" ("Of Monuments and Documents," 161).

This dismantling, however, is only half the story, and not only because it hasn't yet occurred in practice to the extent that it has been achieved in poststructuralist or postcolonial theory. We may live in a postcanonical age, but our age is postcanonical in much the same way that it is postindustrial. The rising stars of the postindustrial economy, after all, often turn out to look a good deal like the older industries: Amazon needs warehouses of bricks and mortar; Apple and Lenovo have built huge assembly-line factories, complete with toxic chemicals and pollution problems, as they crank out an ever-growing number of quickly obsolescing products to overburden our closets and the world's landfills. This recrudescence of old-style industrialization is compounded by a second factor: many of the established industries have proven to do quite well in our postindustrial age. The automobile, icon and mainstay of the old industrial economy, hasn't gone the way of the stagecoach in the age of the Information Highway. There are more cars on the road than ever, and in particular there are more *luxury* automobiles on the road. The Lexus, the Mercedes, and their high-end friends have profited by adding value in the form of dozens of microprocessors that do everything from improving fuel economy to remembering their drivers' preferred seating positions.

Comparative literature presents a similar situation, partly because literary theory stepped in to provide an alternate canon to fill the gap left by the literature it was busy deconstructing and decentering. If we no longer focus largely on a common canon of literary masterworks that we can require our students to study and expect our readers to know, we need some alternate basis to work from. So, it's said, we rely on Butler, Foucault, and Spivak to provide the common basis for conversations formerly underwritten by shared knowledge of Dante, Shakespeare, and Baudelaire. But have these old-economy authors really dropped by the wayside? Quite the contrary: many of them are more discussed than ever, and they continue to be more strongly represented in survey anthologies than almost any of the new discoveries of recent decades. Like the Lexus, the high-end author consolidates his (much more rarely, her) market share by adding value from the postcanonical trends: the James Joyce who used to be a central figure in the study of European high modernism now inspires ambitious collections of articles with titles like *Semicolonial Joyce* and *Transnational Joyce*. Undeniably, comparatists today are giving more and more attention to "various contestatory, subaltern, or marginal perspectives," as the Bernheimer Report urged in 1993 (44), yet most of the older major authors are still very much with us.

How can this be? Something surely has to give. The number of hours in the day and the number of weeks in the semester haven't expanded along with the literary canon, yet we're definitely reading all sorts of works that are beyond the scope of the old "Western Masterpieces." We must be reading them in place of *something:* hence the frequent assumption, especially by opponents of the recent expansion, that we're abandoning Shakespeare for Toni Morrison. But this isn't so. Instead, just as in the postindustrial economy, what has happened is that the rich have gotten richer, while most others just scrape by or see their fortunes diminish. In the process, the canon has morphed from a two-tiered system into a multilevel one. Formerly, national literatures could be fairly cleanly divided into "major" and "minor" authors, and even in the heyday of the masterpiece approach, a range of minor Western authors could still be found accompanying the major authors in anthologies, on syllabi, and in scholarly discussion. The 1956 *Norton Anthology of World Masterpieces* (as it was then called) had no women at all among its seventy-three authors; only in the third edition of 1976 did the editors finally include two pages by a woman, Sappho. Yet they found room for the Russian symbolist Aleksandr Blok and the minor Portuguese realist Raoul Brandão, along with their far more extensive selections from Dante and Dostoevsky.

This two-tiered model of major and minor authors has shifted in recent years. Far from fading away, a few of the old major authors have ascended into what can be called a hypercanon—the equivalent of the increasing wealth of the 1 percent. Again on analogy to socioeconomic classes, the category of "major author" can be subdivided into "upper major" writers and still prominent but less frequently discussed "lower

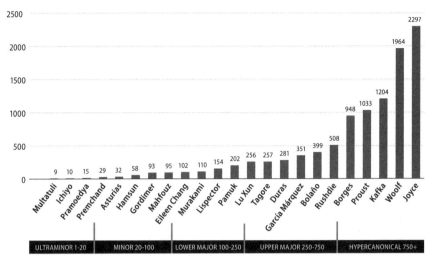

FIGURE 8. Canonicity as shown by citations in the *MLA Bibliography*.

major" figures. Meanwhile, the category of the minor author can be supplemented by a category of *ultraminor* figures. I owe this term to the Faroese comparatist Bergur Moberg, who has coined it in regard to very small
countries or language communities such as his own ("The Ultraminor,"
2017). In a canonical context the term can be applied to individual authors as well. These are often significant, even major figures at home but
are rarely read or discussed by scholars elsewhere.

As a way of charting these divisions, I looked at two dozen authors I've
been recently working on, to see how often they were listed in subject
headings in the *MLA Bibliography* during the decade 2008–2017. I count as
"ultraminor" those writers who have averaged fewer than two subject listings per year over the course of the decade. "Minor" authors are those having 20–100 listings during the decade, "lower major" have 100–250, and
"upper major" have 250–750, while "hypercanonical" writers enjoy more
than 750 listings, and often many more. The results are shown in figure 8.
Needless to say, this is not a comprehensive exercise in data mining, both
because of my very personal choice of authors and because the *MLA International Bibliography*, despite its name, is far from complete in its inclusion
of international scholarship. It has more worldwide listings these days than
it formerly did, with many entries now in Chinese, Japanese, and Arabic,

but it remains heavily weighted toward North American and European journals that report their listings to the MLA. Even so, the chart reveals striking disparities of scholarly attention, disparities that are only partially related to the writers' standing in their homeland or their international recognition as evidenced by such markers as the Nobel Prize.

As the chart indicates, the hypercanon is populated by older major authors who haven't just held their ground but have gained substantially in recent years. Proust, Borges, Kafka, Woolf, and Joyce occupy this category in my sample, and each of them has many more entries than the leading authors in the "upper major" category. It may be noted that most of the upper major authors, as well as all the hypercanonical authors, have written in the same three hegemonic languages identified by Georg Brandes in 1899—English, French, and German—plus one additional global language, Spanish. The power of global English is reflected in the outsized tallies for Joyce and Woolf, who tower above their hypercanonical neighbors, while the persisting advantage of French over most of the world's languages is evidenced in Marguerite Duras's 281 listings, placing her above the Nobel Prize winners Rabindranath Tagore (with 257) and Orhan Pamuk (with 202) as well as China's pivotal modernist Lu Xun (with 256). Duras is an excellent writer, but she hardly has the stature, either at home or abroad, of these major writers in less hegemonic languages.

The overall pattern is clear, though there are exceptions. Neither the Nobel Prize nor the power of global English has kept Nadine Gordimer in the company of these constantly discussed writers. Her stock rose considerably amid the anti-Apartheid struggles in South Africa and her receipt of the Nobel Prize in 1991, and during the decade 1988–1997 she had a substantial set of 202 listings in the *MLA Bibliography*. Then in the following decade she slipped to 135 listings, on the way to her most recent ten-year total of 93, only slightly above the 80 she had received in 1978–87.

At least she was writing in English. As Brandes would have predicted, it remains as challenging as ever to be a major writer in a peripheral country whose language is also peripheral within the world linguistic system. Thus the Nobel Prize winners Naguib Mahfouz and Knut Hamsun languish in the minor category, despite their seminal importance in the literary histories of their countries and their entire regions. All the writers on the list who ended up in the lower major category write in nonhegemonic languages: Arabic, Chinese, Japanese, Portuguese, and Turkish. All are from literary traditions whose importance is widely acknowledged in principle but often neglected in practice outside specialist circles. Even Lu Xun, shown toward the bottom of the upper major category with 256 entries, would fall well down within the range of lower major authors if we subtract the 131 entries that are written in Chinese. The ultraminor category includes Japan's Higuchi Ichiyō, Indonesia's Pramoedya Ananta Toer, and the Dutch writer Multatuli; minor European languages are disadvantaged at roughly the rate of major non-Western languages, just as Brandes found in 1899, when he expressed his profound irritation that third-rate French writers could become better known than the very best Scandinavians.

What is evident from this very selective chart is that many of the old major authors coexist quite comfortably with the new arrivals to the neighborhood. All of my hypercanonical writers were well represented in the *MLA Bibliography* fifty years ago, when none of the others on the list (apart from García Márquez) had more than a handful of listings. Further, all the hypercanonicals have had substantially more listings in the past decade than they did five decades ago. Joyce's and Proust's listings have increased by a third, Borges's have doubled, and Woolf's have multiplied almost fivefold. García Márquez has gained as well, but he still has a lower total now than any of the five hypercanonical figures had half a century ago. Far from being threatened by their unfamiliar neighbors, the old major authors gain new vitality from association with them, and only rarely do they need to admit one of them into their club. By "they," of course, I really mean "we." It is we teachers and scholars who determine which writers will be effectively represented in today's classrooms, at our conferences, and in our journals and books.

As we sustain the system today, it is often the old "minor" authors who fade into the background, becoming a sort of shadow canon that the older generation still knows (or vaguely remembers from long ago), but whom the younger generations of students and scholars encounter less and less. This process can be seen even within the national literatures, where pressures of time and range are much less pronounced than in the larger scales of comparative and world literature. Shakespeare and Joyce aren't going anywhere, and spacious new wings have been added onto the libraries devoted to their work, but Hazlitt and Galsworthy are looking a little threadbare on the rare occasions when they're seen out and about. It may not be long until their cultural capital runs out and their ruined cottages are bought for a tear-down.

This canonical bifurcation is pronounced even within a single country; the disparities of attention are more dramatic still when it comes to world literature, given the severe pressures of time and numbers involved. If we define world literature for this purpose as works that are discussed beyond the ranks of specialists in an author's country or region of origin, we see the hypercanonical impulse extending far beyond older fields formerly closely held by the New Criticism and its offshoots. In world literature, as in some literary Miss Universe competition, an entire nation may be represented by a single author: Indonesia, the world's fifth-largest country and the home of ancient and ongoing cultural traditions, is usually seen, if at all, in the person of Pramoedya Ananta Toer. Jorge Luis Borges and Julio Cortázar divide the honors for Mr. Argentina.

A high degree of selectivity may be understandable in view of world literature's new scope, yet it is remarkable to see how an incipient hypercanon has come to create divisions even among the select group of non-Western authors who have become well known in North America. The field of postcolonial studies has shown rapid growth during the past forty years, and yet this growth has affected authors in very uneven ways, to a degree that seems quite disproportionate to any differences of artistic quality or cultural influence. A few favorite writers have emerged into a postcolonial hypercanon (counting an "upper major" level of listings as the index of hypercanonicity in the specific field of postcolonial studies). Chinua Achebe, J. M. Coetzee, Salman Rushdie, Derek Walcott, and a few others have joined García Márquez—again, a list dominated by men, and predominantly men writing in English. I haven't found many other postcolonial writers with that level of attention. Instead, we fairly soon reach a level of a small handful of entries per year, even for such important writers as Munshi Premchand and the Nobel Prize winner Miguel Ángel Asturias. These infrequently discussed writers could be called the Hazlitts of postcolonial studies—an odd way to think of them, surely, given their excellence as writers and their eminence in their home countries. Yet the numbers suggest that internationally they have the marginal status once accorded to "minor" Romantic poets and essayists.

Some members of this shadow canon formerly loomed larger in discussions of colonial and postcolonial literature but are now being eclipsed by the ascent of other authors into the upper-major ranks: Asturias is overshadowed by García Márquez, R. K. Narayan has been upstaged by Salman Rushdie, Alan Paton gave way in the 1980s to Nadine Gordimer. Gordimer in turn is now being shouldered aside by her fellow Nobel laureate J. M. Coetzee, who was at parity with her during the 1980s but has far outstripped her since then; in 2008–2017, he received 759 listings to her 93. All in all, even without the inherited underpinnings of author-specific journals and special-interest groups (*The Wordsworth Circle*, the Shakespeare Associations of England and of America), it appears that postcolonial studies is reproducing the hypercanonical bias of the older European-based fields.

In 1995 Rey Chow warned that the early efforts to broaden the spectrum of comparative studies weren't so much dismantling the great-power canon as extending its sway by admitting a few new great powers into the alliance:

> The problem does not go away if we simply substitute India, China and Japan for England, France, and Germany. . . . In such instances, the concept of literature is strictly subordinated to a social Darwinian understanding of the nation: "masterpieces" correspond to "master" nations and "master" cultures. With India, China, and Japan being held as representative of Asia, cultures of lesser prominence in Western reception such as Korea, Taiwan, Vietnam, Tibet, and others simply fall by the wayside—as marginalized "others" to the "other" that is the "great" Asian civilizations. ("In the Name of Comparative Literature," 109)

Since then, her warning may have been partially averted at the level of the nation only to return at the level of the celebrity author.

How should we respond to this situation during the years ahead? As readers, we should resist it; as scholars and teachers, we should turn it to our advantage. We now have the resources available, in anthologies and in individual volumes, to read more widely and to present a wider range of materials to our students. Of course Rushdie, like Woolf, is a wonderful figure to discuss for many purposes, but we don't always and everywhere have to come back to the same few figures. In particular, we should take more care than we usually do to coordinate syllabi: far too often, a student will emerge from college having read *Things Fall Apart* three times and *Beloved* four times, but never having read Mahfouz or Ghalib.

We should resist the hegemony of the hypercanon, yet as long as it is a fact of life, we should also turn it to our advantage. Students may not enroll in a course on writers they've never heard of, so if we do want to broaden their horizons, it can be useful to include enough hypercanonical figures to catch their attention—not least because writers enter the hypercanon only when they really are exciting to read and talk about in a wide variety of contexts. Yet our offerings don't have to be all Rushdie all the time, any more than they ever needed to be all Shakespeare all the time. As my anthology co-editors and I have found, hypercanonical and countercanonical works can be grouped together, to the benefit of both.

Outside the hypercanon, surprisingly little cross-cutting work has been done to link writers beyond the boundaries of regional spaces or imperial networks. This was brought home to me some years ago when my graduate students in English at Columbia made a special request for "a Joyce course." As they recognized, Joyce's status is such that a course devoted to him offers valuable training for students interested in modernism, in postmodernism, in postcolonial studies, and in the history of the novel. I readily agreed to offer this course, but as a comparatist I wanted to expand the field, so I surrounded Joyce's works with a range of precursors, contemporaries, and successors. Some of these readings showed direct lines of influence: from Ibsen to Joyce, who learned Dano-Norwegian in order to read his hero in the original; from Joyce in turn to Clarice Lispector. Other choices, such as *Swann's Way,* were intended to suggest something of the modernist "field" within which Joyce was writing. I wanted to start by giving some sense of the ways that realism was dealing with issues of gender in the 1890s as Joyce approached the period of writing *Dubliners,* so I assigned Ibsen's *A Doll's House,* which Joyce knew intimately, together with "Separate Ways," a short story by Higuchi Ichiyō.

Joyce would never have heard of her, but her story is comparable to Joyce's tales of broken families, told in a mode of poetic naturalism. Unexpectedly, Ibsen proved to provide a common term of comparison. In an enthusiastic review of Ichiyō in 1896, the novelist Mori Ōgai declared that in her writing "the characters are not those beastlike creatures one so often encounters in Ibsen or Zola, whose techniques the so-called naturalists have tried imitating to the utmost. They are real, human individuals that we laugh and cry with" (Danly, *In the Shade of Spring Leaves*, 148). Beyond their responses to naturalism, a further ground of comparison between Ichiyō and Joyce can be found in their early involvement with peripheral magazines and newspapers, as will be discussed in the next chapter.

Such strategic conjunctions enable us to avoid the extremes of choosing between a well-grounded but restricted study of direct influences and an ungrounded, universalizing juxtaposition of radically unconnected works, in the mode advocated by Alain Badiou in his *Handbook of Inaesthetics* or the "invariants" championed by Étiemble. Focused comparisons between hypercanonical and non- or countercanonical writers can do much to illuminate familiar and newly visible authors alike, and they can ease the problems of audience faced by anyone who wants to work on either sort of author. If most nonspecialist readers have never heard of Higuchi Ichiyō, how are we to interest them in looking at her work, especially if we don't want to reduce her to yet another peripheral illustration of some Euro-American theorist's master-narrative? Conversely, with no fewer than 10,778 books and articles published on Joyce during the past fifty years, every Irish ballad has already been tracked down, every chapter—almost every sentence—of *Ulysses* lovingly dissected, debated, reinterpreted. What can possibly be left to say if we dream of writing essay 10,779? In this circumstance, cross-cultural comparisons prove to be marvelously illuminating and refreshing. Making them, moreover, can help lessen the radical imbalance of attention given to upper major and hypercanonical writers versus almost everyone else.

Comparisons have regularly been made within the hypercanonical ranks: over the years, a total of 91 books or articles have been published on Joyce and Proust, including 26 just in the past decade. Yet what of Joyce and Clarice Lispector? She is one of the most important writers of the second half of the twentieth century, and she was far more directly in dialogue with Joyce than was Proust, who never read him and who famously had nothing to say to him on the one occasion when they met. Lispector titled her first novel, *Perto do coração selvagem* (*Near to the Wild Heart*), with a phrase from *A Portrait of the Artist as a Young Man*, and her collection of linked short stories *Laços de família* (*Family Ties*) is one of *Dubliners*' most creative successors. She has a substantial number of 154 entries from the past decade in the *MLA Bibliography,* yet not one of these items compares her and Joyce. And what of Tagore? A dominant figure in modern Bengali literature, he shared Joyce's concerns with colonialism, interlinguistic tensions, and the impact of modernity on resistant traditional societies. Yet among the 551 entries for Tagore over the course of the past fifty years—and the more than *10,000* for Joyce—there is only a single article on Tagore and Joyce, published in 1997. Perhaps less surprisingly, given the small number of articles written on Premchand or Ichiyō, there isn't a single article on either of them and Joyce. Still less (if an empty set can have an even emptier subset) are there any articles on Premchand and Ichiyō.

We've come a fair distance in the quarter-century since the Bernheimer Report was published, but we seem to be succumbing too readily to the pressures of time and the attractions of hypercanonical celebrity, both within Western literature and beyond. Perhaps we've been too quick to take the advice of Joyce's elusive, lisping character Sylvia Silence, "the girl detective," in her thinly veiled critique of *Ulysses*: "Though a day be as dense as a decade," she warns us, "you must, how, in undivided reawlity draw the line somewhawre" (*Finnegans Wake,* 292). Not one line but many: lines of connection across the conflicted boundaries of nations and of cultures, and new lines of comparison across the divisions between the hypercanon and the countercanons of world literature.

Literature in the Global Mediascape

Literature has always circulated together with other modes of artistic expression. Painting, sculpture, and music are classic subjects for interarts comparison, more recently supplemented by a growing engagement with film studies, but comparatists have done relatively little with the newer media now in play, leaving them to media studies specialists based in national traditions. Yet it is increasingly clear that literature is in worldwide competition today with the rapidly developing forms of newer media, from cable television to music videos to online games, and literary scholars may have an uneasy sense that literature is losing out in the competition. As readers give way to viewers, the results may be almost unrecognizable even when a literary predecessor is evoked.

Consider the imposing figure of Girugaamesshu (figure 9). This is none other than Gilgamesh, hero of the world's first major work of world literature, now reincarnated as a warrior in Hironobu Sakaguchi's best-selling video game series *Final Fantasy* (*Fainaru Fantaji*), first released by Nintendo in 1987, with around 150 million units sold since then. Global traditions meet in this reincarnated Gilgamesh. His eight arms recall the iconography of ancient Hindu divinities, while his weapons have an international pedigree. A traveling sword collector, he is equipped with "Genji equipment" based on medieval Japanese narratives such as *The Tale of the Heike* (somewhat oddly assimilated to Murasaki Shikibu's poetic Prince Genji), and in the *Final Fantasy* series he is often shown searching for King Arthur's sword Excalibur. What are we to make of such a figure, with its imploding of the world's literary traditions? Can—or should— literary scholars engage with such materials, or are they only so much cultural noise we can just as well ignore? More ominously, do such virtual avatars herald the approaching end of literary studies as we know them? How much value is there to analyzing the *Morte d'Arthur* or debating the inclusion of *Gilgamesh* versus *The Tale of Genji* in our survey courses, if all that our students really want to do is to play the video game?

The overwhelming of literature by the dark electronic arts is a source of anxiety in Haun Saussy's lead essay in the 2006 ACLA report on the state of the discipline. "We live in an era of plentiful information, information

FIGURE 9. *Final Fantasy* Gilgamesh. 7 inch PVC action figure. Square Enix Co., 2008.

so readily available as to be almost worthless," Saussy says, and he asks, "what would Marcel have made of the inaccessibility of Albertine's mind if he had always before him her GPS location, heart rate, probable serotonin level, last 500 Google searches, past year's credit card transactions, status on Friendster, speed-dial list, and 25 most-played songs?" ("Exquisite Cadavers," 31). Saussy observes that an electronic file of *War and Peace*, "downloadable gratis from the Gutenberg Project," takes up the same space on a hard drive as a sixty-second sample from "The Sounds of Moo: The Young Polish Real Electronic Music," and in this context "most of literature looks like a relic of an earlier, data-poor, low-bandwidth era of communications. The reader of literature is a paleontologist, scraping and fitting together a few poor bones to imagine a ten-story beast." He somberly concludes that "the close readings and paradoxes of traditional literary criticism must have been symptoms of the information-poor communications networks of the past, when details mattered" (32).

Even if we share Saussy's concern, we will do better to engage with the new media than retreat into a paleontological stance of regret for the loss of the long, difficult novels now threatened with extinction in the curriculum. Five years after his ACLA report, in fact, Saussy himself co-edited a special issue of the online journal *CLCWeb* devoted to "New Perspectives on Material Culture and Intermedial Practice" (Tötösy de Zepetnek et al., 2011), which includes valuable essays on topics including video games, graphic novels, and remediation in digital media. Such intermedial work is as much a matter of translation as of interpretation. As Karen Littau has said, "a properly 'worldly' account of the place of literature requires, perhaps more than ever, that translation be recast as not irreducibly inter-lingual, but additionally inter- and trans-medial" ("Two Ages of World Literature," 161). Extending our work to the global mediascape can offer new possibilities for comparative study if we adapt our literary-critical skills to these materials and to the new material conditions they reflect.

To date, the rapidly growing field of media studies has predominantly been developed by scholars in disciplines other than literature: in Germany, for instance, by sociologists, political scientists, and film scholars, and in the United States within departments of communication or American Studies. Some scholars in both countries have begun to apply literary analysis to new media, as can be seen in Ernest Hess-Lüttich's "Netzliteratur—ein neues Genre?" and in Corneliussen and Rettberg's collection *Digital Culture, Play, and Identity,* though only one of their thirteen contributors is based in a department of literature. In an early entry into the field by a comparatist, Eric Hayot analyzed the virtual worlds of online games in essays such as "Reading Game/Text" (2004) prior to publishing *On Literary Worlds* in 2012, the year before he became ACLA's president. Comparative literary studies can thrive in the newly expansive media environment, bringing new audiences to some of our favorite authors and offering literary insights and cross-cultural perspectives to new media studies of language, narrative, and representation. The changing mediascape will entail the redirection of some of our approaches, and not all the classics of the pre-internet age will survive the transition. Yet others will: classic works have persisted over the centuries precisely through their adaptability to new times and new media.

Entranced by a bard's performance of the *Iliad*, a listener in the tenth century BCE might have thought it impossible for Homer's poetry to be conveyed effectively in the strange new technology of *graphesis* or writing. A great many songs were certainly lost with the eclipse of the old oral tradition, but through the medium of writing the *Iliad* and *Odyssey* survived long after the death of the last illiterate bard. Buried in the sands of Iraq for two millennia, *The Epic of Gilgamesh* skipped the entire era of the transition from tablet and scroll to the invention of printing. It came to light just at the dawn of the modern media age, which is not an altogether new age, as we can consider as we scroll down our tablet when we read *Gilgamesh* in PDF. Thanks to the new technologies of film and video, millions of viewers have heard Gilgamesh's story retold by *Star Trek*'s Captain Picard to a dying Tamarian on the distant planet of El-Adrel. No mere window-dressing in this scene, "the oldest story in our world" (as Picard calls it) provides a key moment of interspecies understanding, as the Tamarian language consists entirely of metaphors. Having gotten nowhere with direct statements, Picard discovers that he can only communicate through poetic language and storytelling.[3]

As an example of the reframing of the literary canon today, consider *Dante's Inferno*—not the first third of the *Commedia*, but the video game. In December 2009 Electronic Arts, Inc., put out a news release to announce the game's pending arrival:

> Attention PlayStation 3 owners: Satan will see you now! And thank you for waiting!
>
> **SPEND THE HOLIDAYS IN HELL WITH THE DANTE'S INFERNO DEMO!**

Muscular Christianity goes steroidal in this game, in which a heavily armed Dante battles his way through Hell to rescue a buxom Beatrice from

---

[3] "Darmok," episode 102 of *Star Trek: The Next Generation*. www.startrek.com/database _article/darmok (accessed July 10, 2018).

Satan's clutches. The game's "official website" gave the following summary at the time of the demo's release:

> Players will experience fast-paced hack-n-slash combat as they fend off waves of enemies before taking on the ultimate battle against Death. After defeating this boss, Dante will be armed with Death's scythe, a powerful holy cross, and will be ready to tear open the Gates of Hell. . . . "Our main goal from the start of this project has been to create a journey that will make gamers truly feel like they are going through hell," said executive producer Jonathan Knight.[4]

Plundering the classics at will, game makers show signs of an anxiety of influence, though not of a literary nature; instead, their concern is to differentiate themselves from their immediate predecessors in the video game market. Thus the box for *Genji: Days of the Blade* (Sony Computer Entertainment, 2006) announces that the game "unveils beautiful next generation graphics and vastly improved game play on your PlayStation 3. Step away from the traditional gaming experience as you discover a new level of action and adventure for the PS3." Here, "the traditional gaming experience" means "two years ago," and "next generation graphics" means "better than your older brother's." The *Genji* has circulated for centuries in illustrated versions and has been turned into manga and anime in recent decades, but *Genji: Days of the Blade* goes much further, transforming Genji into a sword-wielding samurai, a figure at a radical remove from Murasaki's poetic, perfume-blending hero.

In 2003 Jan Van Looy and Jan Baetens published a collection entitled *Close Reading New Media: Analyzing Electronic Literature,* and students of the new media are increasingly taking what Simon Egenfeldt-Nielsen has described as "a cultural turn in video games studies." He argues that "a close reading of a video game is not only possible, but it also yields interesting insights about how a game that makes use of stories is experienced by a player," and he advocates exploration of "the poetics of game design"

---

[4] www.dantesinferno.com (accessed March 9, 2010). This site no longer exists—a common feature of sites for the fluid gaming world.

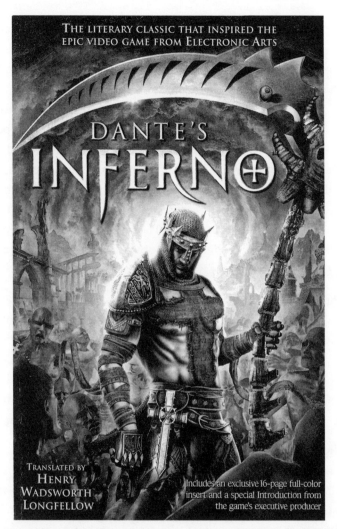

THE LITERARY CLASSIC THAT INSPIRED THE
EPIC VIDEO GAME FROM ELECTRONIC ARTS

DANTE'S
INFERNO✠

TRANSLATED BY
HENRY
WADSWORTH
LONGFELLOW

Includes an exclusive 16-page full-color
insert and a special Introduction from
the game's executive producer

FIGURE 10. Cover for the Electronic Arts edition of Dante's *Inferno* (2010).

(*Understanding Video Games*, 189–92). A substantial symbiosis already exists between digital and print culture. To take the example of *Dante's Inferno*, though its producers took extreme liberties with the original, Electronic Arts also published a paperback edition of Dante's actual *Inferno*, distributed by no less a publisher than Random House. They published their Dante edition three months *before* the release of the video game, as a kind of teaser for the game (figure 10).

In this edition, Electronic Arts supplements the poem with an essay by the game's executive producer, and a color insert juxtaposes scenes from the game with classic images of hell, from Hieronymus Bosch to Gustave Doré, that had inspired their designers. Like the video game box, the front cover is adorned with a warrior Dante in a spiked helmet, naked to the waist and with a blood-red cross painted over his rippling pecs (perhaps a distant echo of Spenser's Red Crosse Knight?). This Samurai Dante holds a huge, gleaming scythe with which he is about to vanquish several zombie-like devils against a Boschian backdrop. Dante's poem becomes the game's prequel, "the literary classic that inspired the epic video game from Electronic Arts," as the cover announces. The back cover displays a prophetic optimism befitting the original epic's upward trajectory, celebrating the video game's smashing success months before its actual release:

> All hell is breaking loose. Electronic Arts' thrilling video game *Dante's Inferno* has exploded on the scene and this is the book that provides unique insight into its creation. Go back to the source with Henry Wadsworth Longfellow's celebrated translation of Dante's epic poem. Presented in its entirety, here is the foundation and inspiration for the game. Then learn how the game's creators turned Dante's notorious Nine Circles of Hell into the hottest game around.

What should we make of this overheated *Inferno*?

Certainly we shouldn't uncritically embrace this marketing ploy, but neither should we piously refuse to engage with Electronic Arts' dark arts, as though the game could appeal only to the most naïve and culturally illiterate consumers. In fact, the major lines of response to the appropriation of Dante's poem were already being debated in the gaming community itself around the time of the game's release. Three postings on the gaming fan site Destructoid.com suggest the range of views. A gamer writing under the name Paustinj clearly felt misled by the prepublication of Dante's text: "WTF is this shit?" he wrote, adding: "Expect alot of that from people who buy this book."[5] Paustinj had apparently been look-

---

[5] www.destructoid.com/blogs (accessed March 9, 2010, though no longer visible).

ing for something more along the lines of the *Dante's Inferno Strategy Guide* published by Prima Games (another division of Random House), and so he was annoyed to have been misled into buying a foundational text of Western culture.

Other postings expressed very different views. A gamer called Uzzy took a high Arnoldian line, declaring: "Words simply cannot express just how wrong this is." Though Uzzy roundly rejected the debasement of the Western canon, another Destructoid blogger presented a more nuanced view. SirMonster210, whose thumbnail photo showed a heavily bearded man wearing sunglasses with scarlet lenses, was a hardcore gamer but hardly an uncritical one:

> this game's pending release did inspire me to read the original work. i dont see the game as "ruining" anything. the poem is great and will continue to be great. and the game might be great too. the book will probably be a quick cash in, but who knows . . . the hardcopy *AVP: three world war* has me by the balls and wallet right now. if i can fall for that marketing scheme, who knows.

SirMonster210 read Dante's poem as a result of Electronic Arts' promotion, but though he was impressed by the poem he remained skeptical concerning the game. He surely wasn't alone. In a major marketing push, Electronic Arts bought a thirty-second advertisement during the 2010 Super Bowl broadcast, the most expensive televised event of the year. On his own, Dante would never have made such a splash on American television, and we can expect that SirMonster210 was only one of many consumers who were brought to Dante by the promotion of the game.

Yet *Dante's Inferno* can be understood as something more than a way to inveigle viewers into reading a classic book. No one would mistake the game's cartoonish characters and violent action for Dante's creation, but its visual artistry is another matter, and it can enrich the experience of the poem for readers of the *Commedia*. The game's visual success stemmed from Electronic Arts' decision to commission designs from Wayne Barlowe, a writer and illustrator known for his Dantesque fantasy work *Barlowe's*

Inferno (1999). One admirer of both Dante and Barlowe wrote online about this fruitful conjunction:

> Honestly, the attention to detail is simply fantastic. The walls made of trapped sinners, Minos shouting out verdicts in the background as you approach, the screams of sinners, a man calls out for Ulysses in the bowels of Charon's boat, the detailed backgrounds such as a giant skull spitting out the corpses of the damned at the start. It's simply on a massive, grand scale and if you've ever read Dante and lived to see his Hell brought to the big screen . . . you will NOT be disappointed playing this video game.[6]

Today's electronic games present remarkably rich worlds for scholars as well as consumers to explore. As Jesper Juul says in his book *Half-Real: Video Games between Real Rules and Fictional Worlds*, "The worlds that video games project are often ontologically unstable, but the rules of video games are very ontologically stable. . . . That the majority of fictional game worlds are incoherent does not mean that video games are dysfunctional providers of fiction, but rather that they project fictional worlds in their own flickering, provisional, and optional way" (169).

Grand Theft Ovid

Teachers as well as scholars can find ways to enter these flickering worlds. An ambitious melding of literature and new media can be found in a performance piece called *Grand Theft Ovid*, which has been presented in various forms in New York City and elsewhere since 2009. *Grand Theft Ovid* is the brainchild of Edward Kim, a drama teacher at a private high school in Connecticut. Kim observed that many of his students, boys especially, were spending more time playing online video games than reading literature, and he decided to challenge them to put these interests together. He assigned his class to pick episodes from Ovid's *Metamorphoses* and adapt them to one or more of their favorite online video games, creating

---

[6] Review by Sammycat, 2/9/2010, amazon.com/Dantes-Inferno-Divine-Playstation-3 /product-reviews/B001NX6GBK (accessed November 9, 2019).

FIGURE 11. Performance of *Grand Theft Ovid*, directed by Edward Kim, Brick Theater, Brooklyn, New York, 2010. Photograph by Michael Gardner.

avatars for each character and then finding appropriate settings and props for each tale. One game the class used was *Grand Theft Auto*, which provided the basis for the work's witty title; other games used included *World of Warcraft* and *Halo 3*.

The assignment was so successful that Kim was able to take the results on the road as a theater piece. I first saw *Grand Theft Ovid* in an experimental theater in New York City, where it was performed live to a packed audience of hipsters, plus myself. Several students were seated at laptop computers connected to the internet (figure 11), while another student read Ovid's text aloud. All the pieces involved line-by-line attention to *The Metamorphoses*, and the students often found inventive settings for the tales (Icarus, for instance, becomes a military pilot whose helicopter crashes). Interesting juxtapositions occurred in scenes set in *World of Warcraft*, where unrelated teams periodically came through the spaces being used by the *Grand Theft Ovid* group. The game allows players to post comments to whoever is online in a given room, and several exchanges took place between Kim's students and puzzled *Warcraft* veterans, some of whom were amused while others were annoyed to learn that Ovid had invaded their mythological realm.

All the episodes were interesting, but particularly effective was the story of Niobe, who refuses to worship the goddess Latona, mother of Apollo and Diana. Niobe boasts that she is more deserving of worship than the goddess, having fourteen children to Latona's two, whereupon the enraged goddess has her son take his bow and kill Niobe's children. The group set this tale within *Halo 3*, a "first-person shooter" game, to give its proper generic designation. This choice had an uncanny effect: we viewers found ourselves in an arid landscape of hills and stone structures, behind the barrel of a machine gun, helplessly joining the unseen god as he pulled the trigger to exterminate Niobe's seven sons and then her seven daughters, as each would appear from some hiding place, seeking to flee or hurrying to comfort a dying sibling. The result was a kind of overlay of the Iraq War and *King Lear*: "As flies to wanton boys are we to th' gods; / They kill us for their sport," as Gloucester grimly remarks late in the play (4.1.36–37).[7]

Grand Theft Ovid's Niobe episode powerfully counters the dulling effect of the virtual-reality violence critiqued in Petra Grimm and Heinrich Badura's collection *Medien—Ethik—Gewalt*. In its live staging of the game play and its accompanying recitation of Ovid, *Grand Theft Ovid* also complicates the imposition of virtuality on reality that Andrzej Kiepas has discussed as "real virtuality" ("Medien in der Kultur"). Changing realities have, in fact, changed *Grand Theft Ovid* itself, as Edward Kim periodically has his students do a new version of the piece, either taking different episodes from Ovid or redoing existing ones. Two of their versions of "Niobe" can be found on YouTube, under the titles "EK Theater—Niobe 2010" (the version described here) and "EK Theater—'Niobe' Halo: Reach." When I invited them to perform their piece at Harvard in April 2016, I found that

---

[7] Appropriately, this quotation provides the title for an online story by a gamer, based on the *Final Fantasy* series (Iknopeiston, "As Flies to Wanton Boys").

they had given "Niobe" an urban setting, no longer suggesting desert warfare but now tied to mass shootings in schools.

Developed through a creative collaboration between a teacher and his students, *Grand Theft Ovid* differs from Electronic Arts' *Dante's Inferno* in its fidelity to its source. The performances restage Ovid in much the way that Peter Sellars gave Mozart's operas new life in the 1980s by using the original scores and libretti but setting *Don Giovanni* in Spanish Harlem and *The Marriage of Figaro,* prophetically, in Trump Tower. *Grand Theft Ovid* also differs from *Dante's Inferno* in its choice of a translation. In publishing their *Inferno* prequel, Electronic Arts used the plodding nineteenth-century rendering by Henry Wadsworth Longfellow, partly for its detailed notes, but no doubt also to avoid paying a permissions fee for one of the excellent contemporary translations. By contrast, *Grand Theft Ovid* used an eloquent modern translation, beautifully read during the performance to a backdrop of minimalist electronic music. Talking later with one of the student performers, I learned that he'd been reading Ovid in his Latin class and was happy to have the chance to consult the original while working on the piece.

Electronic Arts was roundly criticized by Dante specialists for so dramatically altering the poem, especially in the portrayal of Beatrice, who is reduced from Dante's savior to a bare-breasted damsel in distress who needs *him* to save *her*. As Columbia's Teodolinda Barolini sardonically commented in *Entertainment Weekly*—most likely the first time a Dantista had ever appeared in its pages—"Of all the things that are troubling, the sexualization and infantilization of Beatrice are the worst. . . . She's this kind of bizarrely corrupted Barbie doll" ("An Ivy League Professor Weighs In," 79). Yet before he turned to virtual worlds, the game's executive producer, Jonathan Knight, had earned an MFA in drama at Boston University. There he became interested in modern adaptations of the classics, and he directed a production of Tom Stoppard's *15 Minute Hamlet*. In his introduction to the game's published spin-off, Knight says that he wanted to incorporate a strong female character into the game. The obvious choice was Beatrice, but she doesn't appear until the end of the *Purgatorio*, when she takes Virgil's place as Dante's guide to paradise. In order to bring her into the *Inferno*, Knight and his collaborators "decided to create a kind of

Christian Persephone story to layer on top of the poem" (xxi), and so they introduced a backstory in which Satan has abducted Beatrice, as Hades had abducted Persephone to become his underworld bride. At the same time, Beatrice plays Eurydice to Dante's Orpheus, who is incongruously armed with a scythe rather than a lyre as he descends to rescue her, and as the game progresses Dante periodically has tantalizing, sexually charged visions of her awaiting rescue. Such a melding of classical motifs would likely have appealed to Teodolinda Barolini if it had been created by Ariosto, but she was apparently too put off by her first impression of the game to bring her literary-critical skills to bear on its intertextual heritage.

Far from ignoring the insights of literary scholars, Electronic Arts brought in a Dante specialist, Guy Raffa of the University of Texas, who served as the game's literary consultant and wrote commentary for its website. Raffa was a good choice; he had developed an extensive website, *Danteworlds*, "an integrated multimedia journey" (http://danteworlds.laits .utexas.edu). Raffa's site is full of excellent images and information, and it has links to online texts of the *Commedia*, including a bilingual edition that pairs the Italian text with the splendid translation by Robert Hollander. The game has more literary and artistic grounding than Barolini realized, though in an ideal underworld, Raffa could have done more to give Beatrice the Ovidian resonance that Jonathan Knight intended but that Barolini was probably not the only viewer to miss. At the very least, when the time came to prepare the published spin-off, Raffa should have kept Electronic Arts from going with the almost unreadable Longfellow translation. He could have insisted that they follow the lead of his website and use a translation such as Hollander's, whose permissions cost would hardly have strained their lavish budget.

Ovid in the DMZ

More directly literary than video games are the digital narratives now being created on the internet, though these often require differing modes of reading—or viewing—than traditional printed texts. As Jessica Pressman remarks in the 2017 ACLA report, electronic literature is "born digital." Both multimedia and multimodal, it "requires its reader to read and think comparatively" as it challenges generic conventions and disciplinary boundaries alike ("Electronic Literature as Comparative Literature," 248). Such new media represent a significant transformation of what might have been considered under the classic comparative rubric of "literature and the other arts," which would have taken up such topics as ekphrasis or the concept of the baroque in poetry, music, and art. Electronic literature can be as much a visual as a verbal experience, yielding an interarts implosion rather than an ekphrastic moment in a text or an analogue in a separate medium.

As a case in point, we can consider the work of Young-hae Chang and Marc Voge. Since 1999, the Seoul-based pair has uploaded more than a hundred pieces on their website, www.yhchang.com, producing their virtual fictions under the ironic name YOUNG-HAE CHANG HEAVY INDUSTRIES. Rebecca Walkowitz, who devotes the final chapter of her book *Born Translated* to them, has observed that this name mimics those of Korean corporations such as Samsung Heavy Industries. "The very language of the corporate moniker," she writes, "a mixture of Anglicized Korean and business English, encapsulates a transpacific regionalism that is at once utterly Korean and utterly global" (211). Asked by an interviewer about their name, Chang and Voge once replied, "It's pretty evident. YHC for Young-Hae and HI for Marc. We changed Marc into 'HEAVY INDUSTRIES' because Koreans love big companies and Marc doesn't mind being objectified and capitalized on" (Yoo, "Interview").

Their works typically consist of black-and-white text streamed across the screen in five- or ten-minute episodes, accompanied with a soundtrack of classic American jazz. Chang and Voge reject the elaborate technologies and lush virtual worlds favored by video games; instead, as Jessica Pressman has written, their works "resist the alignment of electronic literature with hypertext, evade reader-controlled interactivity, and favor the foregrounding of text and typography, narrative complexity, and an aesthetic of difficulty" ("The Strategy of Digital Modernism," 303). Pressman proposes that Chang and Voge invert the classic modernist requirement of intensive slow reading, as their texts rapidly stream across the screen, creating a complexity based in speed and often involving cognitively disorienting divergences between the primary text, typographical effects, and subtitles in one or more languages.

Visible anywhere in the world, YHCHI's works are never free of context, beginning with the cultural and political contexts provided by their choices of language and of venue. These contexts become something different from the influences long emphasized in comparative studies, or the Kristevan intertexts flowing through works, whether consciously chosen or not by the artist. Chang and Voge engage more in what Elke Sturm-Trigonakis has described as "Global Playing in der Literatur," in her book of that title. Each piece involves an eclectic choice of elements drawn from local and international cultures, strategically mobilized for purposes of the work's theme and also its planned presentation—often in site-specific instantiations as well as on the internet. They compose their texts in English, Korean, or French, each with its very different valences and associations, and they often subtitle them in other languages, usually when they are presenting works in a museum or biennale or on a college campus. Their work is thus globally (re)situated in multiple venues, even as they often reference two very specific worlds: the international art world, whose commercialism and herd mentality they frequently satirize, and the Korean peninsula where they live and work. Wedged into a narrow lot in one of Seoul's few remaining low-rise neighborhoods, their trapezoidal house is appropriately located near the National Museum of Modern and Contemporary Art and also the palatial Blue House, residence of South Korea's prime minister.

YHCHI's works are regularly shown in museums as text-based visual art, but they can equally be read as prose poems, and literary as well as art-world references run through their work. Jessica Pressman's "Strategy of Digital Modernism" discusses their piece "Dakota," which overlays Ezra Pound and Jack Kerouac, while Rebecca Walkowitz notes their self-conscious connection to the author-translators Samuel Beckett and Vladimir Nabokov as well as Pound (*Born Translated*, 228). Older texts can be glimpsed as well. Ovidian myth makes a subterranean appearance in "Miss DMZ," a haunting meditation on life in a divided country. One morning, the episode's narrator finds flyers posted at his corner grocery shop in Seoul, advertising free gifts at a duty-free store. He descends a staircase behind the shop and finds himself in a dimly lit tunnel leading northward, evidently a very long extension of one of the tunnels that North Korea infamously dug beneath the DMZ in preparation for a potential southern invasion. One of these has become a major tourist attraction, where visitors can descend—past a gift shop—to venture along the tunnel until the way is barred by a heavy metal door.

The narrator pushes the door open, and he finds himself in the DMZ Duty-Free Shop, which looks like the lobby of a faded East European hotel. Elegantly dressed customers sip martinis and examine luxury goods in glass cases, and a beautiful young woman invites him to dance, then urges him to try his luck in an adjacent casino. Rather than fleecing him, as we'd expect a bar girl to do, she helps him win a series of hands at chemin de fer. When he cashes in his chips, instead of money he is given a key to a bedroom where he and Miss DMZ spend the night making love. In the morning, she tells him that he has to return home, despite his pleas to stay with her and become one of "the regulars" in the duty-free shop. In one of many instances of failed intercultural connection in Chang and Voge's work, Miss DMZ smiles but says that it is "against the rules" for him to stay, "because you're not one of us." He leaves, determined to return, but the next day he finds that the tunnel has disappeared from the corner store; he is left alone in a basement storeroom filled with boxes of instant ramen.

"Miss DMZ" reverses the common narrative of the deprived North Korean fleeing through the DMZ to reach the good life in South Korea, and it revises its literary predecessors as well. One of these may be the classical Chinese fable "Peach-blossom Spring," composed by Tao Yuanming in 421 CE and often retold, in which a fisherman ventures through a narrow grotto and finds a hidden kingdom of eternal springtime and plenty, but he can never find his way back after he leaves. A more direct forebear is Ovid. At the entrance to the casino, the narrator sees a large painting of "a naked woman reclining on the back of a bull in flight"—the abduction of Europa, most famously portrayed in the second book of the *Metamorphoses*. Overall, "Miss DMZ" inverts the Ovidian myth of Orpheus and Eurydice. Instead of seeking to rescue his beloved, the narrator longs to stay forever in her eerie underworld, which satirically blends North Korean

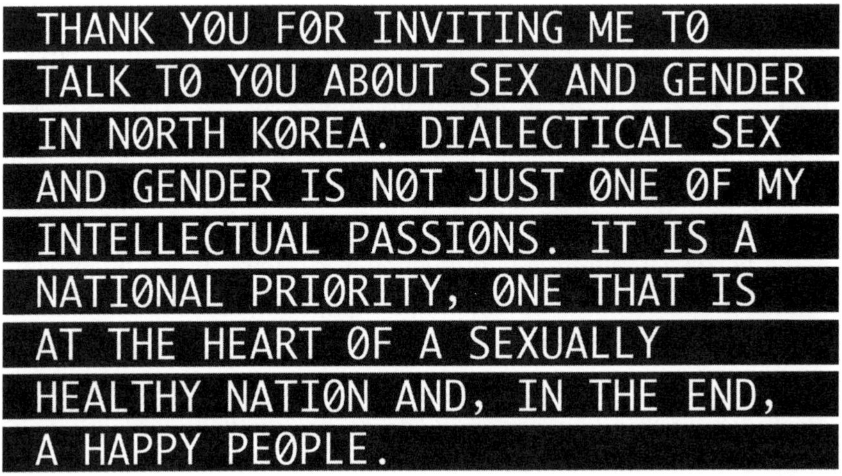

THANK YØU FØR INVITING ME TØ
TALK TØ YØU ABØUT SEX AND GENDER
IN NØRTH KØREA. DIALECTICAL SEX
AND GENDER IS NØT JUST ØNE ØF MY
INTELLECTUAL PASSIØNS. IT IS A
NATIØNAL PRIØRITY, ØNE THAT IS
AT THE HEART ØF A SEXUALLY
HEALTHY NATIØN AND, IN THE END,
A HAPPY PEØPLE.

FIGURE 12. Screenshot from Young-Hae Chang Heavy Industries, "Cunnilingus in North Korea." Courtesy of Young-Hae Chang and Marc Voge.

anticapitalism with the anomie of airport duty-free shops worldwide. No money ever changes hands in the DMZ duty-free, and the narrator isn't being swindled by "the regulars" who pose as customers but are actually employees of the shop. Instead, he receives the gift of free love in this cashless society, but only for a single night. It is against the rules for him to stay, and when he begs Miss DMZ to accept a gift, she replies calmly, "that is especially against the rules." Everyone does their duty in the duty-free shop.

If "Miss DMZ" is both local and global, other works are binational in character, often combining Chang's and Voge's home traditions. One of their signature pieces, "Cunnilingus in North Korea," blends two very different North-South divides: the Korean and the American. This piece purports to be a speech by "our Beloved Leader Kim Jong-Il" praising oral sex as the highest expression of Communist equality (figure 12). He declares that North Koreans have been freed to relate on an elemental human level, thanks to their rejection of the deadening force of consumerism that blights the South. He does acknowledge "certain failings" in running his impoverished country, but he praises his people's ability to make the most of sex, getting "something for nothing."[8] Chang and Voge's parody of Communist officialese was so pitch-perfect that they received an inquiry from the editor of *Harper's* magazine, who wanted to reprint what he thought was an actual speech and wondered how they'd gotten hold of it. When I asked them how they had responded, Voge said that after pondering their options they simply replied, "When he wants to reach us, he knows how to find us."

The beloved leader's speech is accompanied by a soundtrack consisting of "See-line Woman," a song by the African American jazz singer Nina Simone. At first, the words seem completely incongruous, having nothing to do with Korean politics or even with sex: "See-line woman / she drink coffee / she drink tea / and then go home / see-line woman." As the song proceeds, however, we learn that the woman is a powerful seductress, controlling men's desire, their wallets, and even their sanity: "see-line woman / dressed in red / make a man / lose his head." The ballad presents a self-assured woman who asserts her sexuality, vocalizing her pleasure in her wailing and moaning. The soundtrack's transgressive language increasingly erupts into the earnest written text on the screen, as when Kim declares that his attentive North Korean men "know all the tricks of their trade" to satisfy their partners. The text's animation takes on a propulsive rhythm that brings out the sexuality of Simone's "yeah yeah yeah yeah" and her half-moaning delivery of the lyrics. As Walkowitz remarks of another of their pieces, "Perhaps the soundtrack functions like a language? Or, perhaps we should regard the verbal text not as the primary medium but as lyrics attached to a score?" (*Born Translated*, 207). African American jazz provides YHCHI with a powerful counterpoint to Korean rhetoric, sometimes with Kim's words flashing stroboscopically as if they are pulsing with orgasmic energy, undercutting the ideological rigidity of his message.

"See-line Woman" was a southern folk song that Nina Simone popularized as a crossover hit among white audiences located especially in the North (the song is taken from her 1964 album *Broadway Blues Ballads*). As repurposed by YHCHI, the song further unsettles the North-South opposition within Korea itself, brilliantly mocking North and South Korean

[8] www.yhchang.com/CUNNILINGUS_IN_NORTH_KOREA_V.html (accessed May 14, 2019).

social and sexual politics alike. "Cunnilingus in North Korea" sends up the failures of North Korean economic policy, as we see a desperate Kim Jong-Il abandoning his usual repression, reduced to praising oral sex as one of the few pleasures available to the population he has liberated from—or deprived of—the seductions of consumer goods. At the same time, by interweaving North Korean political rhetoric and African American blues, the piece attacks South Korean consumerism and the South's sexual politics, not freed from patriarchal values even in an era of economic progress and political liberalization.

YHCHI's works are at once global and site-specific, and a given piece can change for a new setting. While "Cunnilingus in North Korea" was created as a free-floating work on the internet, in May 2019 Chang and Voge produced a new version for an appearance in Buenos Aires. "Cunnilingus en Corea del Norte (Buenos Aires Tango Version)" uses the prior text (in Spanish translation), but the soundtrack is a tango-based composition, whose languid sexuality produces a very different effect from Nina Simone's lyrics. The pacing is considerably slower, but the more variable rhythm of tango yields disorienting shifts in the size and timing of the text; a series of quick beats, each with a glimpse of one or two words of Kim's speech, can be followed by several lines of text as a lingering note fades away. Meanwhile, the local form of "Buenos Aires Tango" is globalized, with a Japanese koto taking the place of a guitar and a South African vocal line emerging toward the end. Counterpointed against Chairman Kim's earnest speech, the effect is at once ironic and ominous.

Like *Grand Theft Ovid*, Young-Hae Chang Heavy Industries gives literary scholars an ample field for analysis. Both the physical and the virtual worlds are open to comparative studies as never before, in today's version of the unlikely combination of theological treatises, opera libretti, and *sub rosa* erotica with which Provost Prešeren stocked his *knjižnica* in Ljubljana three centuries ago. The Seminary Library made room for Ovid as well, part of the chain of transmission that put his works into the hands of the lovelorn and politically disaffected poet France Prešeren in the nineteenth century. Today, two millennia after Ovid was driven into exile for his own sexual improprieties and political indiscretions, he still thrives in unexpected metamorphoses in our flickering virtual worlds.

7

Worlds

In the opening chapter of *The Fellowship of the Ring*, Bilbo Baggins throws a lavish double birthday party for himself and Frodo, his young cousin and heir. Bilbo has spared no expense for this great event; he is turning 111, while Frodo is crossing the threshold of hobbit adulthood, age 33, and Bilbo has matched the grand total of their ages by inviting "a gross" of 144 guests. Only Bilbo knows, however, that this party will mark his farewell to life in the Shire, as he announces just before he puts the One Ring on his finger and disappears, to the astonishment of everyone still sober enough to be paying attention. Tolkien prepares for this dramatic event with a carefully orchestrated crescendo of details that he narrates in a mode of everyday realism, ensuring that we are fully inside his imaginary world before Hobbiton is invaded by dark forces of which most hobbits know nothing. Thus, Bilbo gives exceptional gifts to the children at the party:

> On this occasion the presents were unusually good. The hobbit-children were so excited that they almost forgot about eating. There were toys the like of which they had never seen before, all beautiful and some obviously magical. Many of them had been ordered a year before, and had come all the way from the Mountain and from Dale, and were of real dwarf-make. (28)

How real can these toys be, when they are made by fairy-tale beings who don't actually exist in the real world?

In thinking about the worldly presence of literary works, we need to consider how they relate to the world around them through the worlds they create. What are the dimensions of the imaginative world built up by a novel, or staged by a playwright, or envisioned by a poet? What are its boundaries, its environment, its history, its sociology or ethnography, its economic and class determinants, its gender relations? What mixture, if any, does it present of the impossible and the everyday, such as the dwarves' subterranean workshop from which the best toys have to be ordered a year in advance?

In *Fictional Worlds* (1986), Thomas Pavel discussed the variable "referential density" that a work can have, the relative wealth or paucity of information given per page, scene, or stanza about the world envisioned by the work. As Umberto Eco has said, "a work encloses us within the boundaries of its world and leads us, one way or another, to take it seriously" (*Six Walks*, 78). A realistic writer such as Leo Tolstoy or Jhumpa Lahiri needs to provide enough referential details to create a persuasive reality effect, but their fictive worlds tally with what we see around us, or what we know from Russian history. Inventors of fantasy worlds have a special burden to persuade us that their elves or their Martians move in a lifelike environment that extends beyond the specific details we're shown.

Building on Pavel, Eco, and his own prior work on video games, in *On Literary Worlds* Eric Hayot focuses on features such as "amplitude" and "completeness" to describe the coordinates and building blocks with which a writer creates a virtual literary world. Tolkien's hobbits, dwarves, and wizards are compellingly believable thanks to the remarkable amplitude and completeness of their world. Middle-earth can be compared to Sir Thomas More's pioneering alternative-reality fiction, *Utopia* (1516), which begins with an exchange of letters between More and several of his real-life friends in Antwerp, building on the account that Amerigo Vespucci had published in 1504 describing his voyages along the coast of Brazil; More and his friends learn of Utopia from Vespucci's supposed crew member Raphael Hythlodaeus. Further grounding his fictional world, as Tolkien would do four centuries later, More provided Utopia with a history, a map, and even a page showing the Utopian alphabet. Yet Tolkien went far beyond him (and quite likely beyond any writer before or since) in creating an entire world beyond the pages of his novel. Thomas More couldn't have conducted a conversation in Utopian to save his life, but Tolkien actually invented Elvish. It is an unreal but fully functioning language, which Tolkien described as endlessly engrossing "in its intimacy, in its peculiarly shy individualism," as a language that no one but he could speak ("A Secret Vice," 213).

Writers often allude to events outside the scope of their work, suggesting that their story isn't just taking place on some cardboard stage set. In *The Case-Book of Sherlock Holmes*, Sherlock refers to a series of never-published cases, including one involving "the giant rat of Sumatra, a story for which the world is not yet prepared" ("The Adventure of the Sussex Vampire," 2). Here Holmes gestures toward a life more fully lived outside the story's boundaries, or more precisely a "case-book" of tales outside the story of "the Sussex Vampire." He is leafing through his case-book looking for guidance, as he doubts that he can handle the situation he is being asked to investigate: a young mother has been discovered sucking blood from her baby's neck. "But what do we know of vampires?" he asks Watson; "really we seem to have been switched on to a Grimm's fairy tale" (2). "Switched" is a railway metaphor here, not an electrical one: Holmes fears that he may be getting diverted onto a horror-story track, derailed from his customary genre of rationally solvable crimes. Fortunately, as he tells Watson at the story's end, he arrived almost instantly at the solution thanks to "the train of reasoning which passed through my mind in Baker Street" (10), even before they boarded the 2:00 train at Victoria Station to head out to Sussex.

Conan Doyle has enhanced his tale's worldliness through a metafictional reference to a nonexistent tale involving an imaginary species on the other side of the globe. The world may not have been prepared to read a Sherlock Holmes story even more outré than one about a vampire mother, but Conan Doyle had fully prepared the world for the *idea* of a story involving a giant rat of Sumatra—so successfully, in fact, that several later writers have written the story for him. And more than that: in 2007, when a new species of large rodent was discovered in Papua New Guinea, the find was announced by the *New York Times* in an article entitled "The Giant Rat of Sumatra, Alive and Well" (Lyons), even though the reporter had to admit that Papua New Guinea is located "a few islands too far to the right"—in actual fact, nearly three thousand miles away. Giant rats may one day turn up on Sumatra itself—smuggled in, if necessary, by de-voted Holmesians—but we know that no vampires will ever be unearthed in Sussex. Though the mother declares that Holmes "seems to have pow-ers of magic" (10), the great detective has discovered an earthly explana-tion for her bizarre behavior (sucking out curare with which a jealous stepsibling is trying to poison his little rival). As Holmes says to Watson, "This agency stands flat-footed upon the ground, and there it must remain. The world is big enough for us. No ghosts need apply" (3). The worldwide network of the Baker Street Irregulars testifies to his devotees' persisting desire to fit his world to the dimensions of our own, even though they privately know that there is no *hors-texte* in either Derrida's or Spivak's sense, no long-lost casebook in a steamer trunk somewhere, beyond the actually existing canon of four novels and fifty-six tales.

By contrast, Tolkien needs us to accept that wizards really do have pow-ers of magic, in a world qualitatively different from anything Sherlock Holmes would encounter in Sussex or on Sumatra. Tolkien grounds his trilogy in a massive archive that he had spent decades composing, and so he can draw with complete naturalness on a fully realized "sub-creation" or "secondary world." He used these terms in 1939, when he was begin-ning *The Lord of the Rings*, in a lecture—a virtual manifesto—"On Fairy-stories." In a wide-ranging defense of the art of fantasy, he argued against Coleridge's Romantic conception of "the willing suspension of disbelief," which Eco has described as the necessary agreement that a reader makes with a writer (*Six Walks*, 75). Tolkien saw the fictional compact differ-ently. What has been called "willing suspension of disbelief," he says,

> does not seem to me a good description of what happens. What really
> happens is that the story-maker proves a successful "sub-creator."
> He makes a Secondary World which your mind can enter. Inside it,
> what he relates is "true"; it accords with the laws of that world. You
> therefore believe it, while you are, as it were, inside. The moment
> disbelief arises, the spell is broken; the magic, or rather art, has
> failed. ("On Fairy-stories," 132)

In Tolkien's view, it is only when a writer has failed that we have to will ourselves to suspend our disbelief, "a subterfuge we use when condescending to games or make-believe" (132). Tolkien didn't want his reader to chuckle knowingly at the idea of toy-making dwarves and then put his book on the shelf with juvenile fiction, or else read on without any serious emotional or ethical engagement. He was intent on creating a fully believable world, though unlike Byron or Joyce he wasn't trying to rival God's creation: hence, Middle-earth is a subcreation, not to be confused with our own.

Both Tolkien's aesthetics and his politics were radically different from Bertolt Brecht's, but his elves and orcs create their own kind of *Verfremdungseffekt*, to recall the term that Brecht had adopted four years before Tolkien delivered his lecture. Neither Brecht nor Tolkien wants us to lose ourselves in a world of melodramatic illusion: we should *find* ourselves instead, gaining a new ethical or political self-awareness. To defamiliarize our ordinary world, Brecht has placards carried on stage and takes us to Szechuan, early modern London, or the Thirty Years' War. Tolkien takes us to a far more distant past, in which "real" people like Aragorn mingle with quasipeople (hobbits), "real" fairy-tale figures (elves, dwarves, wizards), and wholly invented beings (orcs, Ents, Nazgul). These characters collectively populate a world that we can imaginatively enter without ever forgetting that we're in a fictive world of stories that can awaken and guide our moral sympathies.

Tolkien filled his subcreation with a history that stretches deep into antiquity and with a richly envisioned everyday life in the present. Even the brief description of Bilbo's party gifts is unobtrusively calibrated to convey considerable referential density. The best toys are "real dwarf-make," but this phrase doesn't invite us to question the reality of dwarves, as it might in an ironic postmodern tale by John Barth. On the contrary, this detail subtly heightens the reality of Gimli and Glóin, long before we meet them, by positing a world in which only some toys are real dwarf-make. Others must be mere hobbit-make, and some of those may be *imitation* dwarf-make, not the real thing at all. Further, only some of Bilbo's gifts are "obviously magical," which means that others are obviously not magical, and still others are probably magical but don't look it at first. The fourth possibility in this conceptual grid would be toys that seem to be magical but really aren't. These are certainly not among Bilbo's marvelous toys, the like of which the children have never seen before, but the youngsters may well have been given such disappointing baubles at less lavish parties in the past. A world of possibility has been suggested to us in two sentences, which are irrelevant to the plot but fundamental to the creation of Tolkien's world.

I begin with the world created within the literary work in order to emphasize that any substantial work of literature creates its own primary context, its world, which we can explore in itself as well as in its relation to other literary worlds and to the social world outside the text. Comparatists have often been criticized by specialists in national literatures for not knowing enough about the contexts in which the works they discuss were created, and students of world literature have in turn been criticized in similar terms by regionally focused comparatists. Context is always good to have, though as I have argued in chapter 6, the most relevant context for a given approach may be international or transnational rather than local. Yet even before we arrive at any kind of external context, a significant work of literature will work its magic—whether dwarf-made or Tolstoyan—within the context it creates for us. With each of his novels, Kazuo Ishiguro once remarked, "I feel like I'm *closing in on some strange, weird territory* that for some reason obsesses me and I'm not sure what the nature of that territory is, but with every book I'm kind of closing in on this strange territory" (Vorda and Herzinger, "Interview," 150). A fundamental aspect of our work as students, teachers, and scholars of literature is to explore the strange territories created by the authors we study, whatever choice we make of further contexts in which to situate their singular worlds.

The National, the International, the Supranational

The farther we venture into a writer's secondary creation, the more fully we will be able to understand how it reflects—or, better, refracts—the world known to the author, and to see its implications for the world known to us today. As Eric Hayot says, "aesthetic worldedness is the form of the relation a work establishes between the world inside and the world outside the work" (*On Literary Worlds*, 45). Even a novel set in the distant past or on another planet is always connected to the writer's world, however obliquely, but these connections can be conceived in very different ways.

One of the basic choices we have to make concerns the framework within which we pursue our discussion. Here we can follow the Slovak comparatist Dionýz Ďurišin, who in 1992 wrote a book entitled *Čo je svetová literatura?* (What Is World Literature?)—a work whose provenance and date can remind us that the contemporary discussion of world literature is by no means only a North American or post-9/11 phenomenon. In his related essay "World Literature as a Target Literary-Historical Category" (1993), Ďurišin distinguishes among three distinct but interrelated contextual levels: the national, the international, and the supranational. To continue with the example of Tolkien, his works have inspired a great deal of scholarship, but almost all of it has been on the national level. As of April 2019, the *MLA Bibliography* lists no fewer than 2,880 books and articles that include him in their subject listings; these were written with few exceptions by scholars who have focused on Tolkien's fantasy world in itself or in its English context.

The Lord of the Rings is often analyzed as part of an English tradition going back to Victorian fantasy literature and to the Middle English and Anglo-Saxon narratives in which Tolkien was an expert, especially *Beowulf* and *Sir Gawain and the Green Knight*. Tolkien's historical context is also often explored as well, from his experience in the trenches during World War I to the incipient collapse of the British Empire, sometimes with reference to his early childhood in South Africa and the uneasy racial geography of Middle-earth's south and east. Other scholars have explored Tolkien's critique of industrialization, grimly dramatized in Mordor and Orthanc and then brought home in Saruman's takeover of the Shire at the trilogy's end. In this context, *The Lord of the Rings* (begun in 1939, completed in 1954) takes its place in the company of such futuristic English works as Aldous Huxley's *Brave New World* (1932) and George Orwell's *1984* (1949) as well as Mervyn Peake's medievalist *Gormenghast* trilogy (1948–59). No one has yet undertaken a comparison to Huxley, but there are half a dozen articles that discuss Tolkien and Orwell, and a few others compare him to Golding or to Peake.

The Lord of the Rings can equally be studied in an international frame. It has periodically been discussed in relation to Germanic and Nordic mythology and to the genre of the quest romance, yet there is almost no discussion of Tolkien in relation to modern writers outside England. Seeing Tolkien in an international context can help us better understand his Englishness as well as his modernity; it shouldn't be forgotten that Middle-earth maps on to Europe as a whole, not just England. To take the distinctive category of best sellers by medievalists, the trilogy has often been compared to the Narnia series and the Silent Planet trilogy of his close friend C. S. Lewis, but no one has yet discussed Tolkien together with Umberto Eco. Yet *The Name of the Rose* also retrojects contemporary political concerns into a medieval world, complete with intensive discussions of language in a world of inscrutable signs. In such a comparison, Eco and Tolkien could be triangulated with Conan Doyle, given Eco's reworking of Holmes and Watson into William of Baskerville and his sidekick Adso of Melk. Gandalf the Grey too has a good deal in common with Holmes, in detective skills and in many other respects, including heavy tobacco use and coming back to life long after a seemingly fatal plunge into an Alpine abyss when locked in struggle with a mortal enemy.

To take another Italian example, *The Lord of the Rings* could well be compared to Italo Calvino's medievalist trilogy of the 1950s, *The Cloven Viscount*, *The Baron in the Trees*, and *The Nonexistent Knight*, collected in 1960 under the title *I nostri antenati* (*Our Ancestors*). In these fictions, Calvino turned to fantasy as a way to move beyond the neorealism of the early works he'd based on his experience in the Italian Resistance. Tolkien always rather implausibly denied that his trilogy had anything to do with World War II, but he did admit a connection to his traumatic experiences during World War I. He fought in the Battle of the Somme in 1916, and almost all of his close friends were killed in the trenches by the war's end. He began elaborating his vast fantasy world in 1917, after being invalided back to England, starting with a work resonantly titled *The Book of Lost Tales*.

A comparison to Calvino might proceed from his 1950s trilogy to *Invisible Cities*, which blends *Arabian Nights* Orientalism with anachronistic elements of mechanized warfare, overpopulation, and the ecological degradation that also figures prominently in *The Lord of the Rings*. The

Chinese empire's invisible cities, *città invisibili*, gradually become unlivable modern cities, *città invivibili*, as Calvino once remarked ("Presentazione," ix). Narratologically, both authors are centrally concerned with stories about stories within stories. Bound in red on Tolkien's instructions, *The Lord of the Rings* is described on the title page—in both elvish script and dwarves' runes—as based on the *Red Book of Westmarch*, the history-plus-memoir that Bilbo Baggins is struggling to complete at the end of *The Lord of the Rings* itself. For his part, Calvino's Marco Polo describes his series of fantastic cities to Kublai Khan, implicitly anatomizing the one city he never discusses, his own Venice. Thirty-three scholars to date have compared Tolkien and C. S. Lewis, but no one has ever compared the works of Tolkien and Calvino, two of Europe's seminal postwar fantasists.

The absence of comparisons between Tolkien and Calvino or Eco probably stems from certain widely held but too rarely questioned assumptions: for example, that "popular" literature lives in a different universe from truly *literary* writing; that canonized postmodernists have little in common with contemporaries who aren't engaged in rewriting Proust, Joyce, or Cervantes; that politically progressive writers form a closed circle into which antiprogressive writers need not be invited. Yet such exclusions limit our understanding of modern fiction's varied aesthetic and political relations to the postwar world. Modernity has always developed in dialectical relation to various strands of antimodernity, and literature can be modern without being modernist. In recent years, studies of modern British literature have expanded well beyond the self-confirming delimitation that long favored Virginia Woolf, for instance, to the almost total occlusion of her more popular (and in fact very interesting) rival Arnold Bennett. H. G. Wells's brilliant *Tono-Bungay* was rarely discussed together with Conrad's *Heart of Darkness* and *Nostromo*, despite the many ways in which Wells was ringing distinctive changes on "Conradian" themes. Both Wells and Bennett were best-selling authors who wrote linear narratives in accessible prose, but we can now allow that literature in the first decades of the twentieth century had more varied virtues than were admitted within Bloomsbury's precincts. Studies such as Ralph Wood's collection *Tolkien among the Moderns* have begun to explore Tolkien's relations to British modernism, but there has been next to no comparative work on him in a modern context.

As for the frequent identification of *The Lord of the Rings* as popular genre fiction, its massive popularity is undeniable; with sales of 150 million copies to date, it is the best-selling work of literature of the twentieth century, if not all time. Yet popular literature is becoming increasingly visible in comparative and world literary studies, in a return to a Herderian populism long overshadowed by Goethean elitism. This can be seen in collections such as *Crime Fiction as World Literature* (Nilsson et al., 2017), which includes essays on Orhan Pamuk, Nordic Noir, the Mexican narconovela, and Bulgarian translations of Agatha Christie. The scholarly reception of *The Name of the Rose* hasn't been impeded by the fact that Eco cannily built his novel on a detective-story base, gaining in the process a massive worldwide readership, with sales of some 50 million copies to date, surpassing all but the most successful works of pulp fiction. Moreover, Tolkien wasn't so much writing genre fiction as inventing the genre that has come to be known as fantasy fiction, moving far beyond the parameters of the post-Victorian children's writing with which he'd begun. If he had never written his trilogy, *The Hobbit* would be read today only in the company of *The Wind in the Willows* and *Winnie-the-Pooh*, and it would have been filmed by Disney (whose films Tolkien despised) rather than by Peter Jackson.

Beyond the international frames of modern literature or the European theater of war, many of Tolkien's themes are what Dionýz Ďurišin would call supranational. This dimension doesn't rely on national or regional contexts but involves issues that have worldwide scope, as with Tolkien's deeply held environmentalism. He also deals with psychological issues of a general rather than a national or international nature. In "Unheralded Might," Christopher Hinojosa has analyzed the addictive effects of the One Ring, an aspect powerfully brought out in Peter Jackson's film of *The Fellowship of the Ring* when a clearly addicted Bilbo tries to snatch the ring from Frodo. A number of scholars have probed gender issues in Middle Earth, as in Christine Vogt-William's discussion of "hobbit homosociality" in her essay "Brothers in Arms," while Tolkien's Ents have been discussed in terms of the posthuman (Van Curen, "Ecocriticism and the Transcorporeal"). Yet these discussions generally proceed through close readings rather than through comparative analysis, and even the eminently supranational ecological dimension of Tolkien's work has been discussed in relatively local terms, either with reference to his upbringing in rural England or in terms of his "ecomedievalism."

With Tolkien, as with many other writers outside the hypercanon, the field is open for international and supranational comparisons, including to historical fictions of the World War II era such as Yourcenar's *Mémoires d'Hadrien* (1952) or Hermann Broch's *Der Tod des Vergil* (*The Death of Virgil*, 1945). Like Tolkien, both Yourcenar and Broch create a doubly defamiliarized form of historical fiction. Rather than look back into the recent past of their own country, as Toni Morrison did in *Beloved*, they venture much farther away in time and space, setting their works in the ancient Mediterranean—Latin for "Middle (of the) Earth"—where classical languages were spoken long before the creation of the modern vernaculars in which their novels are written.

Looking beyond Europe, we can compare Tolkien's world to the mixture of magic and realism that Alejo Carpentier labeled *lo real maravilloso* in 1949, though for Tolkien it might be better to speak of *magia realista*: realistic magic rather than magical realism. Even with that difference, Tolkien's Shire is similar in various dimensions to the Macondo of García Márquez's *Cien años de soledad* (1967), another invented world that both is and is not part of the wider world from which it is long cut off. Comparisons are often made between Macondo and Faulkner's Yoknapatawpha County, and for good reason, yet there is little magic in Faulkner's realism. Far closer to García Márquez's gypsy Melquíades is the itinerant wizard Gandalf. Both perform magical feats, even to the point of returning from the dead, both are racially other figures who seem suspicious to local citizens, and both are masters of prophetic texts in ancient languages that few but they can read.

A full-scale comparison of the two books would of course include their fundamental differences, including the differential consequences of Tolkien's nostalgic conservatism versus García Márquez's progressive leftism. Yet a pure opposition would be difficult to maintain. Both writers are concerned with the baneful effect of multinational industry invading their rural homeland, though Tolkien speaks of Saruman importing methods learned in Mordor while García Márquez speaks directly of the United

Fruit Company. Tolkien's portrayals of the totalitarian Sauron and his puppet Saruman could well be compared to the Latin American tradition of the dictator novel, inaugurated during the same years by works such as Miguel Ángel Asturias's *El señor Presidente* (1946), which has its own share of mythic motifs, inspired by Asturias's research for his *Leyendas de Guatemala* (1930).

A comparison of Tolkien to his Latin American contemporaries would situate *The Lord of the Rings* more fully in its midcentury literary and political context, helping us to understand its remarkable worldwide success. The comparison would also underscore the fact that a mixture of the magical and the realistic isn't the special province of third-world indigenes who take flying carpets in stride. Nor does it reflect some uniquely Latin American reality—a neo-Orientalist claim that García Márquez made in his Nobel Prize acceptance speech, "The Solitude of Latin America." As comparatists have often recognized, García Márquez can best be understood not only in relation to his Latin American interlocutors but within the supranational contexts of the postwar era and of the modern novel.

Cien años de soledad thus forms the disenchanted conclusion to Franco Moretti's *Modern Epic: The World System from Goethe to García Márquez* (1996), which moves from *Faust* and Wagner's Ring Cycle to *Moby-Dick*, *Ulysses*, *The Waste Land*, and *Cien años de soledad*. Moretti sees these sprawling works as what we might call, revising Lukács, the epics of a world abandoned by epic. Moretti's story could have been expanded in interesting ways if it had included Tolkien's self-consciously modern epic. As an undergraduate, Tolkien had been captivated by the *Kalevala* and neglected his studies in classical Greek in order to teach himself Finnish. He translated *Beowulf* in the 1920s and changed the course of *Beowulf* studies with his essay *"Beowulf:* The Monsters and the Critics" (1936), in which he argued that the poem is not a naïve medieval fantasy but a deep exploration of human destiny. In his *Ring* trilogy he was rewriting Wagner's prior rewriting of Germanic traditions in his Ring Cycle, which Moretti discusses at length; like Wagner, but on his own terms, Tolkien sought to create a mythology appropriate to the modern era. He was out of step with the contemporary world in various respects, a conservative Catholic devoted to lost ages of the world, but Moretti gives space to the equally conservative Anglo-Catholic T. S. Eliot. Tolkien's serious epic endeavor could have served as a valuable counterpoint to Joyce's and García Márquez's ironic anti-epics.

The significant differences between Joyce's Dublin, García Márquez's Macondo, and Tolkien's Middle-earth can help us understand the full range of possibility for modern (as opposed to solely modernist) writing, and can give insight into the specific choices made by each writer individually. This double benefit is why Dionýz Ďurišin considered the supranational level to be the most important area for comparative studies today. Here again, the field is open. García Márquez and Tolkien each have upward of two thousand entries in the *MLA Bibliography*, but though four dozen entries compare García Márquez with Faulkner, there isn't even one for him and Tolkien. To judge from Tolkien's neglect by comparatists, he might as well have written his trilogy in Elvish.

From Literary Worlds to World Literatures

The irreducible variety of literary worlds is a key aspect of what Gayatri Spivak has called "the singularity and unverifiability of 'literature as such'" (*A Critique of Postcolonial Reason*, 176). This singularity provides a check against categorical stereotyping—a temptation for any literary analysis, but one to which comparatists are particularly prone. Specialists in a single tradition are more likely to have a comprehensive knowledge of the variety of works within their tradition of choice, and they may be less inclined to reduce an entire period or country to a univocal definition. Comparatists have to be particularly alert to the danger of creating broad-brush characterizations on the basis of a limited set of examples, in our own version of Ian Watt's extrapolation of the rise of "the novel" from the works of three English novelists.

Too many comparative studies in the last century opposed "French" versus "German" traditions or "Eastern" versus "Western" poetics, amalgamating a multitude of writers within an imperious dichotomy (a theme to which we will return in the next chapter). We hear less these days about "the Orient" or "the Third World," but it is now common to encounter "the Global South."

This term represents a welcome opening up beyond the lingering Orientalism of older "East/West" studies and the heavy focus on linear relations between a former colony and its imperial center, but it risks an even greater homogenization, now on a hemispheric scale. When such stereotyping is dissected, it is usually blamed on the neoliberal "world system," but it may equally be an artifact of the scholar's own selectivity. Spivak has remarked that "I think *the global South* is a reverse racist term, one that ignores the daunting diversity outside Europe and the United States. We decide to define what we are not by a bit of academic tourism" ("How Do We Write, Now?" 166).

As Derrida emphasized, such binaries are rarely neutral. Often, a simplistic version of the less favored term is held as a constant against which to showcase the admirable qualities of the works brought together under the preferred term. In order to avoid reproducing this ingrained tendency, it isn't enough to reject the ahistorical Orient of a Hegel, which can return to haunt scholarship in other guises, even in as progressive a thinker as Benedict Anderson. In *Imagined Communities* (1983), Anderson brilliantly combines European, Southeast Asian, and Latin American examples, creating a far more level playing field for the analysis of modern literatures and cultures than had been usual before him. Yet his argument rests upon a different stereotype: of secular modernity versus otherworldly premodernity.

In his opening chapter, "Cultural Roots," Anderson proposes that modern nationalism grew from premodern religious as well as political roots; the nation strengthened its legitimacy by taking on a quasireligious dimension, giving an earthly and dynamic cast to the timeless imagined communities of Christendom, Buddhism, or the Islamic *ummah*. So far so good, but he discusses religion and nationalism in terms of a sharp historical divide: "in Western Europe the eighteenth century marks not only the dawn of the age of nationalism but the dusk of religious modes of thought" (11). The chapter is marked by this kind of dichotomous thinking, based on what Anderson himself describes as "perhaps simpleminded observations" (11), always to the disadvantage of the fatalistic, antiprogressive premoderns trapped in their cyclical concept of time. Orientalism has been banished from modern Asia only to take refuge in the premodern world.

Scholars today are widely aware of the need to avoid reducing the singularity of works and cultures to a conceptual lowest common denominator. Hence we often speak of "modernisms" rather than "modernism," "sexualities" rather than "sexuality," and "subject positions" rather than "identity." As Bruce Robbins and Paulo Lemos Horta have noted in the introduction to their 2017 collection *Cosmopolitanisms*, "by this point one would almost say that cosmopolitanism would look naked without that final 's'" (1). A comparable evolution has been occurring in world literary studies. A tendency toward theoretical monism can be found in works from the turn of the millennium such as Moretti's "Conjectures on World Literature" (multiple conjectures, to be sure, but revealing a common "law of literary evolution"), Pascale Casanova's *La République mondiale des lettres* (the multiplicity of letters devolves into a single republic, with one "Greenwich Meridian" at any given time), or indeed my own *What Is World Literature?* ("a mode of circulation and of reading"). It was useful at the time to try and formulate a general conception of world literature as the field began to expand beyond Europe, but fairly soon a range of sometimes warring categories emerged within the overall concept.

As Stefan Helgesson and Pieter Vermeulen have observed in the introduction to their volume *Institutions of World Literature* (2016), "much of the confusion around the term arises out of a failure to acknowledge that its meaning and substance will differ, sometimes sharply, depending on who is using it, in which contexts, and for what purposes" (2). Over the past decade and a half, debates on world literature have involved a variety of attempts to specify what the term can mean in various manifestations and contexts. This is a natural way to refine a broad concept, though Eric Hayot sees these efforts as "a symptom of the insolidity and even ghostliness of the world in its contemporary usage, where it seems to appear only to announce its transformation into something other than what it means, its incapacity to assure the very spatial range it seems to promise" (*On Literary Worlds*, 36). As an example, he cites Christopher Prendergast's commonsense observation in *Debating World Literature* (2004) that no one actually studies all the literatures of the world. Hayot concludes that Prendergast's statement "just goes to show that whatever the world in world literature means, among the other things it can mean is 'not the whole world.' Which is, if nothing else, weird" (36). I can only imagine how shaken Hayot must be by the World Series.

After two decades of ongoing discussion, it ought to be possible by now to flesh out the ghostly or vampirish concept of world literature. This shouldn't be done by artificially harmonizing different approaches, still less by ruling most of them out of court, but on the contrary by clarifying the differing worlds they envision and the differing approaches that can come under the umbrella term. As with literary theory, no one will need to utilize every approach to world literature; what we need to know is what choices we are making, and why we make them, when we adopt a given definition of "the world" in world literature, and we should be able to use different definitions for different purposes. In the following pages, I will outline several dimensions of world literature that seem to me particularly salient in making these choices. These involve questions of scope, of context, and of politics.

It is worth beginning with an overall distinction. A confusion exists in English between world literature as a body of primary texts and world literature as a field of study. These are very different things, and these two kinds of world literature don't necessarily fit comfortably together. Thus in 1886 Hutcheson Macaulay Posnett expressed considerable skepticism in his *Comparative Literature* about socially rootless "world-literature," but his own book is unquestionably an ambitious exercise in world literary studies. Though English usage lacks the clarity given in German by the difference between *Weltliteratur* and *Weltliteraturforschung*, it is important always to specify which is meant in a given context. This can be done by referring to the discipline as World Literature in capital letters, as Emily Apter does in *Against World Literature*, or more generally by specifying whether we are referring to a concept, a body of texts, a pedagogical program, or a field of research, as I will do in the following pages.

World Writers' World Literatures

Mads Rosendahl Thomsen has made a useful distinction between theories that are oriented toward individual readers or writers, theories that grow out of pedagogy, and theories that propose a broad research agenda

(*Mapping World Literature*, 20). Most of the recent debates over world literature have focused on scholarship and to a lesser extent on teaching, but little attention has been given to writers' own ideas. It was as a practicing writer, though, that Goethe first elaborated the term *Weltliteratur*, thinking both of the foreign works he was reading and also of how he was being read abroad. As John Pizer and Dieter Lamping have respectively detailed in *The Idea of World Literature* and *Die Idee der Weltliteratur*, many writers since Goethe have evoked or discussed the concept, and they have construed world literature very differently in different times and places.

Writers tend to view world literature as news they can use: they are less interested in what a work may have meant in its home context than in what it can do for them now. In the words of the Romanian poet and novelist Mircea Cărtărescu, "I don't care what country André Breton lived and wrote in. I don't know the spot on the map where Bulgakov's Kiev lies. I haven't read Catullus, Rabelais, Cantemir or Virginia Woolf according to any map, but I have taken them from a library where books stand side by side" ("Europe"). Cărtărescu's approach is an intensified version of what César Domínguez has identified as "the common reader's experience, that is, a reading experience that crosses all kinds of borders (temporal, spatial, linguistic, cultural, etc.) in order to build meaning" (*Introducing Comparative Literature*, xiv). As Albert Guérard remarked in 1940 in his *Preface to World Literature*, "World Literature, for the average reader, is not a theory, but a condition" (5).

When writers step back to theorize about their craft, they often draw on a range of world writers. In "A Defence of Poetry," Percy Shelley references half a dozen English poets but nearly two dozen classical and Continental figures, and he quotes both Dante and Tasso in Italian. Even unusually voracious readers such as Cărtărescu or Orhan Pamuk create for themselves a private canon of works that have deeply affected them and that they plunder, or resist, or often both at once. These personal canons can shift over time. In *The Naive and the Sentimental Novelist*, based on his Norton lectures of 2009, Pamuk gives pride of place to *Anna Karenina*, not surprisingly in view of the fact that he had just completed his highly Tolstoyan *Museum of Innocence*. Had he been giving the Norton lectures in the early 1990s, when he was writing *The Black Book*, Dostoevsky's

The Possessed might well have appeared in place of *Anna Karenina*, while Dante and Calvino would probably have played a greater role if he'd given the lectures at the time he was writing *The New Life*.

A quite limited connection to a world author can have a transformative effect, if it comes at a critical moment for a young writer looking for an alternative to the reigning norms at home. Gabriel García Márquez has said that he found his way as a writer when a friend in college lent him a copy of Kafka's *Metamorphosis*, in Spanish translation:

> The first line almost knocked me off the bed. I was so surprised. The first line reads, "As Gregor Samsa awoke that morning from uneasy dreams, he found himself transformed in his bed into a gigantic insect. . . ." When I read the line I thought to myself that I didn't know anyone was allowed to write things like that. If I had known, I would have started writing a long time ago. So I immediately started writing short stories. ("The Art of Fiction")

A single sentence was enough to show García Márquez his future path, or so he claims, while for Mo Yan this effect was produced by "a few pages" from William Faulkner and from García Márquez himself. As he said in his Nobel Prize lecture in 2012,

> in the course of creating my literary domain, Northeast Gaomi Township, I was greatly inspired by the American novelist William Faulkner and the Colombian Gabriel García Márquez. I had not read either of them extensively, but was encouraged by the bold, unrestrained way they created new territory in writing, and learned from them that a writer must have a place that belongs to him alone. . . . [T]hough I had read little of their work, a few pages were sufficient for me to comprehend what they were doing and how they were doing it, which led to my understanding of what I should do and how I should do it. ("Storytellers")

Another Nobel laureate, Oe Kenzaburo, began his lecture by describing the two books that helped him as a child to deal with the traumas of wartime Japan, when "the whole world was then engulfed by waves of horror" ("Japan, the Ambiguous, and Myself"). Both were foreign stories of an adventurous boy's escape from familiar surroundings: Mark Twain's

Adventures of Huckleberry Finn, and *The Wonderful Adventures of Nils,* by the Nobel Prize winner Selma Lagerlöf, which Oe says gave him the ambition to learn the language of birds and one day to travel to Sweden. Her book had a lasting impact on him, far from its original incarnation in 1906 as *Nils Holgerssons underbara resa genom Sverige* (Nils Holgersson's wonderful journey around Sweden). The name of the country (as well as the hero's family name) disappeared from the Japanese title, as from the English version, but it was integral to the original book. Lagerlöf had been commissioned by Sweden's Lärarförbundet (National Teachers' Union) to write a story to help schoolchildren learn Swedish geography. She devised a plot in which the mischievous Nils is transformed into a *tomte,* a gnome known from Swedish folktales, gifted with the ability to speak with animals. Nils is then carried by geese around each of Sweden's twenty-five provinces, learning about their geography and folklore as he goes.

With its scrappy hero and its folkloristic vignettes, Lagerlöf's book found many readers worldwide. It appeared in English translation already in 1907 and in Japanese in 1916—the first of several Japanese translations that Oe might have read in the 1940s. For readers abroad, what had been Nils's journey (*resa*) through his national landscape turns into a series of "adventures" (as the English title puts it) in an imaginary land.[1] Instead of a geography lesson, the book became something more akin to *The Hobbit.* It thereby gained a new and different force for readers who wouldn't have cared, or even noticed, that Nils doesn't make a stop in one of Sweden's provinces—a dereliction for which Lagerlöf was criticized by unhappy residents of the neglected region. Instead, Oe found in Nils a boy who manages to achieve a mature humanity against all odds. "Mother and Father!" Nils exclaims on finally returning home, now restored to his proper form: "I'm a big boy. I'm a human being again!" Quoting this self-affirmation, Oe says that for many years afterward, in times of suffering, he would repeat these words to himself and draw strength from his early identification with Nils.

---

[1] I am told by Manuel Azuaje-Alamo that the title in Japanese employs the word *fushigi* (wonderful), the same word that had been used in the recent Japanese translation of *Alice's Adventures in Wonderland.*

Oe studied French in college. His mentor was Watanabe Karuo, a specialist in Rabelais, whom Watanabe had translated despite having been warned by his teachers in Paris that *La Vie de Gargantua et de Pantagruel* was "intraduisible." No belletristic exercise, Watanabe's translation was his response to the rise of Japanese militarism. "Surrounded by the insane ardour of patriotism on the eve and in the middle of the Second World War," Oe says in his Nobel lecture, "Watanabe had a lonely dream of grafting the humanist view of man on to the traditional Japanese sense of beauty and sensitivity to Nature." During the war years and the American occupation, Watanabe "did his best to transplant into the confused and disorientated Japan of that time the life and thought of those French humanists who were the forerunners, contemporaries and followers of François Rabelais."

Watanabe's translation inspired Oe to infuse his own writing with what he calls—citing Bakhtin—Rabelais's "grotesque realism" and "the laughter that subverts hierarchical relationships." Oe concludes his lecture by discussing his relationship to contemporary writers elsewhere in Asia. He evokes them not in a mode of hobnobbing at literary festivals but in terms of common political struggles:

> By sharing old, familiar yet living metaphors I align myself with writers like Kim Ji-ha of Korea, Chon I and Mu Jen, both of China. For me the brotherhood of world literature consists in such relationships in concrete terms. I once took part in a hunger strike for the political freedom of a gifted Korean poet. I am now deeply worried about the destiny of those gifted Chinese novelists who have been deprived of their freedom since the Tiananmen Square incident.

Oe is a writer for whom the personal and the political are deeply intertwined. For him, world literature has been a refuge, a resource, and a weapon.

World Literature in the Classroom

Oe Kenzaburo read Rabelais in college, and his understanding of Rabelais and other world writers was shaped thereafter by a developed literary-critical awareness; it isn't every Nobel laureate who quotes Mikhail

Bakhtin in his acceptance speech. High school and college classrooms are where many readers discover world literature, particularly works from earlier times. Many works of world literature stay in print thanks to classroom adoptions, whether as freestanding volumes or in anthologies. The works that regularly appear on syllabi form what Susan Gallagher has called the pedagogical canon that circulates within a country's educational system ("Contingencies and Intersections"). Students encounter these canonical works within a scene of instruction that reflects the instructor's preferred theoretical approach and chosen themes.

A growing number of courses are now offered under the rubric of "world literature" in different countries, often in distinct national configurations. Thus in China "world literature" is usually taught in foreign language departments, while comparative literature courses are offered in Chinese departments, where the focus is on relations of Chinese writers with foreign works. In the United States, courses labeled "world literature" have often taken the form of broad surveys at the freshman and sophomore level, offered within English departments or in interdepartmental general education programs, and are only sometimes taught by trained comparatists or by professors of foreign literatures. In her introduction to a multivolume project entitled *Literatura-mundo comparada: Perspectivas em português*, Helena Carvalhão Buescu notes that the collection was created by scholars in Lisbon, and she says that the results would likely have been quite different if it had been constructed elsewhere in the Lusophone world. She emphasizes that a genuinely global understanding of literature must always be a form of "comparative world literature," reflecting "a historically and comparatively situated reading within the frame of world literature" (*Mundos em português*, 1:25).

The large world literature anthologies produced for the North American market during the past two decades have attracted a good deal of attention from scholars interested in exploring, or critiquing, the ongoing development of world literary studies. As an editor of one of these anthologies, I am naturally pleased to find them receiving scholarly attention in addition to their classroom use, most often in sophomore-level general education courses. Yet it seems to me that the survey anthologies have often been too quickly taken as metonymies of the field at large, whether in celebrations of their inclusiveness or in stern condemnations of their "bulimic, entrepreneurial drive to anthologize and curricularize the world's cultural resources" (Apter, *Against World Literature*, 3). It is less often noted that upper-level courses approach world literature very differently, usually through detailed examination of a given theme or problematic in a restricted number of texts, primarily involving languages that the instructor knows. Even introductory survey courses are much more selective in materials and more thematically focused than can be seen from the bare table of contents of the anthology they use, if they use one at all, as I found when editing a collection for the Modern Language Association (*Teaching World Literature*), where many different approaches can be seen.

The sophomore-level surveys do pose special problems when they include works from many countries and periods, and they have been criticized on both philological and political grounds. A particularly thoughtful critique was mounted by Marshall Brown not long after he had himself served as one of the co-editors of *The Longman Anthology of World Literature*. In his essay, Brown disputes the frequent rhetoric in these courses (and in my own *How to Read World Literature*) of providing students with voyages of discovery into distant cultures. He argues to the contrary that the world as a whole is inaccessible to us, and that our primary experience of the foreign is one of dislocation and dissonance. Brown sees literary meaning as residing in its specificity, and he is quite specific as to what this specificity entails. "Of course," he says, "specificity means localism, and openness to the globe must imply a sacrifice of local rooting. To be made universally comprehensible, a situation must shed its linguistic and social particularities. It must be flattened out, reduced to a common denominator" ("Encountering the World," 357).

Brown illustrates this problem through the ways in which Chinua Achebe, Derek Walcott, and Petrarch have described encounters with the world, which they find *unheimlich*. Brown sees translation as creating an artificial homeliness very different from these writers' fraught worldliness: "world literature begins with a local situation translated into a common language. . . . Yet translation and explanation denature; the aura is lost. Thus commonness inevitably falsifies and so turns into kitsch" (358). He ends his essay by concluding: "World literature, to me, is not writing that gains in translation, but writing that retains its alienness even in the original" (364).

Brown's view stands at the opposite pole from the hermeneutic approach to translation advanced by theorists such as Lawrence Venuti. In place of a Benjaminian nostalgia for lost auras, or the local rootedness that Brown takes as "of course" forming the true locus of literary meaning, Venuti emphasizes a work's reinscription in its new context. These are ultimately irreconcilable views of literary language itself. Galin Tihanov has observed that such divergences go back to early arguments among the Russian formalists, "reenacting the cardinal debate on whether one should think of literature within the horizon of language or beyond that horizon" ("The Location of World Literature," 474). The formalists were in broad agreement that the essence of literary texts inheres in their "literariness," but they disagreed on what literariness really entails. Roman Jakobson considered literariness to be bound up in the work's verbal texture, and in consequence he devoted his literary analyses to poems discussed in the original languages. Very differently, as Tihanov says, Viktor Shklovsky and Boris Eikhenbaum "believed that the effects of literariness are also (and, in a sense, primarily) produced on levels above and beyond language" (474), and they readily worked with translations.

Brown isn't actually arguing against the teaching of survey courses in world literature. Rather, he opposes a mode of teaching that emphasizes a reader's sense of connection with the world evoked by the text; he proposes instead the encounter with a work's "alienness even in the original." Such a perspective clearly would apply to any course one teaches, including on a single literature or even a single author. Thus Brown gives an eloquent reading of Petrarch's sonnet 35, which begins:

Solo e pensoso i più deserti campi
Vo mesurando a passi tardi e lenti;
E gli occhi porto, per fuggire, intenti,
Ove vestigio uman l'arena stampi.

[Alone and pensive, I measure the most deserted fields with heavy steps and slow; and keep my eyes intent on fleeing, wherever a human trace marks the sand.] ("Encountering the World," 358)

The poet experiences the world as a desert, a space of emptiness, not at all as a home away from home. As Brown says, "The outcome of the lyric encounter with the world is enunciated in the last line of the first of the poems in Laura's death, 'Ma 'l vento ne portava le parole'—But the wind carried off the words. The world worlds, but only to end in aphasia" (360).

Petrarch's sonnet, however, has nothing to do with encountering an unfamiliar culture, a distant era, or a foreign language, the problems specific to world literature courses; the issue here concerns the nature of experience and of the poetic language that conveys it. Though Brown denies that translation can convey a writer's meaning without flattening it out, his thesis concerning Petrarch's aphasic poetry is fully illustrated even in the prose translations he gives for the Italian. "But the wind carried off the words" expresses the evaporation of language fully as well as does "Ma 'l vento ne portava le parole," and even gives a version of the alliteration of "portava/parole" with "wind/words." An instructor who wants to emphasize aporias and dissonances can readily do so in a world literature class even when using translations, and indeed it is difficult to imagine teaching Petrarch, or Kafka, any other way. "What have I in common with Jews?" Kafka famously asked himself; "I have hardly anything in common with myself" (*Diaries*, 252). Certainly one could do more with Petrarch's specific wording by using his Italian original, and more with a good verse translation than with a plain prose version. Yet even an introductory survey course can provide originals at least for selected poems, as in fact the *Longman Anthology* does for Petrarch and a variety of other writers, giving not just one but variant translations of poems or passages, so as to enable teachers and students to hear the original and to explore the different effects of the differing renderings.

And what of Petrarch's original context? One reason people use anthologies is that they do provide a good deal of information on the works' cultural and historical context, through introductions, footnotes, and clusters of related readings. Teachers who want more context will either supplement what the anthology offers or will instead choose to assign individual texts, giving fuller readings from fewer authors. Sophomore-level surveys often have a more focused selection in terms of period and region than would be found in the "If it's Tuesday, this must be Renaissance Florence" kind of course. Yet such wide-ranging courses have their own benefits in terms of opening out differing perspectives and modes of literary experience. Petrarch's *Canzoniere* would never have inspired a Petrarchan tradition all around Europe if poets in England, France, and Poland needed to know more about Petrarch's life and times than any good anthology can give in its introduction and notes.

It is an oversimplification to oppose rooted local context to globe-trotting decontextualization, even at the basic level of an introductory survey course. As John Guillory emphasizes in *Cultural Capital*, it is the syllabus itself that provides the primary context in which works are read in a course, shaped by the instructor's thematic emphases, interpretive predilections, and ideological presuppositions. In the case of Petrarch, I teach his sonnets in a threefold context: formal, historical, and theoretical. I juxtapose his sonnet "Una candida cerva sopra l'erba" with Sir Thomas Wyatt's adaptive translation "Whoso list to hunt," inviting the class to explore how Wyatt shifts the sonnet toward his setting in the court of Henry VIII and toward the linguistic resources of English. We then compare both poems to later sonnets by Louise Labé and by Shakespeare, who differently build on and subvert what had become an established Petrarchan tradition. I frame these comparisons in a critique of Moretti's claim in his "More Conjectures" essay that Petrarchism would illustrate his center-periphery theory as well as the novel does. I teach the Italian and French texts in bilingual editions, though most of the points I want to bring out can be seen in the translations, as I try to help students find their way around in Petrarch's uncanny world and in the exfoliating tradition of the sonnet. I would even say that my Petrarch is almost as depressive as Marshall Brown's, even if the poetry itself is not. To me, it is Petrarch's love life that ends in aphasia, not his magnificently crafted and eloquent sonnets, which draw us deeply into his lyrical world of loss and longing.

People who want to teach courses in world literature will need to decide whether to use an anthology, and if so, how best to select the readings. No one ever teaches more than a fraction of the works offered in the six-volume anthologies' six thousand pages. That they have grown so large is partly a result of an expansion of the literary field, but equally their size is a function of the variety of approaches and emphases favored by faculty in many different kinds of institutions, and often by different faculty within one institution, enabling them to create very different pathways through their pages. A world literature anthology produced for a market whose curriculum was set at the national level could achieve all the purposes of the current ones at a quarter of the length.

For all their capaciousness, however, the survey anthologies continue to embody significant limitations in the way world literature is still often taught. As Lawrence Venuti has noted in *Contra Instrumentalism* (51–52), the anthologies do relatively little to sensitize students—or instructors—to the interpretive issues involved in the use of translations. Further, European literatures retain a disproportionate presence in all the current anthologies; the major canonical Western writers are given substantially more space than all but a few non-Western writers. As the anthologies are developed on the basis of surveys of people teaching in the field, these results reflect general expectations among the faculty who will assign the anthology rather than the editors' own preferences. World literature courses in the United States are usually taught by people whose training was in Western literature, and they have a tendency to favor what they know best. Mary Ann Caws and Christopher Prendergast found this out to their regret in the early 1990s, when they spearheaded a resolutely non-Eurocentric anthology, *The HarperCollins World Reader*. Its global table of contents had been welcomed by the publisher's reviewers, but once the anthology came out, very few instructors chose to assign it, given its slender selections from writers such as Dante and Dostoevsky, whom they expected to see strongly represented.

Even for writers whom editors and instructors alike want to include, the anthologies' contents are significantly skewed by the availability or affordability of translations. Many desirable selections are left out because a copyright holder asks an unaffordable permissions fee or even withholds permission at any price. For non-Western authors, especially from earlier periods, it is also common to find only translations that have been made as aids to readers who possess the original language, and often these translations don't work well on their own. As a result of all these factors, analysis of what is included in an anthology needs to be aware of the complicated forces that shape the end result, including the time lag between scholarly developments in an area and their reflection in courses taught by nonspecialists.[2]

Allowing for these correctives to any direct mapping of curricula onto scholarship, it can be useful to look at anthologies and handbooks beyond one's own borders as well as at home, to see how comparative and world literary studies are brought into classrooms elsewhere. Particularly in the United States, there is a tendency for even globally minded comparatists to think mostly of their own national environment when discussing institutional arrangements. The French comparatist Didier Coste made this point in a review essay on Gayatri Spivak's *Death of a Discipline,* in which he noted her heavy focus on "le milieu universitaire étasunien." "In the American university milieu," he comments, "what is construed by American ideology as a major event, which is always recent (the fall of the Soviet Empire, terrorist attacks in New York and Washington), displaces the less recent and occludes the long-term logics of the past as well as the future" ("Votum Mortis"). By contrast, he says, the shape of the discipline has hardly changed for decades in France, despite the pleas of occasional insurgents such as Étiemble.

Whereas comparative literature in the United States has increasingly shifted its emphasis to the twentieth and twenty-first centuries, a very different picture is given in an Italian manual for undergraduates, *Guida allo studio delle letterature comparate* (2013), written by Piero Boitani and Emilia Di Rocco of Rome's Sapienza Università. They begin with an introduction that discusses ancient literature and then proceeds to sections on Patristics, the Middle Ages, and the Renaissance, before closing with an introductory discussion of *Weltliteratur* and modern comparative

---

[2] For a cogent critique of the *Longman Anthology* by an Arabist, see Omar Khalifah's "Anthologizing Arabic Literature," together with my response, "Contextualizing Arabic Literature." For the place of Arabic within comparative studies generally, see Waïl Hassan, "Arabic and the Paradigms of Comparison."

literature. The emphasis on earlier periods is seen throughout the book, as in a chapter on the lyric, whose first four sections proceed from antiquity though the Middle Ages. Only the fifth and final section treats "La lirica moderna," in which the modern period covers an expanse of six hundred years, from Petrarch to the present.

Boitani and Di Rocco's vision of comparative literature is thoroughly Western and largely European, but theirs is not the same Europe that we would find in a student guide from another European country. In part this is because the authors include a much higher proportion of Italian writers than surveys elsewhere would do. Theirs, then, is an Italianate Europe, and they make almost no reference to any non-Western material. When they touch on world literature (*letteratura mondiale*), they do so only in connection with European epics and myths. As they say at the outset, their focus is "fundamentally on Euro-American comparative literature. We wanted in this way to show how one can 'do' comparative literature on the basis of Western texts" (xxi).

In its emphasis on early periods and in its unembarrassed Eurocentrism, the *Guida allo studio delle letterature comparate* may seem to be an Italian version of Didier Coste's unchanging French comparatism, but this isn't actually the case. Breaking with the older nation-based approach implied in their title (the plural term *letterature comparate* literally means "compared literatures"), Boitani and Di Rocco set national traditions aside. Instead, they organize their book first by genres and then by themes. In a further contrast to both American and French comparatism, they give considerable space to religious literature. In the genre-based first half of their book, they devote a chapter to "Il sacro"—though they acknowledge that "the sacred" isn't a genre in any ordinary sense—with sections on Genesis and Hesiod, wisdom literature, and the four gospels. They end the chapter by discussing the gospels' importance to Dante and later writers, from Racine to Dostoevsky and (interestingly) Norman Mailer.

This isn't comparative literature as it is studied either at Columbia or at the Sorbonne Nouvelle. Nor, in fact, is it how *letterature comparate* is studied in Milan. At Milan's private IULM university, comparative studies take place within the university's thriving translation studies program; differently again, the program at the Università di Milano-Bicocca focuses on poetics and cultural studies. A related emphasis on modern European literature and theory is found in *Letterature comparate* (2015), a handbook for students edited by Francesco de Cristofaro, with chapters by himself and nine colleagues from around Italy. Their introductory chapter advances a "rhizomatic" vision of cultural diversity as the field moves beyond its traditional Eurocentrism (13). In keeping with this emphasis, the introduction includes a section on "Una dimensione globale" (14–22), which gives a judicious overview of recent discussions of world literature and postcolonial studies. In the body of the book, however, the focus is almost entirely on the literatures of Europe and the United States. Even the seventh chapter, "Letteratura mondo: Oriente/Occidente," deals largely with European conceptions, with brief discussions of some non-Western writers whom the Europeans were reading. This handbook's rhizome is still rooted in Europe.

Attending to the ways the discipline is taught in other countries can help comparatists find approaches we may want to apply as well, or simply to gain a clearer sense of the wider range of possibility from which our own national discipline has made its choices. Further, looking at the differing emphases found within a single country such as Italy, or even in the single city of Milan, can help attune us to differences within our own national context. People who speak of the field of world literature as a singular entity that "inevitably" has certain limitations (the adverb is used by both Brown and Apter) are ignoring not only the considerable variety to be found worldwide but, in many cases, the significant differences within their own country.

The study of world literature is often taken these days as a rejection of comparative literature's longstanding Eurocentrism, whether this expansion is celebrated as ethically desirable inclusiveness or critiqued as literary tourism. Yet many world literature courses continue to focus largely or entirely on Western literature. Some of these courses use texts such as the two-volume *Norton Anthology of Western Literature*, whose genesis and purposes are cogently analyzed by Sarah Lawall in her essay "The West and the Rest."[3] Other instructors will select only Western works from a more global world literature anthology, or will use individual texts of their own choosing. There is no reason to insist on a singular definition of world literature that denies the still quite common practice of considering European literature as a significant world-literary space, whether in a course labeled "Masterpieces of European Literature" or in a "World Literature" course whose syllabus is predominantly Western.

Outside of classrooms, writers themselves often use "world literature" to refer chiefly to European literatures. Milan Kundera was a lecturer in *Weltliteratur* in Prague and later moved to France to take a position in Rennes as a professor of comparative literature, and his academic experience as well as his novelist's perspective inform his essay *"Die Weltliteratur"* (2005). There Kundera discusses Goethe's concept and its relevance today, adducing a wide range of writing from Norse sagas to works by Kafka, Beckett, Ionesco, and many other Europeans. His focus is entirely on Europe as a world-literary space, an arena of "maximum diversity in minimum space" (31). When he refers to "a faraway country of which we know little" (33), he is ironically quoting Neville Chamberlain's dismissive comment when ceding Czechoslovakia to Hitler at the Munich conference in 1938. For Kundera, the problematics of East/West cultural politics are fully visible in the relations between western Europe and "the European Orient," which he describes as "a whole other *world*, the world of the European East" (43).

In Japan, the novelist Ikezawa Natsuki, winner of both the Akutagawa and Tanizaki prizes, published a series of lectures in 2005 under the title *Sekai bungaku o yomihodoku: Sutandāru kara Pinchon made* (Decoding World Literature: From Stendhal to Pynchon). There he discusses ten foreign novels as well as his own *The Quiet Land*. Five of the foreign authors are from Europe (Stendhal, Tolstoy, Dostoevsky, Joyce, Mann), four from

---

[3] The *Norton Anthology of Western Literature* came out in its ninth edition in 2014. In 2018 Martin Puchner and his co-editors decided against doing a tenth edition, a sign that purely Western world literature courses are decreasing in numbers. The Western edition remains in print, though it is somewhat surreally listed by Amazon together with other classics of "Western literature" such as *The Redemption of the Lonesome Sheriff* and *Gunning for Glory*.

the United States (Melville, Twain, Faulkner, Pynchon), and only one (García Márquez) from anywhere else in the word. Ikezawa then edited a thirty-volume world literature collection, published in 2007–2011 under the title *Ikezawa Natsuki Kojin Henshu Sekai Bungaku Zenshu* (Ikezawa Natsuki's Choice of World Literature, Complete Collection). For this expansive collection he chose personal favorites that he felt should be better known in Japan; Jack Kerouac's *On the Road* was his intriguing choice for the first volume in the series. Two-thirds of the works he selected are European (a proportion comparable to that in the American survey anthologies), and most of his non-European works were written in English, French, or Spanish. Remarkably, the collection sold over four hundred thousand copies. "Japanese people love things in sets," Ikezawa modestly told an interviewer, "like bento boxes" ("Conversation").

More recently, three essays by the great Albanian writer Ismail Kadare have been translated into English under the title *Essays on World Literature* (2018). In these essays, dating from 1985 to 2007, Kadare describes in moving terms how Aeschylus, Dante, and Shakespeare helped him come to terms with corruption and civil conflict as he was growing up under the isolated totalitarian regime of Enver Hoxha. As the book's translator says in a preface, "These essays chart a map of world literature and its geniuses dating back to antiquity with such critical awareness that we may soon see Kadare himself bookending this lineage of geniuses" (xii). Particularly striking is the final essay, in which Kadare reads *Hamlet* together with Albanian history in terms of traditions of blood vengeance. These traditions were formally codified in the fifteenth century in *The Code of Lekë Dukagjini*, still widely used today, which has extensive provisions for when and how one can properly enact vengeance. The term used for "legal code" is *kanun*—taken from Ottoman Turkish, which had taken the term from Arabic, which in turn had borrowed the Greek κανών (rule, standard), the same term that gives us the literary canon as well. In Kadare's account, the Shakespearean and legal canons have regularly overlapped in Albania.

In February 1924 the conservative Prime Minister Ahmet Zogu—who later crowned himself King Zog I—survived an assassination attempt as he entered parliament. The would-be assassin was released from prison after he proclaimed that he wasn't politically motivated but was merely seeking to avenge his uncle's murder. Zogu, however, was sure that the assassination was actually ordered by his chief rival, the liberal party leader Bishop Fan Noli. The bishop was suspect on literary as well as political grounds, for he wrote patriotic poetry and translated many works of world literature as a way of developing and consolidating Albanian as a literary language. As in the then still recent Ottoman era, Albanian conservatives like Zogu were deeply suspicious of such cosmopolitan activities. "The renowned Italian maxim, 'traduttore traditore,'" writes Kadare, "here assumes its basic meaning. Interpreters were accused of treason and attacked" (182). Bishop Noli did become prime minister when Zogu was overthrown four months after the assassination attempt, but he fled into exile when Zogu returned to power at year's end. A year and a half later, Noli produced "one of the most beautiful, if not the most beautiful, translations of *Hamlet* in the world" (185).

Hamlet entered Albanian culture thanks to the bishop's widely read and frequently staged translation, even figuring in a murder trial in 2006. Accused of killing a fellow criminal over drug money, the murderer asserted that he had acted for a very different reason: to avenge the murder of his grandfather, whom his associate had killed. He declared that he was impelled to act by his grandfather's ghost: "Every night the ghost would appear. Avenge my blood, he said. I can't rest until you kill Cuf Kërtalla. . . . He appeared every night, like the ghost of Hamlet" (206–7). Kadare wryly comments that "the trial becomes more difficult than expected. Even the Council of Europe has made remarks about the Albanian *Kanun* and about the lawyers who are apparently advising local Albanian bandits to justify their crimes through Shakespeare's *Hamlet*" (207). In Kadare's account, world literature has come to Albania with a vengeance.

Ismail Kadare, Milan Kundera, and Oe Kenzaburo could fully describe the impact of world literature on their writing, and on their culture, by talking about a selected set of canonical Western figures. In Kadare's rich meditation on *Hamlet* alone, we can find many of the major themes current in larger-scale world literary studies, including center-periphery relations, nationalism and cosmopolitanism, emigration and exile, poetry and politics, translation and betrayal. World literature is no longer

coextensive with Europe, but European literature remains *a* world literature of compelling interest for many writers, readers, and scholars.

This is not to say that every European writer is a devotee of world
literature. As Galin Tihanov has observed, Elias Canetti satirized the
very concept in *Die Blendung* (translated as *Auto-da-Fé*). Canetti's novel is
divided into three sections entitled "Ein Kopf ohne Welt," "Kopflose
Welt," and "Welt im Kopf" (a worldless head, a headless world, the world
in the head). Canetti's antihero Peter Kien knows a dozen Asian languages and has amassed a huge private library, but he withdraws from the
world, even having his windows boarded up to make more room for
books; he ends up committing suicide by setting his books and himself on
fire. Less fatally than his antihero, though, Canetti drew on European as
well as Confucian and Buddhist texts for his novel. As Tihanov says, Kien
is a modern Quixote, driven mad by too much reading ("Elias Canetti,"
412), and we might add that Canetti provided him with a hunchbacked
dwarf as his Sancho Panza and an illiterate wife as his Dulcinea. In his
collection *The Conscience of Words*, Canetti acknowledged his debts to
Kafka, Stendhal, Gogol, and Tolstoy, and unacknowledged debts might
also be traced; Kien converses with the shade of Confucius, much as Machiavelli used to do with his classical predecessors at night in his humanist library. The novel's world-literary imbrications only increased after its
publication in 1935. Kien's suicide-inducing library of world literature has
a good deal in common with Borges's "Library of Babel" (1941), and Kien
could have found a fellow sinologist in Borges's Stephen Albert, mur-
dered in his library in "The Garden of Forking Paths." Borges could even
have seen himself in a scholar-librarian who obsesses about going blind,
though when Canetti won the Nobel Prize in 1981, Borges said that he'd
never read him, and perhaps never had.

Canetti was still ambivalent about world literature in 1981, and he declined to give the usual Nobel lecture making graceful allusions to his
honored predecessors. Instead, he merely offered some remarks at the
banquet in his honor, in which he cited only Kafka and three Austrians
(Karl Kraus, Robert Musil, and Hermann Broch) as inspirations ("Banquet
Speech"). The same Canetti, though, was fluent in five languages and lived
in several different countries around Europe. Born in Bulgaria, he grew

up there and in England, Austria, Switzerland, and Germany, then became a British citizen during a decades-long residence back in England. Late in life he settled in Zurich, where he is buried in the Fluntern Cemetery a few yards away from James Joyce—appropriately enough, as Peter Kien is a Viennese Ulysses; the penultimate chapter of *Die Blendung* is even titled "Listenreicher Odysseus" (guileful Odysseus). Today Canetti is a world author to whose grave other writers make pilgrimages. Their visits in turn can become world texts: Cees Nooteboom describes his cemetery visit to Canetti and Joyce in his *Tumbas: Graven van dichters en denkers* (2007), which can be read in French, German, Italian, and Spanish versions as well as in Dutch.

Canetti's trans-European life was very different from Kadare's in isolated Albania; Europe has always been a shifting congeries of countries and home to differing canons and countercanons. As Mircea Cărtărescu writes in "Europe Has the Shape of My Brain," "There are several Europes, disseminated in time and in space, a multidimensional confederation of Europes. With which of them am I in solidarity? Which of them do I hate?" The Japanese historian Haneda Masashi has observed that imperialists everywhere, including in Asia, have benefited from the fiction that Europe is a stable region with a definite cultural identity. As a result, Haneda prefers to speak of "Europe" within quotation marks or to use "a more neutral term, such as west Eurasia" (*Toward Creation*, 105). If Erich Auerbach had taken fuller account of his Turkish surroundings, a more capacious version of *Mimesis* might well have merited a Haneda-style subtitle: "The Representation of Reality in West Eurasian Literature."

Scale and Scope

A fundamental question for any comparative project is to determine its scale, and world literary studies raise this question with particular force. World literature can be studied through the lens of a single author, as in John Burt Foster's *Transnational Tolstoy* (2013) or Birns and De Castro's *Roberto Bolaño as World Literature* (2017), or even through a single work, as in Michael Emmerich's *The Tale of Genji: Translation, Canonization, and World Literature* (2013) or Hamid Dabashi's *The Shahnameh: The Persian*

Epic as World Literature (2019). At an intermediate scale are studies of a regional world system such as that of East Asia, as in Karen Thornber's *Empire of Texts in Motion* (2009) and *Ecoambiguity* (2012). Wiebke Denecke counterpoints two world regions in her *Classical World Literatures: Sino-Japanese and Greco-Roman Comparisons* (2013), working directly in Greek and Latin as well as Chinese and Japanese. Networks of print and publication can also be studied in global terms, as in Eric Bulson's *Little Magazine, World Form* (2017). Most broadly, world literature can be approached through synthetic studies of worldwide scope, as in Alexander Beecroft's *An Ecology of World Literature* (2015), which extends from local ("choric") literatures to the "panchoric," the cosmopolitan, the vernacular, the national, and finally the global. Beecroft builds on his dual grounding in classics and in ancient Chinese literature and culture, with frequent reference to examples elsewhere; like Posnett's *Comparative Literature*, his book tests the limits of how fully an individual scholar can encompass the globe.

A still broader scope was famously and controversially advocated by Franco Moretti in "Conjectures on World Literature" (2000) and its sequel "More Conjectures" (2003). Drawing on the world-systems theory of Immanuel Wallerstein, Moretti argued that world literature exists in a global network that was established during the nineteenth century and has become dominant today. Yet this system doesn't operate in a "flat" landscape of unimpeded flows of capital, nor does it offer equal access to writers or to readers in different countries. Instead, Moretti says, the world literary system is "simultaneously *one*, and *unequal:* with a core and a periphery (and a semi-periphery) that are bound together in a relationship of growing inequality" ("Conjectures on World Literature," 46). In peripheral cultures, the result was an extended period of disruption of traditional forms, as the foreign imports (chiefly from France and England) had something of the character of invasive species, a Darwinian process that Moretti made explicit in an article on "Evolution, World Systems, *Weltliteratur*" (2006). Eventually, peripheral writers found ways to incorporate local elements into the imported form of the novel and could synthesize the local and the foreign in fully achieved works of art.

Moretti's essays on world literature formed a corrective to neoliberal assertions of the free flow of goods and information, a perspective summed up in the journalist Thomas Friedman's best seller *The World Is Flat* (2005). As Aamir Mufti has more recently said, "Can we really speak of 'literature' as a single world-encompassing space without reference to these material and ideological features of the structures of mobility, and therefore also of *immobility*, across the globe? We clearly cannot" (*Forget English!* 11). In addition to Moretti's early emphasis that the literary world system is built on imbalances of both cultural and financial capital, his essays were valuable for their focus on the politics of literary form. As he says, echoing Pierre Bourdieu in *Les règles de l'art*, "Forms are the abstract of social relationships: so, formal analysis is in its own modest way an analysis of power" (59). It is no coincidence that he published his "Conjectures" essays in *New Left Review*.

Moretti has been criticized for his reliance on translations, and for taking evidence at second hand from literary histories of different countries without considering that the scholars he cites may have problematic biases of their own. He has also been criticized for giving too little credit to the vitality of local traditions in peripheral regions and for presenting a too unified image of Europe itself. Granting that his model can be challenged on various levels, he does offer a way to approach the worldwide spread of the bildungsroman, or the prose poem, or the European idea of "literature," and he doesn't suppose that local cultures are purely passive receivers of metropolitan ideas and forms. On the contrary, he emphasizes that the world system evolved in the nineteenth century as "a system *of variations*. The system was one, not uniform. The pressure from the Anglo-French core *tried* to make it uniform, but it could never fully erase the reality of difference" (56).

While his scientism fuels a schematic drive almost as great as Northrop Frye's, Moretti also takes from the natural sciences an experimental openness to test and revise his theories. In the original "Conjectures" essay, he boldly proposed that the English, French, and Spanish writers credited as exemplifying the rise of the novel were "*not the rule at all, they're the exception*. They come first, yes, but they're not at all typical. The 'typical' rise of the novel is Krasicki, Kemal, Rizal, Maran—not Defoe" (53). In "More Conjectures," however, he takes on the critique leveled by Jonathan Arac ("Anglo-Globalism?") and by Jale Parla ("The Object of Comparison"), who had pointed out that eighteenth-century England itself was a semiperipheral country not unlike Krasicki's Poland, Kemal's Turkey, or Rizal's Philippines. Moretti replied: "Here things are easy: Parla and Arac are right—and I should have known better" ("More Conjectures," 116). How often have we read such an admission from a leading literary theorist?

Moretti has never actually applied to world literature the "distant reading" that he recommends in his "Conjectures" essays and in his subsequent collection *Distant Reading* (2013). At the time he was formulating his "Conjectures," he was in the process of organizing a massive five-volume collection on the novel as a global form, *Il Romanzo* (2001), totaling over four thousand pages in all, yet he didn't attempt to write this on his own on the basis of secondhand information. Instead, he enlisted dozens of specialists in many literatures, who were able to write on the basis of direct knowledge of the works and the topics they were addressing. Since then, the "Literary Lab" he co-created at Stanford has focused almost entirely on British literature for its exercises in data mining.

We can refine Moretti's formal analysis, and rethink the East/West and center-periphery binaries, by attending to the means of literary production, as Graham Huggan has urged in "The Trouble with World Literature." An example would be the global burgeoning of the short story around the turn of the twentieth century. A surprising number of major writers in semiperipheral countries, including James Joyce in Ireland, Lu Xun in China, and Higuchi Ichiyō and Akutagawa Ryūnosuke in Japan, got their start in those years as short-story writers. Each of these writers had quite different literary ambitions, but new printing technologies had produced a flood of illustrated newspapers, magazines, and journals, and these new outlets needed material. Living in urban landscapes increasingly shaped by technologies and fashions imported from the European core, engaging equally with foreign and local literatures, these and other young writers collectively revolutionized the short story, giving new realism and psychological depth to a popular genre that was still mostly published for light entertainment.

To take the Japanese case, an early account of the explosive growth of journals in late Meiji Japan can be found in the writings of Walter Dening.

Born in England, Dening had come to Japan as a Protestant missionary, but after several years he gave up Christianity and embarked on a career as a journalist and teacher of English. In 1892 he published a long article in London that gives one of the first broad surveys of the era's writing. Dening frames his discussion in the context of the new magazines that had been springing up in the previous decade. Like Moretti a century later, he sees a mixed picture of an uneven literary landscape, marked by the disruption of traditional forms and a confused search for new modes of writing:

> It is not for a moment to be expected that an age of transition, such as that in which Japan finds herself at present, should be productive of great literary works. Where men's minds are undergoing a thorough change as to the comparative value of different kinds of knowledge and the best means of diffusing it, and where the language which is the vehicle of men's thoughts is itself in a transitional stage, their writings become to a large extent literary experiments in one direction or another. Few of the books of the first part of the Meiji era will be read ten years after their publication. . . . The temptation to run into print in Japan is great; labour and paper are cheap, and the literary standard is low. ("Japanese Modern Literature," 643)

It is notable that Dening emphasizes the low cost of labor and of paper, in addition to language and literary composition. He goes on to say that the new outlets for publication offer all too many opportunities for writers: "the swarms of journals on every conceivable subject now in circulation are only kept afloat by the efforts of a host of shallow scribblers. It is the decrease, then, and not the increase, of magazines that all lovers of Japanese literature desire to see" (661).

So far, Dening's views directly anticipate Moretti's portrayal of an extended period of imitative uncertainty before a peripheral culture eventually establishes itself on new terms. Yet Dening already sees a positive dimension. Amid the mass of mediocre writing, he says, "there are happily a great many exceptions," for "we live in an age when translations and miscellaneous writings are revolutionizing thought, are imparting breadth of view and liberality of sentiment with a rapidity and to an extent unprecedented in the annals of the nation" (644). Seen in this light, the situation in late Meiji Japan was not so different from that in Ireland, the United States, and even England around the same time, when the proliferation of newspapers and magazines supported the flowering of Anglo-American modernism. Dening notes that most Meiji-era writing would soon be forgotten, but the same can be said of literature anywhere. A time of transition and ferment can be beneficial for writers, breaking the hold of outworn modes of writing and stimulating their creativity. At such times a brilliant peripheral writer can find opportunities for major advances that might not be made by established writers working within a settled literary tradition and a hidebound educational system.

Born in 1872 to a family of modest means in Tokyo, Higuchi Ichiyō received an excellent classical education before her father's fortunes and health declined; he died when she was seventeen. She had shown a precocious talent for composing poetry in classical style and was already determined to become a writer, replacing her given name, Natsuko, with the poetic pen name of Ichiyō, "One Leaf." She had no way to earn a living as a poet, however, and after her father's death she and her mother and sister were living a hand-to-mouth existence as seamstresses on the edge of Tokyo's red-light district. She turned to fiction at age twenty and began publishing a series of increasingly brilliant short stories in new magazines such as *Miyako no Hana* (Flower of the Capital), which Dening describes in his survey as "a journal for light literature" (662).

Ichiyō recorded in her diary the drama of returning home to announce: "Look, mother, I received 10 yen today for my first installment in *Miyako no Hana*!" Her sister declared that "You are now a professional writer," and added: "Who knows? You may become so famous that someday your face will be the one appearing on a Japanese note!" Ichiyō laughed and told her sister not to get carried away—"A woman's face on a note in Japan?" (Kimura, *A Note from Ichiyō*, 83). In an act of true poetic justice, since 2004 she has been featured on the ¥5000 banknote, the third woman ever to be so honored, after an empress and her own favorite writer, Murasaki Shikibu. During Ichiyō's brief, meteoric career before her death from tuberculosis in 1896, the late Meiji magazines made her a professional writer, and they gave her the opportunity to develop her art far beyond the general run of what appeared in their pages.

So too in 1904 the young James Joyce could publish his unsettling first story of Dublin life, "The Sisters," in a far from elite publication, *The Irish Homestead*. Founded in 1895, *The Irish Homestead* was the weekly newspaper of the Irish Agricultural Organization Society, which sought to introduce rural readers to new farming methods and machinery so as to provide a stronger economic base for Irish independence. The twenty-two-year-old Joyce was working on *Stephen Hero*, the first version of what would eventually become *A Portrait of the Artist as a Young Man*, but he was desperately short of funds, and he sent an appeal to several friends asking them to lend him a pound each. One of Joyce's friends, the minor poet George Russell, was *The Irish Homestead*'s literary editor, and though he didn't want to make another loan, he offered to pay a pound apiece for a series of short stories for the paper. As he told Joyce, "It is easily earned money if you can write fluently and don't mind playing to the common understanding and liking for once in a way" (Joyce, *Letters*, 2:43).

Joyce quickly wrote "The Sisters," which ran as "Our Weekly Story" in the issue for August 13, 1904. There it was printed alongside advertisements for Cantrell and Cochran's Mineral Waters and for "Dairy Machinery and Appliances of Every Description," including cream separators, refrigerating machines, and milk pumps. Embarrassed to be publishing in what he called "the pigs' paper" (*Ulysses*, 193), Joyce adopted a pseudonym, "Stephen Daedalus." He only managed to publish two more stories before Russell ended the arrangement after the paper's readers began objecting to them; tales of alcoholism, priestly pederasty, and domestic violence weren't too well suited to the common understanding and liking. Yet *The Irish Homestead*, like *Miyako no Hana* a decade earlier, had offered an impoverished but precocious young writer the opportunity to see his first stories in print.

What Is a World (Literature)?

Implicitly or explicitly, any attempt to delineate world literature entails defining the world—the world created by the text, the world of the text's creator, and the worldly location within which we carry on our studies.

FIGURE 13. World literature in the empyrean and down to earth.

These worlds are all subject to change, and they can interact uneasily. As Joyce said in *Finnegans Wake*—a work designed to be completely unpublishable in *The Irish Homestead*—"the mappamund has been changing . . . since times and races were" (253). Literature and its worldly life can look very different to different observers even at the same time and in the same country, as can be seen from the covers of two recent German publications (figure 13).

Edited by Dieter Lamping of the University of Mainz, *Meilensteine der Weltliteratur* (2015) is a collection of concise essays on 110 canonical writers, from the Enlightenment to the present, grouped in sections organized by period or genre. The essays sketch the author's life and times and then summarize and analyze one or two of the writer's key works. The focus is squarely on European "milestones," defined as works that have had a substantial impact beyond their home country, together with several writers from the Americas and one from South Africa (Nadine Gordimer). The cover shows stacks of books floating in the empyrean, making them unusually light for milestones—the unbearable lightness of *Weltliteratur*? Milan Kundera's *Unbearable Lightness of Being* is in fact one of the works discussed, as is Lagerlöf's *Nils Holgerssons underbara resa*, along with classic texts by Flaubert, Tolstoy, Woolf, and many more.[4]

In sharp contrast, *Die neue Weltliteratur und ihre großen Erzähler* (The New World Literature and Its Great Storytellers, 2014) is a personal assessment of some fifty authors by Sigrid Löffler, a prominent cultural journalist. She likely took the term *neue Weltliteratur* from Elke Sturm-Trigonakis's *Global Playing in der Literatur: Ein Versuch über die neue Weltliteratur* (2007), whose bilingual title announces her interest in multilingual writers of global perspective. Löffler's world literature is decidedly down to earth—the cover shows a sidewalk book stall in Kolkata—and her "new world literature" is written by contemporary migrants into Europe and North America. In place of Lamping's high-flying books in the heavens are the uprooted authors whom Löffler describes as *Luftwurzler* (13)—human epiphytes, literally "air-rooted ones."

There are no overlaps at all between Löffler's 50-plus writers and Lamping's 110, and yet there are some basic commonalities in their methods and perspectives. Both focus on an intermediate scale of presentation, well beyond an emblematic handful of figures but far below a data-mined group of thousands. In their selections, both show a pronounced canonical drive. While Lamping's book seeks to orient students to canonical works from the past three centuries, Löffler stresses the greatness of her "great storytellers," proposing a contemporary canon in formation. For both, the West is the primary scene in which world literature is to be found and read, even if their narratives move in opposite directions: Lamping's collection includes a Moretti-style diffusionist portrayal of Latin American writers

---

[4] *Meilensteine der Weltliteratur* further illustrates the variability of canons of world literature. Germany and Austria are strongly represented, with thirty-three "milestones," versus only sixteen by French writers, a proportion that would be unthinkable in France and unlikely almost anywhere else. Also distinctively German is the inclusion of many writers from the United States—nineteen in all, second only to the Germans, reflecting postwar German fascination with American culture. An interesting choice is the inclusion of a section on Yiddish literature, in keeping with post-Holocaust efforts to deal with the country's Jewish legacy.

building on their European intertexts, while Löffler presents a world literature created by immigrants who come to the metropole and revitalize Western literature itself—a version that can be related to Pascale Casanova's account, although Löffler doesn't cite her.

Löffler also shares with Lamping the widespread German interest in English-language writing. She focuses on migrants into England, the United States, and Canada, whose writing she sees as exemplifying the world-wide literatures of emigration. Though she draws on the work of Edward Said, Homi Bhabha, and Ngũgĩ wa Thiong'o, she presents the English language far more positively than would most Anglophone postcolonialists. Her focus is on literary rebels who transform the once-imperial language in which they now write. Quoting Salman Rushdie's praise of the "enormous flexibility and richness" of English, she presents English as "an especially democratic language" and a resource for subversive immigrants "who want to be visible as world writers" (16). She briefly acknowledges the postcolonial critique of global English as a leveling commercial medium, but she simply sets aside "the strategically planned bestsellers, generated by a massive industry of literature for light entertainment, that constantly flood the bookstores: Global McFiction won't be considered here" (18).

Ironically, it is Global McFiction that predominates in the Kolkata bookstall shown on her cover. The legible literary titles are mostly thrillers by English and American writers such as Robert Ludlum, Jeffrey Archer, and Tom Clancy, together with a Nancy Drew mystery and a couple of popular nineteenth-century classics (*Leaves of Grass*, *The Pickwick Papers*). Ken Kesey is perched on top of the pile. Löffler has excluded the world's most widely read literature from her pages, but it haunts her dust jacket in the precarious stack of dusty paperbacks on a Kolkata sidewalk.

Describing, and Changing, the World

Goethe could envision *Weltliteratur* as a fundamentally harmonious network of enlightened intellectual commerce, but the situation has become more complex since then. As the poet and cultural theorist Hans Magnus Enzensberger has said, "Only in the twentieth century has 'world' become the prefix to every productive and destructive possibility: world war, world economy, world literature—in earnest this time, in deadly earnest, and as a condition of survival. With this the historic process entered a new phase" ("World Language," 50). Critics of world literary studies not infrequently view its exponents as merely describing a world that needs radical change. Graham Huggan is unsparing in asserting that the field "is too much a *symptom* of the often profoundly anti-democratic and neo-imperialist tendencies within globalization that an appropriately 'global' Comparative Literature should make it its business to resist" ("The Trouble with World Literature," 491). The result may be a well-meaning but vague "literary tourism that can only ever be selectively global" (492) or, worse yet, "Anglo-globalist triumphalism masquerading as liberal-democratic global consciousness" (498). How are students and scholars of world literature to avoid succumbing to antidemocratic Anglo-triumphalism?

In *What Is a World? Postcolonial Literature as World Literature* (2016), Pheng Cheah proposes taking a deeper look at the concept of world itself. In his view, too many theorists of world literature take the world for granted, not as a dynamic field that literature can hope to change: "They equate the world with circulatory movements that cut across national-territorial borders. They are primarily concerned with the impact of these spatial movements on the production, reception, and interpretation of literary texts instead of world literature's impact qua literature on the world" (3). In place of such descriptive cartographies, Cheah proposes an approach "that does not merely describe and analyze how literary works circulate around the world or are produced with a global market in mind but that seeks to understand the normative force that literature can exert in the world, the ethicopolitcal horizon it opens up for the existing world" (5). His project highlights contemporary postcolonial novels that envision radical social change and the creation of a new era of human freedom.

Cheah argues that the sociological mappings advanced by Moretti and Casanova portray literature as hardly more than "a passive reflection of the forces at work in a global market" (28), from which literature is "entirely derivative" (35). Not only the literary work but the reader can become "simply dummies through which social forces are ventriloquized" (36). This critique understates the complexity of the relations that Moretti develops between literary form and social formations as well as the dynamism that Casanova ascribes to peripheral writers as engines of innovation. She emphasizes the degree to which writers from "dominated" cultures have to struggle against odds that have long been stacked against them, a perspective that she elaborated in *La Langue mondiale: Traduction et domination* (2005). Hers is far from an apolitical perspective or one that simply accepts the market as a given.

In 2003 Moretti responded somewhat acerbically to a critique similar to Cheah's by Efraín Kristal, who argued that Moretti's "Conjectures on World Literature" minimized the creativity of peripheral writers and their ability to resist foreign domination. Kristal proposed instead that "themes and forms can move in several directions—from the centre to the periphery, from the periphery to the centre, from one periphery to another, while some original forms of consequence may not move much at all" ("Considering Coldly" 74). To this Moretti replied:

> Yes, forms *can* move in several directions. But *do* they? This is the point, and a theory of literary history should reflect on the constraints on their movements, and the reasons behind them. . . . The model proposed in "Conjectures" does not restrict innovation to a few cultures and deny it to the others: it specifies *the conditions under which it is more likely to occur*, and the forms it may take. Theories will never abolish inequality; they can only hope to explain it. ("More Conjectures," 112–13)

Pheng Cheah sets his sights higher than explanation; he wants to change the world. "As an enactment of the opening of worlds by the coming of time," he says, "world literature points to something that will always exceed and disrupt capital" (11). World writers respond "to the need to remake the world as a place that is *open* to the emergence of peoples that globalization deprives of world" (19). Cheah seeks to disrupt the neoliberal global order both through his scholarly analysis and by his construction of the archive to analyze, thereby yielding a synergy between material and method.

So too the Warwick Research Collective selects works that thematize the problems of combined and uneven development that their group wishes to combat. Similarly, Sigrid Löffler's *neue Weltliteratur* is the literature of migrants whose writing embodies her issues of hybridity and creative dislocation. Her intention is both to map and to perform a new vision of the world, creating a mimetic parallel between the voyages undertaken by her novelists and those experienced by her own readers: "Since this book brings into view regions of the world that before now have rarely or never been taken note of, it invites you to a voyage of discovery. Literary landscapes will be mapped in the ways they have been carried over into literary narratives" (19). Introducing his own version of "The New World Literature" (the title of his first chapter), Cheah says that "I have chosen literary narratives concerned with the world-destroying consequences of various modalities of capitalist globalization" (*What Is a World?* 16). His project itself "can also be a form of critical resistance that brings the attention of the wider world to the plight of peoples impacted by global forces and their struggle to safeguard a future for their worlds" (16–17).

Both Löffler and Cheah are more direct than Moretti in seeking to achieve a political effect through their work, but this is a difference of degree rather than of kind. Less overtly activist than either Löffler or Cheah, Moretti is closer to Cheah in another respect. Politically oriented theory is prominent for both of them, though Moretti uses Fredric Jameson, Kojin Karatani, and Roberto Schwarz where Cheah (more conservatively in this respect) uses a European set of references, from Hegel to Derrida. Moretti remains loyal to his Italian Marxist formation, and Verso, which also publishes *New Left Review*, brought out his *Distant Reading* in 2013, the same year they published Emily Apter's *Against World Literature*.

We are often drawn to write about works with which we feel ourselves in sympathy, and it is probably no coincidence that Löffler focuses on the literature of migration and minority experience; she was born in the German minority of what was Czechoslovakia, then emigrated to Austria and eventually to Germany. Yet it would mean a tremendous impoverishment of literary studies if we only studied contemporary world literature, even more if the only contemporary works considered worth studying were novels, and only novels by or about migrants, and if within that micro-canon the only things worth discussing, in writers as rich and complex as Michael Ondaatje or Amitav Ghosh, would be their critiques of imperialism or capitalism.

Comparatists from Herder and de Staël onward have been intent on changing the world, and world literature provides an important venue for our scholarly activism in difficult times. But there are many ways to change the world. This can be illustrated by considering Löffler, Cheah, and Moretti in terms of Mads Rosendahl Thomsen's distinction between theories oriented toward readers, classrooms, or scholars. Though Löffler frames her project within postcolonial theory, including Glissant as well as Anglophone theorists, she wears her scholarship lightly. Free of footnotes, her book is addressed to common readers, and she celebrates her authors' ability to overcome the traumas of war, dislocation, and racism. She discusses figures as various as V. S. Naipaul, Salman Rushdie, Michael Ondaatje, Aleksandar Hemon, Nuruddin Farah, and Dinaw Mengestu, in a strategic mix of well-known figures with others whom few of her readers will have heard of. She makes a point of discussing only works that have been well translated into German, giving no ground in her presentation to global English, even though many of her authors write in English. In this way, she hopes to change the landscape of the German literary field, and she is directly intervening in the roiling debates over the immigration crisis in Germany.

Cheah treats some of the same writers as Löffler, but he does so very differently, through extended discussions of Hegel, Marx, Heidegger, Arendt, and Derrida. Bolstered with nearly three hundred endnotes, many of them substantial, Cheah's "complexly argued" book "makes a significant, timely, and radical intervention," as Wai Chee Dimock and Simon Gikandi (respectively) say on the back cover. Cheah intervenes into scholarly discourse rather than the public sphere, though his book may eventually yield public effects via the classroom, if his academic readers change their syllabi in light of his arguments, and if their students in turn go out into the world infused with a new understanding. Cheah highlights the scene of instruction in his introduction, in which he describes resistance he has experienced from his own students. In 2009 he taught a graduate seminar on postcolonial world literature in the English department at

Berkeley, in an early instantiation of the plan for his book. In their end-of-term evaluations, his students praised the theoretical readings, but they were less impressed by the novels he had chosen. Disappointed, Cheah comments:

> I would have thought that ethical and political issues arising from the impact of contemporary global capitalism on a large part of the world's population would be of interest in a seminar on contemporary world literature. But this would require readers to step outside their comfort zones of familiarity with canonical English literature and learn more about other parts of the world, especially from nonliterary discourses. (16)

Cheah seeks to overcome such resistances by providing scholar-teachers with new ways to present postcolonial perspectives and to get revolutionary novels more widely read. It is likely, in fact, that writing his book helped Cheah hone his presentation and produce this effect in his own seminars. The graduate students who took his course in 2009 were probably quite interested in reading noncanonical literature dealing with the impact of global capitalism (why else would they have signed up?), but for whatever reasons the course didn't achieve the results that Cheah had sought. In the summer of 2018 he taught a related seminar for the Institute of World Literature in Tokyo. Whereas in 2009 his Berkeley students complained that he could have chosen "better" and more "universal" novels, in our end-of-session survey the majority of his Tokyo participants rated the readings as "excellent," the highest of five categories offered, and no one at all listed the readings in the bottom categories of "poor" or merely "fair." The only complaints concerned the substantial theoretical readings (which had been catnip to the Berkeley students), but the respondents in 2018 wished they'd had more readings from some of the same novelists that Cheah's students had resisted in 2009.

In contrast to Löffler's readerly outreach and Cheah's complexly argued philosophical approach, Moretti's program of world-systems analysis via distant reading seems far from the experience of the common reader or even of the classroom. Yet he intends a very direct effect on institutional politics. Though he may only expect theory to explain the world at large, his work in digital humanities represents a frontal assault on business as usual within literary studies. His archive is not a handful but thousands of novels, and he gives as much attention to "the great unread" of popular literature as to canonical works. To accomplish this goal, he set up the Stanford Literary Lab as a scholarly collective whose data mining opposes individual scholars' consumerist close readings. The lab has involved faculty, graduate students, and undergraduates in close collaborations, allowing ideas to percolate up and not just filter down from the top.

One of the most interesting papers to emerge from the first years of the lab's work was "Loudness in the Novel," a study of speech levels in the nineteenth-century British novel. Among other findings, this study yielded the surprising result that as London became noisier over the course of the century, conversations in the novels grew steadily quieter. The paper was written by an undergraduate, Holst Katsma, who came up with the idea. He worked with a graduate student adviser to write code that enabled him to extract a set of terms from some two thousand novels, indicating the volume of a speech or reply (such as whether it was "whispered" or "murmured," "cried" or "shouted," or simply "said"). His project became his senior essay, directed by Moretti. It was published online as the lab's seventh "pamphlet," and it won two university awards, including one of four given for the best honors thesis in any field at Stanford. Katsma's paper is indeed purely descriptive, but through such projects the Literary Lab is doing its part to change the academic world, not only by citing critics such as Raymond Williams and Fredric Jameson but in the pragmatic politics of how the group carries on its work. Moretti is the first to admit that the lab hasn't yet yielded the dramatic results he'd hoped for, but as he said in a 2017 profile in the *New York Times*, "I'd rather be a failed revolutionary than someone who never tried to do a revolution in the first place" (Schuessler, "Reading by the Numbers").

Although Moretti's revolution is located within the library and the lab, his essays have gotten a good deal of wider attention, as his *New York Times* interview shows. *Distant Reading* won the 2014 award for criticism given by the National Book Critics Circle, and they were probably impressed not just by his graphs but also by the introductions he added to each essay in the collection, giving a very personal account of the genesis of each one. Taken together, the introductions create a narrative of intellectual quest and growth—scholarship as Moretti's favorite form, a bildungsroman. Thus the introduction for the opening essay, "Modern European Literature: A Geographical Sketch," alludes to his own geographic and linguistic migration. Shortly after moving from the University of Verona to Columbia University in 1990, he wrote the essay for a nonacademic audience in Italy, then rewrote it for publication in *New Left Review*. As he says,

> This was a happy essay. Evolution, geography, and formalism—the three approaches that would define my approach for over a decade—first came into systematic contact while writing these pages. I felt curious, full of energy; I kept studying, adding, correcting. . . . I was writing in Italian; for the last time, as it turned out—though, at the time, I didn't know it. In Italian, sentences run easier; details, and even nuances, seem to emerge all by themselves. In English, it would all be different. (2)

Sigrid Löffler, Franco Moretti, and Pheng Cheah have had very different personal and intellectual itineraries, yielding distinct spatial and temporal cartographies, based on differing archives and addressed to different audiences. All three writers are academic activists, and whichever parallel or divergent route any of us chooses to take, every comparatist has much to learn from each of them, and from the full range of world literary studies today.

8

Comparisons

On one of Dylan Thomas's alcohol-fueled lecture tours to the United States, he was introduced at a campus reception to a professor of comparative literature, a discipline he'd never heard of. "What do you compare it with?" he asked: "*Shit?*" This at least is what he probably said, though in recounting this anecdote in his 1968 ACLA address, Harry Levin veiled the query in a decorous paraphrase.[1] Even so, Levin obliquely endorsed the poet's suggestion, saying that "the ultimate comparison, as Dylan Thomas may have been obscurely hinting, measures literature against life itself" (6). In *James Joyce: A Critical Introduction*, Levin had mentioned the memorable scene in *Finnegans Wake* in which Shem the Penman mixes ink out of his own urine and excrement to write his "usylessly unreadable Blue Book of Eccles . . . not protected by copriright in the United Stars of Ourania" (*Finnegans Wake*, 179, 185). But a full-scale study—*The Anxiety of Effluents*, perhaps?—would have been a monograph too far.

The difficulties of setting the legitimate boundaries of comparison were as apparent to sober comparatists as they were to inebriated Welsh poets. René Wellek hoped that literary theory could bridge the divides between national traditions in a balanced assessment of similarities and differences that he called "perspectivism," a term that Erich Auerbach favored as well. Yet Wellek was haunted by the specter of comparison spinning out of con-

---

[1] According to Levin, it was an unnamed colleague who provoked the poet's question. "As soon as Thomas learned that my informant was—like most of us—a professor of comparative literature, he asked: 'What do you compare it with?' And in his inimitable, uninhibited, and explosive manner, he went on to offer a monosyllabic suggestion, which we could not permit ourselves to entertain" ("Comparing the Literature," 5).

trol. In one of the chapters he drafted for *Theory of Literature*, he cast this danger in political terms, as the threat of "absolutism" or, worse yet, anarchy:

> Perspectivism means that we recognize that there is one poetry, one literature, comparable in all ages, developing, changing, full of possibilities. Literature is neither a series of unique works with nothing in common nor a series of works enclosed in time-capsules of Romanticism or Classicism. . . . Both absolutism and relativism are false; but the more insidious danger today, at least in England and the United States, is a relativism equivalent to an anarchy of values, a surrender of the task of criticism. (43)

Comparison was in danger of unleashing mere anarchy on the literary world.

It may seem to us today that midcentury comparatists had a fairly easy time of it in constructing their comparisons. Even when discussing an international movement such as Romanticism, they would typically focus on a small handful of European countries whose writers often knew each other's work and had grown up with a broadly shared classical and Enlightenment heritage. In keeping with this emphasis, and with the broader political project of helping put a war-torn Europe back together, comparatists emphasized similarities more than differences. Wellek's fear of critical anarchy led him to place a heavy emphasis on "a close unity which includes all Europe, Russia, the United States, and the Latin-American literatures" (49). He enlisted time as well as space in his unifying comparatism: "One cannot doubt the continuity between Greek and Roman literatures, the Western medieval world, and the main modern literatures," he declared, and he praised Auerbach's *Mimesis* and Ernst Robert Curtius's *European Literature and the Latin Middle Ages* for having demonstrated "the unity of Western civilization" from antiquity onward (49–50).

Others, however, could doubt that unity, even within western Europe and just within a single period. In her essay "Born to Compare," Lilian Furst says that she wrote her first book, *Romanticism in Perspective*, to challenge Wellek's highly unified view of Romanticism (113). Her perspectivism was surely grounded in her childhood dislocations in Europe and her abiding sense of being an outsider in England and again in America. A generation older than Furst, and removed by his early emigration from the direct experience of wartime trauma, Wellek had more confidence in the postwar project of creating a united Europe. Furst's radically perspectival view of Romanticism must have looked dangerously anarchic to him, but she felt that she might not have been relativistic enough. She addresses the problem in her book's conclusion, entitled "Perspective." After making many comparisons among Romantic writers, she has come to feel that

> it is the differences between the faces of Romanticism in England, France and Germany that become apparent rather than the similarities. . . . So much so that it would indeed seem easier to be convinced of the diversity of the Romantic movement than of its fundamental unity in view of its manifold manifestations. This may explain why critics have generally tended to argue in favour of the likenesses in an attempt to introduce some semblance of order and cohesion into the maze that is Romanticism. (277)

For Furst, what "holds the Romantic family together" (280) is a set of family resemblances, rather than a unified program. "At best," she concludes, "the highly intricate web of similarities and differences that forms the fabric of European Romanticism could be characterized in the phrase that Coleridge used to describe beauty: 'Multeity in Unity.' Perhaps we should do Romanticism more justice if we ceased the search for that elusive unity and began rather to appreciate its multeity" (290).

Comparing the Incomparable

Wellek's Euro-universalism was premised on a civilizational approach that excluded most of the world. He does say that one should study Western civilization "without minimizing the importance of Oriental influences, especially that of the Bible" (*Theory of Literature*, 49), yet no influential Orientals appear in his index. Among 1,100 entries, I don't find a single name from outside Europe and North America. Included in principle, Latin America is excluded in practice, and even the Bible doesn't merit an entry.

The question of comparability grew sharper during the 1980s, as comparatists began to give more attention to non-Western literatures and struggled to locate their studies along an expanded spectrum *"Entre lo uno y lo diverso."* This was the title of Claudio Guillén's 1985 introduction to the discipline, translated into English under the less philosophical title *The Challenge of Comparative Literature.* Throughout his book, Guillén asserts the necessity of "keeping in mind the constant to and fro between the unity sought by our discourse or our human consciousness, and the countless historical-spatial differentiations, so real and so tangible in the field of literature, so alluring and fascinating" (104). Writing in Barcelona, where he spent the latter part of his career after many years in the United States, Guillén dedicated his book to René Wellek and Harry Levin, but his vision of *lo diverso* went well beyond Europe. Son of the exiled poet Jorge Guillén—who had given the 1957–58 Norton Lectures on the topic "Language and Poetry"—Guillén drew his examples predominantly from poetry, both in the several languages he could read and in translation. He gave substantial attention to Latin America, including Nahuatl poetry (in Garibay's Spanish translations), and he drew on experiences lecturing in China to discuss classical Chinese poetry. He argued that for all their differences, poets in Tang Dynasty China, Renaissance Europe, and Mesoamerica were all writing what can be identified and discussed as lyric poetry.

Three years later, recognizing the growing interest in Asian literatures among comparatists, Clayton Koelb and Susan Noakes included several essays on "East/West" studies in their collection *The Comparative Perspective on Literature* (1988). At the unity end of the spectrum, an essay by Robert Magliola asserts a close comparability of sexualized religious iconography in the European Renaissance and in tantric Buddhism. With no historical linkage between these distant traditions, Magliola finds his ground of comparison in theoretical discourse. He uses a forthrightly Derridean frame, which he had showcased in his 1984 book *Derrida on the Mend: Buddhist Differentialism.* In his essay, he sees both the European and the Buddhist iconographic traditions as performing a "deconstructive maneuver" on the overt spiritual message of the scriptures they were supposed to illustrate ("Sexual Rogations, Mystical Abrogations," 207).

Magliola's essay follows Pauline Yu's very different "Alienation Effects," a skeptical discussion of the limits of East/West comparability. Noting that "literary 'universals' on close examination almost invariably turn out to be Western ones," Yu argues that "what have been called metaphor and allegory in Chinese poetry are actually grounded in a set of philosophical presuppositions fundamentally different from those out of which the terms arose in the European tradition" (163). She says that "although the Chinese short poem (*shi*) and Western lyric appear analogous in nature, their different roots have given rise to rather different sets of critical concerns" (164).

In 1997 Michael Palencia-Roth, founder of the pioneering program in Comparative and World Literature at the University of Illinois, proposed renaming "comparative literature" as "contrastive literature," so as to break the hold of universalizing ideas of cross-cultural similarity ("Contrastive Literature"). An extended argument for contrastive comparison was mounted a year later by the Princeton-trained, Osaka-based scholar Takayuki Yokota-Murakami in *Don Juan East/West: On the Problematics of Comparative Literature*. He caustically described postwar American comparative literature as a "Marshall Plan" devoted, like the governmental initiative, to the twofold purpose of opposing Communism and extending American hegemony abroad (179–80). Though the Americans had prided themselves on their victory over French positivism, Yokota-Murakami saw their work as a new form of francocentric cosmopolitanism, and he argued that Japanese as well as American accounts of "Japanese Don Juanism" had relied on Western conceptions masquerading as universal values. Throughout his book he critiqued Étiemble's quest for universal forms and motifs, proposing that for all his championing of cultural difference, Étiemble ultimately adopted "the cultural imperialist formulation of 'humanity' in which whatever fits the French (and, in large measure, Western) paradigm will be regarded as part of 'human nature'" (168).

Étiemble was of course very much aware of this problem. Thus when comparing Japanese monogatari to Western novels, rather than subsume the monogatari within the Western term, he proposed "romance" as a more neutral *tertium comparationis*. In Yokota-Murakami's view, this substitution only displaced the problem:

> By resorting to the notion of "Romance," a comparativist can expect to compare "romances" of the world, one form of which happens to be the European novel. But is there an original, ideal "Romance" purely independent of historical contingencies? Is it not that the moment one chooses to utter "romance," the concept is functioning within the hermeneutic horizons of Western literature and literary criticism? (171)

The dominance of hegemonic concepts might be opposed through counteroperations, for example, in narrative studies that could take as their ground of comparison the monogatari, of which the chivalric romance would merely be a European variant. Yet, as Yokota-Murakami observes, such reverse comparisons "have seldom, if ever, taken place" (179). In his concluding section, soberly entitled "The Violence of Comparison," he declares that cross-civilizational comparison "is inevitably an act of violence of some sort. For it cannot be achieved except by a distortion of the object in accordance with the viewer's paradigm. Perception of cultural alterity is already an exercise of power, a political act, that calls for the assimilation, if not the extinction, of the other paradigms" (187).

Though the issue of a leveling unity was already debated within studies of European Romanticism, the differences become all the greater when we attempt cross-cultural comparison. Yet the very heightening of cultural distance can actually make it more likely that comparative study will attend seriously to difference. Yokota-Murakami's own book, in fact, performs the kind of differential comparativism that his polemical conclusion declares to be virtually impossible. His acute awareness of the distinctiveness of Japanese traditions of love and sexual conquest enables him to argue against reducing Murasaki's shining Genji or Ihara Saikaku's amorous Yonosuke to embodiments of "the Japanese Don Juan," and his chapters on "The Introduction of 'Love' into Japan" and on "Sexuality as a Historical Construct" are models of culturally grounded comparative discussion. Yokota-Murakami's practice illustrates the balanced formulation that he offers at the outset: "Comparison on an international scale," he says, is "a tightrope walk which sways between identity, elementary and essential, on the one hand, and difference, contingent and marginal, on the other. A comparativist gains nothing by reaching either end of the rope" (15).

Since the turn of the millennium, comparatists have renewed their efforts to maintain balance as they walk the tightrope of cross-cultural comparison. A particularly suggestive exploration of the problem is a methodological essay by the Belgian classicist Marcel Detienne, *Comparer l'incomparable* (2000, 2009; *Comparing the Incomparable*, 2008). Detienne discusses the work of a group of anthropologists and historians, formed at Johns Hopkins during the 1990s, dedicated to exploring aspects of ancient civilizations around the world. In his second chapter, "Constructing Comparables," Detienne argues that instead of comparing only neighboring societies with close connections, comparatists should look farther afield. Rather than seeking parity or likenesses, the root meaning of terms such as "com*pare*" and "Ver*gleich*," he proposes using a "contrastive approach" with which "one can discover cognitive dissonances; or, to put that more simply, one may bring out some detail or feature that had escaped the notice of other interpreters and observers" (23).

A key moment for Detienne in developing his contrastive approach came when his working group began exploring foundational myths in several widely disparate cultures, looking at ways in which founding figures and sites have been used to establish a territory. For this purpose he brought together a group of classicists and anthropologists working on early cultures of Africa, Japan, and the Americas, as well as the Mediterranean world. The project got off to a good start, but then a problem was raised from the Japanese side of the group: "[W]e experienced a salutary heuristic shock when we discovered what appeared to be an instance of incomparability. One day, two Japanese specialists who had long remained silent as we fumbled our way forward, came to confess, to their chagrin, that, according to the most ancient texts, in Japan there simply was no founding, no founder" (25–26). Rather than inviting the Japanologists to leave the group, Detienne says, "I thanked them warmly and told them that now we could at last begin to think about what 'to found, to establish everlastingly' really meant. Thanks to the provocation caused by that incomparability, a familiar category such as 'founding' was about to become cloudy, to fracture and disintegrate" (26). This experience led the group to practice a "plural comparativism" that could dispel "the misleading transparency of 'founding,'" allowing them to undertake "a conceptual analysis of what 'creating a territory' might mean as it moves from one society to another" (27).

For Detienne, plural comparativism is an ethical as well as an intellectual ideal, the best means to avoid a specious universalism based on our own values projected outward. As a prime example of such self-enclosed scholarship, he cites the work of the *Annales* school of French historians, satirically suggesting that the great Fernand Braudel led his disciples astray by reinforcing a francocentric perspective despite his leftist principles and his broad Mediterranean framework:

> I can imagine a young historian sitting in the metro or on a bench in the Jardin du Luxembourg. For the price of a couple of sandwiches, he has just purchased *L'Identité de France*. Ravenously, he devours the newly minted Academician's introduction, in which Braudel confesses his nostalgia for France, a retrospective France, infinitely rich in its past experiences: a heaven-sent terrain for comparative history. As he chews this over, the young man hastens to read on, wondering "What kind of comparative history?" (37)

A quote from Braudel's book provides the answer: "A history in search of similarities, the real condition of any social science." Detienne then imagines that "a chorus of historians takes up the cry: contexts are neglected; what we should compare is that which is comparable." Gloomily, Detienne concludes, "I tell you, it's like weeds: however much you root out prejudices, some always remain" (37).

Detienne's working group embodied his strategy for rooting out deeply held prejudices. Rather than trying to create an *Annales*-style "school," he chose people of differing backgrounds and perspectives, and they worked intensively together to gradually become a collective *nous-je*. His translator renders this neologism as "a we/I" (27), capturing the pronouns but losing the underlying pun on Greek νοῦς (mind). It isn't enough for the historian to excavate the collective *mentalités* of medieval peasants; the scholar's own mentality needs to be reconfigured as well. Every comparatist "must be at once singular and plural," but scholars can't achieve this state on their own. "For 'a' comparativist to become plural, it is necessary to form a microgroup of ethnologists and historians who are colleagues or even accomplices and who are prepared to think aloud, together" (24).

Detienne returned to the attack on nationalistic scholarship in a considerably expanded second edition of his book (published in 2009, not yet translated), for which he added three chapters that dissect the complicity of French classicists and anthropologists in upholding the myth of an "incomparable" French nation somehow born in an equally exceptional ancient Greece. He ends with a section entitled "Au-delà du Vatican et de ses champs élyséens: Retour sur l'art de construire des comparables" (*Comparer l'incomparable* [2009], 169–73). There he acerbically discusses a meeting in September 2008 between Pope Benedict XVI and Nicolas Sarkozy, whom he refers to not by name but as France's Pontifex Maximus. In their meeting at the presidential palace—the Palais de l'Élysée, which has become an earthly paradise for the visiting pope—the two leaders agreed on the intimate connection between France and Catholicism, born in the marriage of classical Greek thought with Greco-Roman Christianity. Detienne closes his book with a plea for a comparativism of "dissonance" that can enable scholars to dispel such myths of origin and "to place themselves in perspective" in the process. Though he admits that "no comparative anthropology can be a panacea," Detienne affirms that "a comparatism of an experimental and constructive type can contribute effectively to placing us at a distance from ourselves" (173).

Detienne's formulation is appealing, but just how much distance can we actually achieve from ourselves? More particularly, does even an émigré scholar ever fully leave home? After years of teaching at Hopkins, Detienne himself hadn't entirely escaped the gravitational pull of his intellectual formation in France. His description of his scholarly ideal sounds a good deal like what he would have imbibed in the 1960s in the overlapping circle of Parisian classicists and structural anthropologists, including Jean-Pierre Vernant, Nicole Loraux, Pierre Vidal-Naquet, and Claude Lévi-Strauss. In advancing a worldly cosmopolitanism, he champions a kind of global nomadism, scouring the world for illuminating patterns of difference: "A comparativist seeking to construct his subjects must be able to move, without a passport," he writes, "always carrying with him or her a little bunch of questions, as if to sweep over as extensive as possible a field of investigation that is as yet without limits" (*Comparing the Incomparable*, 24, 27). For all Detienne's differences from his former associates, this formulation has clear affinities with the "nomadic science" that Deleuze and Guattari advanced in *Mille plateaux* (1980), and it echoes Lévi-Strauss's ironic description of his scholarly method: "I have a neolithic kind of intelligence. Like native bush fires, it sometimes sets unexplored areas alight; it may fertilize them and snatch a few crops from them, and then it moves on, leaving scorched earth in its wake" (*Tristes Tropiques*, 53). You can take the nomad out of Paris, it seems, but you can't necessarily take Paris out of the nomad.

Comparison without Hegemony

A steady stream of books and articles has been devoted to this problem during the past decade. In 2013, building on two decades of work in China by himself and a group of colleagues, Cao Shunqing published *A Variation Theory of Comparative Literature*. In the book he seeks to free Chinese scholars from the "aphasia" of losing their own voice through a wholesale adoption of Western theories, and he critiques Western comparatists' frequent reading of non-Western works (when they read them at all) in terms of Western conceptions. Disputing the common emphasis on similarities in comparative studies in the 1970s and 1980s, he argues that "another kind of comparability can be constructed through heterogeneity" (230), in a mode of comparison that "creates inspiration and astonishment" (233). For Cao, a cross-cultural comparative literature "with Chinese characteristics" will be based on an integrated awareness of the classical and modern Chinese traditions, not treated in isolation but enriched and modified through a judiciously selective use of elements taken from foreign literatures and theories.

In the same year, a less optimistic discussion of cross-cultural comparison was published by R. Radhakrishnan under the skeptical title "Why Compare?" This was the opening essay in a volume edited by Rita Felski and Susan Stanford Friedman, *Comparison: Theories, Approaches, Uses*. Building on his earlier *Theory in an Uneven World*, Radhakrishnan posits that one of the terms of any comparison tends to dominate the other and, "in enabling a new form of recognition along one axis, perpetuates dire misrecognition along another" (19). His essay is followed by Susan Stanford Friedman's pointed rejoinder, "Why Not Compare?" After listing arguments against comparison, she observes: "We compare because if we do not, there are worse consequences than the political, decontextualizing problems of comparison. What are the ethics of not comparing? To refuse comparison is also a political act, one that can potentially reinstate hierarchies by not challenging them" (36). In his contribution to the volume, Haun Saussy returns to the problem of hegemonic comparatism: "We, like many anthropologists, are sharply aware of hypocritical universalism. The abhorrence we feel toward it makes us suspicious of the whole comparative enterprise." Quoting Radhakrishnan's assertion that comparison "perpetuates dire misrecognition," Saussy asks, "would it not be better to insist that comparison does its job poorly when it reduces too effectively, when it discards too much of the prior context that gave a work its meaning in the first place?" ("Axes of Comparison," 67–68).

A running debate in these years has been the question of how broadly a comparison can extend. Radhakrishnan favors a localized comparatism grounded in a single national or imperial history, while Saussy, who works in both Chinese and European literatures, argues that postcolonialists can't avoid "the demon of comparison" merely by limiting themselves to a single imperial matrix. He adds that cross-cultural comparison is more than ever needed when so many problems and possibilities extend far beyond the frame of the nation: "clinging to the nation as our unit of thought will not help in the task" (73).

For his part, Saussy draws the line at world literature. He says that "the discussion about 'world literature' has been one of the channels for exploring the issue—or, to put it less blandly, one of the subfields that perpetuate the problem" (69). In another contribution to the volume, however, Zhang Longxi defends world literary studies by advancing a version of Saussy's own response to Radhakrishnan. In his essay, "Crossroads, Distant Killing, and Translation," as in his book *From Comparison to World Literature*, Zhang argues that it is when a comparison is done badly, whether within a region or across world cultures, that local context evaporates and that European values are introduced in the guise of universals. Zhang isn't opposed to the idea of universals, in fact, but draws equally on Chinese and on Western traditions to underscore commonalities that can counter the stark confrontations of "East" versus "West" that he had critiqued two decades earlier in his *Mighty Opposites: From Dichotomies to Differences in the Comparative Study of China*.

As I argued in chapter 6, it is no longer necessary to oppose the national to the cross-cultural or the comparative to the global. A nation-based study can treat global issues as they emerge in a given time and place, and the two ends of the local–global spectrum can join when we consider the world within the nation. In *All the Difference in the World*, Natalie Melas discusses Benedict Anderson's success in doing just this, in a series of three essays that he published in *New Left Review* in 2004. These center on a single novel by José Rizal, *El Filibusterismo*. In his earlier novel *Noli me Tangere*, Rizal had expressed his Filipino hero's insecurity vis-à-vis Europe in the phrase *el demonio de las comparaciones*, which Anderson evoked in the title of his book *The Spectre of Comparison* (changing Rizal's demon to a more Marxian spectre haunting comparatists). "Digressive and narrative in form and method," Melas says, Anderson's essays locate *El Filibusterismo* within "an astounding historical network of global intersections" (34). These intersections range from Meiji Japan to Bismarck's Germany to Huysmans and Mallarmé in France, and to many points beyond. As Melas says, "these essays constitute a rigorous account of the comparative underpinnings"—we might equally say, the world-literary relations—"of what would normally be categorized as national literature," which Anderson unfolds "on the 'micro' register of a branching, open-ended narrative, dense with empirical detail" (34).

In a probing article entitled "Comparison without Hegemony," Sheldon Pollock makes a case for "capturing similarities and differences across a limited number of instances in order to understand the cases under discussion, to isolate from the incidental what is 'crucial' and possibly, though less likely, what is 'causal'" (191). His concern is with the danger that the cases discussed by the comparatist will rarely exist on the same plane. Pollock observes that such disparities come about not just as a result of imperial histories or differences in cultural power but because our research tends to move outward from the better known to the less known. As he says:

> Under ideal circumstances of self-awareness the process here can be treated simply as a variant of the hermeneutic circle: B takes on its particular meaning only in the context of ABCD, but that context itself only becomes meaningful if we already know what A, B, C, D individually and somehow independently mean. Like the hermeneutic circle, the comparative circle can be a virtuous one, as I will suggest. Having identified B as an empire (or "empire") through generalization from A, we may then correct our generalization by probing differences between B and A. (198)

Too often, though, "the ideal circumstances are not met and the virtuous circle becomes a vicious one when a particular is elevated into a 'standard'" (198). Pollock gives the example of Hegel's skewed discussion of Sanskrit epic on the basis of norms derived from the *Iliad* and *Odyssey*, which Hegel saw as exemplifying "the true fundamental character of the epic proper" (200). Pollock advocates a constant awareness that "no given model of intellection can be held to be universal. Observing this limit . . . is critical if comparativism is to be saved from itself" (190). He concludes that "if comparison is necessary, the will to domination that sometimes seems built into the comparative method is certainly not" (202).

In a subsequent essay, "Conundrums of Comparison," Pollock goes beyond advocating self-awareness. He proposes what he dubs "methodological cosmopolitanism," a pluralist perspective that might set aside European terms altogether when comparing such forms as Indian *itihada* and Chinese *shi* (282). At a far remove from the search for similarities, such "differential comparison" involves

> new modes of mutual estrangement, so to call it, made possible by off-center comparison. This is something that emerges from the reciprocal illumination of objects of analysis that can now be seen to

be equally different, and neither deficient nor deviant; and, more important, often radically different the one from the other. Comparison unencumbered by delusions about the essential nature of things (what an epic or history or a nation really is) allows you to better capture the particularity, and peculiarity, of a given case. Better put: the true specificity of any given case emerges only against the backdrop of some other. (286)

A searching treatment of the problem of cross-cultural comparison has been provided by Ming Xie in *Conditions of Comparison* (2011). Xie argues that comparativists should frame their comparisons within a second-order reflexivity: "*comparison* in the traditional sense is usually interested in the practical results of its operations—that is, similarities or differences as such—whereas *comparativity* or the *activity* of comparing or thinking about how (not) to compare is more concerned with *how meaning is constituted*" (38–39). He uses "comparativists" not as a synonym for "comparatists" but to designate intensely self-aware inquirers whose comparisons can reveal "the unthought" in their own episteme as well as what hasn't been seen within the foreign culture's self-understanding.

For Xie, "the unthought is akin to the untranslatable, in the sense that the untranslatable does not just signify the 'failure' of translating from one language to another. Rather, it signifies the untranslatable as the ontological condition of translation and knowledge" (44). Citing Kenneth Burke's "perspective by incongruity," Xie argues that "comparativity as an epistemological activity has far-reaching political and ethical implications as a mode of critical inquiry. Critical comparativity is not just about comparing existing ways of thinking but also, more important, comparing *against* them" (49). In the process, we can come to perceive the relativism of our cherished universalisms, and we can arrive at "what may be called a *relativist universalism*—that is, a universalism that sees itself as contingent and contestable" (127).

Such relativistic self-awareness doesn't require abandoning our existing conceptual vocabulary, a quest that would be doomed to failure even if it were desirable. A change of terms won't necessarily create a meaningful change in practice, any more than when President Jimmy Carter chastised his inflation czar Alfred Kahn for warning that high inflation could lead to a new "depression." Kahn temporarily solved the problem by substituting "banana" for the forbidden term, but objections were raised by banana producers, leading Kahn to replace the euphemistic banana with "kumquat." A concept by any other name may taste as bittersweet.

To return to Takayuki Yokota-Murakami, although he sharply criticizes the unexamined application of terms such as "novel" or "romance" to Japanese monogatari and *ukiyo zōshi*, he doesn't shrink from defining the latter genre as "a kind of pulp fiction of the Edo period" (*Don Juan East/West*, 172). He employs Western conceptual vocabulary throughout his book, frequently using terms such as "signifier," "discourse," and "literature," and he allows that "one cannot pursue a transcivilizational comparison without such an Ur-concept" (172). His objection is to the enshrining of a Western version of a form or concept as the norm, with the non-Western cases relegated to the status of minor or stunted variants. This resembles Northrop Frye's impatience in *Anatomy of Criticism* with scholars of European literature who subsume very different forms of narrative under the blanket term "novel." Yet we can still use the term, so long as we don't reduce Murasaki Shikibu to a poor prototype of Jane Austen, or make Cao Xueqin into a not-quite-Proust. Instead, worldly comparatists can deprovincialize the novel by looking well beyond the cultural parameters envisioned by Ian Watt or even Frye.

The same goes for conceptual frameworks. In *What Is a World?* Pheng Cheah explores postcolonial world-making in terms derived from his intensive engagement with Continental philosophy, but he insists that he isn't repeating an older Hegelian or Marxist Euro-universalism:

> The organization of this book can give the wrong impression of a division of labor between European philosophy and literature from the postcolonial South, where postcolonial literary texts have the subordinate function of illustrating the ontological and normative problems concerning worldliness that European philosophy elaborates. In fact, no such division exists. . . . My analyses of postcolonial world literature are not merely examples of this theory. They

inflect and deepen the theory by exploring concrete postcolonial sites where the opening of new worlds is of the greatest urgency. (14)

Cheah uses fictional works to explore and adapt his philosophers' theories, though at times it appears that his novelists only confirm arguments that he had developed through his own revisionary readings of Hegel, Heidegger, Arendt, and Derrida. But the principle is an important one: a prime use of cross-cultural comparison—whether labeled as postcolonial, comparative, transnational, or world literary studies—is to open out and test our concepts against a wider range of historical and cultural forms of expression.

Modernisms and Modernities

At the other end of the scale from the analysis of world-making by individual authors is the study of worldwide genres or movements. In the balance of this chapter, I will illustrate the conceptual difficulties and possibilities of cross-cultural comparison through the issue of periodization. As Emily Apter has observed, a generalized "Eurochronology" has been widely adopted by literary scholars, not only in Europe and America but in much of the world. She proposes that "literary history needs to open up to radical re-sequencing, through anachronic timelines, non-Eurochronic descriptions of duration, and a proliferation of new names for periods as yet unnamed, or which become discernible only as Untranslatables of periodicity" (*Against World Literature*, 65). Even before we begin proliferating the as yet unnamed untranslatables of periodicity, we would do well to test our existing period concepts against works produced beyond the Eurozone where these periodizations were mostly developed. Such revisioning is already under way, as in Schildgen, Gang, and Gilman's collection *Other Renaissances* (2006), which explores the varied ways in which the European term has been appropriated and repurposed for modern settings, from Ireland to Harlem to China to Bengal.

Here I will take up the perennially debated terms "modernism" and "modernity." The challenge for comparatists is to be fully alive to the varieties of modernity around the world, and a singular definition risks swamping all possibilities, excluding large bodies of the actually existing materials produced within the modern era and distorting our understanding of the materials we do study. Particularly in Anglo-American scholarship, the study of literary modernity has often focused largely on works that could be defined as modernist, a close conjunction seen in the title of the journal *Modernism/Modernity*. Modernity is often used as a broad designation for the past two or sometimes three centuries, with modernism as a kind of crystallization in the late nineteenth century in France and England, cresting in the first decades of the twentieth century, and spreading gradually to other parts of the world, even as modernism in the "core" devolved into late or neomodernism and postmodernism. Scholars have begun working to open the concept to varieties of modernism worldwide, in works such as Wollaeger and Eatough's *Oxford Handbook of Global Modernisms* (the plural in their title is noteworthy) and Hayot and Walkowitz's *A New Vocabulary for Global Modernism*. Postcolonialists in particular have questioned the close association of modernization with westernization, and discussions of modernity now extend several centuries back, in the line of inquiry inaugurated three decades ago by Janet Abu-Lughod's *Before European Hegemony: The World System A.D. 1250–1350*.

In *Planetary Modernisms* (2016), Susan Stanford Friedman questions the very idea of modernism and modernity as period concepts:

> To fulfill the promise of the planetary turn, I suggest, we must rethink *modernity* and *modernism* outside the long twentieth century, outside the post-1500 temporal frame commonly understood as the *period* of the *modern* in its stages from early to late. I use the term *planetary* to invoke this greater expanse of time and space, to signal my attempt to break away from periodization altogether. (7)

Building on Braudel but going well beyond him, Friedman reaches out "into a longer *durée* and a wider planetary reach" (9), with case studies drawn from the Tang Dynasty and the Mongol Empire, before she returns in her final section to postcolonial modernisms. In place of any temporal framing, Friedman identifies modernism with "a combination of metaphorical keywords such as *rupture, vortex, mobility, acceleration, system, network, circulation,* and *heterotopia*" (11). Though she acknowledges that her approach "opens a can of worms" (6), particularly for the practical organization of knowledge and academic specialization, she insists that "large-scale perspectives make visible the often unacknowledged assumptions that frame work on modernism/modernity, particularly Eurocentric ones," and she stresses that "this view helps break down the ideological compulsion for European or American exceptionalism that has been central to the formation of the metanarrative of Western modernity" (313).

Friedman is boldly striking out against the presentism of much modernist scholarship, and she isn't the first to do so. In his classic study *Five Faces of Modernity* (1987), Matei Calinescu traces the roots of the term "modernity" back to the fifth century CE, when the Latin *modernus* began to displace the older νεώτερος / *neotericus,* in a heightened contrast to *classicus* or *antiquus* (14). Though Calinescu concentrates on later texts that use or imply the term "modern," he adds an important qualification: "Of course, I am fully aware that such a limitation is artificial and that the 'consciousness of modernity' is not tied down to the use of a specific word or of a set of phrases, similes, or metaphors that obviously derive from it" (10). On this perspective, it can be said that anywhere we find written texts we have a key precondition for the development of a self-consciously modern perspective. As the Egyptologist Jan Assmann has remarked, "Writing caused history to be where myth was"; its invention created "a cultural split into antiquity and modernity" ("Cultural Memory," 389–90).

Ancient writers were often heirs to centuries or even millennia of previous artistic endeavor. The Assyrians of the seventh century BCE thought of themselves as modern by comparison to the Babylonians who had dominated Mesopotamia before them, and the Babylonians in turn saw themselves as modern by comparison to the Sumerians, whom they had supplanted in the early second millennium BCE. Even Sumerian writers hardly thought of themselves as ancients. Four thousand years ago, the world's first known patron of literature, the Sumerian king Shulgi of Ur (r. 2094–2047 BCE), proclaimed himself to be the preserver and restorer of an ancient literary heritage. "My wisdom is full of subtlety," he declares in one of the many encomia he wrote or commissioned for himself, and his subtle wisdom included using the soft power of culture to cement his authority. "I am no fool," he continues, "as regards the knowledge acquired since the time that heaven above set mankind on its path." When he has discovered "hymns from past days, old ones from ancient times," Shulgi says, "I have conserved these antiquities, never abandoning them to oblivion." He ordered the old poems added to his singers' repertoire, "and thereby I have set the heart of the Land on fire and aflame" (Šulgi B, lines 270–80). Shulgi clearly sees himself as a modern, but his archaic modernism doesn't involve a post-Romantic rupture from the past; instead it entails a strategic use of his heritage for present purposes. Granting this difference, Shulgi may help us consider the ways in which our more recent modernists weren't breaking with the past as sharply as they often claimed: in important respects, Virginia Woolf, for example, is less a radical modernist than an eminent post-Victorian.

Two millennia after Shulgi, Roman writers saw themselves as newcomers over against the older traditions of Greece. A prime example of Roman modernism is Apuleius, with his narrative fragmentation, stylistic innovations, intense self-reflexivity, and comic subversions of Greek romance and philosophy. His work even shows elements of what would now be called postmodernism, if we think of his *Metamorphoses* or *Golden Ass* as deconstructing the Roman "high modernism" of Virgil and Ovid before him. Further, Apuleius shapes his tale in opposition to the threatening modernity around him, just as Calinescu would expect of a modernist (*Five Faces of Modernity*, 41). Set in a world of violence, greed, and hypocrisy, his satire is aimed squarely at the cultivated secularism of sophisticates like Ovid, for whom the ancient Greek gods are little more than literary conceits or tropes, colorful characters whose stories give him opportunities to probe purely human concerns and to display his poetic virtuosity. Still less does Apuleius favor the rationalism of Neoplatonists like his contemporary Marcus Aurelius, for whom it was an open question whether the gods actually exist. It is surely no coincidence that the first character to fall victim to the power of witchcraft in Apuleius's tale is a hapless oldster named Socrates.

Yet Apuleius is also concerned about a very different modern threat: the expansionist monotheism that was starting to take hold in Rome and in his adoptive city of Carthage, where a group of Christians were martyred in the year of his death. The Christians were rejecting every religious tradition but their own, subjecting even Judaism to radical revision. Long before Ezra Pound urged poets to "Make it New," the New Testament ended with John's vision of "a new heaven and a new earth"—itself a phrase taken from Isaiah—and with Jesus proclaiming Ἰδοὺ καινὰ ποιῶ πάντα: "Behold, I make all things new" (Revelation 21:1,5). During his wanderings, Apuleius's asinine hero Lucius encounters a dissolute miller's wife who "sacrilegiously feigned bold awareness of a deity whom she proclaimed to be the only God. By devising empty ceremonies she misled the people at large, and deceived her hapless husband by devoting herself to early-morning drinking"—evidently communion wine—"and day-long debauchery" (*Metamorphoses*, 170). Apuleius opposes this debased modernity by turning to the ancient mysteries of Egyptian religion. In his climactic eleventh book, Isis—goddess of the moon and patron of ceaseless transformation—appears to Lucius in a dream-vision, granting his fervent wish to be restored to human form on condition that he be initiated into her mysteries and become her servant. Already in his prologue, Apuleius invites his reader to enjoy his "Greekish tale" (*fabulam Graecanicam*), "as long as you don't disdain to run your eye over Egyptian papyrus inscribed with the sharpened point of a reed from the Nile" (1).

Apuleius can be of particular interest for modernist studies today as he was a migrant writer from Rome's colonial periphery. Born in North Africa of Numidian and Berber parentage, he studied philosophy in Athens and then went to Rome to study law. In the prologue to the *Metamorphoses*, his hero describes himself as a linguistic acrobat, performing "much as a circus-rider leaps from one horse to another" (1). He comically excuses his provincial Latin by asserting that his style is distorted by his bilingual fluency—not in North African Punic but in the culturally prestigious language of Greek. Anticipating Georg Brandes's claim that language is a writer's prime weapon, Lucius uses military terms to describe his linguistic conquests: "at Athens, I served in my first campaigns with the Greek tongue. Later, in Rome, freshly come to Latin studies I assumed and cultivated the indigenous language [*indigenam sermonem*]." He then begs our pardon "if I offend as a crude performer in the exotic speech of the Forum [*exotici forensis sermonis*]" (1). Such peripheral positioning has a history extending to the present day. In a preface to the 2007 reissue of

Provincializing Europe, Dipesh Chakrabarty outlines his migration from India to Australia and his linguistic shift from Bangla to English (xi–xii). Two thousand years before Chakrabarty provincialized Europe, Apuleius opened his book by exoticizing Rome.

Not everyone will want to venture as far from the usual temporal boundaries of modernism as ancient Rome or Tang Dynasty China. What we all do need to consider are the ways in which discussions of literary modernity can be enriched and complicated by including works that don't fit neatly into the existing modern(ist) canon. Entire countries have long been neglected in studies of modern literature, and not only countries outside Europe. Theo D'haen has noted that Dutch literature was sidelined in the older comparative studies because the Netherlands wasn't a major European power, whereas now Dutch literature is ignored because the Netherlands isn't located in the Global South. On the rare occasions when a Dutch author is mentioned, it is likely to be the anticolonial Eduard Douwes Dekker (Multatuli), whereas an important figure such as the modernist poet J. J. Slauerhoff—as global a writer as Conrad—remains almost unknown abroad ("J. J. Slauerhoff").[2]

One scholar begins an essay on Multatuli himself with a note of exasperation: "Must everything in modern Dutch literature begin and end with Multatuli?" (Zook, "Searching for *Max Havelaar,*" 1169). Zook is actually criticizing an overemphasis within Dutch studies; local scholarship isn't free of its own tendentious and exclusionary map-making. As of this writing, the *MLA International Bibliography* lists seventy-eight essays discussing Multatuli, the majority in English, French, or German. For Slauerhoff there are a respectable forty-five citations, but almost all of them are in Dutch, with only nine in any other language. Six of those are focused

---

[2] Slauerhoff spent most of his life working as a ship's doctor on voyages to East Asia and South America. As D'haen observes in "Dutch Interbellum Poetry and/as World Literature," Slauerhoff wrote in dialogue with Chinese as well as European poetry, and he identified with Camões, whose *Lusíads* was the first major work written in Asia by a European poet.

within Dutch studies, with just three comparative essays treating Slauer-hoff with other literatures.

Worldly comparatists today are beginning to feature many neglected modern languages and literatures, from the Low Countries to highland Guatemala, and from eastern Europe to Southeast Asia, but the map of modernism is far from complete. The issue is partly one of national traditions that remain invisible within both postcolonial and world literary studies, but it is equally a matter of programmatic selectivity when works are chosen for discussion. A scholar will naturally need to make choices for any given study, but pervasively selective choices become patterns of exclusion. Timothy Brennan observed this problem twenty years ago. Criticizing the widespread emphasis on socialist realism within postcolonial studies, Brennan complained of

> a lack of interest in the explicitly modernist or experimental writing of those who are considered not to be political enough—those who do not fit the injunction that the third-world writer embody politics in a readily consumable form. This would be the process at work, I think, in the surprisingly weak reception of the Brazilian novelist Clarice Lispector, for instance, with her brilliant psychological portraits of love and loss. (*At Home in the World,* 207)

He returned to this theme toward the end of his book: "In the space between the reading of novels, poems, and essays from Latin America, Africa, and Asia and the reading of postcolonial theory, much is missing. A massive network of emotions and sympathies found in the primary work does not always find itself exhibited in the criticism" (310). Natalie Melas has commented that "in other words, 'difference' is not so different after all." She agrees with Brennan, though with a caveat: "The argument seems unassailable to me, except in its polemical overstatement. Is it really possible, I wonder, to seek 'real,' absolute difference? Doesn't any object brought into the sanctioned discourse of the university by that very fact conform to some rule of recognizability?" (*All the Difference in the World,* 237n.74).

It isn't easy to expand a field of inquiry to works that are occluded by what Shu-mei Shih has called our technologies of recognition ("Global

Literature"). Yet scholarship often advances precisely by directing attention to neglected works that can refine an argument or reshape a field. Thus the Warwick Collective's *Combined and Uneven Development* responds to Brennan's critique by looking beyond the norms of realism and exploring modes of "irrealism" developed by contemporary writers. The collective's Neil Lazarus himself has criticized postcolonial studies for a selective "exaltation of migrancy, liminality, hybridity, and multiculturality" ("The Politics of Postcolonial Modernism," 33). Yet the Warwick group is still interested only in writers whose politics closely resemble their own, in novels that illustrate the theme of combined and uneven development, which the group has derived from a particular Marxist tradition. A writer such as Clarice Lispector, deeply interested in the uneven politics of gender and in center-periphery relations both within and beyond Brazil, doesn't figure in their account. Nor, in fact, does any woman writer—a surprising omission in the work of a resolutely progressive group, and one that includes women as well as men.

Particularly when looking beyond the Euro-American sphere, comparatists have to be wary of cherry-picking the most easily assimilated works, to the exclusion of others that might challenge or complicate their argument. As David Der-wei Wang has written concerning the sharply differing—but often equally selective—accounts of modern Chinese literature by mainland and overseas scholars, "Is it not a paradox that critics can subscribe to a 'politics of marginality' and pontificate about a 'clash of empires' and 'global contextualization,' all the while rigidly marginalizing forms of Chinese modernity and historicity that do not emerge within some preconceived mainstream?" ("Introduction," 27).

As an Asian example within the sphere of global modernity, consider *Four Reigns*, the neglected masterpiece of the important Thai writer Kukrit Pramoj (1911–1995, commonly referred to by his first name). Kukrit's novel describes Thailand's transition into modernity, beginning in the 1890s during the reign of the reformist King Rama V and ending with the sudden death of Rama VIII in 1946. As seen through the eyes of the book's heroine, Mae Phloi, *Four Reigns* offers a distinctively Southeast Asian perspective on the complex relations of tradition and modernity during the first half of the twentieth century. Kukrit was concerned with preserving traditional culture and values, even as he actively promoted modernization. Descended from Rama II and the king's Chinese wife, he held the title Mom Raja-wongse (the honorable), and he remained loyal to the monarchy throughout his life. He was a prolific journalist and writer, author of some forty books in all. In addition to novels and short stories, he wrote books on Thai history and art, and he founded a classical Thai dance company for which he was a lead dancer. He pursued his varied artistic endeavors during troubled times. In 1932, when he was twenty-one, a military coup replaced absolute rule with a nominally democratic but fundamentally authoritarian system, in which an elected parliament was controlled by the military and a small group of wealthy families. Kukrit viewed the monarchy as the best check on military-oligarchic control, and *Four Reigns* mounts an understated but far-reaching critique of the new pseudodemocratic order.

Kukrit was what could be called a conservative progressive. Like many of the Thai aristocracy of his era, he was educated in England, earning an Oxford degree in philosophy, politics, and economics. He was committed to Thailand's development as a modern and independent nation, and he had no patience with exoticizing Western representations of his country as a timeless land of Oriental splendor. His first book, written in English with his brother Seni Pramoj, was *The King of Siam Speaks* (1948). The book was inspired by their irritation at the representation of King Rama IV in the 1946 Hollywood film *Anna and the King of Siam*, which starred Rex Harrison as the king and Irene Dunne as the British governess who tries to wean him from his barbarian ways. The brothers showed that, far from being the hidebound autocrat portrayed in the film, Rama IV was a promoter of women's rights and a modernizer who had sought to resist Western expansionism by developing science and technology during his reign (1851–68), very much in parallel to his Japanese counterpart, the Emperor Meiji.

A year after publishing *The King of Siam Speaks*, Kukrit founded a newspaper, *Siam Rath* (Thai Nation), for which he wrote a widely read column; his newspaper became (and remains) a leading venue for political and cultural reporting. Among his multifarious activities, Kukrit was also a playwright and actor, and in 1973 he created and starred in a stage version of *Rashōmon*, based on Akira Kurosawa's film. A decade earlier, he had co-starred with Marlon Brando in the Hollywood film *The Ugly American*, in which Brando played the morally compromised American ambassador to the Indochinese nation of "Sarkhan," while Kukrit played the country's prime minister.

Kukrit became increasingly involved in politics himself. He founded a conservative political party and was elected to parliament, then actually became prime minister in real life in 1975–76. While in office, he mediated conflicts between rightists and leftists, and he kept a wary distance from both China and the United States at the close of the Vietnam War. Asked how Thailand had avoided the "domino effect" when Vietnam and then Cambodia were taken over by China-backed Communists, Kukrit replied, "We do not belong to the same set of dominoes. Perhaps we play cards" (Warren, "Cool Hand in Thailand").

Kukrit was a major presence in Thai literature and politics for several decades, and his newspaper gave him a base of operations in both arenas. A year after founding *Siam Rath*, he began serializing *Four Reigns* in his paper; the novel came out in book form in 1953. It was characteristic of his wish to place literature in the service of social transformation that he chose to publish his most ambitious novel in his general-circulation newspaper, rather than a small magazine or literary press. With *Four Reigns* and many other works, Kukrit gradually developed a substantial reputation beyond his own country. In 1990 he was one of the first recipients of the newly established Fukuoka Prize in Japan for contributions to the development of Asian culture. Appropriately, Kurosawa was one of the three other recipients that year.

In *Four Reigns*, Kukrit uses his heroine, Mae Phloi, as his vantage point, and he presents a sensitive portrayal, tinged with satire, of her struggle to make and then remake her life in a rapidly changing but still stubbornly patriarchal society. Phloi is a traditionalist at heart who reluctantly adapts to changing times, symbolized by such everyday details as new fashions in clothing. Using her apolitical viewpoint enables Kukrit to indirectly critique the growing authoritarianism among the military/business interests after 1932. One way Phloi experiences the effects of the new governmental order is through dictates on what to wear. One of her sons has bought in to the new regime and its propaganda, and as World War II commences, he proudly tells his mother that Thailand "nowadays seems to be acting as big as Japan, the Great Power" (589). He says that to complete the process of catching up to Japan, Thailand must adopt "culture" (*wathanatham*, a neologism). When Phloi asks what that word means, her son replies: "We must wear hats" (590). The middle-aged Phloi says that young women may like trying a new fashion, but such a change would make her feel like a clown. To this her son makes a chilling reply:

> "Clown or no clown, you'll have to do it, my girl."
> "And if I don't?"
> "The police will get you." (590)

Mae Phloi has little understanding of politics, in which her husband and sons become actively involved on conflicting sides, and so she rarely criticizes what she sees happening, but here as elsewhere Kukrit takes the opportunity to suggest his views in the very process of having his heroine "not understand" the dictates of the regime.

Throughout *Four Reigns*, in classic modern(ist) style, language becomes a prime arena of contestation. One of Phloi's sons comes home from Paris with a French wife, who is sympathetically shown trying with only partial success to master the nuances of Thai language and customs, but the marriage has difficulties. Things get worse when Phloi's sons become sharply divided over politics: whereas one joins the puppet government set up under Japanese occupation, another son joins the resistance to the new government. Without expressing an opinion on political events as such, Phloi focuses on the language her arguing sons use, criticizing "these violent words—incredibly violent" (467). A page later, she tries to absorb the new loan-word *khonsatituchan* (from English "constitution"), which sounds in Thai like *satituchan*, "person." "Very confusing," thinks Phloi (468). Kukrit's novel is subtly but deeply antiauthoritarian, and he portrays the oligarchic coup against the monarchy as cloaked in Orwellian euphemisms: the coup is only "a change of system," a manifestation of "progress," and an advancement of "democracy"—a term that the brothers can't agree how to translate into Thai (474).

The novel ends in deep uncertainty, with Phloi dying on June 9, 1946—the very day that the twenty-year-old King Rama VIII suddenly died in his palace bedroom. Had he been assassinated? Had his brother accidentally shot him while they were examining his pistol, not realizing it was loaded? Or had he been depressed and committed suicide? To this day, public discussion of this question is forbidden in Thailand. *Four Reigns* only hints at people's shock and uncertainty at this tragedy, which occurred just as the country was beginning to pull itself together after the wartime occupation by Japan.

Kukrit Pramoj is a writer of considerable interest from many points of view, yet he has never received the attention given to his Indonesian counterpart Pramoedya Ananta Toer. Both wrote ambitious multigenerational novels that encapsulate the development of their modern nation; Kukrit's *Four Reigns* can well be compared with Pramoedya's four-volume *Buru Quartet* (1973–75), from questions of politics to language to clothing; both works even have chapters depicting a sudden fad for bicycles. With its rich portrayal of the coming of modernity to Indonesia, *The Buru Quartet* figures prominently in Pheng Cheah's *Spectral Nationality*, in Peter Hitchcock's *The Long Space*, and in Christopher GoGwilt's *The Passage of Literature*, whereas Kukrit isn't mentioned in any of those books, or so far as I know in any other scholarly studies outside Thailand.

A writer needs influential champions to become known worldwide, as William Marling argues in *Gatekeepers: The Emergence of World Literature and the 1960s*, where he gives detailed accounts of the variety of actors in the international field who made "world writers" out of a favored few figures such as García Márquez and Murakami while sidelining most of their contemporaries. Kukrit's standing in postcolonial studies might well be higher if Benedict Anderson, who did much to draw Anglophone postcolonialists' attention to Southeast Asia, had showcased him in his books together with Pramoedya. Anderson specialized in Thai as well as Indonesian politics and culture, and he made a translation of modern Thai stories shortly after publishing *Imagined Communities*. Kukrit would have been a perfect figure to take up in that book, given Anderson's emphasis on the role of newspapers and novels in creating the imagined community of the modern nation.

Anderson later wrote about the decade during which Kukrit had his stint as prime minister, and with reference to another of Bangkok's leading newspapers he emphasized that "the importance of the press should not be underestimated; above all, that of the popular newspaper *Thai Rath*, which, with its huge nationwide readership, represents another kind of imagined national community, alongside those conjured up by parliamentary institutions or the Nation-Buddhist-Monarchy shibboleth of the old regime" ("Murder and Progress in Modern Siam," 108). Yet neither he nor anyone else outside Thailand has ever analyzed Kukrit's novels and stories. As of October 2018, Pramoedya has forty-four citations in the *MLA Bibliography*, almost all of which are essays or book chapters devoted entirely to him or drawing comparisons with world figures such as Joseph Conrad and José Rizal. Kukrit has a grand total of two citations: a five-page entry in a dictionary of Southeast Asian literary biography, and a book review of *Four Reigns* and two other Thai novels, published in the *New York Review of Books* in 1992, eleven years after the translation had actually appeared.

A self-consciously modern writer, a kind of feminist, and a skeptically engaged observer of political and social change, Kukrit seems to have only two strikes against him: he was a royalist rather than a leftist, and he was a Buddhist rather than a secularist. Kukrit's Buddhism comes to the fore in *Many Lives,* a linked set of short stories that trace the karmic paths that lead each character onto a ferryboat that sinks amid a violent storm on the Chao Phraya River, which runs through the heart of Bangkok. In *Four Reigns*, Mae Phloi's death is portrayed at the novel's end in distinctly Buddhist terms: "It was in the late afternoon of that Sunday, the ninth of June 1946, when the tide was low in Khlong Bang Luang, that Phloi's heart stopped beating and her transient joys and suffering in this life came to an end" (656). Khlong Bang Luang is a tributary canal of the Chao Phraya. On the opening page of the novel, Phloi had ventured downriver from her home along the canal, sent by her mother to seek her fortune as an attendant in the royal court. On the novel's final page, situating a very specific and traumatic day under the aegis of eternity, *Four Reigns* beautifully comes full circle.

Benedict Anderson was actually well aware of Kukrit's work, but he gave him only a footnote in the seventy-five-page introduction to his anthology of Thai stories, *In the Mirror*. In his footnote, Anderson mentions *Four Reigns* as a "significant novel" but then turns to a lesser work, *Red Bamboo*, noting that it was translated into English with support from the United States Information Service, thanks to its anti-Communist theme (10n.). The writers whom Anderson chooses for his collection are all younger "subversive" and "non-conforming" figures whose work was shaped by their reading of Western Marxists and Asian Maoists (18, 28). Their stories are dotted with appropriate political lessons: "The land of Thai is broad and wide," one narrator remarks, "but today every inch of it is someone's property" (236). "The more he thinks about this business of capital," we're told of a story's hero, "the more bitter he feels" (254). In his essay on "Murder and Progress in Modern Siam," quoted above, Anderson dismisses anyone of Kukrit's outlook in his remark about "the Nation-Buddhist-Monarchy shibboleth of the old regime," but this throwaway line hardly does justice to those deeply ingrained elements of Thai life. A novel that Anderson himself describes as significant deserves attention even if it is written by a Buddhist monarchist, if we want to better understand the interwoven strands of literary modernity in Thailand and beyond.

Whether he has been neglected for political reasons or simply through a lack of awareness abroad, Kukrit offers a distinctive perspective on Asian modernity. His four-generation saga makes a natural comparison to Pramoedya's, and the comparison could extend beyond them. No modern writer was more concerned—even obsessed—with the ambiguous impact of modernity than Yukio Mishima, and he too turned to historical fiction as a way to explore his concerns, most notably in his *Sea of Fertility* tetralogy (1968–71). He is often studied in relation to such European figures as Nietzsche, Mann, and Proust, but as far as I know, he has never been discussed in relation either to Kukrit or to Pramoedya, both of whom offer closer models than Proust or Mann for a multigenerational history of modernity seen in semiperipheral perspective.

With his ironic wit, Kukrit had none of Mishima's militaristic fanaticism, but they shared several fundamental qualities, including an involvement with drama and film as well as fiction, a royalist nationalism, and a drive to preserve premodern traditions amid a rapidly changing world.

They were both highly political writers, and Kukrit actually had a leading political role of a kind that Mishima only dreamed of. While Kukrit's novel registers Japan's cultural and political impact on Thailand, Mishima's tetralogy in turn draws on Thai history and religion. Mishima spent several months in Thailand in 1965 and visited again in 1967 as he was working on *The Sea of Fertility*, whose third volume takes its title from Bangkok's iconic Temple of Dawn. Mishima could well have met Kukrit on one of his visits, and even without a meeting in person he would have been struck by Kukrit's combination of literary and political prominence. *The Temple of Dawn* features the Thai Princess Moonlight, Ying Chan, as the second reincarnation of Kiyoaki Matsugae, doomed hero of the first volume, *Spring Snow*. Two of the characters in *Spring Snow* are Thai princes, and they are linked to two of the kings of Kukrit's *Four Reigns*. Chao Pattanadid is a son of Rama VI, the second of Kukrit's four monarchs, and he and his cousin Kridsada have gone to school in Lausanne together with the future Rama VIII, the ill-fated young monarch in the final chapters of *Four Reigns*. Interestingly, we learn that the Thai princes have been sent from Lausanne to study in Japan because Pattanadid's father is afraid that their cousin, the future king, is becoming too westernized in Switzerland, and he looks to the Peers School in Tokyo to provide the best balance of East and West.

Religion provides a further basis of comparison. Though not a believer like Kukrit, Mishima too found in Thai Buddhism a cyclical counterweight to the modern march of progress. He illustrates this theme through the young princes in the first volume and then with the reincarnation of Kiyoaki as Ying Chan in *The Temple of Dawn*. The *Sea of Fertility* tetralogy is almost an encyclopedia of strategies for interweaving a premodern Asian past and a global modernity, and Thai religion and culture provide an important frame of reference for Mishima's epic tale. For a further basis of comparison, we could consider Mishima, Kukrit, and also Pramoedya in terms of their intertextual blending of Asian and European predecessors. Mishima's tetralogy references *The Tale of Genji* together with Proust, while Kukrit was steeped in Victorian literature as well as Thai folk traditions. Pramoedya's hero, Minke, hopes to become the Indonesian Multatuli, and at the same time he wants to give his writing the flavor of a classical *wayang* shadow play.

A whole new panorama of modernity opens up as we begin to look beyond the usual suspects. Of course, a history of literary modernity that would include *Four Reigns* at the cost of suppressing the magnificent *Buru Quartet* would be no improvement at all. Yet it is important also to include a figure such as Kukrit Pramoj in our accounts, precisely because he doesn't fit neatly into the narratives that Western critics typically want to create for literature of "the third world," "the Global South," "the postcolony," "the world system," or "the periphery"—terms of varied connotations but similar singularity. What we need are pluralistic studies that admit materials which challenge and modify the aesthetic, political, and historiographic frameworks we bring to them. This is the best way to practice a comparison without hegemony, as we build our glass houses in what the troubled narrator of Pramoedya's *House of Glass* describes as "that new jungle called the modern age" (227–28).

Conclusion

Rebirth of a Discipline

In 2001, when Gayatri Spivak delivered the Wellek Library lectures that became *Death of a Discipline*, she was registering a feeling that had been growing among American comparatists for some time. It appeared to many that comparative literature had lost the sense of definition and mission that it had enjoyed during the postwar European reconstruction of the 1950s and then the theory boom of the 1960s and 1970s. In 1993 the Bernheimer Report described the discipline as "anxiogenic" and as already "defensive and beleaguered" by the mid-1970s (41), caught between its Eurocentric aestheticism and the very different approaches being developed outside the precincts of comparative literature in the burgeoning fields of women's, ethnic, cultural, and postcolonial studies.

A sense of decline and anomie could be felt at the annual meetings of the ACLA during the 1980s and well into the 1990s. They were very modest events, often held in chilly locales in March, with some 150 papers presented in disjointed and poorly attended panel sessions. At the 1993 annual meeting in Bloomington, Indiana, Stuart McDougal devoted his presidential address to urging the association to find ways to revitalize itself. He laid particular stress on the fact that few prominent comparatists were bothering to join the ACLA, a point reiterated in the Bernheimer Report (42). McDougal wasn't the first to voice such concerns. When Thomas Greene began his term as ACLA's president in 1985, I asked him what he felt was the major challenge facing the association. He replied with a single word: "Mediocrity."

The 1994 annual meeting, held in Claremont, California, featured a slight increase to 180 papers, but the association still wasn't drawing a wide attendance. A grand total of three papers were delivered by scholars based in other countries—one each from Canada, England, and Germany. Even the meeting's national scope was limited, as most of the speakers that year came from the West Coast. Outreach efforts led to a somewhat broader national and international attendance the next year at the University of Georgia; among the 223 papers, a total of nineteen were given by speakers from abroad, coming from ten countries in all. The participation declined the following year, however, when the association met at Notre Dame, with a total of 177 papers given. Only nine were presented by speakers from abroad, six of them from neighboring Canada.

This attenuated institutional picture finally began to change in 1997, for an interlocking set of intellectual, institutional, and political reasons. In that year, the association's board resolved to become international not just in theory but in practice, and we held our first meeting abroad, in Puerto Vallarta. At the same time, we shifted to what has become ACLA's ongoing format of three-day seminars, which give the opportunity for sustained discussion from multiple perspectives. In proposing this format, I had both practical and political goals. In order for people to attend in a location that almost everyone would have to fly to, it would help them get travel funds if they were delivering a paper. The seminar format meant that everyone who attended could be a presenter, which had the further advantage of breaking down the hierarchies of presenters versus mere attendees and of plenary stars versus those relegated to "breakout" sessions: all of the attendees were speakers, and all were in seminars together.

The format proved to be a success, allowing for more developed conversations and also for an easier mixing of graduate students and faculty, though in time we did relax our structural egalitarianism to the extent of including some plenary sessions. People started inviting friends from other departments and other countries, and by the time my department hosted ACLA's meeting in 2009, our organizing committee had to find space for 2,100 papers on a kaleidoscopic array of topics—a tenfold increase in just a dozen years. The participants came from all around the United States and from fifty different countries, from Azerbaijan to Belgium, Malaysia, and Peru. Our annual meetings since then have had as many as 3,000 participants; apart from the MLA Convention, which encompasses all fields, the ACLA's meetings are among the largest literature conventions anywhere.

Good formats, and good weather, can only do so much. The acceleration of globalization has certainly had a major impact as well, making comparative literature a good setting to explore interests and concerns arising from the conflictual transformation of the world's economic and cultural landscape. Equally important has been the increase in international communication and travel fostered by the internet and by deregulated airfares, enabling far-flung scholars to organize seminars and then to collect frequent-flier points as they gather to critique neoliberalism. Yet these large-scale changes wouldn't have led people to ACLA if the association had continued to confine itself to "card-carrying" comparatists and to accept only papers dealing with material in two or three languages. The ACLA seminars are as comparative as ever, whether in terms of languages, countries, arts, or disciplines, but many individual papers have a single focus. This enables specialists in one literature to present their papers within the comparative context created by the seminar as a whole. Whether the topic concerns migrant identities or lyrical temporalities, presenters frequently gain insights from other traditions than the ones they know. Many more people, languages, and literatures are now present at our annual meetings than when Harry Levin could speak of comparing "the literature."

Given the continuing shrinkage in the humanities, though, and the political turmoil in much of the world, the revitalized discipline of comparative literature remains in a precarious position. To continue to thrive, comparatists need to continue to scrutinize our practices, to reach out more effectively to colleagues beyond our programs and to the public beyond our campuses, and to work together in ways that create synergies among disparate perspectives. A theme running throughout this book has been that the different strands of comparison that we find today have long been intertwined, including philologically based close reading, literary theory, colonial/postcolonial studies, and the study of world literature. They can and should become better integrated than they have yet been, even while their practitioners maintain significant differences in archives, approaches, and perspectives.

Many constructive ideas are put forward in the most recent ACLA report, overseen by Ursula Heise—the first of the reports to be chaired by a woman, and the first by a faculty member at a public university. The evolving shape of the discipline is also indicated in the fact that Heise is a comparatist who works extensively on American literature. She isn't even located in a comparative literature department but is affiliated with UCLA's English department and also with its Institute of the Environment and Sustainability, reflecting the evolution of her work from early studies of postmodernist narrative (*Chronoschisms*) to ecological literature and film (*Sense of Place and Sense of Planet* and *Imagining Extinction*). Furthermore, thanks to the initiative of Eric Hayot, this was the first ACLA report to take the form of a website (https://stateofthediscipline.acla.org), featuring dozens of essays grouped under a variety of headings (Paradigms, Practices, Ideas of the Decade, and Futures). The essays were contributed by graduate students as well as faculty, both in the United States and abroad, and were supplemented by threads of readers' comments. A print version was published in 2017 under Heise's overall editorship; its plural title, *Futures of Comparative Literature*, expresses well the discipline's open-endedness, and the collection offers many ideas that comparatists can use going forward.

What comparatists do *not* need in future are yet more restrictive position-takings insisting that only one kind of literature, one theoretical approach, or one brand of politics is intellectually or ethically worth our while. It is natural for scholars to focus on the materials they find most useful for the questions they want to ask and to employ the theories they favor. It is another matter for people to issue sweeping calls against alternative approaches and to insist that the discipline's true future lies only along their particular path. When Werner Friederich noted the irony in 1960 that comparatists were mostly discussing only a quarter of the NATO-nations, it would have been better if he had called for opening out the field, at the very least to the other NATO-literatures, instead of arguing against the use of the term "world literature." Paul de Man's declaration in 1979 that deconstructive analyses "will in fact be the task of literary criticism in the coming years" (*Allegories of Reading*, 17) hasn't set a lasting agenda for the discipline as a whole, even though his insights continue to be productive for a substantial number of comparatists. In her survey of the field in 1993, Susan Bassnett roundly declared that "Comparative literature as a discipline has had its day," and proposed that we "should look upon translation studies as the principal discipline" (*Comparative Literature*, 161). Bassnett herself has modulated her claim since then, even as translation studies has begun to make a greater and long-overdue appearance in our programs. Efforts today to promote one or another approach against all others are unlikely to have a longer shelf life than their polemical predecessors.

The kind of bridge-building that we need is seen in the opening of Peter Hitchcock's *The Long Space: Transnationalism and Postcolonial Form* (2010): "This book began several years ago as a means to understand how postcolonial writing might be thought differently within world literature (and, indeed, how world literature itself would be changed in that relation)" (xi). This is one of several recent attempts to think through the interactions between postcolonial and global or world literary studies. In addition to the works previously discussed by Apter, Cheah, Friedman, and Löffler, these include Suman Gupta's *Globalization and Literature* (2009), Paul Jay's *Global Matters* (2010), Moser and Simonis's *Figuren des Globalen* (2014), Pascale Casanova's *La Langue mondiale* (2015), Debjani Ganguly's *This Thing Called the World* (2016) and her *Cambridge History of World Literature* (2020), Aamir Mufti's *Forget English!* (2016), Hayot and Walkowitz's *A New Vocabulary for Global Modernism* (2016), Levine and Lateef-Jans's *Untranslatability Goes Global* (2017), Baidik Bhattacharya's *Postcolonial Writing in the Era of World Literature* (2018), and Weigui Fang's collection *Tensions in World Literature* (2018).

In terms of the heritage of Continental theory, a model for Harvard's Institute for World Literature has been Cornell's School for Criticism and Theory, on whose website Hent de Vries describes the program as "an annual scholarly and intellectual platform on which the drama of the somewhat fruitless theory wars and the questionable virtue of vain polemics is resolutely sidestepped." He advocates "a climate of rigorous investigations and courteous debate" among scholars willing to move beyond "the infatuation with identities and cultures, national literatures and cosmopolitanisms, humanisms and antihumanisms . . . while never forgetting the concrete political responsibilities that more abstract reflections entail" ("Director's Welcome"). Some of the issues that de Vries mentions, such as national literatures and cosmopolitanisms, are very active areas of investigation within comparative studies, but for ACLA and the IWL as for the SCT, rigorous investigations and debates don't mean burying disagreements or artificially harmonizing divergent approaches. More productive is the kind of engagement amid diversity that Helena Buescu has called "experiência do incomum como forma de comunidade"—the experience of the uncommon as a mode of community (*Experiência do incomum*, 7).

Many of the best comparative studies today involve novel intersections of perspectives that haven't always been in conversation, as can be seen in the forward-looking work now often being pursued by comparatists in their first or second books. Here I will cite just four examples among many. In *A Common Strangeness* (2012), Jacob Edmond examines globalization through case studies in experimental Chinese, Russian, and American poetry. In place of either universality or untranslatability, Edmond seeks uncommon commonalities among poets who participate in an international movement from within very distinct cultural spheres. Lital Levy's *Poetic Trespass: Writing between Hebrew and Arabic in Israel/Palestine* (2014), published by Princeton in Emily Apter's Translation/Transnation series, is a comparative study that is equally a contribution to translation theory, Middle Eastern studies, and colonial/postcolonial studies. Levy explores "a poetics of in-betweenness" in "the Hebrew-Arabic no-man's-land, the zone of poetic trespass, whose impossibility is the essential condition of imagination" (143, 297). Very differently, Delia Ungureanu's *From Paris to Tlön: Surrealism as World Literature* (2017) is a sociologically based interarts study that traces the rival strategies by which André Breton and Salvador Dalí sought to conquer the world, first in Paris and then in New York. She uses archival research to trace the forgotten routes of transmission by which surrealist ideas of the oneiric object migrated from avant-garde poetry into painting and then came to infuse pivotal works by many world writers, including Borges, Nabokov, and Pamuk. Those three writers always denied any connection to surrealism, but the archives show otherwise.

The question of archives returns us to the tale of two libraries in chapter 1 and the tale of two *knjižnici* in chapter 6: the history of comparative literature is to a considerable extent a story of libraries and collections built and preserved, lost or destroyed. This is the subject of my fourth example, Venkat Mani's *Recoding World Literature: Libraries, Print Culture, and Germany's Pact with Books* (2017), which as it happens begins with epigraphs from both Borges and Pamuk. Mani discusses what he calls "bibliomigrancy"—the physical movement of books across borders. In his introduction, he recalls childhood memories of a Soviet bookmobile that appeared in his home town north of Delhi, filled with "a veritable smorgasbord for the hungry small-town readers" (3). From this mobile library Mani bought *Aparādha aura Danda* (Crime and Punishment) by an author he'd never heard of, opting for Dostoevsky because this satisfyingly thick book was priced at only ten rupees. Fortunately, he hadn't encountered Thomas Greene's stern warning against comparative literature being "purveyed in the style of a smorgasbord at bargain rates" (Greene Report, 31). Looking at the politics of culture via the materiality of physical books, Mani argues that the Germans' massive investment in acquiring world literature provided a substitute for the territorial empire they lacked. In Mani's account, Germany's "pact with books" was in many ways a Faustian bargain.

These four books can suggest the range of themes, approaches, and materials that are found in comparative studies today. They also indicate several ways in which comparatists are working across the discipline's long-standing fault lines. In terms of the old opposition between national and comparative literary studies, it is noteworthy that two of these books have received prizes from individual literature associations (Levy's in Jewish Studies, Mani's in German Studies), while Ungureanu has received prizes both in comparative literature and in humanities, and Levy also received the MLA's prize for the best book in any field. All four combine global perspectives with local rootedness, detailing the often tense intersections of languages and cultures in Moscow and Beijing, in Tel Aviv and on the West Bank, in Paris and New York, in East and West Berlin. All four scholars are interested in the politics of culture and the complexities of translation as writers and their works cross—or fail to cross—internal and external borders. They all combine theoretical discussion with illuminating readings of poems, stories, and novels. All four have taught seminars for the Institute for World Literature, from very different perspectives. Finally, all of them understand literature as an aesthetic experience as well as a repository of philosophical or political ideas, and their own writing is vivid and full of life. Only after selecting my examples did I reflect that three of the four came to English as their second or even third language; the fourth, Jacob Edmond, is a New Zealander for whom English isn't the same native language that it is for a New Englander like myself. Through their close engagement with poetry and prose in the original languages as well as in translation, they all counter the hegemony of global English even as they make eloquent use of it in their work.

As we have seen throughout the preceding chapters, we all have our work cut out for us as we reshape comparative literary studies in a rapidly changing world, amid the many pressures we face on and off our campuses. As we bring literature to bear on issues of migration and displacement, ecological crises, rising ethno-nationalisms, and the general coarsening of political debate, it is worth recalling Horace's dictum that literature should be *dulce* as well as *utile*. Along with the lessons that poems, plays, and novels convey, they offer us unique and lasting pleasures of language at its richest, of haunting poetic voices, of engrossing characters and plots, as they take us out of our immediate environment and concerns. Comparative literature intensifies this process by setting our home tradition in a differential frame or by taking us out of our culture altogether, offering us the provisional freedom to imagine our world, and ourselves, differently.

The experience of literature in a global age is at once dauntingly excessive and radically incomplete. This duality can be seen in *Discussing the Divine Comedy with Dante*, a massive painting twenty feet long by nearly nine feet high, painted in 2006 by three Chinese artists, Dai Dudu, Li Tiezi, and Zhang An (figure 14). A black-and-white reproduction doesn't do justice to their panorama, but it can be seen on websites such as Aziz's "Art Fact" blog on the *China Daily* website. In place of the *Commedia*'s hundred cantos, the painting presents a hundred figures from many eras and walks of life. Many, such as Mao Zedong, Albert Einstein, and Michael

FIGURE 14. Dai Dudu, Li Tiezi, and Zhang An, *Discussing the Divine Comedy with Dante* (2006).

Jordan, are instantly recognizable anywhere in the world. Others would be meaningful only in a Chinese context—the rock star Cui Jian, or Norman Bethune, a Canadian doctor who treated members of Mao's forces, for whom Mao wrote an elegy after his death in 1939. Juan Antonio Samaranch, former president of the International Olympic Committee, is probably included thanks to the awarding of the 2008 Summer Olympics to Beijing. This is the world seen from a distinctly Chinese vantage point.

Literature and philosophy are well represented in this capacious compendium, from Homer, Confucius, and Socrates to the drunken Tang Dynasty poet Li Bai (now equipped with a typewriter, perhaps in a nod to Lin Yutang), and on to writers including Shakespeare, Pushkin, Goethe, Nietzsche, Lewis Carroll, Gorky, and Tagore. They are mixed in with everyone from Genghis Khan to Napoleon to Elvis Presley to George W. Bush, who fails to see Osama bin Laden behind him. Cinema is represented by Charlie Chaplin, Shirley Temple, Bruce Lee, Marlon Brando as the Godfather, and Audrey Hepburn reclining on Chopin's piano, while Steven Spielberg watches Picasso studying Abraham Lincoln, who is looking quizzically at Mao. Other painters include Leonardo, Michelangelo, and a modern watercolorist, Qi Baishi. Next to the Empress Dowager Cixi, Salvador Dalí is shown looking up toward the mural's painters, who have given themselves cameos, surveying the scene together with Dante from a rampart in the upper right corner of the canvas.

According to Dai Dudu, "we wanted to represent world history within a single painting. We wanted to showcase the world's story, and let viewers feel as if they were flipping the pages of a history book" (quoted in Aziz, "Art Fact"). Everyone who is (or was) anyone, it seems, gets their fifteen centimeters of fame in their visual storybook. Of course, "everyone" isn't there; the hundred figures are a tiny sampling from world history and culture. Yet even so, they present an overwhelming mélange. The three artists themselves look rather depressed as they try to make sense of the scene, in poses reminiscent of some of M. C. Escher's puzzled observers of impossible architectural constructions.

Comparatists can well share the artists' mixed emotions as we survey the crowded panorama of the literatures extending around us and before us. Libraries help us organize our materials, but only up to a point. In *Recoding World Literature*, Venkat Mani emphasizes that libraries are never simply treasuries of culture, as they always exclude—or repress—more than they preserve. As Jan Assmann has said, writing "gives rise to a dialectic of expansion and loss. . . . The positive new forms of retention and realization across the millennia are counterbalanced by the negative forms of loss through forgetting and through suppression by way of manipulation, censorship, destruction, circumscription, and substitution" (*Cultural Memory and Early Civilization*, 9). In a discussion of the destruction of Ashurbanipal's great library at Nineveh, Martin Puchner observes that the subsequent loss of the cuneiform script, and with it the entire body of Mesopotamian literature, "suggests a painful truth about literature: The only thing that can assure survival is continual use. Don't put your trust in clay or stone. Literature must be used by every generation. Overly impressed by the endurance of writing, the world forgot that everything was subject to forgetting, even writing" (*The Written World*, 44).

Comparatists face two nearly unsurmountable limits: the paucity of extant early literatures, and the overwhelming abundance of modern writing.

"The history of the Victorian Age will never be written," as Lytton Strachey famously remarked; "we know too much about it" (*Eminent Victorians*, 1). Our capacious libraries and our exploding internet archives are daunting but deceptive; they can lead us to think that we have it all, when we never do—not only because so many books never made it into the library or have later been deaccessioned, but because we leave so many shelves untouched. True, we can't read even a fraction of what our libraries hold, and though archival activists periodically discover significant long-forgotten works, I don't mind leaving to the Stanford Literary Lab the task of mining the data in thousands of obscure as well as eminent Victorian novels, in the service of the comprehensive history that couldn't be written in Strachey's day. But comparatists have barely begun to explore neglected byways, and even overgrown highways, in less well-trodden areas. I would like to suggest as a basic principle that any literary theory or critical method is valuable if it enables us to expand our archive in useful ways, and to read newly recovered as well as long-familiar works with appreciation, deepened understanding, and a critical edge. Conversely, any theory or any method whatsoever is problematic if one of its prime results—or its goal— is to wall off entire corridors of the library.

These concerns are ones of overabundance, but we face the opposite problem with early literatures, whose libraries were so often destroyed or simply left to decay. Anyone who works in ancient literature is likely to be haunted by the works we know of that have been lost, even by so famous a figure as Sophocles; of the hundred and twenty plays he wrote in his long life, seven survive. Worse, we have lost entire bodies of works whose very loss is unknown to us. It is often said, for instance, that Mesopotamian literature ossified by around 800 BCE, and that scribes thereafter largely confined themselves to copying and recopying a canon of earlier texts; but how can we possibly be sure? It is clear that cuneiform signs pressed onto clay tablets ceased to be the vehicle for many new literary creations, but it is hard to imagine that generations of scribes in the area's sophisticated urban centers never felt inspired to compose a poem or write a story. It is far more likely that their literature fell victim to a change of technology: the popular new alphabets were written on perishable papyrus and parchment rather than baked on clay. Unlike the lost plays of Sophocles and the entire body of late Assyro-Babylonian literature, the Bible and the two Homeric epics survived only because people never stopped recopying them before their existing copies disintegrated.

Those losses are not without their advantages. Specialists in classical Greece, in ancient Egypt, or in Mesopotamia can hold the extant corpus of their literature on a single bookshelf or in a few megabytes on their hard drive, supposing they entrust their texts to that even more ephemeral medium. We have still less from the pre-Conquest Americas, thanks to the conquistadors' wholesale destruction of "idolatrous" codices. Only a handful of them remain today, together with a few works such as the *Popol Vuh* that survived by being written down in the Roman alphabet. The very paucity of primary materials, however, encourages a holistic approach to ancient cultures. It isn't uncommon for an Egyptologist or a Mesoamericanist to have a comprehensive personal library of scholarship in several disciplines, and to be comfortable working on history, art, and archaeology as well as on literature. Even the lacunae in our archives and in the surviving manuscripts offer their own rewards. The Australian scholar Inga Clendinnen ended her magisterial *Aztecs: An Interpretation* (1991) with a brief one-paragraph epilogue, in which she expresses the paradoxical fascination of a largely lost history:

There is a long and painful distance between the lived Mexica world and the small clutter of carved stones and painted paper, the remembered images and words, from which we seek to make that world again. Historians of remote places and peoples are the romantics of the human sciences, Ahabs pursuing our great white whale, dimly aware that the whole business is, if coolly considered, rather less than reasonable. We will never catch him, and don't much want to: it is our own limitations of thought, of understandings, of imagination we test as we quarter those strange waters. And then we think we see a darkening in the deeper water, a sudden surge, the roll of a fluke—and then the heart-lifting glimpse of the great white shape, its whiteness throwing back its own particular light, there, on the glimmering horizon. (275)

Whether we work on older or newer literatures, on cultures close to those we grew up in or farther away, comparatists of all kinds can experience the pleasures of revealing the particular shape of long-submerged works and of seeing a favorite writer in the unfamiliar light of a novel comparison.

In his polemical introduction to *Anatomy of Criticism,* Northrop Frye urged the critics of his day to suspend preset value judgments and to cast their nets more widely than they had been doing, but he adds that such capacious inquiries should not "progress toward a general stupor of satisfaction with everything written, which is not quite what I have in mind" (28). Certainly today no scholar is in danger of succumbing to a general stupor of satisfaction, whether regarding our materials, our methods, or the world around us. As a motto for comparatists, I would like to propose a quotation from an important early work of cultural comparison, the *Kitab al-Khazari* by the Iberian poet and philosopher Judah ha-Levi (1075– 1141). Written in Judeo-Arabic at the end of his life, in times at least as troubled as our own, *The Book of the Khazars* takes the form of a dialogue organized by the king of the Khazars, a pagan people living along the Black Sea who were said to have converted to Judaism in the eighth century. Judah ha-Levi imagines the king having had a disquieting dream, in which he is told that his intentions are good but his deeds are not. The king decides to bring together a Christian, a Muslim, a Greek philosopher, and a rabbi to make their case for the best system of belief. The rabbi wins the debate through a mixture of historical, philological, and philosophical arguments; he places special emphasis on the claim that the Hebrews alone have written records describing the entire history of the world. Though I admire the rabbi's archival enthusiasm, what I would propose as a motto is the king's explanation for seeking understanding through dialectical debate and a search into sources. "Tradition in itself is a fine thing, if it satisfies the soul," the king says, "but a perturbed soul prefers research" (*The Kuzari,* 5.1).

Lacking a library, the king conducts his comparative research in the form of an oral examination, in an inverted version of the doctoral orals that would one day trouble the dream of a graduate student's spouse, in the anecdote with which I opened this book. In place of an orals committee of four scholars examining the student, here the royal inquirer responds to his own unsettling dream by examining his four scholars; as always, comparison reveals difference together with similarity. Yet the king's reply holds good, nine hundred years after Judah ha-Levi wrote his dialogue. From Herder and de Staël to Auerbach and beyond, the perturbed souls we have examined in this book can help us chart our course forward as we seek new and better ways to compare the literatures today.

Bibliography

Abu-Lughod, Janet L. *Before European Hegemony: The World System A.D. 1250–1350.* New York: Oxford University Press, 1989.

Adorno, Theodor. *Minima Moralia: Reflexionen aus dem beschädigten Leben.* Frankfurt am Main: Suhrkamp, 1951. *Minima Moralia: Reflections from Damaged Life.* Tr. E. F. N. Jephcott. London: New Left Books, 1974.

Anderson, Benedict R. O'G. *Imagined Communities: Reflections on the Origin and Spread of Nationalism.* Rev. ed. London: Verso, 2016.

——. "In the World-Shadow of Bismarck and Nobel." *New Left Review* 28 (2004): 85–129.

——. "Jupiter Hill: José Rizal: Paris, Havana, Barcelona, Berlin—3." *New Left Review* 29 (2004): 91–120.

——. "Murder and Progress in Modern Siam." In *Exploration and Irony in Studies of Siam Over Forty Years*, 101–15. Ithaca, NY: Cornell Southeast Asia Program Publications, 2014.

——. "Nitroglycerine in the Pomegranate." *New Left Review* 27 (2004): 99–118.

——. *The Spectre of Comparison: Nationalism, Southeast Asia, and the World.* London: Verso, 1998.

Anderson, Benedict R. O'G., and Ruchira C. Mendiones, eds. and tr. *In the Mirror: Literature and Politics in Siam in the American Era.* Bangkok: Editions Duang Kamol, 1985.

Apter, Emily. *Against World Literature: On the Politics of Untranslatability.* London: Verso, 2013.

——. "Global Translatio: The 'Invention' of Comparative Literature, Istanbul, 1933." *Critical Inquiry* 29.2 (2003): 253–81. Repr. in *The Translation Zone*, 41–64.

——. *The Translation Zone: A New Comparative Literature.* Princeton: Princeton University Press, 2006.

Apuleius. *Metamorphoses (The Golden Ass).* Ed. and tr. J. Arthur Hanson. Loeb Classical Library. 2 vols. Cambridge, MA: Harvard University Press, 1989, 1996. *The Golden Ass.* Ed. and tr. P. G. Walsh. Oxford World Classics. Oxford: Oxford University Press, 1994.

Arac, Jonathan. "Anglo-Globalism?" *New Left Review* 16 (July–August 2002): 35–45.

Arantes, Paulo Eduardo. *Sentimento da dialética na experiência intelectual brasileira: Dialética e dualidade segundo Antonio Candido e Roberto Schwarz.* São Paulo: Paz e Terra, 1992.

Assmann, Jan. *Cultural Memory and Early Civilization: Writing, Remembrance, and Political Imagination*. Tr. David Henry Wilson. Cambridge: Cambridge University Press, 2011.

———. "Cultural Memory and the Myth of the Axial Age." In Robert N. Bellah and Hans Jonas, eds., *The Axial Age and Its Consequences*, 366–407. Cambridge: Cambridge University Press, 2012.

Asturias, Miguel Ángel. *El señor Presidente*. Madrid: Cátedra, 1997. *The President*. Tr. Frances Partridge. London: Gollancz, 1963.

———. *Leyendas de Guatemala*. 3rd ed. Madrid: Cátedra, 2002.

Auerbach, Clemens. "Summer 1937." In Barck and Treml, eds., *Erich Auerbach*, 495–500.

Auerbach, Erich. "Epilegomena zu *Mimesis*." *Romanische Forschungen* 65 (1953): 1–18. "Epilegomena to *Mimesis*." Tr. Jan M. Ziolkowski. *Mimesis* (2003 ed.), 559–74.

———. *Mimesis: Dargestellte Wirklichkeit in der abendländischen Literatur*. 2nd ed. Bern: Francke, 1959. *Mimesis: The Representation of Reality in Western Literature*. Tr. Willard R. Trask. Princeton: Princeton University Press, 1953. Fiftieth-anniversary edition, 2003.

———. "The Philology of World Literature." In James L. Porter, ed., *Time, History, and Literature: Selected Essays of Erich Auerbach*, 253–65. Tr. Jane O. Newman. Princeton: Princeton University Press, 2014.

———. "Über das Studium der Romanistik in Istanbul." In Christian Rivoletti, ed., *Kultur als Politik: Aufsätze aus dem Exil zur Geschichte und Zukunft Europas (1938–1947)*, 89–92. Tr. Christophe Neumann. Konstanz: Konstanz University Press, 2014.

Aziz. "Art Fact: Dai Dudu, Li Tie Zhi, Zhang An." https://blog.chinadaily.com.cn /forum.php?mod=viewthread&tid=717218&page=1&authorid=650995 (accessed August 8, 2019).

Badiou, Alain. *Petit manuel d'inesthétique*. Paris: Éditions du Seuil, 1998. *Handbook of Inaesthetics*. Tr. Alberto Toscano. Stanford: Stanford University Press, 2005.

Bakhtin, Mikhail M. *The Dialogic Imagination: Four Essays*. Ed. and tr. Michael Holquist and Caryl Emerson. Austin: University of Texas Press, 1983.

Balakian, Anna. "How and Why I Became a Comparatist." In Gossman and Spariosu, eds., *Building a Profession*, 75–87.

———. *The Snowflake on the Belfry: Dogma and Disquietude in the Critical Arena*. Bloomington: Indiana University Press, 1994.

Banoun, Bernard. "Notes sur l'oreiller occidental-oriental de Yoko Tawada." *Études Germaniques* 65.3 (2010): 415–29.

Barck, Karlheinz, and Martin Treml, eds. *Erich Auerbach: Geschichte und Aktualität eines europäischen Philologen*. Berlin: Kulturverlag Kadmos, 2007.

Barlowe, Wayne. *Barlowe's Inferno*. Beverly Hills, CA: Morpheus, 1998.

Barolini, Teodolinda. "An Ivy League Professor Weighs In: Expert View." *Entertainment Weekly* 1091 (February 26, 2010): 79.

Barthes, Roland. *Roland Barthes par Roland Barthes*. Paris: Éditions du Seuil, 1975. *Roland Barthes by Roland Barthes*. Tr. Richard Howard. New York: Hill and Wang, 2010.

———. *S/Z*. Paris: Éditions du Seuil, 1970. *S/Z: An Essay*. Tr. Richard Miller. New York: Hill and Wang, 1975.

Bassnett, Susan. *Comparative Literature: A Critical Introduction*. Oxford: Blackwell, 1993.

———, ed. *Translation and World Literature*. Abingdon: Routledge, 2018.

Beecroft, Alexander. *An Ecology of World Literature: From Antiquity to the Present Day*. London: Verso, 2015.

Beil, Ulrich J. "Zwischen Fremdbestimmung und Universalitätsanspruch: Deutsche Weltliteraturanthologien als Ausdruck kultureller Selbstinterpretation." In Helga Essmann and Udo Schöning, eds., *Weltliteratur in deutschen Versanthologien des 19. Jahrhunderts*, 261–310. Berlin: Erich Schmidt Verlag, 1996.

Bender, Thomas. "Lionel Trilling and American Life." *American Quarterly* 42.2 (1990): 324–47.

Berczik, Árpad. "Hugó von Meltzl." *Német Filológiai Tanulmányok* 12 (1978): 87–100.

Bermann, Sandra, and Catherine Porter, eds. *A Companion to Translation Studies*. Oxford: Blackwell, 2004.

Bermann, Sandra, and Michael Wood, eds. *Nation, Language, and the Ethics of Translation*. Princeton: Princeton University Press, 2005.

Bernheimer, Charles, ed. *Comparative Literature in the Age of Multiculturalism*. Baltimore: Johns Hopkins University Press, 1995.

———, et al. "The Bernheimer Report, 1993: Comparative Literature at the Turn of the Century." In Bernheimer, ed., *Comparative Literature in the Age of Multiculturalism*, 39–48.

Bess, Michael. "Power, Moral Values, and the Intellectual: An Interview with Michel Foucault." *The Daily Californian*, November 10, 1980. www.michaelbess.org/foucault-interview (accessed March 14, 2018).

Bhabha, Homi. *The Location of Culture*. London and New York: Routledge Classics, 2004.

Bhattacharya, Baidik. "On Comparatism in the Colony: Archives, Methods, and the Project of *Weltliteratur*." *Critical Inquiry* 42.2 (2016): 677–711.

———. *Postcolonial Writing in the Era of World Literature: Texts, Territories, Globalizations*. Abingdon and New York: Routledge, 2018.

Binet, Laurent. *La Septième fonction du langage*. Paris: Grasset, 2015. *The Seventh Function of Language*. Tr. Sam Taylor. New York: Farrar, Straus and Giroux, 2017.

Birns, Nicholas, and Juan E. De Castro, eds. *Roberto Bolaño as World Literature*. New York: Bloomsbury Academic, 2017.

Blessing, James H. "Comparative Literature and Title IV of the National Defense Education Act." *Comparative Literature Studies*, special advance number (1963): 127–33.

Bloom, Harold. *The Anxiety of Influence: A Theory of Poetry*. 2nd ed. New York: Oxford University Press, 1997.

Boitani, Piero, and Emilia Di Rocco. *Guida allo studio delle letterature comparate*. Bari: Laterza, 2013.

Boym, Svetlana. *Another Freedom: The Alternative History of an Idea*. Chicago: University of Chicago Press, 2012.

———. *The Future of Nostalgia*. New York: Basic Books, 2002.

———. *The Off-Modern*. New York: Bloomsbury Academic, 2017.

Braider, Christopher. "Of Monuments and Documents: Comparative Literature and the Visual Arts in Early Modern Studies, or The Art of Historical Tact." In Saussy, *Comparative Literature in an Age of Globalization*, 155–74.

Brandes, Georg. *Hovedstrømninger i det nittende Aarhundredes Litteratur (1872–1890)*. 6 vols. Copenhagen: Jespersen and Pio, 1966. *Main Currents in Nineteenth Century Literature*. Tr. Diana White and Mary Morison. 6 vols. New York: MacMillan; London: Heinemann, 1906.

———. "Weltliteratur." *Das litterarische Echo* 2.1 (1899): 1–3. "World Literature." Tr. Haun Saussy. In Thomsen, *Mapping World Literature*, 143–47. Repr. in Damrosch et al., *Princeton Sourcebook*, 61–66.

Brennan, Timothy. *At Home in the World: Cosmopolitanism Now*. Cambridge, MA: Harvard University Press, 1997.

Breton, André. "The Surrealist Situation of the Object." In *Manifestoes of Surrealism*, 261–310. Tr. Richard Seaver and Helen R. Lane. Ann Arbor: University of Michigan Press, 1972.

Broch, Hermann. *Der Tod des Vergil*. Frankfurt: Suhrkamp, 1994. *The Death of Virgil*. Tr. Jean Starr Untermeyer. New York: Vintage, 1995.

Bronner, Yigal, David Dean Shulman, and Gary A. Tubb, eds. *Innovations and Turning Points: Toward a History of Kāvya Literature*. New Delhi: Oxford University Press, 2014.

Brooke-Rose, Christine. *Between* (1968). In *The Christine Brooke-Rose Omnibus: Four Novels*, 391–575. Manchester and New York: Carcanet, 1986.

———. "Exsul." *Poetics Today* 17.3 (1996): 289–303.

Brooks, Peter. *Reading for the Plot: Design and Intention in Narrative*. Rev. ed. Cambridge, MA: Harvard University Press, 1992.

Brooks, Peter, Shoshana Felman, and J. Hillis Miller, eds. *The Lesson of Paul de Man*. *Yale French Studies* 69 (1985).

Brown, Marshall. "Encountering the World." *Neohelicon* 38 (2011): 349–65.

Buescu, Helena Carvalhão. *Experiência do incomum e boa vizinhança*. Porto: Porto Editora, 2013.

——— et al., eds. *Literatura-mundo comparada: Perspectivas em português*. Vol. 1: *Mundos em português*. Ed. Helena Carvalhão Buescu and Inocência Mata. Lisbon: Tinta da China, 2017.

Bulson, Eric. *Little Magazine, World Form*. New York: Columbia University Press, 2017.

Calinescu, Matei. *Five Faces of Modernity: Modernism, Avant-Garde, Decadence, Kitsch, Postmodernism*. Durham: Duke University Press, 1987.

Calvino, Italo. *I nostri antenati: Il cavaliere inesistente, Il visconte dimezzato, Il barone rampante*. Turin: Einaudi, 1960. *Our Ancestors*. Tr. Archibald Colquhoun. New York: Vintage, 2009.

———. *Le città invisibili* (1972). Milan: Mondadori, 1993. *Invisible Cities*. Tr. William Weaver. San Diego and New York: Harcourt, Brace, 1974.

———. "Presentazione." In *Le città invisibili*, v–xi.

Candido, Antonio. *Formação da literatura brasileira: Momentos decisivos* (1959). 2 vols. Belo Horizonte: Editora Itatiaia, 1975.

———. *On Literature and Society*. Ed. and tr. Howard S. Becker. Princeton: Princeton University Press, 2014.

Canetti, Elias. "Banquet Speech." www.nobelprize.org/prizes/literature/1981 /canetti/speech (accessed March 13, 2019).

———. *Die Blendung: Roman*. Munich: C. Hanser, 1992. *Auto-da-fé: A Novel*. Tr. C. V. Wedgwood. New York: Farrar, Straus and Giroux, 1984.

———. *The Conscience of Words*. Tr. Joachim Neugroschel. New York: Seabury, 1979.

Cao, Shunqing. *The Variation Theory of Comparative Literature*. Berlin: Springer, 2013.

Cărtărescu, Mircea. "Europe Has the Shape of My Brain." www.icr.ro/pagini /europe-has-the-shape-of-my-brain/en (accessed September 12, 2018).

Casanova, Pascale. *La Langue mondiale: Traduction et domination*. Paris: Éditions du Seuil, 2015.

———. *La République mondiale des lettres*. Paris: Éditions du Seuil, 1999. *The World Republic of Letters*. Tr. M. B. DeBevoise. Cambridge, MA: Harvard University Press, 2004.

———, ed. *Des littératures combatives: L'internationale des nationalismes littéraires*. Paris: Éditions Raisons d'agir, 2011.

Caws, Mary Ann, and Christopher Prendergast, eds. *The HarperCollins World Reader*. New York: HarperCollins, 1994.

Chakrabarty, Dipesh. *Provincializing Europe: Postcolonial Thought and Historical Difference*. Princeton: Princeton University Press, 2007.

Cheah, Pheng. *What Is a World? On Postcolonial Literature as World Literature*. Durham, NC: Duke University Press, 2016.

Ch'ien, Evelyn Nien-Ming. *Weird English*. Cambridge, MA: Harvard University Press, 2004.

Chou, Min-chih. *Hu Shih and Intellectual Choice in Modern China*. Ann Arbor: University of Michigan Press, 1984.

Chow, Rey. "In the Name of Comparative Literature." In Bernheimer, *Comparative Literature in the Age of Multiculturalism*, 107–16.

Clendinnen, Inga. *Aztecs: An Interpretation*. Cambridge and New York: Cambridge University Press, 1991.

Coletti, Vittorio. *Romanzo mondo: La letteratura nel villaggio globale*. Bologna: Il mulino, 2011.

Corneliussen, Hilde G., and Jill Walker Rettberg, eds. *Digital Culture, Play, and Identity: A "World of Warcraft" Reader*. Cambridge, MA: MIT Press, 2008.

Correira dos Santos, Carolina. "Brazilian Literary Theory's Challenge before the Non-human: Three Encounters and an Epilogue." In May Hawas, ed., *The Routledge Companion to World Literature and World History*, 334–47. Abingdon and New York: Routledge, 2018.

Coste, Didier. "Votum Mortis." *Fabula: La recherche en littérature*. www.fabula.org /cr/449.php (accessed August 24, 2018).

Croce, Benedetto. *L'Estetica come scienza dell'espressione e linguistica generale* (1902). *Aesthetic as Science of Expression and General Linguistic*. Tr. Douglas Ainslie. London: Vision Press, 1953.

Culler, Jonathan. "Comparability." *World Literature Today* 69.2 (1995): 268–70.

Culler, Jonathan, and Pheng Cheah, eds. *Grounds of Comparison: Around the Work of Benedict Anderson*. London and New York: Routledge, 2003.

Dabashi, Hamid. *The Shahnameh: The Persian Epic as World Literature*. New York: Columbia University Press, 2019.

Damrosch, David. "Contextualizing Arabic Literature: A Response to Omar Khalifah's 'Anthologizing Arabic Literature.'" *Journal of World Literature* 2.4 (2017): 527–34.

———. *The Buried Book: The Loss and Rediscovery of the Great Epic of Gilgamesh*. New York: Henry Holt, 2006.

———. *How to Read World Literature*. 2nd ed. Oxford: Blackwell, 2017.

———. *What Is World Literature?* Princeton: Princeton University Press, 2003.

———, ed. *Teaching World Literature*. New York: Modern Language Association, 2009.

———, ed. *World Literature in Theory*. Oxford: Wiley Blackwell, 2014.

Damrosch, David, Natalie Melas, and Mbongiseni Buthelezi, eds. *The Princeton Sourcebook in Comparative Literature*. Princeton: Princeton University Press, 2009.

Damrosch, David, and Katharina Piechocki. "Spitzer's Rabelais." https://youtu.be /8vND65MF69Y (accessed August 1, 2019).

Damrosch, David, David L. Pike, et al., eds. *The Longman Anthology of World Literature*. 6 vols. 2nd ed. New York: Pearson, 2008.

Damrosch, David, and Gayatri Chakravorty Spivak. "Comparative Literature / World Literature: A Discussion." *Comparative Literature Studies* 48.4 (2011): 455–85.

Danly, Robert Lyons. *In the Shade of Spring Leaves: The Life of Higuchi Ichiyō, with Nine of Her Best Stories*. Rev. ed. New York: W. W. Norton, 1992.

Dante Alighieri. *Dante's Inferno*. Tr. Henry Wadsworth Longfellow. Introduction by Jonathan Knight. New York: Ballantine Books / Del Rey, 2010.

David, Jérôme. *Spectres de Goethe: Les métamorphoses de la 'littérature mondiale'*. Paris: Les Prairies ordinaires, 2011.

De Cristofaro, Francesco, et al. *Letterature comparate*. Rome: Carocci Editore, 2015.

Deleuze, Gilles, and Félix Guattari. *Mille plateaux: Capitalisme et schizophrénie 2*. Paris: Éditions de Minuit, 1980. *A Thousand Plateaus: Capitalism and Schizophrenia*. Tr. Brian Massumi. Minneapolis: University of Minnesota Press, 1987.

De Man, Paul. *Allegories of Reading: Figural Language in Rousseau, Nietzsche, Rilke, and Proust*. New Haven: Yale University Press, 1979.

———. "Criticism and Crisis." In *Blindness and Insight: Essays in the Rhetoric of Contemporary Criticism*, 3–19. Minneapolis: University of Minnesota Press, 1971.

———. "Reading History." Introduction to *Toward an Aesthetic of Reception*, by Hans Robert Jauss. Repr. in *The Resistance to Theory*, 54–72.

———. *The Resistance to Theory*. Minneapolis: University of Minnesota Press, 1986.

Denecke, Wiebke. *Classical World Literatures: Sino-Japanese and Greco-Roman Comparisons*. Oxford: Oxford University Press, 2013.

———. *The Dynamics of Master's Literature: Early Chinese Thought from Confucius to Han Feizi*. Cambridge, MA: Harvard University Press, 2011.

Dening, Walter. "Japanese Modern Literature." In E. Delmar Morgan, ed., *Transactions of the 9th International Congress of Orientalists (Held in London, 5th to 12th September 1892)*, 2:642–67. London: International Congress of Orientalists, 1893.

Denton, Kirk A. "Lu Xun Biography." *MCLC Resource Center*, 2002. http://u.osu.edu/mclc/online-series/lu-xun (accessed December 17, 2018).

Department of Education. "The History of Title VI and Fulbright-Hays: An Impressive International Timeline." www2.ed.gov/about/offices/list/ope/iegps/history.html (accessed February 16, 2018).

Derrida, Jacques. *De la grammatologie*. Paris: Éditions de Minuit, 1967. *Of Grammatology*. Tr. Gayatri Chakravorty Spivak. Rev. ed. Baltimore: Johns Hopkins University Press, 2016.

———. *La Carte postale: De Socrate à Freud et au-delà*. Paris: Flammarion, 1980. *The Post Card: From Socrates to Freud and Beyond*. Tr. Alan Bass. Chicago: University of Chicago Press, 1987.

———. "La Différance." In *Marges de la philosophie*, 1–29. Paris: Éditions de Minuit, 1972. "Différance." In *Margins of Philosophy*, 1–27. Tr. Alan Bass. Chicago: University of Chicago Press, 1982.

Detienne, Marcel. *Comparer l'incomparable*. Rev. ed. Paris: Points, 2009. *Comparing the Incomparable*. Tr. Janet Lloyd. Stanford: Stanford University Press, 2008.

Détrie, Muriel. "Connaissons-nous Étiemble (né en 1909)?" *Revue de Littérature Comparée* 74.3 (2000): 413–25.

De Vries, Hent. "Director's Welcome." http://sct.cornell.edu/about/directors-welcome (accessed September 20, 2018).

D'haen, Theo. "Dutch Interbellum Poetry and/as World Literature." In D'haen, ed., *Dutch and Flemish Literature as World Literature*, 218–29. New York: Bloomsbury Academic, 2019.

———. "J. J. Slauerhoff, Dutch Literature, and World Literature." In José Luis Jobim, ed., *Literature e cultura: do nacional ao transnacional*, 143–57. Rio de Janeiro: UERJ, 2013.

———. *The Routledge Concise History of World Literature*. Abingdon and New York: Routledge, 2011.

D'haen, Theo, David Damrosch, and Djelal Kadir, eds. *The Routledge Companion to World Literature*. Abingdon and New York: Routledge, 2012.

D'haen, Theo, César Domínguez, and Mads Rosendahl Thomsen, eds. *World Literature: A Reader*. Abingdon and New York: Routledge, 2012.

Domínguez, César, Haun Saussy, and Dario Villanueva. *Introducing Comparative Literature: New Trends and Applications*. Abingdon and New York: Routledge, 2015.

Douglas, Mary. *How Institutions Think*. Syracuse, NY: Syracuse University Press, 1986.

Doyle, Arthur Conan. "The Adventure of the Sussex Vampire" (1924). www.dfw
-sherlock.org/uploads/3/7/3/8/37380505/1924_january_the_adventure_of
_the_sussex_vampire.pdf (accessed August 16, 2018).

Ďurišin, Dionýz. *Čo je svetová literatura?* Bratislava: Obzor, 1992.

———. *Sources and Systematics of Comparative Literature.* Tr. Peter Tkáč. Bratislava: Univerzita Komenského, 1984.

———. *Theory of Interliterary Process.* Tr. Jessie Kocmanová and Zdenek Pištek. Bratislava: Veda, 1989.

———. *Theory of Literary Comparatistics.* Tr. Jessie Kocmanová. Bratislava: Veda, 1984.

———. "World Literature as a Target Literary-Historical Category." *Slovak Review* 2.1 (1993): 7–15. Corrected repr. in D'haen et al., *World Literature: A Reader,* 150–59.

Durrans, Stéphanie. "The Translation in the Closet: Marguerite Yourcenar and Willa Cather." *Willa Cather Newsletter and Review* 50.2 (2015): 50–55.

Eagleton, Terry. *Literary Theory: An Introduction.* Minneapolis: University of Minnesota Press, 1983.

Eco, Umberto. *Il nome della rosa.* Bologna: Bompiani, 1980. *The Name of the Rose.* Tr. William Weaver. New York: Harcourt, 1983.

———. *Six Walks in the Fictional Woods.* Cambridge, MA: Harvard University Press, 1994.

Edelstein, Ludwig. Review of *Mimesis,* by Erich Auerbach. *Modern Language Notes* 65.6 (1950): 426–31.

Edmond, Jacob. *A Common Strangeness: Contemporary Poetry, Cross-cultural Encounter, Comparative Literature.* New York: Fordham University Press, 2012.

Egenfeldt-Nielsen, Simon, Jonas Heide Smith, and Susana Pajares Tosca. *Understanding Video Games: The Essential Introduction.* Abingdon and London: Routledge, 2008.

Emmerich, Karen. *Literary Translation and the Making of Originals.* New York: Bloomsbury Academic, 2017.

Emmerich, Michael. *The Tale of Genji: Translation, Canonization, and World Literature.* New York: Columbia University Press, 2013.

Enzensberger, Hans Magnus. "The World Language of Modern Poetry." In Michael E. Roloff, ed., *The Consciousness Industry: On Literature, Politics, and the Media,* 42–61. New York: Seabury, 1974.

Étiemble, René. *Comment lire un roman japonais (Le Kyôto de Kawabata).* Paris: Eibel-Fanlac, 1980.

———. *Comparaison n'est pas raison: La crise de la littérature comparée.* Paris: Gallimard, 1963. Repr. in *Ouverture(s) sur un comparatisme planétaire,* 59–146. *The Crisis in Comparative Literature.* Tr. Herbert Weisinger and Georges Joyaux. East Lansing: Michigan State University Press, 1966.

———. *Lignes d'une vie: Naissance à la littérature ou Le meurtre du père.* Paris: Arléa, 1988.

———. *Ouverture(s) sur un comparatisme planétaire.* Paris: Christian Bourgois, 1988.

———. *Parlez-vous franglais?* Paris: NRF/Gallimard, 1964.

————, et al. *Le Mythe d'Étiemble: Hommages, études et recherches inédits*. Paris: Didier Érudition, 1979.

Ette, Ottmar. *Der Fall Jauss: Wege des Verstehens in eine Zukunft der Philologie*. Berlin: Kulturverlag Kadmos, 2016.

Fang, Weigui, ed. *Tensions in World Literature: Between the Local and the Universal*. Singapore: Palgrave Macmillan, 2018.

Fassel, Horst, ed. *Acta Comparationis Litterarum Universarum, Jahrgang 1 (1877)*. Cluj-Napoca: Institutul German al Universității Babeș-Bolyai, 2002.

————. *Hugo Meltzl und die Anfänge der Komparatistik*. Stuttgart: Steiner, 2005.

Felski, Rita, and Susan Stanford Friedman, eds. *Comparison: Theories, Approaches, Uses*. Baltimore: Johns Hopkins University Press, 2013.

Ferris, David. "Indiscipline." In Saussy, ed., *Comparative Literature in an Age of Globalization*, 78–99.

Foster, John Burt, Jr. *Transnational Tolstoy: Between the West and the World*. New York: Bloomsbury Academic, 2013.

Friederich, Werner. "Ferdinand Baldensperger." *Yearbook of Comparative and General Literature* 11 (1962): 41–44.

————. "On the Integrity of Our Planning." In Haskell Block, ed., *The Teaching of World Literature*, 9–22. Chapel Hill: University of North Carolina Press, 1960.

Friedman, Susan Stanford. *Planetary Modernisms: Provocations on Modernity across Time*. New York: Columbia University Press, 2015.

Frye, Northrop. *Anatomy of Criticism: Four Essays*. Princeton: Princeton University Press, 1957.

————. *The Educated Imagination*. The Massey Lectures, Second Series. Toronto: Canadian Broadcasting Corporation, 1963.

Furst, Desider, and Lilian R. Furst. *Home Is Somewhere Else: Autobiography in Two Voices*. Albany: State University of New York Press, 1994. Lilian R. Furst und Desider Furst. *Daheim ist anderswo: Ein jüdisches Schicksal, erinnert von Vater und Tochter*. Frankfurt: Campus Verlag, 2009.

Furst, Lilian R. "Freud and Vienna." *Virginia Quarterly Review* 77.1 (2001): 49–62.

————. *Random Destinations: Escaping the Holocaust and Starting Life Anew*. New York: Palgrave Macmillan, 2005.

————. *Romanticism in Perspective: A Comparative Study of Aspects of the Romantic Movement in England, France and Germany*. London: Macmillan, 1969.

Galadewos. *The Life and Struggles of Our Mother Wallata Petros: A Seventeenth-century African Biography of an Ethiopian Woman*. Ed. and tr. Wendy Laura Belcher and Michael Kleiner. Princeton: Princeton University Press, 2015.

Gallagher, Susan VanZanten. "Contingencies and Intersections: The Formation of Pedagogical Canons." *Pedagogy* 1.1 (2001): 53–67.

Ganguly, Debjani. *This Thing Called a World: The Contemporary Novel as Global Form*. Durham, NC: Duke University Press, 2016.

————, ed. *The Cambridge History of World Literature*. 2 vols. Cambridge: Cambridge University Press, 2020.

García Márquez, Gabriel. *Cien años de soledad*. Buenos Aires: Editorial Sudamericana, 1967. *One Hundred Years of Solitude*. Tr. Gregory Rabassa. New York: Harper and Row, 1970.

———. "The Solitude of Latin America." Nobel Prize lecture, 1982. www .nobelprize.org/prizes/literature/1982/marquez/lecture (accessed September 5, 2018).

García Márquez, Gabriel, and Peter H. Stone. "The Art of Fiction No. 69." *Paris Review* 82 (1981). www.theparisreview.org/interviews/3196/gabriel-garcia -marquez-the-art-of-fiction-no-69-gabriel-garcia-marquez (accessed August 24, 2018).

Genette, Gérard. *Figures I–III*. Paris: Éditions du Seuil, 1966, 1969, 1972. *Figures of Literary Discourse*. Tr. A. Sheridan. New York: Columbia University Press, 1981. *Narrative Discourse: An Essay in Method*. Tr. Jane E. Lewin. Ithaca, NY: Cornell University Press, 1983.

Gervinus, Georg Gottfried. *Geschichte der poetischen National-Literatur der Deutschen*. 5 vols. Leipzig: Engelmann, 1835–42.

GoGwilt, Christopher. *The Passage of Literature: Genealogies of Modernism in Conrad, Rhys, and Pramoedya*. Oxford: Oxford University Press, 2010.

Gossman, Lionel, and Mihai I. Spariosu, eds. *Building a Profession: Autobiographical Perspectives on the Beginnings of Comparative Literature in the United States*. Albany: State University of New York Press, 1994.

Graff, Gerald. *Professing Literature: An Institutional History*. Chicago: University of Chicago Press, 2007.

Green, Geoffrey. *Literary Criticism and the Structures of History: Erich Auerbach and Leo Spitzer*. Lincoln: University of Nebraska Press, 1983.

Greene, Roland. "Their Generation." In Bernheimer, *Comparative Literature in the Age of Multiculturalism*, 143–54.

Greene, Thomas M. "Versions of a Discipline." In Gossman and Spariosu, *Building a Profession*, 37–48.

———, et al. "The Greene Report, 1975: A Report on Standards." In Bernheimer, ed., *Comparative Literature in the Age of Multiculturalism*, 28–38.

Grimm, Jacob. *Geschichte der deutschen Sprache*. Leipzig: Weidmannsche Buchhandlung, 1848. 2 vols. Repr. Hildesheim: G. Olms, 1980.

Grimm, Petra, and Heinrich Badura. *Medien—Ethik—Gewalt*. Stuttgart: Steiner, 2011.

Guérard, Albert. "Comparative Literature?" *Yearbook of Comparative and General Literature* 7 (1958): 1–6.

———. *Preface to World Literature*. New York: Henry Holt, 1940.

Guillén, Claudio. *Entre lo uno y lo diverso: Introducción a la literatura comparada*. Barcelona: Editorial Crítica, 1985. *The Challenge of Comparative Literature*. Tr. Cola Franzen. Cambridge, MA: Harvard University Press, 1993.

Guillory, John. *Cultural Capital: The Problem of Literary Canon Formation*. Chicago: University of Chicago Press, 1993.

Gumbrecht, Hans Ulrich. "'Methode ist Erlebnis': Leo Spitzers Stil." *Vom Leben und Sterben der großen Romanisten: Karl Vossler, Ernst Robert Curtius, Leo Spitzer, Erich Auerbach, Werner Krauss*, 72–151. Munich: Carl Hanser Verlag, 2002.

Gupta, Suman. *Globalization and Literature*. Cambridge: Polity Press, 2009.

Ha-Levi, Judah. *The Kuzari = Kitab al-Khazari: An Argument for the Faith of Israel*. Tr. Hartwig Hirschfeld. New York: E. P. Dutton, 1905. Repr. New York:

Schocken, 1964. https://en.wikisource.org/wiki/Kitab_al_Khazari (accessed October 25, 2018).

Hamacher, Werner, and Neil H. Hertz, eds. *Responses: On Paul de Man's Wartime Journalism.* Lincoln: University of Nebraska Press, 1988.

Haneda Masashi. *Toward Creation of a New World History.* Tr. Noda Makito. Tokyo: Japan Publishing Industry for Culture, 2018.

Hartley, L. P. *The Go-Between.* New York: New York Review Books, 2002.

Hartman, Geoffrey. "Looking Back at Paul de Man." In Waters and Godzich, *Reading de Man Reading,* 3–24.

Hassan, Waïl S. "Arabic and the Paradigms of Comparison." In Heise, *Futures of Comparative Literature,* 187–94.

Hatcher, Anna Granville. *Reflexive Verbs: Latin, Old French, Modern French.* Baltimore: Johns Hopkins University Press, 1942.

Hausmann, Frank-Rutger. *Vom Strudel der Ereignisse verschlungen: Deutsche Romanistik im "Dritten Reich".* 2nd ed. Frankfurt am Main: Klostermann, 2008.

Hayot, Eric. *On Literary Worlds.* New York: Oxford University Press, 2012.

Hayot, Eric, and Rebecca Walkowitz, eds. *A New Vocabulary for Global Modernism.* New York: Columbia University Press, 2016.

Hayot, Eric, and Edward Wesp. "Reading Game/Text: EverQuest, Alienation, and Digital Communities." *Postmodern Culture* 14.2 (2004): 50–73.

Heise, Ursula. *Chronoschisms: Time, Narrative, and Postmodernism.* Cambridge and New York: Cambridge University Press, 1997.

———. *Imagining Extinction: The Cultural Meanings of Endangered Species.* Chicago: University of Chicago Press, 2016.

———. *Sense of Place and Sense of Planet: The Environmental Imagination of the Global.* New York and London: Oxford University Press, 2008.

———, et al., eds. *Futures of Comparative Literature: ACLA State of the Discipline Report.* London and New York: Routledge, 2017.

Helgesson, Stefan. "'Literature,' Theory from the South, and the Case of the São Paulo School." *Cambridge Journal of Postcolonial Literary Inquiry* 5.2 (2018): 141–57.

Helgesson, Stefan, and Pieter Vermeulen, eds. *Institutions of World Literature: Writing, Translation, Markets.* London and New York: Routledge, 2016.

Herder, Johann Gottfried. *Briefe zu Beförderung der Humanität.* Ed. Hans Dietrich Irmscher. *Werke,* ed. Martin Bollacher et al., vol 7. Frankfurt am Main: Deutscher Klassiker Verlag, 1991.

———. *Briefe Gesamtausgabe 1763–1803.* Ed. Karl-Heinz Hahn et al. 18 vols. Weimar: Böhlau, 1977–2016.

———. "Shakespeare." In Gregory Moore, ed., *Selected Writings on Aesthetics,* 291–307. Princeton: Princeton University Press, 2006.

———. *Volkslieder Übertragungen Dichtungen.* Ed. Ulrich Gaier. *Werke,* ed. Martin Bollacher et al., vol 3. Frankfurt am Main: Deutscher Klassiker Verlag, 1990.

Hess-Lüttich, Ernest W. B. "Netzliteratur—ein neues Genre?" In Michael Stolz, Lucas Marco Gisi, and Jan Hoop, eds., *Literatur und Literaturwissenschaft auf dem Weg zu den neuen Medien: Eine Standortbestimmung,* 225–43. Zurich: Germanistik.ch, 2007.

Higonnet, Margaret. "Introduction." In Higonnet, ed., *Borderwork: Feminist Engagements with Comparative Literature*, 1–16. Ithaca, NY: Cornell University Press, 2018.

Hill, Geoffrey. *Selected Poems*. New Haven: Yale University Press, 2010.

Hinojosa, Christopher. "Unheralded Might: J. R. R. Tolkien's One Ring and the Gift of Power." PhD diss., University of Louisiana at Lafayette, 2013.

Hitchcock, Peter. *The Long Space: Transnationalism and Postcolonial Form*. Stanford: Stanford University Press, 2010.

Horkheimer, Max, and Theodor W. Adorno. *Dialectic of Enlightenment*. Tr. Edmund Jephcott. Stanford: Stanford University Press, 2007.

Howard, Joan E. *We Met in Paris: Grace Frick and Her Life with Marguerite Yourcenar*. Columbia: University of Missouri Press, 2018.

Huggan, Graham. "The Trouble with World Literature." In Ali Behdad and Dominic Thomas, eds., *A Companion to Comparative Literature*, 490–506. Malden, MA: Wiley-Blackwell, 2011.

Hu Shih. *An Autobiographical Account at Forty and "Reminiscences of Dr. Hu Shih."* In Li Tu-ning, ed., *Two Self-portraits: Liang Chi-ch'ao and Hu Shih*, 32–263. New York: Outer Sky Press, 1992.

Ikezawa Natsuki and Yuichi Kinoshita. "Conversation: Facing the Classics—Literature and Theater." https://dento.jfac.jp/en/conversation06112016/2 (accessed September 10, 2018).

Iknopeiston. "As Flies to Wanton Boys." www.fanfiction.net/s/2637122/1 (accessed July 20, 2018).

Ingalls, Daniel H. H., Jeffrey Moussaieff Masson, and M. V. Patwardhan, eds. and tr. *The Dhvanyaloka of Anandavardhana with the Locana of Abhinavagupta*. Harvard Oriental Series 49. Cambridge, MA: Harvard University Press, 1990.

Jameson, Fredric. "Third-World Literature in the Era of Multinational Capitalism." *Social Text* 15 (1986): 65–88.

Jansen, Monica, and Clemens Arts. "L'approdo americano: un'altra storia, un altro esilio." In Luciano Curreri, ed., *L'Europa vista da Istanbul: Mimesis (1946) e la ricostruzione intellettuale di Erich Auerbach*, 71–82. Bologna: Luca Sossella, 2014.

Jaques, Zoe, ed. *Children's Literature and the Posthuman: Animal, Environment, Cyborg*. New York: Routledge, 2015.

Jauss, Hans Robert. "Response to Paul de Man." In Waters and Godzich, eds., *Reading de Man Reading*, 202–8.

Jay, Paul. *Global Matters: The Transnational Turn in Literary Studies*. Ithaca, NY: Cornell University Press, 2010.

Jencks, Christopher, and David Riesman. *The Academic Revolution*. 3rd ed. New York: Doubleday, 1977.

Jones, William. "The Third Anniversary Discourse. Delivered 2 February, 1786, by the President, at the Asiatick Society of Bengal." www.unifi.it/testi/700/jones/Jones_Discourse_3.html (accessed September 1, 2018).

Joyce, James. *Finnegans Wake*. New York: Viking, 1959.

———. *Letters*. Ed. Richard Ellmann. 2 vols. New York: Viking, 1966.

———. *Ulysses*. New York: Vintage, 1961.

"Jože Plečnik." http://erasmuskrize.splet.arnes.si/files/2015/10/PLECNIK-ppt-ang
.pdf (accessed September 15, 2018).

Juul, Jesper. *Half-Real: Video Games between Real Rules and Fictional Worlds*. Cambridge, MA: MIT Press, 2005.

Juvan, Marko. "Peripherocentrism: Geopolitics of Comparative Literatures between Ethnocentrism and Cosmopolitanism." In Jean Bessière and Judith Maar, eds., *Histoire de la littérature et jeux d'échange entre centres et peripheries: Les identités relatives des littératures*, 53–66. Paris: Harmattan, 2010.

Kadare, Ismail. *Essays on World Literature: Aeschylus, Dante, Shakespeare*. Tr. Ani Kokobobo. New York: Restless Books, 2018.

Kadir, Djelal. "Auerbach's Scar." In *Memos from the Besieged City: Lifelines for Cultural Sustainability*, 19–40. Stanford: Stanford University Press, 2011.

———. "To World, to Globalize: Comparative Literature's Crossroads." *Comparative Literature Studies* 41.1 (2004): 1–9.

Kafka, Franz. *The Diaries of Franz Kafka, 1910–1923*. Tr. Joseph Kresch and Martin Greenburg. New York: Schocken, 1976.

Kaplan, Alice. *French Lessons: A Memoir*. Chicago: University of Chicago Press, 1993.

Karátson, André. "Étiemble et les langues." In Étiemble et al., *Le Mythe d'Étiemble*, 123–32.

Katsma, Holst. "Loudness in the Novel." https://litlab.stanford.edu/LiteraryLab Pamphlet7.pdf (accessed September 7, 2018).

Key, Alexander. "Kavya: Prospects for a Comparative Poetics." *Comparative Studies of South Asia, Africa and the Middle East* 38.1 (2018): 163–70.

Khalifah, Omar. "Anthologizing Arabic Literature." *Journal of World Literature* 2.4 (2017): 512–26.

Khan, Muhammad Muhsin, ed. and tr. *Interpretation of the Meanings of the Noble Qur'an in the English Language*. Riyadh: Darrussalam, 2011.

Kiepas, Andrzej. "Medien in der Kultur der realen Virtualität—zwischen Freiheit und Unterdrückung." In Grimm and Badura, *Medien—Ethik—Gewalt*, 249–56.

Kilito, Abdelfattah. *Je parle toutes les langues, mais en arabe*. Arles: Sindbad/Actes Sud, 2013.

———. *La Langue d'Adam*. Casablanca: Éditions Toubkai, 1996. *The Tongue of Adam*. Tr. Robyn Creswell. New York: New Directions, 2016.

———. *Lan tatakalama lughati*. Beirut: Dar al-tali'a, 2002. *Thou Shalt Not Speak My Language*. Tr. Waïl S. Hassan. Syracuse, NY: Syracuse University Press, 2008.

Kim, Edward, et al. "EK Theater: Niobe 2010." www.youtube.com/watch?v= pQiVnRcPXe4 (accessed April 25, 2019).

Kim Jaeyong. "From Eurocentric World Literature to Global World Literature." *Journal of World Literature* 1.1 (2016): 63–67.

Kimura, Rei. *A Note from Ichiyō*. Chandler, AZ: Booksmango, 2017.

Klawitter, Arne. "Ideofonografie und transkulturelle Homofonie bei Yoko Tawada." *Arcadia* 50.2 (2015): 328–42.

Klemperer, Victor. *LTI—Notizbuch eines Philologen* (1947). 3rd ed. Leipzig: Reklam, 1975. *The Language of the Third Reich: LTI: Lingua Tertii Imperii*. Tr. Martin Brady. New York: Bloomsbury, 2013.

Koch, Max. "Zur Einführung." *Zeitschrift für vergleichende Litteraturgeschichte* 1 (1877): 1–12. "Introduction." Tr. Hans-Joachim Schulz and Phillip H. Rhein. In Schulz and Rhein, eds., *Comparative Literature*, 63–77.

Koelb, Clayton, and Susan Noakes, eds. *The Comparative Perspective on Literature: Approaches to Theory and Practice*. Ithaca: Cornell University Press, 1988.

Konuk, Kader. *East-West Mimesis: Auerbach in Turkey*. Stanford: Stanford University Press, 2010.

Krishnaswamy, Revathi. "Toward World Literary Knowledges: Theory in the Age of Globalization." *Comparative Literature* 62.4 (2010): 399–419.

Kristal, Efraín. "Considering Coldly . . . A Response to Franco Moretti." *New Left Review* 15 (May–June 2002): 61–74.

Kundera, Milan. "Die Weltliteratur." In *The Curtain: An Essay in Seven Parts*, 31–56. Tr. Linda Asher. New York: HarperCollins, 2007.

Lagerlöf, Selma. *Nils Holgerssons underbara resa genom Sverige*. Stockholm: Albert Bonniers Förlag, 1998. *The Wonderful Adventures of Nils Holgersson*. Tr. Paul Norlén. London: Penguin, 2018.

Lamping, Dieter. *Die Idee der Weltliteratur: Ein Konzept Goethes und seine Karriere*. Stuttgart: Kröner, 2010.

———. *Internationale Literatur*. Göttingen: Vandenhoeck und Ruprecht, 2013.

———, ed. *Meilensteine der Weltliteratur: Von der Aufklärung bis in die Gegenwart*. Stuttgart: Kröner, 2015.

Las Casas, Bartolomé de. *Brevíssima relación de la destrucción de las Indias* (1552). *The Tears of the Indians: being an historical and true account [. . .] written in Spanish by Casaus, an eye-witness of those things; and made English* by J. P. Tr. John Phillips. London: Printed by J. C. for Nathaniel Brook, 1656.

Lawall, Sarah. "The West and the Rest." In Damrosch, ed., *Teaching World Literature*, 17–33.

Lazarus, Neil. "The Politics of Postcolonial Modernism." In *The Postcolonial Unconscious*, 21–88. Cambridge: Cambridge University Press, 2011.

Leerssen, Joep. "Comparing What, Precisely? H. M. Posnett and the Conceptual History of Comparative Literature." *Comparative Critical Studies* 12.2 (2015): 197–212.

———. *Komparatistik in Großbrittanien 1800–1950*. Bonn: Bouvier, 1984.

———. "Some Notes on Hutcheson Macaulay Posnett (1855–1927)." In Maureen O'Connor, ed., *Back to the Future of Irish Studies: Festschrift for Tadhg Foley*, 111–19. Dublin: Peter Lang, 2010.

Lennon, Brian. *In Babel's Shadow: Multilingual Literatures, Monolingual States*. Minneapolis: University of Minnesota Press, 2010.

Lerer, Seth, ed. *Literary History and the Challenge of Philology: The Legacy of Erich Auerbach*. Stanford: Stanford University Press, 1996.

Lévi-Strauss, Claude. *Tristes Tropiques*. Paris: Pocket, 2001. *Tristes Tropiques*. Tr. John and Doreen Weightman. New York: Penguin, 1981.

Levin, Harry. "Comparing the Literature." *Yearbook of Comparative and General Literature* 17 (1968): 5–16.

———. *The Implications of Literary Criticism*. Ed. Jonathan Hart. Paris: Honoré Champion, 2011.

———. *James Joyce: A Critical Introduction.* New York: New Directions, 1941.

———. "Toward World Literature." *Tamkang Review* 6.2/7.1 (1975–76): 21–30.

———, et al. "The Levin Report, 1965: Report on Professional Standards." In Bernheimer, ed., *Comparative Literature in the Age of Multiculturalism,* 21–27.

Levine, Suzanne Jill, and Katie Lateef-Jan, eds. *Untranslatability Goes Global: The Translator's Dilemma.* London: Routledge, 2017.

Levy, Lital. *Poetic Trespass: Writing between Hebrew and Arabic in Israel/Palestine.* Princeton: Princeton University Press, 2014.

Lin Yutang. *Between Tears and Laughter.* New York: John Day, 1943.

———. *Confucius Saw Nancy, and Essays about Nothing.* Shanghai: Commercial Press, 1936.

———. *From Pagan to Christian.* Cleveland: World Publishing, 1959.

———. *Memoirs of an Octogenarian.* Taipei: Mei Ya, 1975.

———. *My Country and My People.* New York: John Day, 1935.

———. *The Pleasures of a Nonconformist.* Cleveland: World Publishing, 1962.

Lispector, Clarice. *Laços de família.* Rio de Janeiro: Rocco, 1998. *Family Ties.* In *Complete Stories,* 103–231. Tr. Katrina Dodson. New York: New Directions, 2018.

———. *Perto do coração selvagem.* Rio de Janeiro: Rocco, 1998. *Near to the Wild Heart: A Novel.* Tr. Giovanni Pontiero. New York: New Directions, 1990.

Littau, Karen. "Two Ages of World Literature." In Bassnett, ed., *Translation and World Literature,* 159–74.

Llovet, Jordi, Robert Caner, Nora Catelli, Antoni Martí Monterde, and David Viñas Piquer. *Teoría literaria y literatura comparada.* Barcelona: Ariel, 2005.

Löffler, Sigrid. *Die neue Weltliteratur und ihre großen Erzähler.* Munich: C. H. Beck, 2014.

Lowth, Robert. *De sacra poesi Hebraeorum.* Oxford: Clarendon Press, 1753. *Lectures on the Sacred Poetry of the Hebrews.* Tr. G. Gregory (1787). Cambridge: Chadwyck-Healey, 1999.

Lukács, Georg. *Theory of the Novel: A Historico-Philosophical Essay on the Forms of Great Epic Literature.* Tr. Anna Bostock. Cambridge, MA: MIT Press, 1971.

Lyons, Patrick J. "The Giant Rat of Sumatra, Alive and Well." *New York Times,* December 17, 2007. https://thelede.blogs.nytimes.com/2007/12/17/the-giant -rat-of-sumatra-alive-and-well (accessed August 16, 2018).

Mack, Maynard, and Sarah Lawall, eds. *The Norton Anthology of World Masterpieces: Expanded Edition.* New York: W. W. Norton, 1995.

Magliola, Robert. *Derrida on the Mend: Buddhist Differentialism.* West Lafayette, IN: Purdue University Press, 1984.

———. "Sexual Rogations, Mystical Abrogations: Some Données of Buddhist Tantra and the Catholic Renaissance." In Koelb and Noakes, *The Comparative Perspective on Literature,* 195–212.

Mallette, Karla. "Sanskrit Snapshots." *Comparative Studies of South Asia, Africa and the Middle East* 38.1 (2018): 127–35.

Mani, B. Venkat. *Recoding World Literature: Libraries, Print Culture, and Germany's Pact with Books.* New York: Fordham University Press, 2016.

Márai, Sándor. *Casanova in Bolzano.* Tr. George Szirtes. New York: Knopf, 2004.

———. *Embers.* Tr. Carol Brown Janeway. New York: Knopf, 2001.

———. *Memoir of Hungary, 1944–1948.* Tr. Albert Tezla. Budapest: Corvina, 1996.

———. *Portraits of a Marriage.* Tr. George Szirtes. New York: Knopf, 2011.

Marling, William. *Gatekeepers: The Emergence of World Literature and the 1960s.* New York: Oxford University Press, 2016.

Marno, David. "The Monstrosity of Literature: Hugo Meltzl's World Literature and Its Legacies." In Karen-Margrethe Simonsen and Jakob Stougaard-Nielsen, eds., *World Literature and World Culture*, 37–50. Aarhus: Aarhus University Press, 2002.

Martí Monterde, Antoni. *Un somni europeu: Història intel·lectual de la Literatura Comparada.* València: Publicacions de la Universitat de València, 2011.

Martinez, Anne M. "Elvencentrism: The Green Medievalism of Tolkien's Elven Realms." In Karl Fulgelso, ed., *Ecomedievalism*, 31–42. Cambridge: Brewer, 2017.

Melas, Natalie. *All the Difference in the World: Postcoloniality and the Ends of Comparison.* Stanford: Stanford University Press, 2006.

Meltzl, Hugo. "An unsere Leser." *Acta Comparationis Litterarum Universarum* New Series 1.1 (1879): 18.

———. "Islaendisch-Sizilianische Volkstradition in Magyarischen Lichte." *Acta Comparationis Litterarum Universarum* New Series 1.3 (1879): 117–18.

———. "Vorläufige Aufgaben der vergleichenden Litteratur." *Acta Comparationis Litterarum Universarum* 1 (January 1877): 179–82, and 2 (October 1877): 307–15. "Present Tasks of Comparative Literature." Tr. Hans-Joachim Schulz. In Damrosch et al., *The Princeton Sourcebook in Comparative Literature*, 41–49. Repr. from Schulz and Rhein, eds., *Comparative Literature*, 53–62.

Menand, Louis. "The de Man Case." *New Yorker* 90.5 (2014): 87–93.

Meyer, Richard. "Über den Refrain." *Zeitschrift für vergleichende Litteraturgeschichte* 1 (1877): 34–47.

Miller, D. A. *Bringing Out Roland Barthes.* Berkeley: University of California Press, 1992.

Milton, John. *Paradise Lost.* Ed. Merritt Y. Hughes. Indianapolis: Odyssey Press, 1962.

Miner, Earl. *Comparative Poetics: An Intercultural Essay on Theories of Literature.* Princeton: Princeton University Press, 1990.

Moberg, Bergur. "The Ultraminor to Be or Not to Be: Deprivation and Compensation Strategies in Faroese Literature." *Journal of World Literature* 2.2 (2017): 196–216.

Moberg, Bergur, and David Damrosch. "Defining the Ultraminor." *Journal of World Literature* 2.2 (2017): 133–37.

Moretti, Franco. "Conjectures on World Literature" and "More Conjectures." *New Left Review* n.s. 1 (2000): 54–68, and 20 (2003): 73–81. Repr. in *Distant Reading*, 43–62, 107–20.

———. *Distant Reading.* London: Verso, 2013.

———. "Evolution, World Systems, *Weltliteratur*." In Gunilla Lindberg-Wada, ed., *Studying Transcultural Literary History*, 113–21. Berlin: de Gruyter, 2006. Repr. in *Distant Reading*, 121–35.

———. *Modern Epic: The World System from Goethe to García Márquez*. London: Verso, 1996.

Morrison, Toni. *Beloved*. New York: Knopf, 1987.

Moser, Christian, and Linda Simonis, eds. *Figuren des Globalen: Weltbezug und Welterzeugung in Literatur, Kunst und Medien*. Göttingen: V&R Unipress, 2014.

Mo Yan. "Storytellers." www.nobelprize.org/prizes/literature/2012/yan/25452 -mo-yan-nobel-lecture-2012 (accessed August 24, 2018).

Mufti, Aamir R. *Forget English! Orientalisms and World Literature*. Cambridge, MA: Harvard University Press, 2017.

Mullaney, Thomas S. *The Chinese Typewriter*. Cambridge, MA: MIT Press, 2017.

Murasaki Shikibu. *The Tale of Genji*. Tr. Royall Tyler. New York: Viking Penguin, 2001.

Murugan, Perumal. *One Part Woman*. Tr. Aniruddhan Vasudevan. Delhi: Penguin India, 2013. London: Penguin, 2014. New York: Grove, 2018.

Nathan, Leonard. *The Transport of Love: The Meghadūta of Kālidāsa*. Berkeley: University of California Press, 1976.

Nilsson, Louise, David Damrosch, and Theo D'haen, eds. *Crime Fiction as World Literature*. New York: Bloomsbury Academic, 2017.

Nooteboom, Cees. *Tumbas: Graven van dichters en denkers*. Amsterdam: Atlas, 2007.

Norris, Christopher. *Paul de Man: Deconstruction and the Critique of Aesthetic Ideology*. Abingdon and New York: Routledge, 1988.

Oe Kenzaburo. "Japan, the Ambiguous, and Myself." www.nobelprize.org/prizes /literature/1994/oe/lecture (accessed August 23, 2018).

Oesterley, Hermann. "Die Abenteuer des Guru Paramártan." *Zeitschrift für vergleichende Litteraturgeschichte* 1 (1877): 48–72.

Ovid. *The Poems of Exile: Tristia and the Black Sea Letters*. Ed. and tr. Peter Green. Berkeley: University of California Press, 2005.

Özbek, Yasemin. "Heimat im Exil: Alltagsleben am Bosporus in den Briefen von Traugott Fuchs und Rosemarie Heyd-Burkart." In Stauth and Birtek, eds., *Istanbul*, 159–90.

Palencia-Roth, Michael. "Contrastive Literature." *Journal for the Comparative Study of Civilizations* 2 (1997): 21–30.

Pamuk, Orhan. *The Naive and the Sentimental Novelist*. The 2009 Norton Lectures. Tr. Nazim Dikbaş. Cambridge, MA: Harvard University Press, 2010.

Parla, Jale. "The Object of Comparison." *Comparative Literature Studies* 41.1 (2004): 116–25.

Pavel, Thomas G. *Fictional Worlds*. Cambridge, MA: Harvard University Press, 1986.

Peyre, Henri. "Avant-propos." In A. G. Hatcher and K. L. Selig, eds., *Studia Philologica et Litteraria in Honorem L. Spitzer*, 7–9. Bern: Francke Verlag, 1958.

———. "A Glance at Comparative Literature in America." *Yearbook of Comparative and General Literature* 1 (1952): 1–8.

Phillips, Henry. *Volk-songs: Translated from the Acta Comparationis Litterarum Universarum*. Philadelphia: n.p., 1885.

Pizer, John. *The Idea of World Literature*. Baton Rouge: Louisiana State University Press, 2006.

Pollan, Michael. *In Defense of Food: An Eater's Manifesto*. New York: Penguin, 2009.

Pollock, Sheldon. "Comparison without Hegemony." In Hans Joas and Barbro Klein, eds., *The Benefit of Broad Horizons: Intellectual and Institutional Preconditions for a Global Social Science*, 185–204. Festschrift for Björn Wittrock. Leiden: Brill, 2010.

———. "Conundrums of Comparison." *Know: A Journal on the Formation of Knowledge* 1.2 (2017): 273–94.

———. "Small Philology and Large Philology." *Comparative Studies of South Asia, Africa and the Middle East* 38.1 (2018): 122–27.

———, ed. *A Rasa Reader: Classical Indian Aesthetics*. New York: Columbia University Press, 2016.

———, ed. *Literary Cultures in History: Reconstructions from South Asia*. Berkeley: University of California Press, 2003.

Pollock, Sheldon, Benjamin A. Elman, and Ku-ming Kevin Chang, eds. *World Philology*. Cambridge, MA: Harvard University Press, 2015.

Posnett, Hutcheson Macaulay. *Comparative Literature*. London: Kegan, Trench, 1886.

———. "The Science of Comparative Literature." *Contemporary Review* 79 (1901): 855–72.

Pramoj, Kukrit. *Four Reigns*. Tr. Tulachandra. Chiang Mai, Thailand: Silkworm Books, 1981.

———. *Many Lives*. Tr. Meredith Borthwick. Chiang Mai, Thailand: Silkworm Books, 1999.

Prešeren, France. "Zdravljica (A Toast)." www.vlada.si/en/about_slovenia/political_system/national_insignia/france_preseren_zdravljica_a_toast (accessed August 10, 2018).

Pressman, Jessica. "Electronic Literature as Comparative Literature." https://stateofthediscipline.acla.org/entry/electronic-literature-comparative-literature-0 (accessed January 14, 2019). Repr. in Heise, *Futures of Comparative Literature*, 248–57.

———. "The Strategy of Digital Modernism: Young-Hae Chang Heavy Industry's *Dakota*." *Modern Fiction Studies* 54.2 (2008): 302–26.

Pritchett, Frances W. *A Desertful of Roses: The Urdu Ghazals of Mirza Asadullah Khan "Ghalib."* www.columbia.edu/itc/mealac/pritchett/00ghalib (accessed June 5, 2018).

———. *A Garden of Kashmir: The Ghazals of Mir Muhammad Taqi Mir.* www.columbia.edu/itc/mealac/pritchett/00garden/index.html (accessed June 5, 2018).

Pritchett, Frances W. *Igbo Language and Literature: Resources for Study.* www.columbia.edu/itc/mealac/pritchett/00fwp/igbo_index.html (accessed June 6, 2018).

Puchner, Martin. *Poetry of the Revolution: Marx, Manifestos, and the Avant-Gardes*. Princeton: Princeton University Press, 2006.

———. *The Written World: The Power of Stories to Shape People, History, Civilization*. New York: Random House, 2017.

———, et al., eds. *The Norton Anthology of Western Literature*. 9th ed. 2 vols. New York: Norton, 2014.

———, et al., eds. *The Norton Anthology of World Literature*. 4th ed. 6 vols. New York: Norton 2018.

Qian, Suoqiao. *Liberal Cosmopolitan: Lin Yutang and Middling Chinese Modernity*. Leiden: Brill, 2011.

Quint, David. "Thomas M. Greene." http://archive.yalealumnimagazine.com/issues /2004_01/greene.html (accessed February 16, 2018).

Radhakrishnan, R. *Theory in an Uneven World*. Malden, MA: Blackwell, 2003.

———. "Why Compare?" In Felski and Friedman, eds., *Comparison*, 15–33.

Raffa, Guy. *Danteworlds*. http://danteworlds.laits.utexas.edu (accessed May 12, 2018).

Readings, Bill. *The University in Ruins*. Cambridge, MA: Harvard University Press, 1996.

Ricci, Ronit. *Islam Translated: Literature, Conversion, and the Arabic Cosmopolis of South and Southeast Asia*. Chicago: University of Chicago Press, 2011.

Richmond-Garza, Elizabeth. "Detecting Conspiracy: Boris Akunin's Dandiacal Detective, or a Century in Queer Profiles from London to Moscow." In Nilsson et al., eds., *Crime Fiction as World Literature*, 271–89.

Robbins, Bruce. "Prolegomena to a Cosmopolitanism in Deep Time." *Interventions* 18.2 (2016): 172–86.

Robbins, Bruce, and Paulo Lemos Horta, eds. *Cosmopolitanisms*. New York: New York University Press, 2017.

Rodowick, D. N. *Elegy for Theory*. Cambridge, MA: Harvard University Press, 2015.

Rosso, Stefano. "An Interview with Paul de Man." In de Man, *The Resistance to Theory*, 115–21.

Said, Edward W. *Beginnings: Intention and Method*. New York: Basic Books, 1975.

———. "Interview: Edward W. Said." *Diacritics* 6.3 (1976): 30–47.

———. *Joseph Conrad and the Fiction of Autobiography*. Cambridge, MA: Harvard University Press, 1966.

———. "News of the World." *Village Voice Literary Supplement* 68 (October 1988): 14.

———. "Opponents, Audiences, Constituencies, and Community." *Critical Inquiry* 9.1 (1982): 1–26.

———. *Orientalism*. New York: Vintage, 1978.

———. "Reflections on Recent American 'Left' Literary Criticism." *boundary 2* 8.1 (1979): 11–30. Repr. as "Reflections on American 'Left' Literary Criticism," in *The World, the Text, and the Critic*, 158–77.

———. "Secular Criticism." In *The World, the Text, and the Critic*, 1–30.

———. "Travelling Theory." *Raritan* 1.3 (1982): 41–67. Repr. in *The World, the Text, and the Critic*, 226–47.

———. "Travelling Theory Reconsidered." In Robert M. Polhemus and Roger B. Henkle, eds., *Critical Reconstructions: The Relationship of Fiction and Life*, 251–65. Stanford: Stanford University Press, 1994.

———. *The World, the Text, and the Critic*. Cambridge, MA: Harvard University Press, 1983.

Sauer, Elizabeth. "Toleration and Translation: The Case of Las Casas, Phillips, and Milton." *Philological Quarterly* 85.3–4 (2006): 271–91.

Saussy, Haun. "Axes of Comparison." In Felski and Friedman, eds., *Comparison*, 64–76.

————. "Exquisite Cadavers Stitched from Fresh Nightmares: Of Memes, Hives, and Selfish Genes." In *Comparative Literature in an Age of Globalization*, 3–24.

————, ed. *Comparative Literature in an Age of Globalization*. Baltimore: Johns Hopkins University Press, 2006.

Savigneau, Josyane. *Marguerite Yourcenar: Inventing a Life*. Tr. Joan E. Howard. Chicago: University of Chicago Press, 1993.

Schildgen, Brenda Deen, Zhou Gang, and Sander L. Gilman, eds. *Other Renaissances: A New Approach to World Literature*. New York: Palgrave Macmillan, 2006.

Schuessler, Jennifer. "Reading by the Numbers: When Big Data Meets Literature." *New York Times*, October 30, 2017. www.nytimes.com/2017/10/30/arts/franco-moretti-stanford-literary-lab-big-data.html (accessed September 7, 2018).

Schuessler, Jennifer, and Boryana Dzhambazova. "Bulgaria Says French Thinker Was a Secret Agent. She Calls It a 'Barefaced Lie.'" *New York Times*, April 1, 2018. www.nytimes.com/2018/04/01/arts/julia-kristeva-bulgaria-communist-spy.html (accessed April 12, 2018).

Schulz, Hans-Joachim, and Phillip H. Rhein, eds. *Comparative Literature: The Early Years; An Anthology of Essays*. Chapel Hill: University of North Carolina Press, 1973.

Schurr, Georgia Hooks. "Marguerite Yourcenar et le 'drame noir' américain." In Michèle Goslar, ed., *Marguerite Yourcenar et l'Amérique*, 27–57. Brussels: Centre International de Documentation Marguerite Yourcenar, 1998.

Schwarz, Roberto. *Um mestre na periferia do capitalismo: Machado de Assis*. São Paulo: Editora 34, 2000. *A Master on the Periphery of Capitalism: Machado de Assis*. Tr. John Gledson. Chapel Hill: Duke University Press, 2001.

————. *Misplaced Ideas: Essays on Brazilian Culture*. Tr. John Gledson. London: Verso, 1992.

Shakespeare, William. *King Lear*. Ed. Alfred Harbage. Baltimore: Penguin, 1969.

Shelley, Percy Bysshe. "A Defence of Poetry." *A Defence of Poetry and Other Essays*. www.gutenberg.org/files/5428/5428-h/5428-h.htm (accessed September 15, 2018).

Shih, Shu-mei. "Global Literature and the Technologies of Recognition." *PMLA* 119.1 (2004): 16–30.

Shirane, Haruo. *The Bridge of Dreams: A Poetics of "The Tale of Genji."* Stanford: Stanford University Press, 1988.

Shklovsky, Viktor. "Art as Technique." In Lee T. Lemon and Marion J. Reis, eds., *Russian Formalist Criticism: Four Essays*, 5–22. Lincoln: University of Nebraska Press, 1965.

Shulgi of Ur. "Šulgi B." Electronic Text Corpus of Sumerian Literature (ETCSL). http://etcsl.orinst.ox.ac.uk/cgi-bin/etcsl.cgi?text=t.2.4.2.02# (accessed October 24, 2018).

Siskind, Mariano. *Cosmopolitan Desires: Global Modernity and World Literature in Latin America*. Evanston, IL: Northwestern University Press, 2014.

Spitzer, Leo. *Essays in Historical Semantics*. New York: S. F. Vanni, 1948. Repr. New York: Russell & Russell, 1968.

————. *Essays on English and American Literature*. Princeton: Princeton University Press, 1962.

———. "The Formation of the American Humanist." *PMLA* 66.1 (1951): 39–48.

———. *Fremdwörterhatz und Fremdvölkerhaß: Eine Streitschrift gegen die Sprach-reinigung.* Vienna: Manzsche Hof-, Verlags- und Universitäts-Buchhandlung, 1918.

———. "Geistesgeschichte vs. History of Ideas as Applied to Hitlerism." *Journal of the History of Ideas* 5:2 (1944): 191–203.

———. *Linguistics and Literary History: Essays in Stylistics.* Princeton: Princeton University Press, 1948.

Spivak, Gayatri Chakravorty. *A Critique of Postcolonial Reason: Toward a History of the Vanishing Present.* Cambridge, MA: Harvard University Press, 1999.

———. *Death of a Discipline.* New York: Columbia University Press, 2003.

———. "'Draupadi' by Mahasveta Devi." *Critical Inquiry* 8.2 (1981): 381–402.

———. "Finding Feminist Readings: Dante-Yeats." In Ira Konigsberg, ed., *American Criticism in the Poststructuralist Age,* 42–65. Ann Arbor: University of Michigan Press, 1981.

———. "How Do We Write, Now?" *PMLA* 133.1 (2018): 166–70.

———. "Marginality in the Teaching Machine." In *Outside in the Teaching Machine,* 58–85. Abingdon and New York: Routledge, 1993.

———. "The Politics of Interpretations." *Critical Inquiry* 9.1 (1982): 259–78.

———. "Reading the World: Literary Studies in the 80s." *College English* 43.7 (1981): 671–79.

———. "Rethinking Comparativism." In Felski and Friedman, eds., *Comparison,* 253–70. Rev. version in *An Aesthetic Education in the Era of Globalization,* 467–83. Cambridge, MA: Harvard University Press, 2012.

Staël, Germaine de. *De la littérature: Considérée dans ses rapports avec les institutions sociales.* In *Oeuvres complètes* 1.2, *De la littérature et autres essais littéraires,* 67–388. Ed. Stéphanie Genand et al. Paris: Honoré Champion, 2013. Chapter 9, "Of the General Spirit of Modern Literature," tr. David Damrosch. In Damrosch et al., *The Princeton Sourcebook in Comparative Literature,* 10–16.

———. "Réflexions sur le suicide." In *Oeuvres complètes* 1.1, *Lettres sur Rousseau, De l'influence des passions, et autres essais moraux,* 339–95. Ed. Florence Lotterie. Paris: Honoré Champion, 2008.

———. *Ten Years of Exile.* Tr. Avriel H. Goldberger. Dekalb: Northern Illinois University Press, 2000.

Stauth, Georg, and Faruk Birtek, eds. *'Istanbul': Geistige Wanderungen aus der 'Welt in Scherben'.* Bielefeld: Transcript Verlag, 2007.

Steiner, George. *After Babel: Aspects of Language and Translation.* 3rd ed. Oxford: Oxford University Press, 1998.

Sterne, Laurence. *The Life and Opinions of Tristram Shandy, Gentleman.* New York: Boni and Liveright, 1960.

Strachey, Lytton. *Eminent Victorians.* Harmondsworth: Penguin, 1990.

Sturm-Trigonakis, Elke. *Global Playing in der Literatur: Ein Versuch über die neue Weltliteratur.* Würzburg: Königshausen & Neumann, 2007. *Comparative Cultural Studies and the New Weltliteratur.* Tr. Athanasia Margoni and Maria Kaisar. West Lafayette, IN: Purdue University Press, 2013.

Szabó, Levente T. "Negotiating World Literature in the First International Journal of Comparative Literary Studies: The Albanian Case." *Studia Universitatis Babes-Bolyai—Philologia* 2 (2012): 33–51.

Szentivanyi, Christina. "'Anarchie im Mundbereich': Übersetzungen in Yoko Tawadas *Überseezungen*." In Vittoria Borsò and Reinhold Goerling, eds., *Kulturelle Topographien*, 347–60. Stuttgart: Metzler, 2004.

Tageldin, Shaden. "Untranslatability." https://stateofthediscipline.acla.org/entry /untranslatability (accessed September 15, 2018). Repr. in Heise, ed., *Futures of Comparative Literature*, 234–35.

Tanoukhi, Nirvana. "The Scale of World Literature." *New Literary History* 39.3 (2008): 599–617.

Tawada, Yoko. *Akzentfrei*. Tübingen: Konkursbuch Verlag Claudia Gehrke, 2016.

———. *Überseezungen: Literarische Essays*. Tübingen: Konkursbuch Verlag Claudia Gehrke, 2002.

Thomsen, Mads Rosendahl. *Mapping World Literature: International Canonization and Transnational Literatures*. London: Continuum, 2008.

Thornber, Karen Laura. *Ecoambiguity: Environmental Crises and East Asian Literatures*. Ann Arbor: University of Michigan Press, 2012.

———. *Empire of Texts in Motion: Chinese, Korean, and Taiwanese Transculturations of Japanese Literature*. Cambridge, MA: Harvard University Asia Center, 2009.

Tihanov, Galin. "Elias Canetti (1905–1994): A Difficult Contemporary." In Jacques Picard et al., eds., *Makers of Jewish Modernity: Thinkers, Artists, Leaders, and the World They Made*, 407–22. Princeton: Princeton University Press, 2016.

———. "The Location of World Literature." *Canadian Review of Comparative Literature / Revue Canadienne de Littérature Comparée* 44.3 (2017): 468–81.

Toer, Pramoedya Ananta. *The Buru Quartet: This Earth of Mankind, Child of All Nations, Footsteps*, and *House of Glass*. Tr. Max Lane. 4 vols. London and New York: Penguin, 1996.

Tolkien, J.R.R. "Beowulf: The Monsters and the Critics" (1936). In *The Monsters and the Critics and Other Essays*, 5–48. Boston: Houghton Mifflin, 1983.

———. *The Lord of the Rings*. 2nd ed. 3 vols. London: Allen and Unwin, 1966.

———. "On Fairy-stories." *Tree and Leaf*, 11–70. London: Allen and Unwin, 1964. Repr. in *The Monsters and the Critics*, 109–61.

———. "A Secret Vice." In *The Monsters and the Critics*, 198–223.

Tötösy de Zepetnek, Steven, Asunción López-Varela, Haun Saussy, and Jan Mieszkowski, eds. "New Perspectives on Material Culture and Intermedial Practice." *CLCWeb: Comparative Literature and Culture* 13.3 (2011): https://doi.org /10.7771/1481–4374.1783 (accessed January 9, 2019).

Trilling, Diana. "Lionel Trilling, a Jew at Columbia." *Commentary* 67.3 (1979): 40–46.

Trivedi, Harish. "Translation and World Literature: The Indian Context." In Bassnett, ed., *Translation and World Literature*, 15–28.

Tsu, Jing. *Sound and Script in the Chinese Diaspora*. Cambridge, MA: Harvard University Press, 2010.

Turner, James. *Philology: The Forgotten Origins of the Modern Humanities*. Princeton: Princeton University Press, 2015.

Tyler, Royall. "Translating *The Tale of Genji*." http://nihongo.monash.edu /tylerlecture.html (accessed May 22, 2018).

Ungureanu, Delia. *From Paris to Tlön: Surrealism as World Literature*. New York: Bloomsbury Academic, 2017.

Untermeyer, Louis. *Robert Frost: A Backward Look*. Ann Arbor: University of Michigan Library, 1964.

Valerio, Anthony. *Bart: A Life of A. Bartlett Giamatti, by Him and about Him*. New York: Harcourt, Brace, Jovanovich, 1991.

Vālmīki. *Rāmāyaṇa. Book One: Boyhood*. Tr. Robert P. Goldman. Clay Sanskrit Library. Cambridge, MA: Harvard University Press, 2005. *The Rāmāyaṇa: An Epic of Ancient India. Volume 1: Balakanda*. Introduction and tr. by Robert P. Goldman. Annotation by Robert P. Goldman and Sally J. Sutherland. Princeton: Princeton University Press, 1997.

Van Curen, Garrett. "Ecocriticism and the Trans-Corporeal: Agency, Language, and Vibrant Matter of the Environmental 'Other' in J. R. R Tolkien's Middle Earth." MA thesis, Montclair State University, 2019. https://digitalcommons .montclair.edu/etd/224 (accessed March 29, 2019).

Van Looy, Jan, and Jan Baetens, eds. *Close Reading New Media: Analyzing Electronic Literature*. Leuven: Leuven University Press, 2003.

Venuti, Lawrence. *Contra Instrumentalism: A Translation Polemic*. Lincoln: University of Nebraska Press, 2019.

———. *The Scandals of Translation: Towards an Ethics of Difference*. Abingdon and New York: Routledge, 1998.

———. *Translation Changes Everything: Theory and Practice*. Abingdon and New York: Routledge, 2013.

———. *The Translator's Invisibility: A History of Translation*. Abingdon and New York: Routledge Classics Edition, 2017.

———, ed. *The Translation Studies Reader*. 3rd ed. Abingdon and New York: Routledge, 2012.

Vialon, Martin. "Die Stimme Dantes und ihre Resonanz: Zu einem bisher unbekannten Vortrag Erich Auerbachs aus dem Jahr 1948." In Barck and Treml, eds., *Erich Auerbach*, 46–56.

———, ed. *Erich Auerbachs Briefe an Martin Hellweg (1939–1950): Edition und historisch-philologischer Kommentar*. Tübingen: Francke, 1997.

Vidmar, Luka. *And Yet They Read Them: Banned Books in Slovenia in the Early Modern Age from the National and University Library Collection*. Tr. Jason Blake and Sonja Svoljšak. Ljubljana: Narodna in Univerzitetna Knjižnica, 2018.

Vogt-William, Christine. "Brothers in Arms: Death and Hobbit Homosociality in *The Lord of the Rings*." *Inklings: Jahrbuch für Literatur und Ästhetik* 34 (2017): 81–95.

Vorda, Allen, and Kim Herzinger. "An Interview with Kazuo Ishiguro." *Mississippi Review* 20.1–2 (1991): 131–54.

Walkowitz, Rebecca. *Born Translated: The Contemporary Novel in the Age of World Literature*. New York: Columbia University Press, 2015.

Wang, David Der-wei. "Introduction: Worlding Literary China." In *A New Literary History of Modern China*, 1–28. Cambridge, MA: Harvard University Press, 2017.

Warren, William. "Cool Hand in Thailand." *New York Times*, October 5, 1975. www.nytimes.com/1975/10/05/archives/cool-hand-in-thailand.html (accessed July 20, 2018).

Waters, Lindsay, and Wlad Godzich, eds. *Reading de Man Reading*. Minneapolis: University of Minnesota Press, 1989.

Weinrich, Harald. "Chamisso, Chamisso Authors, and Globalization." Tr. Marshall Brown and Jane K. Brown. *PMLA* 119.5 (2004): 1336–46.

Wellek, René. "The Crisis of Comparative Literature." In Stephen G. Nichols, ed., *Concepts of Criticism*, 283–95. New Haven: Yale University Press, 1963.

———. "Memories of the Profession." In Gossman and Spariosu, eds., *Building a Profession*, 1–12.

Wellek, René, and Austin Warren. *Theory of Literature*. 3rd ed. New York: Harcourt, Brace and World, 1956.

Wells, H. G. *Tono-Bungay*. London: Penguin, 2005.

White, Edmund. Review of *Marguerite Yourcenar*, by Josyane Savigneau. *New York Times Book Review*, October 17, 1993. nytimes.com/books/97/09/14/reviews/16211.html (accessed August 20, 2018).

White, Hayden. "Criticism as Cultural Politics." *Diacritics* 6.3 (1976): 8–13.

Wilson, Horace Hayman. *The Mégha Dúta; or Cloud Messenger; A Poem, in the Sanscrit Language: by Cálidása*. Calcutta and London: Black, Parry, 1814.

Wollaeger, Mark, and Matt Eatough, eds. *The Oxford Handbook of Global Modernisms*. New York: Oxford University Press, 2013.

Wood, Ralph C. *Tolkien among the Moderns*. South Bend, IN: University of Notre Dame Press, 2015.

Woolf, Virginia. *A Room of One's Own and Three Guineas*. Oxford and New York: Oxford World's Classics, 1998.

WReC (Warwick Research Collective). *Combined and Uneven Development: Towards a New Theory of World-Literature*. Liverpool: Liverpool University Press, 2015.

Xie, Ming. *Conditions of Comparison: Reflections on Comparative Intercultural Inquiry*. New York: Continuum, 2011.

Yokota-Murakami, Takayuki. *Don Juan East/West: On the Problematics of Comparative Literature*. Albany: State University of New York Press, 1998.

Yoo, Hyun-joo. "Interview with Young-Hae Chang Heavy Industries." www.dichtung-digital.de/2005/2/Yoo/index-engl.htm (accessed August 5, 2018).

Young-Hae Chang Heavy Industries (Young-hae Chang and Marc Voge). "Cunnilingus en Corea del Norte (Buenos Aires Tango Version)." www.yhchang.com/CUNNILINGUS_EN_COREA_DEL_NORTE_BUENOS_AIRES_TANGO_VERSION_V.html (accessed May 14, 2019).

———. "Cunnilingus in North Korea." www.yhchang.com/CUNNILINGUS_IN_NORTH_KOREA_V.html (accessed May 14, 2019).

———. "Miss DMZ." www.yhchang.com/MISS_DMZ_V.html (accessed May 14, 2019).

Yourcenar, Margaret. *Mémoires d'Hadrien*. Paris: Plon, 1951. *Memoirs of Hadrian*. Tr. Grace Frick. New York: Farrar, Straus and Giroux, 1954.

Yu, Pauline. "Alienation Effects: Comparative Literature and the Chinese Tradition." In Koelb and Noakes, eds., *The Comparative Perspective on Literature*, 162–75.

Zabel, Blaž. "Posnett and the Comparative Approach." *Journal of World Literature* 4.3 (2019): 330–49.

Zaremba, Michael. *Johann Gottfried Herder: Prediger der Humanität: eine Biografie.* Cologne: Böhlau, 2002.

Zhang Longxi. *Allegoresis: Reading Canonical Literature East and West.* Ithaca, NY: Cornell University Press, 2005.

———. "Crossroads, Distant Killing, and Translation: On the Ethics and Politics of Comparison." In Felski and Friedman, eds., *Comparison*, 46–63.

———. *From Comparison to World Literature.* Albany: State University of New York Press, 2014.

———. *Mighty Opposites: From Dichotomies to Differences in the Comparative Study of China.* Stanford: Stanford University Press, 1998.

Zilberman, Regina. "Memórias de tempos sombrios." *Estudos de Literatura Brasileira Contemporânea* 52 (Sept.–Dec. 2017): 9–30.

Zook, Darren C. "Searching for *Max Havelaar:* Multatuli, Colonial History, and the Confusion of Empire." *Modern Language Notes* 121.5 (2006): 1169–89.

Index